## Praise for Michael Kazin's AMERICAN DREAMERS

"*American Dreamers* is Kazin's bid to reclaim the left's utopian spirit for an age of diminished expectations. An editor at *Dissent* magazine and one of the left's most eloquent spokesmen, Kazin presents his book as an unapologetic attempt to give the left a history it can celebrate. . . . *American Dreamers* is not a prescriptive book, offering instructions based on the past. Lessons nonetheless have a way of creeping into its text." —*The New York Times*

"Kazin, a distinguished historian, provides an entertaining journey through some of the fascinating byways of American radicalism. . . . His writing is fluid, avoids professional jargon, and is often witty. Unlike many of his colleagues in history with whom he shares a left-wing orientation, Kazin is fair to conservative critics of radicalism." —*National Review*

"Kazin, a history professor at Georgetown University and an editor at *Dissent* magazine, tells this story clearly and with some muscle in his prose. He's not afraid to tarnish the halos of social democracy's secular saints." —*The Plain Dealer*

"Kazin argues, in this lively and informative account of radicalism in the United States, American dreamers had a substantial impact on culture, society and politics, expanding the meaning of equal opportunity, equal rights and personal liberty and pushing their fellow citizens to reevaluate the nation's role in the world." —*San Francisco Chronicle*

"A work of honest rigor. . . . Kazin understands the limitations of the left, its self-destructive divisions, its difficulty in establishing an American presence within an international movement. . . . It is, to say the least, timely." —*Los Angeles Times*

"For the political junkie as well as those simply curious about the saga of the left, his book is helpfully crammed with numerous informative portraits of famous as well as more neglected figures." —*The Washington Monthly*

Michael Kazin

## AMERICAN DREAMERS

Michael Kazin is professor of history at Georgetown University. He is the author of several books on American politics and social movements, coeditor of *Dissent*, a frequent contributor to numerous publications, and the recipient of a Guggenheim Foundation fellowship, among others.

www.michaelkazin.com

# AMERICAN DREAMERS

*How the Left Changed a Nation*

## Michael Kazin

**VINTAGE BOOKS**
A Division of Random House, Inc.
New York

The Library of Congress has cataloged the Knopf edition as follows:
Kazin, Michael.
American dreamers : how the left changed a nation / by Michael Kazin.
p. cm.
1. Radicalism—United States—History.
2. Social change—United States—History.
3. United States—Social conditions. I. Title.
HN90.R3K39 2011  320.530973—dc22  2011013886

**Vintage ISBN: 978-0-307-27919-4**

*In memory of Roy Rosenzweig*

# Contents

# Acknowledgments

I hope this book, like its subject, invites plenty of argument and debate—be it passionate, reasonable, or both. In writing it, I have tried to follow the advice of one of my favorite historians, the late Richard Hofstadter: "If a new or heterodox idea is worth anything at all it is worth a forceful overstatement . . . This is one of the conditions of its being taken seriously."[1]

What's beyond dispute is how dependent I was on the accumulated scholarship and journalism of nearly two centuries of writing about the left—by partisans, opponents, and academics with smart things to say. That debt is acknowledged in the reference notes and in the indispensable sources listed near the back of the book.

But several individuals deserve more than collective words of praise. Gary Gerstle, Joseph McCartin, and Todd Gitlin—three good friends who are also superb historians—read the entire manuscript and made sound criticisms, most of which I tried to address. My sometime co-author and longtime comrade, Maurice Isserman, interrupted his pursuit of mountaineering history to help me understand the nuances of the American Communist Party. Eric Alterman threw a few necessary challenges and bits of encouragement my way. My agent, Sandy Dijkstra, was again a font of enthusiasm and common sense—and suggested the title of the book.

Several audiences of scholars and activists helped me work out what I thought about the topic. Thanks to Ira Katznelson and Casey Blake at Columbia University, Lisa McGirr at Harvard University, the directors of the Institute for the Study of the Americas at the University of London, and Jean-Christian Vinel at Paris Diderot University for their invitations and excellent suggestions. My colleagues in the history department at Georgetown did what they could to teach me to think beyond national boundaries. And my comrades at *Dissent* reminded me that, in good times and bad, the left can endure, even prosper, as an intellectual endeavor. And thanks to a fellowship from the National Endowment for the Humanities, I was able to spend a year writing and rewriting the manuscript.

The people at Alfred A. Knopf are masters at publishing a book well. I am grateful to Ash Green for accepting the original proposal and to my editor Andrew Miller for knowing how to combine praise with gentle suggestions for sharpening my ideas and refining my prose. Andrew Carlson passed along essential guidance on the illustrations and a good deal else; while Kathleen Fridella expertly managed the production, Jason Booher designed a jacket that turns metaphor into meaning, and Susanna Sturgis copyedited the manuscript with erudition, precision, and wit.

My son Danny and my daughter Maia let me work, or pretend to work, as much as I desired. On occasion, they even humored me into thinking that people of their generation might learn something from what I would write. Zoe sprawled elegantly next to my desk, snoring or barking as the spirit moved her. Beth's intelligence, compassion, and beauty thrill me as much as they did when we began living together, one summer in 1978. She's a damn fine editor, too.

This book is dedicated to a friend who died at the height of his powers, and those powers were very great indeed. Roy Rosenzweig was a brilliant organizer, researcher, writer, teacher, and the best sort of intellectual—one who brought the public into the historical conversation and persuaded historians to think about how to explain their work to ordinary people. In a profession full of large and fragile egos, Roy was the soul of generosity and empathy. He epitomized what the left has been at its best and might become again. Live like him.

# WHAT DIFFERENCE DID IT MAKE?

The free development of each is the condition for the free development
of all.

—Marx and Engels

You have to describe the country in terms of what you passionately hope
it will become, as well as in terms of what you know it to be now. You have
to be loyal to a dream country rather than one to which you wake up every
morning.

—Richard Rorty[1]

In dreams begin responsibility.

—William Butler Yeats

THIS BOOK WAS INSPIRED by Dr. Seuss. Around the time the Supreme
Court helped elect George W. Bush in 2000, I took refuge from political despair by thinking about the books my mother had read to me in
the 1950s, several of which I also read to my children forty years later.
Seuss, whose real name was Theodor Seuss Geisel and who had neither
an M.D. nor a PhD, got his start in the cartoon business illustrating ads
for an insecticide company, but he soon turned his talent to political
purposes. Although he never seems to have joined a left organization,
Seuss was a man of the Popular Front, that broad left vessel anchored by
the Communist Party. For two years in the early 1940s, he was a regular cartoonist for the left-wing New York City daily *PM*, contributing
hundreds of drawings that skewered such figures as Charles Lindbergh
for warming up to Hitler and flagrant racists like Governor Eugene Tal-
madge of Georgia.[2]

After the war, Seuss began to produce children's books that used

Dr. Seuss at his desk, 1957. Seuss, whose real name was
Theodor Geisel, put forth the ideas of the left with great wit,
hipness, and insight—and his books remain popular,
years after his death.

witty rhymes and fluid, fanciful drawings to convey the best principles
and some of the fondest aspirations of the left. He kept this up until his
death in 1989. The books, which have sold millions of copies, include
*The Sneetches*, a brief for racial equality; *Yertle the Turtle*, a satire of fascist tyranny; *The Lorax*, a plea to save nature from corporate greed; *The
Butter Battle Book*, a fable in support of nuclear disarmament; and *Horton
Hears a Who!*, a parable about the need to act against genocide. His most
famous book, *The Cat in the Hat*, while less overtly political, introduced a
sublimely destructive feline who did his bit to inspire the counterculture
of the 1960s.

Seuss made great children's literature out of the essential critique and
vision of the left. He married the ideal of social equality to the principle of personal freedom. As the journalist E. J. Kahn Jr. put it: "In his
books, might never makes right, the meek inherit the earth, and pride
frequently goeth before a fall, usually a pratfall." Seuss crafted "messages" with more wit, hipness, and color than any movement activist I
have ever known. But he rarely took part in protests or campaigns, and

few of his readers appreciated that he was illustrating a coherent and quite political worldview.[3]

Seuss's work was an underappreciated accomplishment in the long, if often difficult, history of the American left. Radicals in the U.S. have seldom mounted a serious challenge to those who held power in either the government or the economy. But they have done far better at helping to transform the moral culture, the "common sense" of society—how Americans understand what is just and what is unjust in the conduct of public affairs. And that is no small thing. "The most enduring aspects of a social movement," writes the historian J. F. C. Harrison, "are not always its institutions but the mental attitudes which inspire it and which are in turn generated by it."[4]

Leftists who articulated big dreams of a different future did much to initiate what became common, if still controversial, features of American life. These included the advocacy of equal opportunity and equal treatment for women, ethnic and racial minorities, and homosexuals; the celebration of sexual pleasure unconnected to reproduction; a media and educational system sensitive to racial and gender oppression and which celebrates what we now call multiculturalism; and the popularity of novels and films with a strongly altruistic and anti-authoritarian point of view.

Some of these cultural radicals were famous, or infamous, in their own time and remain staples of classroom lectures today: the abolitionists Harriet Beecher Stowe and Frederick Douglass, the class-conscious utopians Edward Bellamy and Henry George, the sexual radicals Margaret Sanger and Emma Goldman, the pro-Communist entertainers Paul Robeson and Woody Guthrie, the feminist writer Betty Friedan, and the black power orator Stokely Carmichael. Others, like Max Eastman, editor of *The Masses*, are familiar mainly to academics who understand how critical that magazine was to the rise of a modernist sensibility in the early twentieth century.

A focus on what the left did to alter American culture can provide a partial answer to the most important question one can raise about any movement in history: What difference did it make to the nation and the world?*

---

*A few words of definition and context about the term "left": In contemporary discourse, it generally connotes what "liberal" meant in the 1950s and '60s. In the mass media, most Democratic elected officials seemingly belong to "the left," as do the overwhelming majority of university professors.

The ability of radicals to develop a culture of rebellion, of alienation from domestic authorities, and to expand the meaning of equality
appealed to many Americans who gave little or no thought to actually
voting for a left candidate or joining a radical party. The cultural left
articulated outrage about the state of the world and the longing for a different one in ways the political left was unable to do.

A caveat is necessary here. Culture and politics are not separate
spheres; a cultural change can have important political consequences.
For example, the feminist awakening of the 1960s and '70s began a
process that led to more liberal state abortion laws and then to *Roe v.
Wade*—as well as to funding for child-care centers, laws against sexual
harassment, and an increase in women running for and getting elected
to public office. Conversely, a profound shift in the political sphere can
alter private opinions and behavior. The Civil War did away with human
bondage, which made it possible, albeit in painfully slow steps, to establish a new common sense about the moral imperative to treat individuals
equally, regardless of their race.

But when political radicals made a big difference, they generally did
so as decidedly junior partners in a coalition driven by establishment
reformers. Abolitionists did not achieve their goal until midway through
the war, when Abraham Lincoln and his fellow Republicans realized that
the promise of emancipation could speed victory for the North. Militant unionists were not able to gain a measure of power in mines and

---

But this usage muddies historical distinctions that remain critical to an understanding of the
context in which American politics takes place. If Barack Obama and Noam Chomsky are both
on "the left," then how does one make sense of their opposing views on U.S. foreign policy, and
a good many other subjects?

So I adhere to the classical definition: The left is that social movement, or congeries of mutu-
ally sympathetic movements, that are dedicated to a radically egalitarian transformation of society. There is, of course, a broad spectrum of ways to attempt such a transformation—from quietly
distributing anti-capitalist leaflets on street corners to organizing a revolutionary army to smash
the state.

Coined in 1789 to designate where the radical faction sat in the French National Assembly,
"left" did not come into general use in the United States until the 1930s. It often had a foreign
ring, and many of the Americans who fit the definition did not use it to describe themselves. They
often preferred "radical" or "revolutionary" or "progressive"—or a narrower term like "socialist," "anarchist," or "communist" which proclaimed their membership in one of the ideological
families that populated the tumultous village of the left.

But the egalitarian dreamers who form an unbroken chain from the 1820s to the present need
a common name. "Left" is what their counterparts in other nations would call themselves, and
there is something to be said for adhering to international custom. A useful work on this subject
is Norberto Bobbio, *Left and Right: The Significance of a Political Distinction*, trans. Allan Cameron
(Cambridge, UK, 1996), 72. Also see Rhodri Jeffreys-Jones, "Changes in the Nomenclature of
the American Left," *Journal of American Studies* 44 (2010): 83–100.

factories and on the waterfront until Franklin Roosevelt needed labor votes during the New Deal. Only when Lyndon Johnson and other liberal Democrats conquered their fears of disorder and gave up on the white South could the black freedom movement celebrate passage of the Civil Rights and Voting Rights acts. For a political movement to gain any major goal, it needs to win over a section of the governing elite (it doesn't hurt to gain support from some wealthy philanthropists as well). Only on a handful of occasions has the left achieved such a victory, and it never occurred under its own name.

The divergence between political marginality and cultural influence stems, in part, from the kinds of people who have been the mainstays of the American left. During just one period of about four decades—from the late 1870s to the end of World War I—could radicals authentically claim to represent more than a tiny number of Americans who belonged to what was, and remains, the majority of the population: white Christians from the working and lower-middle classes. At the time, this group included Americans from various trades and regions who condemned the growth of corporations for controlling the marketplace, corrupting politicians, and degrading civic morality.

But this period ended after World War I—due partly to a epochal split in the international socialist movement. Radicals lost most of the constituency they had gained among ordinary white Christians and have never been able to regain it. Thus, the wage-earning masses who voted for Socialist, Communist, and Labor parties elsewhere in the industrial world were almost entirely lost to the American left—and deeply skeptical about the vision of solidarity that inspired the great welfare states of Europe.

During the rest of U.S. history, the public face and voice of the left emanated from an uneasy alliance: between men and women from elite backgrounds and those from such groups as Jewish immigrant workers and plebeian blacks whom most Americans viewed as dangerous outsiders. This was true in the abolitionist movement, when such New England brahmins as Wendell Phillips and Maria Weston Chapman fought alongside Frederick Douglass and Sojourner Truth. And it remained the case in the New Left of the 1960s, an unsustainable alliance of white students from elite colleges and black people like Fannie Lou Hamer and Huey Newton from the ranks of the working poor.

It has always been difficult for these top-and-bottom insurgencies to present themselves as plausible alternatives to the major parties, to convince more than a small minority of voters to embrace their program for sweeping change. Radicals did help to catalyze mass movements. But furious internal conflicts, a penchant for dogmatism, and hostility toward both nationalism and organized religion helped make the political left a taste few Americans cared to acquire.

However, some of the same qualities that alienated leftists from the electorate made them pioneers in generating an alluringly rebellious culture. Talented orators, writers, artists, and academics associated with the left put forth new ideas and lifestyles that stirred the imagination of many Americans, particularly young ones, who felt stifled by orthodox values and social hierarchies. These ideological pioneers also influenced forces around the world that adapted the culture of the U.S. left to their own purposes—from the early sprouts of socialism and feminism in the 1830s to the subcultures of black power, radical feminism, and gay liberation in the 1960s and 1970s. Radical ideas about race, gender, sexuality, and social justice did not need to win votes to become popular. They just required an audience. And leftists who were able to articulate or represent their views in creative ways were often able to find one.

Arts created to serve political ends are always vulnerable to criticism. Indeed, some radicals deliberately gave up their search for the sublime to concentrate on the persuasive. But as George Orwell, no aesthetic slouch, observed, "the opinion that art should have nothing to do with politics is itself a political attitude."[5]

This book seeks to explain what the left won, what it lost, and why. The last objective requires some preliminary thoughts. In a sense, the radicals who made the most difference in U.S. history were not that radical at all. What most demanded, in essence, was the fulfillment of two ideals their fellow Americans already cherished: individual freedom and communal responsibility. In 1875, Robert Schilling, a German immigrant who was an official in the coopers', or cask-makers', union, reflected on why Socialists were making so little headway among the hardworking citizenry:

Everything that smacks in the least of a curtailment of personal or individual liberty is most obnoxious to [Americans]. They believe that every individual should be permitted to do what and how it pleases, as long as the rights and liberties of others are not injured or infringed upon. [But] this personal liberty must be surrendered and placed under the control of the State, under a government such as proposed by the social Democracy.[6]

Most American radicals grasped this simple truth. They demanded that the promise of individual rights be realized in everyday life and encouraged suspicion of the words and power of all manner of authorities—political, economic, and religious. Abolitionists, feminists, savvy Marxists, all quoted the words of the Declaration of Independence, the most popular document in the national canon. Of course, leftists did not champion self-reliance, the notion that an individual is entirely responsible for his or her own fortunes. But they did uphold the modernist vision that Americans be free to pursue happiness unfettered by inherited hierarchies and identities.

At the same time, the U.S. left—like its counterparts around the world—worked to establish a new order animated by a desire for social fraternity. The labor motto "An injury to one is an injury to all" rippled far beyond picket lines and marches of the unemployed. But *American* leftists who articulated this credo successfully did so in a patriotic and often religious key, rather than by preaching the grim inevitability of class struggle. Such radical social gospelers as Harriet Beecher Stowe, Edward Bellamy, and Martin Luther King Jr. gained more influence than did those organizers who espoused secular, Marxian views. Particularly during times of economic hardship and war, radicals promoted collectivist ends by appealing to the wisdom of "the people" at large. To gain a sympathetic hearing, the left always had to demand that the national faith apply equally to everyone and oppose those who wanted to reserve its use for privileged groups and undemocratic causes.

But it was not always possible to wrap a movement's destiny in the flag. "America is a trap," writes the critic Greil Marcus, "its promises and dreams . . . are too much to live up to and too much to escape." In a political culture which valued liberty above all, the left had more difficulty arguing for the collective good than for an expansion of individual rights. Advocates of the former could slide into apologizing for totalitarian rule in the Soviet Union and elsewhere. But to give primacy to "freedom" could deprive the left of its very reason to exist.[7]

In trying to advance both ideals, radicals confronted a yawning contradiction: in life as opposed to rhetoric, the desire for individual liberty routinely conflicts with the yearning for social equality and altruistic justice. The right of property holders and corporations to do what they wish with their assets clashes with environmentalists' desire to preserve the natural habitat, with the desire of labor unionists to restrict an employer's right to hire and fire, and with the freedom of consumers of any race to buy any house they can afford. Leftists who claimed to favor both liberty and equality could not resolve such conflicts. Neither could major-party politicians. But Whigs, Republicans, and Democrats basked in the glow of legitimacy, which often shielded them from the same charges of hypocrisy that bedeviled the left.

Without political power, radicals inside the U.S. never had the opportunity to become tyrants. But they could fight to expand the "politics of the possible" without losing their utopian edge. And in that effort, the makers of words, music, and images were as essential as minor-party officials and grassroots organizers.

Taken together, leftists were American dreamers in three senses of that oft-used phrase. They dreamed about a different kind of society and culture; their visions were the extensions of a larger, far more consensual dream; and, like most dreams, theirs came true only in part and usually not in ways they would have preferred. Such are the inevitable ironies of history.

What follows is a pragmatic narrative, one that clashes with the traditional view of the U.S. left as a failure, whether heroic or otherwise. "Radicalism in the United States has no great triumphs to record," wrote Christopher Lasch, "but the sooner we begin to understand why this should be so, the sooner we will be able to change it." Without political power or honor as prophets, leftists still helped to make the United States a more humane society. I am concerned with victories, however partial, and consequences, sometimes unintentional, of a left that is often written off as a lost cause.[8]

I begin with the abolitionists and other smaller, though no less vibrant, forces who, in the early decades of the nineteenth century, crusaded for causes beyond the emancipation of the slaves: the freedom of women and of workers, and the growth of socialist colonies on the land. These were the first radical social movements in U.S. history, and they created a capacious agenda for all those which followed. Next, I take up the question of how far erstwhile abolitionists, black and white, were able to push the nation during and after the Civil War to accept the full equality of the races. Then I bring the story into the industrial era, when celebrated radicals proposed solutions to "the labor question" that eschewed violence and class hatred. The narrative next moves into the twentieth century, when there coexisted three types of socialist movements—two of which appealed to "producers" across the land, plus a clique of urban bohemians who linked social change to personal liberation. I then examine the paradox of U.S. Communism, a movement that yoked itself to Stalin's despotism while advancing racial democracy and inspiring memorable arts of protest at home. Next, I balance the political blunders of the New Left against its remarkable imprint on American culture. Finally, I sketch a portrait of a left that, since the 1970s, has made a sharp and clever critique of the existing order but is unable—at least so far—to construct a political movement worthy of the name.

I do not attempt to offer a comprehensive or inclusive account of a radical tradition as long and complex, if not as well-known, as that of any other modern nation. Among the significant groups about which I say little or nothing are Catholic radicals, pacifists, the farmer-laborites of the 1920s and 1930s, and democratic socialists from the New Deal years to the present. I happen to sympathize strongly with the latter group. But I cannot claim for it a historical significance it did not possess.

Richard Flacks, a founder of Students for a Democratic Society, has written astutely, "Lefts everywhere confront the fundamental problem that they are calling on human beings to realize a potentiality which people, as a result of their everyday experience, do not readily perceive in themselves." I hope this book shows how radical dreamers in my country have done their part.[9]

# AMERICAN
# DREAMERS

*Chapter One*

# FREEDOM SONGS, 1820s–1840s

Right is of no Sex—Truth is of no Color—God is the Father of us all, and we are all brethren.

> —motto of the *North Star*, edited by
> Frederick Douglass and Martin Delany

Nothing remarkable was ever discovered in a prosaic mood. The heroes and discoverers have found more than was previously believed, only when they were expecting and dreaming of something more than their contemporaries dreamed of, or even themselves discovered, that is, when they were in a frame of mind fitted to behold the truth.

> —Henry David Thoreau[1]

### MEANS OF PROTEST

THE AMERICAN LEFT, like all modern political movements, began with printed words. Three pamphlets that appeared in the fall of 1829 imbued native radicalism with a critique and a vision its inheritors still share. In Manhattan, Frances Wright published her *Course of Popular Lectures*, comprised of talks she had recently delivered in several big cities. A few blocks away, Thomas Skidmore issued a lengthy pamphlet with a lengthy name: *The Rights of Man to Property! Being a Proposal to Make It Equal Among the Adults of the Present Generation* . . . That fall, in Boston, David Walker self-published his *Appeal . . . to the Coloured Citizens of the World, But in Particular, and Very Expressly, to Those of the United States of America.*

All three documents are passionate examples of radical prose: they denounce the existing order in sweeping phrases and lay out flamboyant plans for liberating humanity. Each author, as it happens, grew to adulthood within a distinctly different social milieu. The thirty-four-year-old

Wright was a Scottish lady with an inherited fortune and political connections to lofty figures on both continents: Thomas Jefferson, Andrew
Jackson, and the Marquis de Lafayette. Skidmore, aged thirty-nine, was
a self-educated machinist and teacher from an impoverished family of
Connecticut small farmers. Walker, aged forty-four, was a free black
man born in the slave South who owned a used-clothes shop on the Boston waterfront.

Their backgrounds did much to shape their beliefs and their prescriptions. Frances Wright aimed to free the urban masses from what she
considered to be their backward, Bible-dependent ways of thinking. The
first woman in the U.S. to lecture to audiences of both sexes, she urged
them to reject the falsehoods of religious texts and authorities and to seek
the truths of nature and society for themselves: "Turn your churches into
halls of science," she pleaded, "and devote your leisure day to the study
of your own bodies, the analysis of your own minds, and the examination
of the material world which extends around you!" At the same time, she
scolded American men for not allowing women to "assume the [equal]
place in society" and claimed that young wives were "as completely at the
disposal and mercy of an individual, as the negro slave who is bought for
gold in the slave mkt of Kingston or New Orleans."

David Walker, in paragraphs studded with exclamation points and
quotations from scripture, condemned the violence and hypocrisy of
liberty-loving Americans who owned slaves or apologized for those
who did. "I appeal to Heaven," declared Walker, an elder of the African
Methodist Episcopal Church (AME), ". . . who knows that my object is,
if possible, to awaken in the breasts of my afflicted, degraded, and slum-
bering brethren, a spirit of inquiry and investigation respecting our miseries and wretchedness in this *Republican Land of Liberty!!!!!!*." Walker
implored his fellow blacks to rise up against the slave system, emulating
the Haitian revolutionaries who had freed their land from French rule.
Only through righteous violence could they force whites to treat their
fellow Americans as equal and independent—and escape the punishment
that God would surely visit on a sinful nation.

Thomas Skidmore trained his fury on the holders of accumulated
wealth. "As long as property is unequal . . . ," he wrote, "then those who
possess it *will* live on the labor of others." A republic founded on such
a basis was a crime against nature and natural rights: "Why not sell the
winds of heaven, that man may not breathe without price? Why not sell

the light of the sun, that a man should not see without making another rich?" Skidmore insisted that the only remedy was to abolish all inheritances and to carry out a "General Division" of property, in roughly equal parts, to all Americans. The result, he promised, would be a society in which there would be "no lenders, no borrowers; no landlords, no tenants; no masters, no journeymen; no Wealth; [and] no Want."[2]

These were hardly the first documents written by radicals in America. Wright, Walker, and Skidmore all borrowed ideas from earlier figures who had helped win independence from Britain and defined that independence as securing equal rights to all: Thomas Paine, Thomas Jefferson, and such lesser-known figures as the farmer-philosopher William Manning and Richard

A thoughtful Frances Wright, sometime in the 1830s. Wright was a pioneer of feminism, secularism, sexual freedom, and radical abolitionism. Her critics dubbed her "the Great Red Harlot of Infidelity."

Allen, founder of the AME Church—as well as European thinkers like Mary Wollstonecraft and Jean-Jacques Rousseau. Skidmore borrowed his title, *The Rights of Man*, from Paine's famous defense of the French Revolution. But in America, there was no landed aristocracy to dethrone. Such wealthy merchants as John Hancock and large planters as James Madison actually enhanced their status by becoming leaders of the anti-colonial struggle. The Founders also helped establish the ideal of a moral commonwealth ruled by and for ordinary citizens, a promise whose appeal has never waned.

Not until the late 1820s and the 1830s did Americans form social movements that resemble the kinds which still exist today. Activists built organizations capable of surviving a spasm of protest or a period of defeat. These groups performed a tactical repertoire that remained more or less intact through the twentieth century: written constitutions, elected leaders, regular meetings, petitions, public rallies and street protests, and a movement press full of news and controversy. In all these venues, radicals declared that the founding ideals of the nation must become realities in the lives of all Americans—and offered a bold agenda for making that happen.

The first movements of the left were emerging at the dawn of modern America itself. The nation was undergoing an upsurge of democracy. In contrast to Europe, all white men were gaining the right to vote. "Penny newspapers" stoked mass interest in public affairs, while evangelical revivals did the same for matters of the soul. The mines and water-powered mills of the first industrial revolution were presenting radicals with both opportunities and potential barriers to growth. Catholic immigrants from Europe swelled the cities and workshops of the East and Midwest, generating social divisions of class but also ones of ethnicity and creed. All radicals could agree about the immorality of holding African Americans in slavery. But anyone who dreamed of transcending the contemporary order had to compete for attention with the political parties—Democrats and Whigs—that deftly appealed to plebeian voters.

Wright, Walker, and Skidmore believed a new world was both urgently needed and entirely possible—a dream more Americans may have shared in the thirty years before the Civil War than at any time since. But no member of the trio became the leader of a large or successful movement. Walker died a year after his *Appeal* came out, probably of tuberculosis, although many of his admirers suspected murder. Frances Wright's ambitious plans to set up a network of free, secular schools and an interracial, cooperative settlement in Nashoba, Tennessee, were utter failures. She and Skidmore were both active, briefly, in the Workingmen's Party of New York City—perhaps the first group in history to seek votes in the name of labor. But Wright and Skidmore disagreed with one another's major proposals—and the Workingmen soon split into two factions, neither of which had electoral success. Skidmore died in 1832, leaving more enemies than followers. Wright lived into the 1850s, but she was often overseas, and her reputation as "the Great Red Harlot of Infidelity" made it difficult for her to gain much of a hearing in the United States.

Yet through the nineteenth century and into the twentieth, their main ideas would be echoed within the ranks of the left and beyond. Walker's wrath against racist America inspired such abolitionist leaders as William Lloyd Garrison and Frederick Douglass, and may have sparked a slave rebellion or two. Indeed, John Brown's raid on Harpers Ferry and then the outbreak of the Civil War made the used-clothes dealer seem like a prophet. Wright's aggressive secularism helped spawn an anticlerical tradition—and such creators of the women's rights movement as Elizabeth Cady Stanton and Susan B. Anthony considered her a pioneer. Skidmore's denunciations of class inequality presaged those made by labor unionists and farmer insurgents for over a century after his death.

It is not surprising, however, that the life and work of Wright and Walker continue to attract talented historians and biographers, while we know few details about Skidmore's life, and he rates only a brief mention in scholarly works. Skidmore didn't call for the abolition of private property; he wanted only to ensure that every man and woman would enjoy an equal share of it, guaranteed by their labor. Yet neither that perspective nor an explicitly socialist one has ever won the allegiance of more than a minority of wage earners in the U.S.—or spawned a strong and durable labor left. The idea of taking from the haves to give to the have-nots violates the ideal, or myth, that any American can ascend to a much higher class by working with diligence and cunning. As James Michael Curley, the Boston Irishman who was one of the most successful local politicians in U.S. history, allegedly quipped, "Redistribution of the wealth would be all right, but in America the best we can achieve is redistribution of the graft."[3]

On the other hand, racial injustice has haunted and tantalized the U.S. throughout its history. Slowly and relentlessly, it cut a canyon of mistrust and rivalry between North and South, climaxing in one of the bloodiest civil wars in modern history—the one great exception to the otherwise stable political order established by the framers of the Constitution. Moreover, what Marxists called "the woman question" was salient in public language and activism in the U.S.—from temperance to anti-polygamy to suffrage—decades before it became a central issue in the politics of industrializing Europe. Narratives by radicals about slavery, Jim Crow, and conflict in the erogenous zone were attracting large audiences even before *Uncle Tom's Cabin* gained millions of readers in the U.S. and abroad. Yet, with rare exceptions, comparable works about class conflict have found readers only within left-wing circles—and often not even there.[4]

The three-part overture of 1829 thus introduced major themes that would instruct, inspire, and frustrate the hopes of several generations of radical activists and their followers. Adept at stirring up controversy, Wright, the wealthy immigrant, and Walker and Skidmore—her plebeian, native-born brethren—also showed their successors how to attract a large audience, whether outraged or supportive. But they failed to solve the perennial problem of the left: how to convert this attention into a movement capable of winning the allegiance of millions and bending the powerful to its will—or, even better, erecting a new moral order in its place.

## SACRED CAUSES

Antebellum radicals first had to decide what God wanted them to do. Fanny Wright outlived David Walker by a quarter century, but his evangelical style propelled far more nineteenth-century Americans, white and black, into activism than did her trust in the power of the rational mind. In their spiritual lives, Walker and his compatriots were products of the Second Great Awakening, the storm of romantic revivalism that began gathering at the end of the eighteenth century and kept blowing through the nation until the eve of Civil War. The awakening transformed the religious landscape: it swelled the number of church members and ordained preachers; Baptists and Methodists, whose theology asked little of converts but a passion for salvation, grew the most. Revivalist preachers encouraged the idea that God smiled on American ideals of liberty and self-rule and made agnostics and atheists seem like moral pariahs. "In the United States, people do not believe that a man without religion might be an honest man," reported Gustave de Beaumont, who accompanied Alexis de Tocqueville on his nine-month tour of the country in 1831, one of the more iconic visits in U.S. history.[5] For most American Protestants, leading a moral life meant reading the Bible, attending church whenever possible, and trying to behave as the Book and one's minister instructed.

But a determined minority took their faith a giant step further. "God wills all men to be free!" declared William Lloyd Garrison in 1838. For Garrison and his radical comrades, freedom was a remarkably expansive goal. It stretched beyond abolition, the era's most urgent moral cause, to embrace a variety of reforms that, if enacted, would go far towards making the U.S. a Christian nation in spirit as well as demography. Their demands included the complete equality of blacks and women in both public and private life, an end to the conquest of Indian lands, free public education, humane treatment of prisoners and the mentally ill, abstention from the use of alcohol (and, eventually, a ban on producing and selling it), and the peaceful resolution of all disputes, whether between nations or individuals.[6]

The goal of this embryonic social gospel, shared with utopian dreamers past and future, was a *perfected* society. Christian radicals borrowed the term from a Methodist sect whose members preached that anyone could aspire to "holiness." Inspiration also came from Charles Grandison Finney, the Presbyterian firebrand who preached that because sinners had chosen to do evil, they could reverse themselves and aspire to "entire sanctification." This decisive break with Calvinism, whose fatalist doctrine had disciplined Protestants for two centuries on both sides of the Atlantic, opened the gates of free will to all who dared rush through them. Down the road shimmered the prospect of earning divine love and redemption by serving one's fellow man, woman, and child.[7]

Most radicals before the Civil War thus perceived the salvation of society as akin to salvation of the soul; both were essentially dramas of individual conversion. Abolitionists insisted that slaveholders should free their human property if they wished to avoid damnation. Garrison and his followers called for Christians to "come out" of any church that did not denounce the vile institution. Feminist speakers cited the Sermon on the Mount to justify the claim that women—who were the "pure in heart" and the "peacemakers" in both family and society—should enjoy all the rights currently reserved to men.[8] Even Christian socialists, who put their faith in collective experiments, relied on itinerant agitators to pull new members, one by one, out of their towns and churches.

Antebellum radicals did not confine their vision of freedom to the boundaries of their own nation. Well-financed orators of both races often traveled to the United Kingdom, where they spoke to large and supportive audiences. The British Parliament's 1833 vote to abolish slavery at home and in its colonies smoothed their way. Such figures as the English abolitionist George Thompson and the Irish nationalist Daniel O'Connell returned the favor. Papers edited by Garrison and Douglass routinely included news of conventions, parliamentary reforms, and democratic insurrections in Europe. "My country is the world; my countrymen are mankind," Garrison announced on the masthead of *The Liberator.*[9]

After all, none of the injustices U.S. radicals cared about—from slavery to intemperance—had originated on American soil. An internationalism of soulful humanitarians came naturally to activists steeped in classical philosophy and the scriptures, as well as the writings of Charles Dickens and Thomas Carlyle. To their minds, the mid-nineteenth century was a time of wondrous opportunities and great dangers: the future shape of Western society seemed open; industry and technology, the penny press, railroads and factories could liberate men and women or enchain them in new systems of tyranny more brutal and more seductive than the older kind. Radicals thought they could only prevent the worst by convincing millions of their fellow citizens to understand the truth and change their lives accordingly. There was certainly no time to waste.

Armed with absolute self-confidence, radicals refused to tolerate error, compromise, and moral backsliding. Even freethinkers like Frances Wright had a messianic temperament that rarely harbored doubts or ambivalence about the course they had taken. Radicals made no apologies for using language that drew a sharp line between the sinful and the righteous—and their limitless sympathy for the oppressed was seldom matched by any empathy with their critics. Their approach was proudly illiberal.

Enemies recoiled at the breadth of their ambitions. A leading Southern conservative, the Presbyterian minister James Henley Thornwell, declared ominously: "The parties in this conflict are not merely Abolitionists and Slaveholders. They are atheists, Socialists, Communists, Red republicans, and Jacobins on one side, and the friends of order and regulated freedom on the other. In one word, the world is the battleground."[10]

While most radicals were, in fact, practicing Christians, a number did adopt eccentric habits, as if to demonstrate their zeal for both self-liberation and self-control. Some men grew their hair unfashionably long, some women donned pantaloons, and some couples swore by a strict diet of water, raw vegetables, and whole grains—and refrained from having sex more than once a month. When on speaking tours in the 1850s, the abolitionist Parker Pillsbury routinely woke up at sunrise and took a stroll in the nude. As a consequence, outsiders could equate irregular personalities with risky politics and reject the whole package.[11]

The rigorous moralism of radicals and their defiance of established interests sparked a fury of hostility and violence. They were shouted off podiums, splattered with rotten eggs and pelted with rocks, and sometimes barred from polite society. Mobs attacked their offices and interracial gatherings and, on occasion, destroyed their presses and burned down their meeting halls. But their scorn for convention—and their talent at articulating their views—challenged Americans to think hard about issues critical to America's future. Were they not citizens of a nation founded on the lofty ideals of liberty, self-government, and equality under God? Then how could they stand for politicians who routinely mouthed those principles while refusing to apply them to slavery and the unequal status of women and wage earners? Abolitionists, in particular, forced Americans to consider how to square those ideals with the existence of an institution so central to the nation's business and politics.

Yet for a long time, the influence of radicals was limited to the circulation of their publications and petitions and the crowds who attended their lectures. Radicals could pass no laws, and the candidates they nominated for public office won few votes. Only in their speaking and writing—and, indirectly, through their personal relationships—did they succeed in advancing their causes. Finally, in the 1850s, some abolitionists gained a foothold in national politics, but it was not in their own name.

These American dreamers endured bitter splits over doctrine and strategy and carped from the fringes of national politics. But the fire of their individual consciences never cooled. "The starting point and power of every great reform must be the reformer's self," declared Theodore Weld, a prominent abolitionist. "He must first set himself apart its sacred devotee, baptised into its spirit, consecrated to its service, feeling its profound necessity, its constraining motives, impelling causes, and all reasons why."[12]

## WHO WERE THE ABOLITIONISTS?

What kind of people devoted their lives to the crusade against slavery? Weld's own biography suggests some answers. The charismatic orator and propagandist was born in Connecticut in 1803 to a strict Congregationalist pastor and a warm, forgiving mother—and struggled to earn his father's respect. At the age of twenty-three, Weld attended one of Charles Finney's sermons, only to ridicule the evangelist for preaching a lax theology in an unruly manner. But all that night, the young man wrestled with his feelings. Finally, at dawn, he heard a voice calling on him to repent. Finney had won a new crusader.

Weld did not immediately bring his energy and eloquence to the abolitionist movement. During the late 1820s, he lectured for temperance throughout New England and the Empire State. While enrolled in a reform-minded, biracial seminary at Oneida, New York, the handsome, muscular Weld became an apostle of manual labor for the young, bookish, and privileged. By cutting wood and running to every task, they would prepare their bodies for the rigors of changing the world and appreciate how most people earned their daily bread. Gradually, the logic of Weld's perfectionist creed turned him into a full-time advocate for the liberation of the enslaved. God had created "every being" as "*a free moral agent*," Weld wrote to Garrison in 1833. Thus "he who robs his fellow man of this tramples upon right . . . and sacrilegiously assumes the prerogative of God."[13]

For the next three years, Weld was on the road almost constantly, winning souls for abolition while enduring hecklers, stonings, and snarling dogs. Often, he slept in the homes of free black families and worshipped at their churches. Weld courted the contempt of local grandees by dressing like a common workingman and wearing his hair long and uncombed. Near the end of his journeys, he boasted, "The Lord enabled me to move deliberately onward until the truth triumphed gloriously."[14]

Weld's path to radical abolitionism was similar to that taken by a good number of his white compatriots, of both sexes. Most were born at the turn of the nineteenth century either in New England or upper New York state to families of middling means or better. Raised in strict Calvinist homes, they converted in their teens or early twenties to the romantic gospel preached by Finney and his ilk. Often, a young evangelical would start campaigning against "the liquor traffic" or demand that businesses adhere to the Sabbath—before throwing him- or herself into the more urgent vocation of ending human bondage.[15]

Weld was not among the sixty-two men and women who founded the American Anti-Slavery Society (AAS) at a December 1833 meeting held in a Philadelphia hall owned by a black fraternal group. Police warnings about a violent response to "the amalgamationist conclave" had scared away local whites from offering another facility. Echoing the founding statement of 1776, the abolitionists, three of whom were black, signed a Declaration of Sentiments which pledged "to secure to the colored population of the United States, all the rights and privileges which belong to them as men, and as Americans—come what may to our persons, our interests, or our reputation—whether we live to witness the triumph of Liberty, Justice, and Humanity, or perish untimely as martyrs in this great, benevolent, and holy cause."[16]

Free blacks like David Walker had launched the first local anti-slavery groups, but, as the movement grew, it resembled a cross-section of successful Protestants, of both races, from the fast-growing North. Among the early leaders of the AAS were such upper-class Bostonians as Wendell Phillips, who had been president of the most elite student clubs at Harvard, and Maria Weston Chapman, principal of an exclusive girls' school and wife of a rich merchant. Wealthy men such as Gerrit Smith and Arthur Tappan, the organization's first president, contributed lavishly to the movement. But Garrison was its leading spokesman and editor of its most influential journal, *The Liberator*. And he was the son of an alcoholic sailor who earned his living as a job printer.

Despite its difficult birth, the organization grew to over a hundred thousand members by the end of the 1830s. Many who appeared on its books were nominal adherents who just signed a petition or made a small contribution. But among that throng, skilled workers, factory hands, and housewives outnumbered employers and professionals. The great majority of the abolitionist faithful lived in an arc that stretched north from Philadelphia to the Adirondacks and east to Boston. There, manufacturing and commerce via ocean and canal had created a bustling preview of the modern society most Americans would inhabit by the end of the nineteenth century. Inevitably, most AAS members were native-born parishioners of an evangelical church—visible saints equipped for an age of steam engines and a mass market in ideas as well as goods.[17]

In occupation and religion, black abolitionists were remarkably similar to their white counterparts. Most were born free in the North, worshipped at a Methodist or Baptist church, and earned enough income, at a trade or small business, to make an avocation of activism possible. They signed temperance pledges and pursued other forms of moral uplift with as much fervor as did Weld and Garrison. "While our paper shall be mainly Anti-Slavery," announced Frederick Douglass in the first issue of the *North Star*, "its columns shall be freely opened to the candid and decorous discussion of all measures and topics of a moral and humane character, which may serve to enlighten, improve, and elevate mankind."[18]

Frederick Douglass, c. 1847.
The Maryland-born Douglass
escaped from slavery and became a
leading abolitionist and, after
the Civil War, the most prominent
black man in the nation.

Although slavery no longer existed in the Northern states, its influence on the daily lives of black Americans there was too painful to ignore. Almost everywhere in the "free" states, black men and women were excluded from public schools, restaurants, first-class railway cars, and membership in any churches they had not established themselves. In Northern cities, the presence of ex-slaves, their numbers increasing every year, also kept the horrors of sadistic patrollers and the potential sale of one's children fresh in the minds of the freeborn as well as among refugees from bondage.

Most white radicals imagined themselves to be free of prejudice. But every black abolitionist could point to white allies whose condescending manner, impatience with flawed grammar, and allegedly superior grasp of politics betrayed their notion that slaves were minor actors in the great struggle between cruel masters and white emancipators. When Frederick Douglass decided to issue his own newspaper in 1847, he angered white Garrisonians who believed that, as a refugee from slavery, he was too inexperienced to embark on such a weighty task. They counseled him to stick to the lecture platform, where he usually appeared alongside white patrons. "I think he mistakes his vocation and will regret his course," explained Samuel J. May, a wealthy Unitarian minister. The abolitionists' most common image, first produced by the British industrialist Josiah Wedgwood in the 1780s, was that of a kneeling slave, clothed only at the waist, his wrists in chains and his eyes gazing upward as he pleads, "Am I not a man and a brother?"[19]

But supplication was not a fit posture for free men and women. Some black abolitionists responded by meeting separately in Negro conventions and all-black affiliates of the AAS. In such gatherings, the roots of black nationalism were irrigated with rhetoric about lifting up the race without relying on white benefactors. In 1849, after working for two years as co-editor of the *North Star*, the physician Martin Delany resigned in protest of Douglass's biracial strategy and began to promote the idea of emigration to Africa. "The white man will not live without a country, though he must gain it by usurpation and blood—" he wrote, "the colored man is content to sojourn . . . denied of every right and privilege tending to make him equal to his fellows." Yet most black abolitionists believed there was no alternative—practically or morally—to struggling alongside their white comrades to earn respect and gain the triumph of their common cause.[20]

Despite its growing size and influence, the freedom movement could never break through a stubborn barrier that divided it from a critical section of the emerging white working class. Over four and a half million people emigrated from Europe to the United States between 1830 and 1860. Irish Catholics were both the largest and the poorest group; most had no options other than to clean houses, fix streets, build houses and canals, or toil twelve hours a day in a mine or textile factory. They did know they were white, however, and so few Irish joined a crusade to end the oppression of another race, whose members, if freed, might soon be competing with them for jobs and living space. Instead, Irish Americans quickly became urban mainstays of the Democratic Party, whose ideology counterposed the interests of ordinary whites to that of the "inferior races."[21]

Most abolitionists did show compassion for the newcomers who had suffered under imperial rule and fled a great famine, only to face discrimination and menial work on the other side of the ocean. Both black and white Garrisonians denounced British colonialism and believed a fair day's labor deserved a fair day's wage. They forged a bond with Daniel O'Connell, leader of the movement for Catholic emancipation in Ireland, who condemned what he called the "aristocracy of the skin" as vehemently as any American. In 1842, a throng of five thousand crowded into Boston's Faneuil Hall to cheer an address, signed by O'Connell and many of his fellow Hibernians, that called on their compatriots in the U.S. to "treat the colored people as your equals, as brethren" and to "*cling by the abolitionists.*" "How marvelously Providence works!" exulted Garrison, who chaired the gathering. Surely, the gulf between the two freedom movements would now begin to close.[22]

He was mistaken. As the sectional crisis heated up, Irish Americans grew more estranged from anti-slavery activists and more hostile to blacks themselves. They resented prosperous abolitionists who contrasted the limitless prospects of free labor with the feudal degradation endured by slaves. Trade unionists, from Ireland and elsewhere, accused such wealthy pillars of the movement as Arthur Tappan and his brother Lewis of shedding tears over those suffering in the faraway South but ignoring the abysmal conditions of laborers in Northern cities.

Democratic politicians drew cheers from immigrant voters when they claimed that a life of drudgery for wages was no better than one spent on a plantation where the master at least provided food, shelter, and clothing. "No man devoid of all other means of support but that which his labor affords him can be a freeman," claimed Mike Walsh, an Irish-born New York City legislator, who later became a pro-South member of Congress. As apostles of individual opportunity, abolitionists could not abide the notion that wage earning was a kind of slavery. They were repulsed as well by Walsh's roughneck style—"a hard-drinking brawler and workingman dandy—with his disheveled clothes, diamond ring, and silver-tipped cane," as one historian describes him. Walsh's image was the antithesis of the code of simplicity and self-control evangelical activists tried to live by.[23]

In a militantly Christian nation, the religious differences may have been the most intractable ones. Daniel O'Connell died in 1847, leaving no successor eager to maintain the transatlantic alliance with the Garrisonians. Over the next decade, the influx of a million famine refugees intensified the fears of evangelicals who wanted the U.S. to remain a Protestant republic. American Catholic bishops inflamed the situation when they endorsed Pope Pius IX's resistance to both secular reform and religious pluralism. The Church, vowed New York archbishop John Hughes, aims "to convert the world,—including the inhabitants of the United States . . . the Legislatures, the Senate, the Cabinet, the President and all!"[24]

Abolitionists had sworn to comfort the oppressed and to defend the rights of all. But as Protestant radicals, they were not immune from the hostility to "the whore of Rome" that had helped fuel three centuries of European wars and massacres. As temperance supporters, they also cringed at the Irish fondness for good whiskey. And they bristled at demands by Archbishop Hughes and other prelates that local governments fund Catholic schools. In one form or another, this cultural clash persisted into the twentieth century, separating middle-class radicals from the millions of Catholics who became the core of the industrial working class and the largest bloc of voters in the nation's biggest cities. Protestant and secular radicals would keep appealing *to* them, but a movement that did not spring *from* them could never come close to winning a share of national power.

### THE POLITICS OF PURITY

For almost two decades following the publication of David Walker's *Appeal*, abolitionists toiled on the margins of the political universe. Until the outbreak of war with Mexico in 1846, they concentrated on building their movement and nurturing an internal culture that sustained its members and presented an alternative to the amorality of a slaveholding society. They also had to weather an ideological conflict that led to one of those internal splits that have always plagued partisans of the left.

In 1840, several prominent activists founded the Liberty Party to give true "friends of freedom" a way to protest the unwritten agreement between Whigs and Democrats to keep the question of abolition from getting in the way of their competition for white voters. The new party—among whose leaders were Gerrit Smith, Lewis Tappan, the poet John Greenleaf Whittier, and Henry Stanton (husband of Elizabeth Cady)—nominated candidates for federal office who were committed to doing away with the wicked institution. The slogan "Vote as you pray and pray as you vote" underlined its evangelical convictions. But Liberty men made one vital compromise: they refrained, for the present, from demanding that the federal government abolish slavery where it already existed. That step, they feared, would touch off a civil war. On all other questions, including racial equality under the law, they made clear they would not dilute their principles to win votes. Americans responded in kind; just seven thousand cast ballots for the Liberty presidential ticket of James G. Birney and Thomas Earle.

Adherents of the Liberty Party believed they comprised the more practical wing of the movement—which indicates the strength of the perfectionist creed. In the spring of 1840, they lost control of the AAS to the Garrisonians after a prolonged and nasty debate at the group's annual convention. Soon Liberty men formed a new group, grandly named the American and Foreign Anti-Slavery Society. Garrison and his allies, who were based in Boston and included most female abolitionists, claimed emancipation would never be achieved by trimming doctrinal sails or consorting with evil men or institutions. They stuck by positions which they knew most of their fellow citizens abhorred: full legal equality for women as well as blacks, "coming out" of any denomination or church that allowed slaveholders to be members, absolute pacifism (or "non-resistance"), and refusal to contest elections as long as the national state was under the thumb of slave masters and their political lackeys.

In contrast, Birney and Tappan's faction argued that the movement should campaign solely for abolition, welcoming any Americans, regardless of their opinions on other matters, who were willing to take such an unpopular stand. They also accused the Garrisonians of disrespecting the clergy and forcing women to speak and act in mannish ways that undermined their moral status in the family. But the new group entirely failed to live up to its ambitious name; it attracted few members and by the mid-1850s had quietly disbanded. While most black abolitionists sided with Garrison, they continued to work amicably at the local level with members of the opposing faction.

The split actually did little damage to the movement as a whole. External events were attracting supporters faster than the internecine spat could push them away. The federal courts began to act more aggressively to return fugitive slaves to their masters, which troubled Northerners who had evaded the issue before. The impending annexation of Texas gave the white South a major victory that persuaded Americans in other regions that "the slave power" held a whip hand over national affairs. Southern planters giddy about expanding their holdings in the West now seemed to be imperiling the future of ordinary whites who could never hope to compete with bound labor. As a recruiting argument for the anti-slavery movement, self-interest was proving mightier than Christian altruism.

The response of each camp of abolitionists reflected the same arguments that had caused the split. During the 1844 presidential campaign, Liberty Party orators talked as much about the unelected "oligarchy" of a quarter-million slaveholders as they did about the immorality of slavery. This stance helped increase the size of their popular vote to almost seventy thousand. In contrast, Garrison decided it was time to make a radical break with evil. It would be better, he declared, for the free states to secede from the union altogether than to remain in a nation where slavery was not just undisturbed but growing. At rallies, he even took to burning a copy of the Constitution, calling it "a covenant with Hell." But the growing alarm in the North about "the slave power" still gained him new respect and followers.

While not a major blow to the abolitionist cause, the schism of 1840 did reveal an inescapable aspect of left tradition, and that of any other ideological movement: the ongoing clash between self-righteous purists and anxious opportunists. To outsiders, such distinctions often seem trivial or bewildering. Why couldn't Garrison tolerate the Liberty Party as an experiment in gaining popular support? Why couldn't Birney simply decline to attend meetings addressed by women? But as Max Weber would later point out, the difference between "an ethic of responsibility" and "an ethic of ultimate ends" is intrinsic to any enterprise in visionary politics. Unless it takes state power, a radical movement only advances when it finds a way to combine the two approaches or, at least, manages to soften the antagonism between them.[25]

### THE CULTURE OF A FREE CHURCH

In their personal lives, many abolitionists were quite able to transcend the dilemma of means and ends. They found ways to make their activism innovative, pleasurable, and even economically viable. Shunned by most traditional institutions, they created vibrant alternatives of their own. Ostracized for violating racial and sexual taboos, they behaved in ways that might instruct and perhaps convert their critics. And the arts of abolitionism proved remarkably popular, appealing to far more people than the AAS and the Liberty Party could have reached on their own.

Perhaps the best place to glimpse the abolitionist community on display, and at play, was at an anti-slavery bazaar. Inside venues as large as Faneuil Hall and as small as a rural church, abolitionists exhibited and purchased garments and handicrafts made by friends of the cause, heard an array of speakers and singers, promoted books and tours, circulated petitions, mingled with supporters of different races and classes and religions—and raised most of the funds that kept their journals and organizations alive. "It was a lesson to the partisan and the sectarian; to the tyrant and the demagogue," declared Maria Weston Chapman about one Boston bazaar, "*This* was indeed, a FREE CHURCH. *This* was, in truth, an EVANGELICAL ALLIANCE; for were they not all gathered together in the name that gives deliverance to the captive? Then, surely by his own promise, there is he in the midst of them . . ."[26]

These fairs—the largest took place at Christmastime—showed that abolitionists rejected only the selfish ethic of market society, not the individual joys of consumption. With the talent and resources the movement possessed, there was no reason for activists not to dress well, read good books and magazines, and attend entertaining lectures and theatrical performances. Indeed, such conscientious consumption was an excellent way to win new people to the cause—and to demonstrate its moral superiority to the hydra-headed "slave power."

Abolitionist orators, as carriers of the evangelical spirit, were the most ubiquitous face of the movement. Nearly every prominent male activist and many a female one appeared frequently on the lecture platform, usually before paying customers. Antebellum Americans had a limitless appetite for public speaking. They flocked to sermons and campaign rallies and evaluated orators as cannily as we now discuss actors in films and on television. Lyceums thrived in cities and towns everywhere but the lower South, where the authorities feared abolitionists would find their way onto podiums. Tocqueville marveled that "even the women . . . listen to political harangues as a recreation from their household labors. Debating clubs are, to an extent, a substitute for theatrical entertainments."[27]

Anti-slavery was controversial fare, but that only swelled the size of the crowd whenever mobs did not threaten to disrupt a skillful orator. In 1836, Theodore Weld recruited and trained seventy agents to give lectures for the AAS, as well as to sell subscriptions to *The Liberator* and other journals. Seventy was, he pointed out, the same number of "lambs" or disciples that Jesus had sent to live among the "wolves" of ancient Israel in order to inform them that the "kingdom of God" was near. But the most celebrated abolitionists were natural preachers who didn't need much tutoring.[28]

Perhaps the most gifted and tireless performers were Wendell Phillips and Frederick Douglass. The speaking style of the Boston brahmin differed little from that of the erstwhile fugitive from bondage. Both men were steeped in classical models—Phillips from his education at Boston Latin and then at Harvard, Douglass from memorizing a copy of *The Columbian Orator* he fished out of the trash while he was still a slave, living in Baltimore. Both drew on the repertoire of the evangelical ministry, from the balm of romantic homilies to the fire of jeremiads.

Both also delighted audiences by mixing satire into otherwise stern condemnations of slavery. Phillips portrayed an ancient steel sword "as so flexible that it could be put into a scabbard like a corkscrew, and bent every way, without breaking—like an American politician." Douglass mimicked a white Southern preacher telling a group of slaves, "Oh, consider the wonderful goodness of God! Look at your hard, horny hands, your strong muscular frames, and see how mercifully he has adapted you to the duties you are to fulfil! While to your masters, who have slender frames and long delicate fingers, he has given brilliant intellects, that they may do the *thinking*, while you do the *working*."[29] Unlike most other abolitionists who retired from public speaking after emancipation, both Phillips and Douglass continued to mount platforms regularly until their deaths late in the nineteenth century. Each was an acclaimed orator for over fifty years.

Wendell Phillips, as photographed by Mathew Brady, mid-1850s. Phillips was a Boston brahmin who became a stirring orator for abolitionism and, after the Civil War, for the rights of labor.

But the distinctions between the two men illuminated the achievements—and limits—of their common movement. Phillips was an urbane, relaxed conversationalist who invited listeners to share his urgent concerns about the state of the world and how virtuous individuals could participate in healing it. "He projected great physical authority," writes a biographer, "for he was full framed and athletic looking, with thinning sandy hair and a profile that grew more rugged with age." Douglass struck a more dramatic presence, particularly before white audiences. With passionate words and gestures, he graphically described his own experiences as a slave and connected them to the arduous narratives of other black Americans. He frequently challenged his listeners—Christians to denounce the sins of their churches, voters to reject the immoral two-party system, men to support rights for women. That Douglass was a dignified, handsome black man (who didn't turn fifty until after the Civil War) conveyed an eroticism that captivated many and threatened others. One young female admirer reported that he was "a rather light mulatto of unusually large, splendid and powerful build." Abolitionists were fortunate to have such extraordinary spokesmen. But,

"The Fugitive's Song," written in 1845 by one
of the Hutchinson Singers and dedicated to
Frederick Douglass. The Hutchinsons wrote and
performed songs against slavery for huge audiences
all over the antebellum North.

given their backgrounds, neither Phillips nor Douglass could gain the
sympathies of most white men and women. That left a yawning gap for
future radicals to fill.[30]

The music of abolitionists may have reached as many Americans as
turned out to hear anti-slavery speakers. In the 1840s, the Hutchinson
Family Singers, three brothers and a sister raised on a small New Hampshire farm, demonstrated a new way to agitate while entertaining. The
Hutchinsons started out adapting temperance lyrics to hymns they had
learned in church. In 1842, Nathaniel Rogers, the leading Garrisonian
in their home state, heard one of their concerts and convinced them to
write anti-slavery songs in the same spirit.

The result was explosive. The Hutchinsons quickly became the main attraction at abolitionist conventions, where they mixed freedom songs with patriotic and religious ditties. In 1844, they performed a mostly apolitical repertoire in Washington for President John Tyler and several members of Congress. Abashed at the praise they received from the president and other pro-slavery politicians, the Hutchinsons returned to New England and wrote "Get Off the Track!" The militant song became their theme until they broke up fifteen years later. Its sentiments, wrapped in a metaphor of industrial power and progress, echoed many an anti-slavery speech and editorial:

> Hear the mighty car wheels humming!
> Now look out! *The Engine's coming!*
> Church and statesmen! Hear the thunder!
> Clear the track! Or you'll fall under . . .
> > Get off the track! All are singing.
> > While the *Liberty Bell* is ringing.

> On triumphant, see them bearing
> Through sectarian rubbish tearing;
> Th' Bell and Whistle and the Steaming,
> Startles thousands from their dreaming . . .
> > Look out for the cars, while the bell rings
> > Ere the sound your funeral knell rings.

No commercial publisher would touch the song, so the Hutchinsons had to print and distribute it themselves. Several daily papers predicted that the quartet's flourishing career was "doomed."[31]

But in harmony with their melodramatic lyrics, the controversy only stiffened their resolve and increased their popularity. Until the early 1850s, the troupe performed thousands of times—in some of the largest concert halls in the nation as well as for charity groups and fellow abolitionists. They wrote new songs like "The Bereaved Slave Mother" and "The Fugitive Slave" (the latter dedicated to their friend Frederick Douglass). They insisted on playing before integrated audiences, which caused some theaters to cancel their shows and inspired one New York City paper to brand them "Garrison's Nigger Minstrels."[32]

The smear was inaccurate as well as insulting. The Hutchinsons deliberately presented themselves as a moral alternative to the racy comic actors in blackface who outdrew every other type of entertainer in the land. Reporting on one of their concerts before an interracial gathering in Rochester, New York, Douglass contrasted the Hutchinsons' appeal to "a common brotherhood" with that of the minstrels "who have stolen from us a complexion denied to them by nature, in which to make money, and pander to the corrupt taste of their white fellow-citizens."[33] Although the Hutchinsons gave more than ten thousand performances, they could not compete with the clever stereotypes, low humor, and boisterous song-and-dance routines that made minstrelsy so popular. But they did give the corked-up set a run for their money.

Literary abolitionists did better than that. New England, the region where the movement was strongest, was also home to some of the nation's most inventive and esteemed writers. Ralph Waldo Emerson, Henry David Thoreau, Margaret Fuller, and Henry Wadsworth Longfellow rarely consorted with radical activists, but all wrote eloquently about the evils of slavery and occasionally took actions to back up their beliefs. Thoreau refused to pay poll tax during the Mexican War, and both he and Emerson eulogized John Brown after he was executed for trying to foment a slave insurrection. All but Longfellow belonged to the intellectual vanguard against the old Calvinist and Federalist establishment; the rising stream of transcendental and romantic ideas flowed naturally into the waters of radical reform.

The most popular attacks on slavery came from the pens of activists who had devoted years to the cause. In 1839, Theodore Weld assembled *American Slavery As It Is* from a thousand personal testimonies and brutal accounts that appeared in Southern newspapers. That year, the thick volume sold over a hundred thousand copies and was the key source for refuting claims that most planters were kind and most slaves were happy. *The Narrative of the Life of Frederick Douglass, an American Slave Written by Himself*, published in 1845, did not just demonstrate its author's literary talent. It disproved the notion that black writers could only clumsily imitate white models and created an audience for a new genre of firsthand accounts of oppression that benefited Harriet Jacobs, Sojourner Truth, and scores of other black autobiographers. The poets John Greenleaf Whittier and Frances Ellen Watkins, both of whom were longtime activists in the American Anti-Slavery Society, recited before large crowds and published best-selling collections of their work. Watkins, a black woman dubbed "the Bronze Muse," had a knack for composing memorable, agitational verses. After hearing that white residents of Cleveland had helped catch a fugitive slave, she wrote:

> There is blood upon your city—
> Dark and dismal is the stain;
> And your hands would fail to cleanse it,
> Though you should Lake Erie drain.[34]

Of course, the popularity of *Uncle Tom's Cabin* dwarfed that of every other abolitionist production. Harriet Beecher Stowe's sentimental 1852 exposé outsold every other novel in the nineteenth-century United States and gradually became as much a cultural touchstone as the Gettysburg Address. It inspired more than a dozen books by pro-slavery critics; eight different stage versions, some with music; and innumerable posters, cartoons, advertisements, and even miniature cabins produced for the tourist trade. Minstrels freely adapted its characters, heedless of the irony. Translated into dozens of languages, including Wallachian and Illyrian, *Uncle Tom's Cabin* was unrivaled in the Victorian era as an icon of American moral sensibility. Stowe did not possess the literary gifts of Dickens, Hugo, Tolstoy, or George Eliot. But to millions of readers around the world, she, like them, represented the better angels of her nation.

Its achievements, however, did not match its acclaim. Less than a decade after Stowe's book was published, the carnage of civil war destroyed her hope that Jesus-loving pacifists would vanquish the sin of slavery. One can appreciate *Uncle Tom's Cabin* as a paradigm of "sentimental power," a woman's novel that spurred both men and women to take meaningful actions to end the outrageous treatment of black Americans. But by the time the book came out, the abolitionist movement was already emerging from the political wilderness, and it isn't clear how much her saintly stereotypes—the indomitable mother, the redeemed wild child, the Christlike hero—did to advance the more difficult aim of racial equality. Stowe's famous book was the splendid finale of two decades of earnest propaganda in print, image, and song. To set it apart misses all the cultural artisans—from David Walker onward—who made it possible.[35]

The most radical acts which abolitionists performed were more elusive than votes for a third party or the appeal of a provocative book or extraordinary speaker. To a remarkable degree, anti-slavery militants seem to have practiced what they preached: they tried to lead interracial lives. Black and white activists wrote for the same publications, spoke from the same platforms, worshipped in the same churches, insisted on eating in the same restaurants and sleeping in the same hotels when on tour, and stayed in one another's houses. They also sent their children to the same schools (when local laws made that possible) and attended each other's weddings and funerals. A few even chose a spouse of a different race. These relationships did not resolve differences of perspective about which race should lead the struggle for freedom; if anything, the lack of an internal color line made it harder to brush away slights and misunderstandings. But the abolitionists' personal decisions were still unique and courageous: no other sizable group of Americans had ever lived as if the color bar did not apply to them—and should not matter to anyone else.

Their determination was motivated by a common faith as much as by a common humanity. "Bible politics," Gerrit Smith and his close friend James McCune Smith, a black physician, called it. "The heart of the whites must be changed," wrote James to Gerrit in 1846, "thoroughly, entirely, permanently changed." Any other path would violate the belief in free will, the "self-sovereignty" that was a gift from God. This stamped interracialism with a greater conviction than did the idea that "all men are created equal." Jefferson had said nothing about a *fellowship* of equals, and besides, he was a lifelong slave master and thus a terrible hypocrite.[36]

Some white abolitionists refused to maintain any distinction between the races. William Lloyd Garrison told African-American audiences that he felt and spoke "as a black man," and free black readers composed the majority of subscribers to *The Liberator* in its early years. Each evening, a group of black comrades made sure the notorious white editor got home safely through Boston's dark and narrow streets. John Brown imagined he could lead an insurrection of slaves because he identified so strongly with their suffering—and he convinced a number of black abolitionists that he was not afraid to kill and die to win their people's freedom. "Did not my Master Jesus Christ come down from Heaven and sacrifice himself upon the altar for the salvation of the race," Brown asked a white skeptic, "and should I, a worm, not worthy to crawl under His feet, refuse to sacrifice myself?"[37]

Such acts could not, however, minimize the stark inequality of resources between the races. Gerrit Smith donated large parcels of the million acres he owned in rural New York to black abolitionists and thus created an interracial colony. But he did not divest himself of the wealth that allowed him to decide who was worthy of his philanthropy and who was not.

Neither did the color-blind aspirations of white activists prevent many of them from instructing black activists how to gain entrance into middle-class society. "Establish for yourselves a character of industry, sobriety & integrity," the New England AAS advised a black convention in 1832. That same year, Garrison let slip his concern that African Americans would not "rank as equals" until they achieved the "knowledge and cultivation" of middle-class whites. A decade later, Lydia Maria Child, a prominent abolitionist author, was introduced to Charles Remond, an elo-

John Brown in the 1850s. Brown imagined he could lead an insurrection of slaves because he identified so strongly with their suffering—and convinced many black abolitionists he was willing to kill and die to win freedom for their people.

quent black orator. In a letter to Wendell Phillips, she confessed, "He is the first colored person I have met, who seemed to be altogether such a one as I would have him. He carries ballast enough for his sails, and that is unusual."[38] Understanding why most black people were not like them did not stop white radicals like Child from insisting that they strive to become equally perfect.

Predictably, sex across the color line was the most difficult matter for abolitionists of either race to accept. In millions of words and thousands of speeches, they condemned the license of slave owners to seduce and rape black women. Of all the crimes permitted to masters, none was so morally heinous as the coerced intimacy that produced a huge population of mulattos deprived of paternal affection, guidance, and their rightful inheritance. The abolitionists' foes habitually accused them of lusting after the racial other. Freedom activists vigorously denied it, whether because they feared their own desires or because they wanted to avoid a debate that, in a culture fraught with anxieties about race mixing, they could not hope to win.[39]

Yet real life did occasionally trump reticence. Some degree of sexual attraction was inevitable between people who struggled together for a great purpose—as it was for other Americans who lived in biracial communities. In 1832, Garrison and Child demanded repeal of a Massachusetts law against interracial marriage. "The government ought not to control the affections, any more than the consciences of citizens," Child declared. Still, few black or white abolitionists before the Civil War took such a leap across the color line themselves.

One who defied the prohibition was Frederick Douglass. He often flirted with white women and had long and close friendships with two young European abolitionists: the Englishwoman Julia Griffiths and Ottilie Assing from Germany. Both women were attractive, well-educated, and aggressive—in both their working and personal lives. To safeguard his reputation, Douglass never revealed whether the friendships grew into affairs, but many of his fellow activists suspected they had.

So, it seems, did Douglass's wife, Anna, a freeborn black woman eight years his senior whose savings had helped finance his escape to freedom in 1838. Although their marriage lasted until her death in 1882, it was seldom joyful. Anna Douglass never learned to read and was ill at ease among white people. While her husband traveled the world, she organized his household and raised their children. Eighteen months after she died, Douglass, then sixty-six, married Helen Pitts, a college-educated white clerk in her mid-forties. Pitts's family disowned her, and the press—both black and white—denounced him. Douglass quipped to the press that "his first wife was the color of my mother, and the second, the color of my father." But in a letter to a friend, he fumed, "What business has the world with the color of my wife." When Ottilie Assing heard the news on a lovely summer day in Paris, she left her hotel, walked to the Bois de Boulogne, and swallowed a vial of cyanide.[40]

Few abolitionists were as brave, or foolhardy, as Douglass in bending the bars of custom that imprisoned black people, slave and free, up to the Civil War and beyond. Yet his desire for personal happiness mirrored the larger battle that abolitionists had begun to wage for full equality in law and society, as well as in personal life. That lofty demand went unfulfilled, even after slavery ended, and not every activist adhered to it in practice. Moreover, as Douglass demonstrated, pursuing it could harm innocents along the way. But in establishing the left's reputation for universal empathy, fueled by a romantic faith, abolitionists built a foundation for every radical movement to come.

## "WHAT IF I AM A WOMAN!"

One of the few old comrades who congratulated Frederick Douglass on his second marriage was Elizabeth Cady Stanton. Her good wishes came with a sarcastic jab directed at anyone who criticized his choice of a bride: "After all the terrible battles and political upheavals we have had in expurgating our constitutions of that odious adjective 'white' it is really remarkable that you of all men should have stooped to do it honor." Then she added, "If a good man from Maryland sees fit to marry a disfranchised woman from New York, there should be no legal impediments to the union."[41]

Stanton's scorn for bigoted conventions epitomized the spirit of the women's rights campaign she did as much as anyone to create and lead. Beginning in the 1840s, her movement fought for a long list of specific changes: the right for women to control their own property and gain custody of their children in a divorce, to do the same work and be paid the same wages as men, to become ordained ministers and speak to mixed audiences, and to win the right to vote and hold office. A few states enacted these reforms before the Civil War; full legal equality was not achieved until the late twentieth century. But the primary success of the first feminist movement was to rebut, with a potent arsenal of wit and learning and common sense, the idea that men should decide what women should be allowed to do. That simple challenge struck at the foundations of civilization and gradually reverberated around the globe.

The emergence of women's rights from within the abolitionist crusade has become something of a historical cliché. Most of the key figures who forged the critique of male domination—including Stanton, Lydia Maria Child, Susan B. Anthony, Angelina and Sarah Grimké, Lucretia Mott, and Sojourner Truth—did indeed adapt to their new insurgency the language and tactics they had learned in battling slavery. For several years, every letter each Grimké, apostate daughters of a rich South Carolina planter, wrote to the other concluded, "Thy sister in the bonds of woman and the slave."[42]

But the roots of the early feminists were deeper and more varied than

Elizabeth Cady Stanton and
her daughter, Harriot.
from a daguerreotype 1856.

Elizabeth Cady Stanton, holding her
daughter Harriot, 1856. Stanton wrote
and agitated tirelessly for women's rights
from the 1840s until her death in 1902.
Harriot continued her work, helping to
win woman suffrage in 1920.

that. The evangelical yearning for perfection provided kindling for their work, just as it did for their abolitionist brethren. Some female activists echoed Frances Wright's fierce attack on organized religion. But few were willing to abandon the faith that God lived "in every person," as the Quakers put it—and this gave them confidence to keep climbing the ethical path, however long and arduous the trek might be.

Beginning in the 1820s, female Christian firebrands spoke out on issues they viewed as sinful analogues to slavery. In New York City, Boston, and hundreds of northeastern villages, the Female Moral Reform Society condemned the clients and merchants of prostitution. They insisted "that immediate and vigorous efforts should be made to create a public sentiment in respect to this sin" and "that the licentious man is no less guilty than his victim, and ought, therefore, to be excluded from all virtuous female society." Reform Society activists entered taverns and brothels to hold prayer meetings and established refuges for women willing to leave the benighted trade. They dared to solicit the names of male clients from prostitutes and published them in their journal.

Temperance also claimed the energies of thousands of women who later became advocates of women's rights. Their motivation was practical as much as spiritual: the lure of strong drink drove men to squander their money, beat their wives, neglect their children, and fall under the sway of saloon owners and the politicians who let them operate wherever and for as many hours as they pleased. By opposing prostitution and liquor, evangelical women believed they were defending their homes and the future of the race—as well as pointing the way to a more Christian society. In New England and New York state, many temperance women also belonged to an abolitionist society. Slavery, they believed, came in many forms; each one had to be exposed and eradicated.[43]

To do so, genteel women spoke out aggressively, breaking the code that confined them to the kitchen and the nursery. Their oratory against social evils became an issue in itself and led, indirectly, to the first gatherings that explicitly advocated equal rights for women. The local controversy Frances Wright had touched off late in 1829 mushroomed into a national debate during the following decade.

Talks by female abolitionists to "promiscuous" or mixed audiences drew the most controversy. In 1832, Maria Stewart, a domestic worker from Boston, lectured a group of her fellow black women on the need for them to take a leading role in battling slavery. "What if I am a woman!" she declared. "Did not Queen Esther save the lives of the Jews? And Mary Magdalene first declare the resurrection of Christ from the dead?" Although Stewart declared herself a disciple of David Walker's, her talk didn't curdle public opinion since neither black men nor white people were present. In 1836, however, Angelina Grimké embarked on a speaking tour of New England; the following year, her older sister, Sarah, joined her on the platform. Making radical statements in a refined southern drawl, the Grimkés drew huge crowds and recruited hundreds of people to the movement. But the animus they aroused was just as notable.[44]

As the superior performer, Angelina was the prime object of both acclaim and derision. In a poised yet emotional voice, the thirty-two-year-old described her plantation upbringing as a test of the soul which gave her a special mission to bring women into the struggle. She spoke in explicit detail about the sexual liberties male planters took with their female chattels. She urged Northern women not just to cease buying products made by slave labor; they should also "extend the right hand of fellowship" to "our oppressed colored sisters, who are suffering in our very midst." Ministers, even some who were abolitionists, denounced her for talking about "things which ought not to be named." Angelina was barred from speaking in the Congregational churches of Massachusetts, the largest denomination in the state. From press and pulpit came demands that the freedom movement prevent women from leaving their "natural" sphere, where it was assumed they chatted prettily about domestic concerns.

In the spring of 1837, the Grimké sisters defied the critics when they helped to organize a convention of two hundred female abolitionists in Manhattan. What may have been the first public gathering of activist women in U.S. history began with a reading of the Twenty-seventh Psalm: "The Lord is my light and my salvation, whom shall I fear?" A

Angelina Grimké, c. 1840s.
Grimké broke away from
South Carolina plantation society
to become a dynamic orator for
abolitionism and women's rights.

majority of delegates voted in favor of a strong resolution stating that "certain rights and duties are common to all moral beings"—first among them, the right to advocate the overthrow of slavery. The following winter, Angelina Grimké became the first woman to address the Massachusetts legislature. "We Abolition Women are turning the world upside down," she told the lawmakers.[45]

Yet a few months later in Philadelphia, her speaking career came to a dramatic end. On May 14, 1838, several hundred abolitionists dedicated Pennsylvania Hall, a lavish new structure just a few blocks from where the Declaration of Independence had been signed. The hall was built with contributions from over two thousand reformers and radicals. Never again would the lovers of liberty have to beg anxious or hostile property owners to rent them space for a meeting. After the opening ceremonies, another convention of anti-slavery women was scheduled to begin. But some Philadelphians saw the gathering of blacks and whites, as well as of women and men, as an affront to their racial pride. On the third day of the meeting, just as Angelina rose to speak, a mob of thousands—most of whom were white migrants from the South or from Ireland—encircled the building and prepared to attack it.

"These voices without tell us that the spirit of slavery is *here*," she began, as stones rattled against the tall windows. Every citizen had a duty to resist the evil in their midst, she claimed, but American women had an additional fight to wage. "Men who hold the rod over slaves rule in the councils of the nation . . . they deny our right to petition and remonstrate against abuses of our sex and our kind. We have these rights, however, from our God. Only let us exercise them . . . There is . . . no cause for doubting or despair."

A day later, the mob forced activists to leave their proud new structure; then they burned it to the ground. Whether out of fear or frustration, Angelina, who had recently married Theodore Weld, never spoke in public again. In 1840, the hot debate about whether women should speak to mixed audiences contributed to the schism between the Garrisonians and the Liberty Party. It then cooled down gradually until the coming of the Civil War pushed questions of gender propriety out of the headlines.[46]

However, a feminist movement was quietly developing on two continents. During the 1840s and early 1850s, advocates of women's rights in the U.S. cultivated working friendships with a few dozen of their counterparts in Britain, France, Germany, and Scandinavia. They wrote for each other's publications and attended one another's conventions. Some authored popular books or long essays on the female condition— Margaret Fuller's *Woman in the Nineteenth Century*, Harriet Taylor's "Enfranchisement of Women," Fredrika Bremer's novel *Hertha, or the Story of a Soul*—which helped influence the debate about the proper role and desires of their gender.

European feminists were more attracted to socialism and far less likely to belong to an evangelical church than were their American sisters. But all agreed on a long list of reforms that would bring about "the vindication of the right of Woman to civil and political equality," as two French activists put it in 1850. Their agenda ranged from changing laws that discriminated against women in marriage, at work, in education, and in government to the wearing of wide "Turkish" trousers over a short skirt instead of tightly cinched dresses that reached to the floor. Journalists dubbed the new costume "bloomers" after Amelia Bloomer, editor of a leading temperance and feminist paper, who wore and publicized it. This affectionate network of the like-minded anticipated the "global sisterhood" hailed by feminists during the 1960s and after, but the antebellum forerunners had neither the coherence nor the muscle of an organization to advance their ends.[47]

Not until the revolutionary year of 1848 did American crusaders for women's rights have the opportunity and the courage to hold a meeting to declare themselves as such. The significance of that famous July gathering in Seneca Falls, New York, was less in the Declaration of Sentiments signed by the one hundred participants (one-third of whom were male, including the chairman) than in the fact that the gathering took place at all. Seneca Falls was a prosperous haven of reform where no liquor could be sold, and the Liberty Party, spearheaded by local resident Henry Stanton, was strong. But the only institution in town willing to host the meeting was the Wesleyan Chapel, spiritual home of abolitionists who had "come out" of the regular Methodist church.[48]

"We hold these truths to be self-evident: that all men and women are created equal," began the declaration, the first in a long chain of documents by radicals who would refashion Jefferson's draft for purposes the third president, who died in 1826, would probably have rejected. Of the ten resolutions protesting "repeated injuries and usurpations on the part of men toward woman" discussed inside the Wesleyan Chapel, just one failed to win unanimous approval: the right to vote. "Those who took part in the debate," recalled Elizabeth Cady Stanton and the other editors of *The History of Woman Suffrage* decades later, "feared [that] demand . . . would defeat others they deemed more rational, and make the whole movement ridiculous." The resolution carried by a slim margin. Frederick Douglass, the most prominent man in attendance, spoke up for it, which may have made the difference. He knew what it was like to be a disenfranchised citizen.[49]

Why did universal suffrage, now regarded as the cornerstone of any true democracy, appear "ridiculous" even to some radical activists in the middle of the nineteenth century? All the other resolutions passed at Seneca Falls repeated principled stands the Grimké sisters and their fellow activists had taken a decade before. They claimed the right for women to speak in public and for both sexes to be judged by the same standard of "virtue, delicacy, and refinement of behavior"; they declared that women and men were equal before God. Like the right of married women to own property, these were positions feminists could defend before a broader public. None threatened the domination of men over the public sphere—at a time when partisan politics was waged with a passion akin to combat.[50]

More than oratory, the marketplace, the workshop, or the streets, American government in the nineteenth century was the near-exclusive province of strong men. To change that image and reality would take seven decades of hard campaigning—and a shift to the right in the rhetoric of most suffragists, who largely ceased defending the rights of black men and new immigrants. In 1917, when New York state finally gave the other half of its citizens the right to vote, just one woman who had signed the Declaration of Sentiments was still alive to cast a ballot.[51]

Like most antebellum radicals, the participants at Seneca Falls took their religion very seriously. All but one had been born a Protestant, and the lone exception—fourteen-year-old Susan Quinn—was the daughter of an Irish Catholic father who had decamped for the Episcopalians a few years earlier. While the feminists eagerly, and often wittily, rebutted ministers who told them to keep silent, most did so by appealing to the same higher authority. Sarah Grimké wrote in her pioneering *Letters on the Equality of the Sexes*, "All I ask of our brethren is, that they will take their feet from off our necks, and permit us to stand upright on that ground which God has designed us to occupy."[52]

Not all Grimké's comrades agreed that Christianity would liberate women. Frances Wright was only the best-known, and most notorious, freethinking skeptic in the early feminist movement. In fact, echoes of the anticlerical animus then common on the European left may have rung louder among female activists in the U.S. than among their male counterparts in the abolitionist crusade. That nearly every American churchman deplored women speaking out on any topic, religious or political, inevitably angered their targets.

In 1852, the issue was fervently, if briefly, joined at a women's rights convention held in Syracuse. Antoinette Brown, a recent graduate of both Oberlin College and its seminary, challenged the idea that scripture barred women from entering the ministry. She interpreted Paul's injunction to the Corinthians, "Let your women keep silence in the churches," as forbidding only the *untutored* from asking "questions which did not edify the assembly." She doubted that God would have "approved" so "many prophetesses" if he meant to bar women from giving sermons and leading prayers. "The Bible is truly democratic," Brown concluded, "Do as you would be done by . . . recognizing neither male nor female in Christ Jesus."[53] Elizabeth Cady Stanton, who would later publish the controversial *Woman's Bible*, described these as "good points"; most delegates at the convention probably agreed. They felt comfortable with Brown, the daughter of good abolitionists and faithful churchgoers, who had attended one of the only colleges to admit both women and black people. Her theology was of a piece with her politics—and she had as much right as any man to preach it.

But they had to respect the next speaker too, even though she cut a unique figure in an assembly of native-born Protestants. "For my part," declared Ernestine Rose, "I see no need to appeal to any written authority, particularly when it is so obscure and indefinite as to admit of different interpretations." If the makers of the American Revolution had quoted from the Bible to justify their actions, Rose argued, their British rulers "would have answered them, 'Submit to the powers that be, for they are from God.' " Women should instead demand equal rights "as an act of justice." That "is as self-evident as that two and two makes four."[54]

Rose's distaste for Christian apologetics stemmed, in part, from her upbringing: she was raised in a Polish shtetl, the rebellious daughter of the wealthy Rabbi Potowski. Born in 1805, the girl studied Jewish texts with her father but saw no reason to abide by rules or laws she considered irrational. When Ernestine was sixteen, the rabbi tried to betroth her to one of his friends. Enraged, she argued the matter before a secular court and won. She then left home, never to return. In Berlin, to support herself, she invented an early deodorizer, a "chemical paper to perfume apartments." She moved from there to London, where she married an Englishman, William Rose; in 1836, the couple moved to New York City. Once settled in America, Ernestine Rose began giving speeches for women's property rights and a freethinking socialism. She took on clergymen in public debates about the authority and value of scripture, and fellow abolitionists and feminists who put their faith in electoral politics. Occasionally, she shared a stage with Fanny Wright.[55]

Ernestine Rose was an exemplar of international feminism, a woman who recognized neither gods, nor masters, nor the relevance of national borders. Although little known today, she passed her legacy on to such later activists as Emma Goldman and Louise Bryant, women whose uncompromising secularism and calls for revolution made them notorious but also big hits in the press and on the lecture circuit. But in antebellum America, Rose may have been, as Susan B. Anthony observed, "too much in advance of the extreme ultraists even to be understood by them."[56]

A year after the Syracuse convention, Antoinette Brown was ordained by the Congregational church—the first woman to achieve that honor. Yet before long, the church's Calvinist doctrine of salvation for the few and damnation for the rest rankled her humanitarian sensibilities. She underwent a spiritual crisis, leaving to become a minister in the Unitarian church, home of many northeastern reformers and radicals. After the Civil War, Brown remained a pillar of the women's movement, which increasingly focused on the demand for suffrage. In contrast, Ernestine Rose, then in late middle age, spent time debating the editor of a prominent free-thought paper in Boston who contended that Jews were "totally unfit for progressive people like the Americans among whom we hope they may not spread." In 1869, she essentially gave up the struggle and moved back to London, where she died.[57]

Despite the stark differences in their views and backgrounds, Brown and Rose enjoyed an advantage few non-radical American women of their time could imagine: husbands who warmly supported their political and intellectual careers. William Rose was a quiet man whose Manhattan jewelry shop made it possible for Ernestine to travel and agitate. In his spare time, he compiled a thick scrapbook of her clippings. After Brown was ordained, she married Samuel Blackwell, a British-born abolitionist. Antoinette Blackwell worried marriage might clip her activist wings. "Only leave me free," she assured him, "as free you are

Ernestine Rose, c. 1850s.
The daughter of a Polish rabbi, Rose migrated to the United States and spoke out for women's property rights and a freethinking socialism. She took on clergymen in public debates about the authority and value of scripture and fellow abolitionists and feminists who put their faith in electoral politics.

and everyone ought to be, and it is giving up nothing." Bringing up five children did limit her preaching and traveling. But she became a prolific author who stayed active in feminist causes until her death in 1920.[58]

In the antebellum movement, such stories were commonplace. Abolitionist men tended to marry abolitionist women, and both love and ideology gave their wives the freedom to continue their work in public, if that was their desire. In this intense community of would-be equals, marriage ceremonies often had a countercultural flavor. No minister or magistrate presided at the 1838 wedding of Angelina Grimké and Theodore Weld. Before guests of both races, they took one another's hand as the groom promised "to love, honor and cherish and in all things to recognize your equality with me." A Unitarian minister, the writer Thomas Wentworth Higginson, married Lucy Stone and Henry Blackwell (Samuel's younger brother) in 1855. But the couple wrote their own ceremony, which included a vow to disobey laws that "refuse to recognize the wife as an independent, rational being." Lucy insisted on keeping her own surname—a step that seemed, to many Americans, almost as radical as a woman running for president.[59]

Of course, not all activist marriages were happy ones, and not every advocate of women's rights got wed. Rearing a family inevitably took energy and time away from the movement. While Elizabeth Cady Stanton gave birth to seven children, only a corps of servants enabled her to take off for the meeting room, the lecture hall, and her writing desk. One reason agitation for women's rights stagnated between 1840 and the Seneca Falls meeting in 1848 is that many of its leaders had children during those years. Without effective birth control, biology could trump the best intentions of big dreamers.[60]

For some activists, intimacy with men was neither practical nor desirable. They forged enduring, loving partnerships with other women. Mary Grew, a leading abolitionist and feminist in Pennsylvania, shared a home and bed for decades with a teacher, Margaret Burleigh. It appears that Susan B. Anthony longed for such a relationship too. During the 1860s, she wrote dozens of ardent letters to Anna Dickinson, a beautiful young radical orator. Anthony addressed her as "My Dear Chicky Dick Darling" and wrote that her "plain quarters" had a "double bed . . . big enough and good enough to take you in." All forms of homosexuality were strictly illegal in the nineteenth century. Either out of discretion or inhibition, these women did not reveal if their attachments involved genital sex. Perhaps it did not matter. "Love is spiritual, only passion is sexual," wrote Mary Grew to a close friend. Foes of their movement routinely charged that only "mannish" women were unhappy with their status in American society. Feminists who loved other women quietly defied this slur and seeded a new definition of freedom that future generations of activists would harvest.[61]

The same can be said for the antebellum women's rights movement as a whole. A serious campaign to win the vote didn't begin until after the Civil War, when women also began to push their way into labor unions, universities, and the professions, and to form a female network of clubs and other supportive institutions. Yet, more than a century before modern feminists declared that "the personal is political," many of their forerunners were preaching and practicing their own version of that credo. "It is a settled maxim with me," asserted Elizabeth Cady Stanton, "that the existing public sentiment on any subject is wrong." She and her comrades had taken the first step to transforming what the rest of the world believed women could and should accomplish.[62]

## SOCIALISM STILLBORN

The first American socialists had an even grander ambition. They yearned to replace the emerging order of relentless competition with a realm of perfect cooperation. In their view, capitalism, while an engine of growth, generated untold profits and luxuries for a lucky elite and poverty, anxiety, and war for everyone else. It also valued human beings merely as cogs in the dynamo of material progress, relentlessly dividing each occupation into smaller and more specialized tasks. "The state of society," Emerson wrote in 1837, "is one in which the members have suffered amputation from the trunk, and strut about like so many walking monsters—a good finger, a neck, a stomach, an elbow, but never a man." In the antebellum years, this critique was shared by thousands of Americans who were repulsed by the inequalities that mill owners and free-market ideologists had created. Why not, asked socialists, try to remake the world into a harmonious, loving place in which the benefits of science and technology could be enjoyed, in roughly equal shares, by all?[63]

Early socialists, like their sometime partners, the abolitionists, believed the best way to persuade Americans of their ideas was to carry them out in practice. From the mid-1820s to the late 1840s, several hundred communities or "socialisms" were founded, most in the northeastern states. Those who joined one typically performed collective housework, entered into egalitarian marriages or none at all, rotated necessary tasks from milking cows to building houses, and shed all or most of their private property to embrace a "community of goods." They frowned on segregation, whether by race or gender. Although their aim was a perfect society, socialists believed the only way to get there was to pursue a rational plan to transform how individuals worked with and treated one another. "We estimate the man by his acts rather than his peculiar belief," explained John A. Collins, leader of the colony in Skaneateles, New York. "We say to him, Believe what you may, but act as well as you can."[64]

A number of prominent writers were smitten, however briefly, with these glimmerings of utopia. Emerson, Hawthorne, and Fuller all spent time at Brook Farm, the experimental community near Boston that attracted some of that city's intellectual luminaries. Elizabeth Cady Stanton came close to joining the Raritan Bay Union in New Jersey. "All our talk about woman's rights is mere moonshine," she declared, "so long as we are bound by the present social system." Frederick Douglass made friendly visits to the communities of Hopedale and Florence in rural Massachusetts. The latter, he enthused, was "a protest against sectarianism and bigotry, and an assertion of the paramount importance of human brotherhood."[65]

Horace Greeley, editor of the *New-York Tribune*, the most popular daily newspaper in the country, also did whatever he could to publicize the cooperative vision. A self-educated farmer's boy from New England, Greeley was appalled by the hurly-burly ruthlessness he glimpsed on the streets and in the workshops of Manhattan. There was, he wrote in 1842, "no more ruinous, demoralizing, antisocial and anti-Christian principle than that of FREE COMPETITION." In electoral politics, Greeley was a faithful booster of the Whig Party. But he was, at the same time, a convert to the utopian designs of Charles Fourier, the French exponent of passionate communitarianism who gained few followers in his own land before his death in 1837. Greeley opened the pages of his newspaper to a lengthy series of columns by Albert Brisbane, himself the son of a wealthy landowner, who advocated Fourierism as an alternative to the system of wages and capital. Brisbane carefully avoided mentioning either the deceased sage's ardor for free love or his anti-Semitism. During the 1850s, the *Tribune* also ran close to five hundred articles by Karl Marx, who was free to comment on any political or economic issue. "It was the most regular employment he held in his entire life," observes one historian.[66]

For a brief time, socialism became rather fashionable in high political circles as well as lofty intellectual ones. During the winter of 1825, Robert Owen, the Welsh manufacturer who had recently established the socialist colony of New Harmony in rural Indiana, presented his ideas to a joint session of Congress. "This is a revolution from a system in which individual reward and punishment has been the universal practice," he told the legislators, "to one, in which individual reward and punishment will be unpracticed and unknown, except as a grievous error of a past wretched system." President James Monroe and President-elect John Quincy Adams both stopped by to listen. Their curiosity was a sign that the market system, for all its promise of plenty, was not yet a settled reality for all men of wealth and standing.[67]

Across the ocean, a young German socialist read everything he could find about the new movement, then urged his radical comrades to emulate it. "This much is . . . certain," declared Frederick Engels in 1845, "the Americans, and particularly the poor workers in the large towns of New York, Philadelphia, Boston, etc., have taken the matter into their hearts and founded a large number of societies for the establishment of such colonies . . . The Americans are tired of continuing as the slaves of the few rich men who feed on the labour of the people; and it is obvious that with the great energy and endurance of this nation, community of goods will be introduced over a significant part of their country."[68]

Engels, who didn't visit the United States until the 1880s, was far too sanguine. Some artisans, whose trade unions were beset by hostile judges and employers, did warm to the classless vision, whether articulated by Owen or by Brisbane. The New York printer George Henry Evans, a British immigrant, published essays by both Owen and Frances Wright. But not many American workers were eager to join settlements whose economic prospects were uncertain and whose organizers handled a pen more deftly than an ax or a hammer. Far more were attracted to the idea of the government handing out free plots of land in the West, which Evans promoted as leader of a group called the National Reform Association. A socialism that included few wage earners could not long endure.[69]

Meanwhile, American workers were beginning to organize themselves. They increasingly resented "master" employers who, in an expanding marketplace, no longer had to dirty their own hands in manual toil. Nascent labor unions demanded such reforms as a ten-hour day, higher wages, and the abolition of imprisonment for debt, all of which could be satisfied without threatening the rights and privileges of property, as radicals like Evans and Thomas Skidmore were doing. By the mid-1830s, dozens of local unions had blossomed in every major city from Boston to Cincinnati; in 1835, a general strike in Philadelphia for shorter hours briefly closed down nearly every factory and building site in what was then the third largest city in the nation.

While labor insurgents were quite willing to halt urban commerce, they did not mount a serious challenge to the emerging two-party system, then represented by Jacksonian Democrats and their opponents, the Whigs. In November of 1829, the new, local Workingmen's Party did manage to poll close to one-third of the vote in New York City. The "Workies" scored heavily in districts occupied by artisans and laborers, with a platform that emphasized free public schools and legal protection for unions and railed against "men who fatten on the fruits of your industry." Skidmore, who was one of the party's leaders, came within twenty-three votes of winning a seat in the state assembly. But a few months after the election, factional disputes threw the party into a terminal crisis; most of its voters and activists migrated to the Democrats, whose own fierce populist rhetoric kept Northern white workers in an unholy alliance with most slaveholders in the cotton South.[70]

The contempt the early socialists showed toward religion also prevented them from luring many recruits across class lines. The freethinking Evans was the exception in plebeian neighborhoods where evangelical Protestants mingled uneasily with immigrant Catholics. Like Garrisonian abolitionists, many union activists dismissed established churches as havens for hypocrites and patronizers. But most longed to fulfill the promises of Christianity, not reject them as myths. Jesus, according to George Lippard, an intensely class-conscious Philadelphia mystery writer and labor pamphleteer, longed "to redress the wrongs of the poor" and to suppress "the rich, the proud, the oppressor." For Americans seeking a just society, free thought would finish a distant second to the Sermon on the Mount.[71]

Notwithstanding Douglass's brief enthusiasm, the early socialists were no more successful among blacks, free or slave. During the 1840s, with the help of abolitionists, fugitives from bondage had established a string of communal settlements near the Great Lakes. But these were profit-making concerns and restricted physical labor to men and household chores to women. Two decades earlier, sexual scandal and venal leadership had brought a disastrous, much-publicized end to the settlement of slaves, free blacks, and whites that Frances Wright had begun in Nashoba, Tennessee. Wright transported the remaining slaves to Haiti, where she emancipated them. To most free African Americans, self-help seemed a wiser and more practical solution.[72]

But nearly all the black collective experiments shared the fate of their more ambitious, white-run counterparts. Whatever their philosophy, most lasted only a few years before succumbing to a variety of common ailments: bad management, insufficient funds, untrained and inefficient workers, and a high turnover of members. Residents balked at doing sweaty, repetitive jobs and cherished their right to have an opinion on everything. To paraphrase Bertolt Brecht, those who wished to lay the foundations of selflessness could not abandon their own selfish ways.

The best-financed, best-planned socialist colonies were twenty-four "phalanxes" which Albert Brisbane organized in the 1840s, based on rigid principles and organizational charts he adapted from the writings of Fourier. But together, these communities attracted only about four thousand residents; just two phalanxes survived more than five years. Emerson wrote to Thomas Carlyle in 1840, "We are all a little wild here with numberless projects of social reform. Not a reading man but has a draft of a new community in his waistcoat pocket." A decade later, most of the plans had scattered to the winds. The individualist ethic had triumphed, at least for a while. Not many abolitionists or feminists looked forward to residing in a collectivist utopia.[73]

These stillborn socialisms did make one signal contribution to American culture. To break the chains of patriarchal marriage, many communalists experimented with "free love," both in doctrine and practice. This both titillated and horrified most Americans—judging from the charges of "harlotry," rape, and child abuse that routinely steamed out of the press. Sexual radicals defended themselves by echoing Shelley's romantic prescription from 1813: "a husband and wife ought to continue so long united as long as they love each other; any law which should bind them to cohabit for one moment after the decay of their affection would be a most intolerable tyranny . . ."[74]

The spectrum of sexual philosophies and behaviors among early socialists was actually quite broad, although each colony set down rules of conduct whose rigor would have baffled the libertine commune-dwellers of the 1960s and '70s. At one pole were a handful of radicals, like Bronson Alcott at the Fruitlands community, who sought to remain celibate. Like the Shakers, they believed sexual intercourse bred only jealousy and possessiveness. It spelled the triumph of the needy flesh over the altruistic spirit. At the other extreme—and more common—were those like John Humphrey Noyes of the Oneida colony who preached a loose form of serial monogamy, stipulating only that true affection should accompany desire. Noyes, whose community in upstate New York endured for three decades, took a liberated deity for his model. After Jesus rose to heaven, wrote Noyes, "he had the passions of an ordinary lover" and was "morally free to do as He saw fit." The young women at Oneida took part in a "sexual apprenticeship" program. In order to regulate pregnancies, Noyes counseled men to practice coitus interruptus, but it is questionable whether he followed his own advice. Late in life, he fathered ten children with several different partners.[75]

Perhaps predictably, few women were so eager to break with romantic conventions. Frances Wright's brief espousal of free, interracial love in the late 1820s had gotten her branded a "Great Red Harlot of Infidelity," and she never took such a public stand again. Although socialist men shunned traditional marriage more rigorously than did many feminists, most did so in order to liberate their carnal selves. This clashed directly with the ideology of "true womanhood" on which their wives and sisters, however radical their politics, had been raised. When a husband and wife joined a community, it was usually the man who took the lead. "For such couples," writes one historian, socialisms "were no more than hopeful rehabilitation centers for marriages gone awry."[76]

Yet the notion that liberty included the freedom to decide for oneself whether to have sex and with whom was a radical departure from every norm of religion and custom. Previously, only randy aristocrats had exercised such freedom, and they were not in the habit of proclaiming it as a right every man and woman should enjoy. Early socialists failed to counter the individualist strivings of most Americans or to develop an embryo of a new world that did not include the flawed elements of the old. But zealous for liberty as well as lustful pleasure, they stretched the belief in an autonomous self, basic to the Protestant creed, about as far as it could go.

In their passionate idealism, abolitionists, feminists, and labor radicals also forced their way into the hot center of public debate, if not yet into partisan clubhouses or chambers of state. Often embattled and always controversial, they made millions of their fellow citizens aware of the illiberal and unequal elements that were as intrinsic to their booming society as were textile mills, steamboats, and penny newspapers. In so doing, the antebellum left shook up the body politic; the tremors are with us still.

*Chapter Two*

# THE HALFWAY REVOLUTION,
# 1840s–1870s

God does not intend for one part of his people to feel that they are superior to another part.

> —John B. Rayner, black politician
> from North Carolina[1]

No people will ever be republican in spirit and practice where a few own immense manors and the masses are landless.

> —Thaddeus Stevens, radical leader in the
> House of Representatives, c. 1865[2]

Those who make revolution half way only dig their own graves.

> —Louis de St. Just, French Jacobin, c. 1793

## THE AMERICAN 1848

UNTIL MIDCENTURY, Frederick Engels and his fellow European radicals could reasonably assume that the United States was in the vanguard of a transatlantic upheaval. The communal sprouts of socialism seemed impressive, advocates for women's rights were holding spirited conventions and publishing popular tracts, and abolitionists were challenging the governing elite with a movement whose size, self-confidence, and cultural ingenuity radicals on the other side of the ocean could not match.

Then came the spring revolutions of 1848. From Paris to Cracow, workers, shopkeepers, and students took to the streets to demand universal suffrage, civil liberties, and an end to the rule of arbitrary monarchs. Wage earners and radical intellectuals also called for a republic that would guarantee work and a decent income to all. "The political is being merged in with the social struggle," Margaret Fuller reported to the *New-York Tribune* from Rome. "It is well," she added, "whatever blood is to be shed, whatever altars cast down." The inchoate alliance of plebeian democrats was rent by differences of class and ideology and lacked sufficient arms; it was brutally suppressed by professional militaries, then seduced and divided by such populist demagogues as Louis Napoleon of France. Yet, in the embers of defeat, a class-conscious left was born. "Society was cut in two," shuddered Alexis de Tocqueville. "Those who had nothing united in common envy, and those who had anything united in common terror."[3]

Within a generation, tribunes of the envious would create mass socialist parties united by the vision of a world run by the men and women who did its labor. Although that quest went unfulfilled, the new organizations did secure the right to vote for working-class men and planted the seeds for the luxuriant welfare states of the mid-twentieth century. The one essential scripture of this egalitarian faith was *The Communist Manifesto*, published just weeks before the revolutions of 1848 began. Engels, collaborating with the more eloquent Karl Marx, repudiated the same socialists he had praised just three years before. To build their "castles in the air," the "utopians," claimed the *Manifesto*, had to court sympathetic members of the bourgeoisie and to "violently oppose all political action on the part of the working class." It was an unkind and unfair description of fellow radicals who attempted to offer practical evidence that "wage slavery" could be transcended. In fact, Marx and Engels continued to imagine their ideal future in the same romantic terms as did Robert Owen and John Humphrey Noyes. The *Manifesto* concluded, "The old bourgeois society, with its classes and class conflicts, will be replaced by an association in which the free development of each will lead to the free development of all." But for the next century, their analysis of the capitalist order and labor-centered strategy for forging a new one would be the main credo of the European left and spread its influence to the rebellious subjects of European empires.

For American radicals, 1848 had quite a different meaning. In the U.S., white working men already had the right to vote, and they exercised it with gusto in a republic whose ideals they cherished. But slavery was the bane of that republic, and in 1848, the United States began its descent into the inferno of civil war. That February, for a paltry

$15 million, American diplomats, under the direction of President James K. Polk, forced the Mexican government, which the U.S. had just defeated in war, to abandon its dominion over what is now California and most of the Southwest. The new territories brought the issue of slavery to a crisis point. Whatever politicians, in and out of Congress, did over the ensuing decade—from the Compromise of 1850 to the Kansas-Nebraska Act to the collapse of the Whig Party and the rise of the Republicans—only temporarily delayed the outbreak of war between North and South.

The American 1848 did not immediately alter the perceptions of anti-slavery leaders. In that fall's election, the new Free Soil Party—which opposed extending slavery to the territories but stopped short of calling for abolition—won 10 percent of the popular vote. But it did so with a nominee, former president Martin Van Buren, whom abolitionists, until recently, had considered an incorrigible foe. Winning not a single electoral vote, the Free Soilers made little difference in the outcome. Zachary Taylor, a Whig slaveholder from Louisiana, narrowly captured the White House.

After hearing the results, Frederick Douglass, who had given Van Buren his tepid endorsement, counseled his fellow radicals to steel themselves for countless years in the wilderness. As "a moral movement," they "will always be too odious . . . to be regarded as suitable candidates for offices of emolument or honor," he wrote. But they should have no regrets, for "they have a higher and better reward—the assurance that they have not lived for themselves."[4]

Over the next decade, socialists and feminists had to seek similar comfort as most utopian colonies disbanded, and women's rights stalled at the propaganda stage. In Europe, too, their radical counterparts were in retreat; conservatives regained the political initiative, and the workers' movement had to trim its demands to narrow material improvements which well-off employers could plausibly satisfy. In 1852, Marx's friend Joseph Weydemeyer and several of his fellow expatriate German socialists, part of a surge of militant refugees from the defeated uprisings in their homeland, began publishing a New York City paper, bravely entitled *Die Revolution*. At the same time, they established the first Marxist organizations on U.S. soil: the Proletarierbund and the American Workers League. But *Die Revolution* appeared just twice, and their equally short-lived groups conducted most of their business in German.[5]

Nor did the growing power of the Republican Party make Douglass and his compatriots more confident about the prospects for freedom. Despite electing scores of congressmen from the North and West, the Republicans could do nothing to curb the expansion of the slave power, and most were opposed to calling for an end to slavery where it already existed. Some principled abolitionists did win seats in Congress, most notably the eloquent senators Charles Sumner from Massachusetts and Salmon Chase from Ohio. But throughout the North, federal marshals were still required to enforce the odious Fugitive Slave Law, a key provision of the Compromise of 1850 that had been intended, ironically, to cool sectional hostilities.

Outraged at the new law, radicals decided that they could no longer turn the other cheek. In Boston, abolitionists routinely hid escaped slaves and harassed the "man stealers" in every way they could. "Our white brethren cannot understand us unless we speak to them in their own language," declared James McCune Smith, after runaway slaves battled with slave-catchers in Pennsylvania, "They will never recognize our manhood until we knock them down a time or two . . ." Frederick Douglass agreed: "The only way to make the Fugitive Slave Law a dead letter is to make half-a-dozen or more dead kidnappers."[6]

The fury against this "immoral and irreligious statute" marked a watershed in the movement's history. For the first time since David Walker's *Appeal*, a sizable number of abolitionists rejected the principle of non-resistance. If evil men were going to force their fellow Americans back into bondage, perhaps the only moral stance was to commit violence in the cause of freedom. In 1855, the new Radical Abolition Party, founded in Syracuse, defined slavery as "a state of war." The party was never more than an electoral cipher. But the delegates in Syracuse voted to donate money for guns to a stern-faced, fifty-five-year-old activist who was on his way to Kansas, where pro- and anti-slavery settlers were battling for control of the territory. John Brown, one of the few strict Calvinists in the movement, sincerely believed God had chosen him to wage holy war. "Without the shedding of blood," he quoted from Hebrews, "there is no remission of sin."[7]

Brown had long advocated a bloody end to slavery. In 1848, he helped reissue David Walker's fiery pamphlet; in 1851, he formed the League of Gileadites, a mostly black group dedicated to defending fugitive slaves from recapture. Other abolitionists—most notably the celebrated minister Henry Ward Beecher, brother of Harriet Beecher Stowe—raised money to arm his side in "Bleeding Kansas." But Brown took the warrior path first and never strayed from it. He was also a budding Christian socialist who believed, according to one of his sons, in a "community plan of cooperative industry, in which all should labor for the common good and share 'all things in common' as did the disciples of Jesus in his day." In October of 1859, Brown nailed his place in history when he led a botched raid on the federal arsenal at Harpers Ferry, Virginia. Six weeks after surrendering, Brown went to the gallows and instantly became a martyr to the cause. Writing half a century later, W. E. B. DuBois hailed him as a "prophet" who understood that slavery "had to die by revolution, not by milder means."[8]

Historians continue to debate whether the raid on Harpers Ferry sped the coming of emancipation or just made big trouble in the 1860 campaign for Republicans needing to win over Northern voters who did not favor a preemptive war against the slave power. What is beyond dispute is that Brown's audacious if ill-planned act convinced such abolitionist leaders as Douglass, Phillips, and Gerrit Smith (but not yet Garrison) that war was now the only solution. They were appalled when Abraham Lincoln, in supporting the decision to execute Brown, argued, "We have a means provided for the expression of our belief in regard to Slavery, it is through the ballot box."[9]

### A WAR FOR FREEDOM

Soon after his inauguration, Lincoln had to change his mind. The bloodiest conflict in U.S. history would bring about the end of slavery that radicals had not been close to achieving on their own. Militant abolitionists gained unprecedented status and influence during the war. John Andrew, who as an attorney had raised money for John Brown's defense, served as governor of Massachusetts throughout the war. Andrew helped Frederick Douglass persuade Lincoln to allow black men to serve in the Union Army; over 180,000 eventually did so, suffering a higher casualty rate than their white comrades. Martin Delany, Douglass's erstwhile comrade, put aside his deep skepticism about interracial cooperation to recruit black soldiers. In 1865, he became the first African-American major in U.S. history.

The war turned other anti-slavery firebrands into respectable figures.

Garrison and his allies spoke before huge, enthusiastic crowds. The president and several members of Congress attended talks by Wendell Phillips, whom they had previously shunned as a dangerous agitator; he was even introduced on the floor of the Senate, to generous applause. Conservative newspapers reported on abolitionist meetings with respect instead of derision. Such legitimacy, together with the Union's victory at Antietam in the fall of 1862, gave Lincoln the political backing he needed to issue the Emancipation Proclamation. Salmon Chase became Chief Justice of the United States. Blue-clad troops marched into battle singing "John Brown's body lies a-mouldering in the grave" but "his truth is marching on." In 1863, an integrated detachment of white, black, and Cherokee soldiers—commanded by a former associate of John Brown—battled Confederate troops for control of the Indian Territory (which later dissolved into the state of Oklahoma).[10]

Meanwhile, most feminists and socialists recast themselves as patriotic partisans. They did so as much out of conviction as expediency. After all, the Confederacy stood resolutely against equal rights in the home and workplace as well as between the races. Elizabeth Cady Stanton and other champions of women's rights suspended their separate campaigns and devoted their formidable energies to the Union cause. "All that heroic women dared and suffered through those long dark years of anxiety," Stanton and her co-authors wrote later, "should have made 'justice to woman' the spontaneous cry on the lips of our rulers," once the North had won. Joseph Weydemeyer, a veteran of the Prussian army, ceased agitating for a workers' world and turned to fighting Confederates in Missouri. He rose to the rank of lieutenant colonel and joined the Republican Party. At his death in 1866, the erstwhile revolutionary socialist was serving as the elected auditor of St. Louis County.[11]

At his second inaugural, Abraham Lincoln sounded, for a few eloquent moments, as if he were paraphrasing John Brown:

> Fondly do we hope, fervently do we pray, that this mighty scourge of war may speedily pass away. Yet, if God wills that it continue until all the wealth piled by the bondsman's two hundred and fifty years of unrequited toil shall be sunk, and until every drop of blood drawn with the lash shall be paid by another drawn with the sword, as was said three thousand years ago, so still it must be said "the judgments of the Lord are true and righteous altogether."

That evening, Frederick Douglass and a friend became the first black Americans to attend a presidential reception. At the entrance to the White House, Douglass recalled, "two policemen . . . took me rudely by the arm and ordered me to stand back, for their directions were to admit no persons of my color." But he refused to back down and sent word to the president that he and his companion were being "detained." Soon, the president was grasping Douglass's hand, curious to know what he thought of the inaugural address. "There is no man whose opinion I value more than yours," he told the veteran abolitionist. "Mr. Lincoln, that was a sacred effort," replied Douglass.[12]

Yet radicals' enlistment in the bloody common cause did not achieve the sacred goal of racial equality they had worked so long and passionately to achieve. Most whites who fought for the Union, whether with arms or on the home front, despised haughty slave masters but had little knowledge of or affection for the slaves. Northern soldiers tended to support emancipation because they wanted to punish a rebellious landed elite for gaining wealth and privilege by keeping their laborers in chains. "We of the free states have yielded to this peculiar institution," complained a blue-clad private from Connecticut early in 1863, ". . . until it has become so deeply rooted that [removing] it will shake the nation and our institutions to the very center."[13]

For that shaking to occur, millions of white Americans would have had to leap far beyond their immediate self-interest. Punishing the "rebels" by abolishing their right to hold human chattel did not jeopardize the dominance of whites in either the marketplace or the government, or challenge their assumption of racial superiority. But to open their jobs, polling booths, schools, churches, and homes up to freedpeople was quite a different matter: would the despised minority suddenly gain power over the majority, the proud sinews of the republic? "Hello, Massa; bottom rail on top dis time," a black soldier told his former owner when they met during the war. Many Unionists feared that prospect nearly as much as did hardened Confederates.[14]

Alarm in the North was greatest, inevitably, among those who had never warmed to the abolitionist cause. In the fast-growing cities, Catholic workers—most of whom were of Irish or German ancestry—saw no reason to cheer emancipation; few had voted for the Republican president who was now requiring all young men to sign up for a draft that would send most of them into combat. During the war, prices rose 20 percent higher than wages, and tenement districts became even more crowded, unhealthy, and dangerous. Workers who went on strike usually had to face police clubs and employer blacklisting—despite Lincoln's oft-stated support for the rights of labor. The fact that most urban employers were Protestant and Republican added fuel to an already combustible situation.

In July 1863, the largest city in the nation exploded. For five days, thousands of plebeian white men, most from Catholic backgrounds, rampaged through the streets of Manhattan, burning, looting, and lynching. The riot began as a peaceful protest against the start of the draft lottery in the city but quickly devolved into an assault on both New York's white elite and its free black residents. Small groups—composed, in the main, of young, unmarried men—invaded the homes of well-to-do reformers, destroying furniture and works of art. Larger mobs set upon the Colored Orphan Asylum and individual African Americans. Hundreds of black people were beaten; dozens were raped or murdered and mutilated, their body parts brandished overhead or dragged through the streets as emblems of white power and vengeance. Only with the arrival of troops fresh from the battle of Gettysburg did the authorities suppress the mobs and end the violence.[15]

The draft riots were not the only evidence that class hostility was closely linked with racial hatred in the minds of many wage-earning Americans. In the 1850s, several midwestern states had banned blacks from voting; some even passed unenforceable laws prohibiting them from taking up residence at all. The initiators of most of these statutes were Democratic officeholders whose votes came largely from white men who worked with their hands, in factories, in mines, and on farms. Their notion of a republic run by and for ordinary people excluded anyone who did not spring from European roots.

In rebuttal, abolitionists, who had flocked to the Republican banner after the attack on Fort Sumter, urged racists to appreciate their common humanity. But this sentiment appealed to only a small number of white working-class activists, most of whom were already friendly to the anti-slavery cause. Some Irish nationalists in the Fenian Brotherhood kept alive the egalitarian ideals of Daniel O'Connell; they volunteered for the Union Army and sided with the radical faction in the Republican Party. But the Catholic Church denounced the group as a band of freethinking revolutionaries, and a series of failed raids by Fenians on British outposts in Canada during the late 1860s diverted them from mobilizing Irish workers in the U.S. for any other purpose.[16]

However, across the Atlantic, American leftists could applaud acts of solidarity which they could only dream about at home. In Britain, nearly all British labor activists and millions of ordinary wage earners supported both Lincoln's government and the cause of abolition. This required many to ignore their immediate self-interest in the name of a higher good. Increasingly, the health of the British economy depended upon manufacturing; textile mills that spun Southern cotton into cloth were essential to the nation's growth. To most parliamentarians and profit-minded businessmen, it made sense to recognize the new nation led by slaveholders or, at least, to do nothing either to help Lincoln's government or to speed emancipation. For their part, the landed gentry felt a kinship with the big planters in Dixie who admired the status and envied the estates of hereditary lords and ladies.

But spokesmen for working-class Britons resolutely maintained that human rights should trump every other consideration. In 1862, a mass meeting in the crowded Marylebone district of London condemned the pro-business *Times* for promoting the Southern cause. One speaker proposed a motion to "denounce the war policy of the organ of the stock exchange swindlers and to express sympathy with the strivings of the Abolitionists for a final solution of the slave question." It carried unanimously. Although many British textile factories had to shut down for lack of cotton, few of their hungry employees called on the government to recognize the Confederacy. At year's end, U.S. ambassador Charles Francis Adams wrote that the humbler classes "sympathise with us" because they view the Civil War as "an era in the history of the world, out of which must come . . . a general recognition of the right of mankind to the produce of labor and the pursuit of happiness."[17]

British workers were hardly free of prejudice. As citizens of an empire that held sway over millions of "darker peoples," few doubted the superiority of their own race and culture. But since Britain had abolished slavery thirty years earlier, it seemed hypocritical and cruel to prop up another regime that depended on bondage. Dark-skinned migrants from Barbados and Jamaica were not yet streaming into London and Manchester, so wage earners there had no urge to emulate the rioters in Manhattan. Thus, activists who proclaimed the common bond of toilers carried the day—and played a critical part in preventing their govern-ment from aiding the breakaway nation where cotton was king.

## HOW RADICAL WAS RECONSTRUCTION?

The end of the war, followed a few months later by ratification of the Thirteenth Amendment, left abolitionists with soaring hopes for the future but no consensus about how they wanted the nation to change. With freedom now enshrined in the Constitution, William Lloyd Gar-rison suspended publication of *The Liberator* and called for the American Anti-Slavery Society to disband as well. The great work of individual liberation, he claimed, was done; Americans of goodwill should now work quietly on their own to help the freedmen and -women build new lives. "For the battering ram we must substitute the hod and trowel," counseled an ally of Garrison's, "we have passed through the pulling down stage of our movement." Most rank-and-file abolitionists probably agreed with his logic. It had been a long, exhausting struggle, and the war had persuaded most of them that only the Republican Party could protect the nation from its enemies.[18]

But other veteran crusaders, much like the European Forty-Eighters, were determined to broaden the meaning of freedom in order to trans-form America along truly egalitarian lines—even if doing so clashed with their individualist ideals. Wendell Phillips, Parker Pillsbury, and their allies refused to abandon their organization with so much left for it to do. "We have abolished the slave, but the master remains," Phillips insisted. He took the helm of the AAS, vowing to win suffrage, land, and education for the former slaves. Ever ambitious, Phillips added the uplift of wage earners of every race to his political agenda. "We protected the *black* laborer," he told a crowd in Boston in the fall of 1865, "and now we are going to protect the laborer, North and South, labor everywhere."[19]

For a time, other ex-abolitionists shared his class-conscious sympa-thies. Nearly all endorsed the eight-hour day, which emerged after the war as the central demand of a growing movement of skilled workers. Some, like Garrison, warned unhappy wage earners to petition their lawmakers instead of going on strike to press their case. A sprinkling of anti-slavery radicals joined the International Workingmen's Associa-tion (IWA), which, on Karl Marx's behest, had moved its headquarters from London to New York in the late 1860s. While only about two thousand Americans signed up with the IWA, its public events attracted "a bewildering assortment of suffragists, Spiritualists, trade unionists, land reformers, greenbackers, cooperationists, communists, and even proto-anarchists" before its demise in 1872.[20]

From his home in Britain, Marx blasted the coterie of "bogus reformers, middle-class quacks and trading politicians" for undermining the proletarian rigor he thought essential to raising socialist consciousness. But most American radicals were an optimistic lot, averse to excluding anyone from their ranks on the basis of doctrine alone. In 1871, Theodore Tilton, editor of *The Independent*, one of the most influential magazines in the nation, even compared the Communards of Paris to the Founding Fathers: "The central idea of communism is the same that George Washington spent seven years in killing his fellow-countrymen to achieve—the same which Alexander Hamilton wrote into a constitution which survives to this day."[21]

At the same time, most men on the left were not prepared to extend their sympathies to woman suffrage. In 1866, Lucy Stone, Elizabeth Cady Stanton, and Susan B. Anthony launched the American Equal Rights Association, dedicated to removing all barriers to suffrage throughout the nation. It is "the desire of [my] heart," declared Stanton at the founding convention, "that all who have worked together thus far, may still stand side by side in this crisis in our nation's history."[22]

Her qualifying adverb revealed how reluctant many radicals were to stand up for a principle they had earlier held close to their hearts. "One question at a time," cautioned Wendell Phillips as he assumed the presidency of the Anti-Slavery Society, "This hour belongs to the Negro." In rage, Stanton responded, "Do you believe the African race is composed entirely of males?"[23]

She knew suffragists were swimming against a powerful current of politics and history. By the end of the war, nearly every abolitionist had cast his or her lot with the Republican Party—including those who warmed up to militant unions. In the brewing conflict over how to reconstruct the South, the party's male officeholders and male voters remained the only force that advocated turning emancipation into equality of opportunity and had the power to back up its words. Suffragists had ceased their agitation during the war and were just beginning to create a movement that could force their demand onto the national agenda. "African" women were all but invisible in that effort, and votes for women would never become a priority for the black female activists who spearheaded anti-lynching campaigns and protested the lack of jobs and decent housing for all their people.

So Stanton and her small band of allies were stuck on their own, pleading for a return to the steadfast moralism of antebellum days when radicals had had little else to sustain them. By the end of the decade, the Republican Congress passed the Fourteenth and Fifteenth amendments, the two most significant changes in the Constitution since the Bill of Rights. Everyone born in the U.S. now had the same rights under law as every other citizen. But the amendments did not include the right of women to vote; that remained a matter for each state to decide.

The isolation of suffragists from their old comrades did force them to try out fresh strategies for change. Stanton and Anthony sought new allies among female wage earners in the industrial North. The Working Women's Association they founded in 1868 neither gained many members nor was able to allay the fears of craftsmen about competition from a new source of cheap labor. But it did prove how eager women activists were to transcend their comfortable backgrounds and undertake the work of building a broader coalition. A year later, realizing that no party or movement run by men would assist them, the veteran crusaders organized the National Women's Suffrage Association—the first group dedicated to achieving votes for women throughout the U.S. Over the next half century, it spawned hundreds of sophisticated, frustrating, increasingly successful campaigns to change the suffrage laws of each state and then the nation. Finally, in 1920, with ratification of the Nineteenth Amendment, every American woman won the most basic right of a democratic society.[24]

But for many radicals in the aftermath of Civil War, democracy meant more than the freedom to cast a ballot or run for office. "If the South is ever to be made a safe republic," asserted Representative Thaddeus Stevens of Pennsylvania, "let her lands be cultivated by the toil of the owners or the free labor of intelligent citizens. This must be done even though it drives her nobility into exile! If they go, all the better."[25] When he gave that speech, Stevens was in his mid-seventies and seriously ill. But the aging firebrand's echo of the language and demands of French revolutionaries was probably deliberate. To remake the South would require a mass uprising of the lower orders.

His fellow Republicans agreed that those who had rebelled against the Union deserved stiff political punishment. In 1867, Congress, which their party firmly controlled, wrested from President Andrew Johnson the power to reconstruct the states that had left the Union. The seductive wiles of former Confederates and Johnson's own racist impulses had led the president, a former Democrat from Tennessee, to oppose nearly every attempt to aid ex-slaves. Over the president's veto, Congress passed a series of Reconstruction acts that, in theory, ripped the power of the state away from white planters and gave it to black people and that minority of whites who embraced the new order (the so-called "scalawags" from the South and "carpetbaggers" from the North). Less than three years after the abolition of slavery, African-American men had suddenly gained the right to vote and run for office throughout the former Confederacy.[26]

"Now is the black man's day," exulted a leading activist in South Carolina, "—the whites have had their way long enough—now is *our time.*"[27] With the protection of federal troops, African Americans began to mobilize politically in their churches, neighborhoods, and workplaces. Black men were soon campaigning and winning elections in districts where their people formed a majority. When Reconstruction ended in the mid-1870s, roughly two thousand African Americans had served in legislatures and city councils, as justices of the peace and judges of state courts, as auditors and as delegates to conventions that tore up state constitutions written during slavery days and wrote new, color-blind ones. Sixteen blacks were elected to the U.S. House of Representatives and two to the Senate. "It is hard to imagine a more momentous occasion, at once deeply conservative and boldly revolutionary . . . ," one historian reflects about the first time freedmen cast a ballot. "With that act African Americans ended an age-old history of elite privilege and popular subservience. They stood up and brought their states into the modern world."[28]

What was pathbreaking about black suffrage is obvious, but the conservative element deserves attention too. For most African Americans, Reconstruction meant a chance to exercise the same rights white citizens had long taken for granted: to keep the money one earned, to marry whom one pleased, to speak and assemble and worship freely as well as to take part in politics (even though only men could vote and hold office). They wanted, in other words, to fulfill the promise of liberal capitalism, long denied them because of their race. Their desire, their need, was hardly revolutionary; only the brutal resistance of whites made it appear that way.

The new state governments elected primarily with black votes did pass laws that nudged the South into the modern, industrial age. They constructed schools and hospitals, levied hefty taxes on landholdings, and funded railroads to connect individuals and local businesses to the national economy. All this spending inevitably produced deficits and fostered corruption; politicians who had recently owned nothing but the clothes on their backs were not always paragons of ethics. And those who preached the new "gospel of prosperity" made no meaningful attempt to improve the work lives of black laborers or to give them more access to the ownership of land or capital—the fundamental resources of any agricultural society.

The failure to advance *economic* democracy lent fragility to the impressive political achievements of African Americans. As long as most black people worked directly or indirectly (as sharecroppers) for illiberal whites, they would remain poor—and their influence in government would be vulnerable to attacks, both legal and violent, by the unreconstructed sons and daughters of Dixie.

A small number of radicals, both black and white, grasped the problem and proposed a simple way to begin to solve it: confiscate the lands of planters who had fought for the Confederacy or served in its government. Thaddeus Stevens asked the pertinent rhetorical question: "How can republican institutions . . . exist in a mingled community of nabobs and serfs?" In the spring of 1867, Stevens, despite his failing health, struggled to convince Congress to enact what would have been the most massive redistribution of wealth in American history. His plan was to transfer millions of acres owned by former rebels to freedmen and their families in forty-acre lots. The federal government would hold the land in trust for ten years, then deed it to the ex-slaves who worked it.

Confiscation had long been accepted as an act of war, and Stevens clearly hoped recent precedents would help make his case. In the summer of 1862, when Lee's army had briefly gained the upper hand, Congress passed an act calling for the "seizure of all the estate and property" of anyone committing treason against the United States. But civilian authorities could do little to enforce the measure during wartime. So some commanders in the field took it upon themselves to seize the property of rebels and allow slaves who had fled to Union lines to live on and farm it. Generals Ben Butler and John Pope began the practice in small parts of Virginia early in the war; during the final months of the conflict, William Tecumseh Sherman extended it to the Sea Islands and plantations from Charleston south to Jacksonville. To keep order in the conquered regions, President Lincoln and his top commanders rescinded all these orders, but that did not diminish their popularity among the freedpeople.[29]

Thaddeus Stevens, c. 1850s. In 1867, the stern-faced Pennsylvania congressman led a failed attempt to redistribute the lands of big Southern planters to their former slaves.

At the close of the war, without official sanction of any kind, some blacks occupied plots of arable land that retreating Confederates had abandoned. Though most of the squatters were illiterate, they expressed the same moral claim that had inspired such radical artisans as Thomas Skidmore and the early socialists. "We has a right to the land were we are located," argued Bayley Wyat, who spoke for a group of occupiers in Yorktown, Virginia. ". . . Our wives, our children, our husbands has been sold over and over again to purchase the lands we now locates upon; that the reason we have a divine right to the land. . . . And then didn't we clear the land, and raise the crops of corn, of cotton, of tobacco, of rice, of sugar, of everything?" Many white Southerners feared the federal authorities would agree. One defeated Texas soldier told his family he expected "that all the lands in the Confederacy will be taken away from the white people to pay their war expenses then given in small 160 acre lots to the negroes." What force could prevent this calamity?[30]

Rescue would come from an unlikely source: the U.S. Congress, in which Republicans held almost 80 percent of the seats. On behalf of his confiscation bill, Stevens, whose admirers dubbed him "the Commoner," made the last stand of a career that had begun in the 1820s when, as a Gettysburg lawyer, he protested against the "tyranny" of both the Masonic order and President Andrew Jackson. Former rebels, argued the seventy-three-year-old congressman, were guilty of "unrepented crimes" and deserved no more mercy than any other felons. His fellow congressmen had to prop Stevens up to speak; his voice was too feeble to be heard in the gallery. "His face grew thinner day by day," wrote a contemporary biographer, "his lips were bloodless, and his dark wig, with its hair hanging by the pale cheeks, gave him the appearance of a corpse." In the end, only a handful of members from his own party endorsed the bill; it did not even come up for a vote.[31]

The task would have been just as difficult for a young and vigorous man. Historians call the plan which Congress imposed on the white South "Radical Reconstruction." Yet not many "radical" Republicans, even veterans of the anti-slavery movement, were willing to endorse a proposal that would have fundamentally altered their view of what the state should do to advance economic equality. After all, the Emancipation Proclamation had advised black people to "labor faithfully for reasonable wages." To guarantee the freedmen's civil and political rights put them on a par, at least legally, with other Americans. But to award them property that belonged to other citizens—even ones who had taken up arms against the state—would have defied a central, if unwritten, rule of the capitalist system. It would imply, argued *The Nation*, then a leading "radical" journal, that "there are other ways of securing comfort or riches than honest work."[32]

Stevens and his small band of supporters protested that they only wanted to give black Southerners the same opportunity for economic independence that whites in the North took for granted. When Senator William Fessenden of Maine, the Republican leader in the Senate, declared that confiscation "is more than we do for white men," Charles Sumner replied, "White men have never been in slavery." Stevens clumsily compared his aim to Czar Alexander's decree, seven years earlier, that had emancipated the serfs. While the Russian monarch did allot some land to the people he freed, he took none away from the Russian aristocracy, and no civil war had forced his hand.[33]

Fear of labor unrest in the North also helped stiffen resistance to Stevens's plan. Wage earners now composed two-fifths of the American workforce, and the privations and ideological promises of a war for "free labor" had whetted their appetite for change. Trade union membership had been surging since 1863, as wage earners forced demands for an eight-hour day and a closed shop on employers who were slow to organize in kind. Strikes became common, and skilled workers were able to sustain national unions that had barely existed before the war. Talk of confiscating property could only add fuel to these flames of discontent. Would Irishmen and Germans claim they were the rightful owners of the great railroads they had built and the marbled banks they had erected?

Along with Wendell Phillips, a few Republicans on the far left of their party did side with the rising labor movement. In 1867, Benjamin Wade of Ohio—who, in his youth, had helped construct the Erie Canal and now, as president pro tempore of the U.S. Senate, stood next in line to the presidency—told a home-state crowd that Congress should not just aid the freed slaves but also pay heed to "the terrible distinction which exists between the man who labors and him that does not." But most federal lawmakers belonged to the latter class. They would not allow reconstruction to slip into revolution.[34]

Thaddeus Stevens lived one more year, just long enough to play a minor part in the impeachment of President Andrew Johnson. A troop of black soldiers stood guard over the Commoner's coffin as he lay in state in the Capitol, and Washington, D.C., was blanketed in the fabrics of mourning. Then, Stevens, according to his wishes, was interred in the sole integrated burial ground that existed in his hometown of Lancaster, Pennsylvania. "Finding other Cemeteries limited as to Race . . . ," the inscription on his headstone reads, "I have chosen this that I might illustrate in my death The Principles which I advocated through a long life EQUALITY OF MAN BEFORE HIS CREATOR."[35]

Meanwhile, down south, clusters of landless African Americans were keeping the dream of confiscation alive. They protested orders to relinquish the property of Confederate planters that Union troops had seized during the war. The idea that the federal government had promised each black family "forty acres and a mule" quickly passed from rumor to hope to folk legend. Inevitably, Southern whites suspected revenge was the prime motivation of their former slaves. As one Arkansas paper put it, "scarcely a grown up man or woman of African extraction . . . but believes that he or she will very shortly be placed . . . in possession of the comfortable homes and broad acres of his or her white master or mistress."[36] The idea of confiscation, whether as wish or fear, remained vital long after Reconstruction had passed into history.

As a political demand, however, it gained little more support in the postbellum South than it had in Congress. The African Americans who were elected to public office during Reconstruction generally fit the classic model of the self-made man. Whether born free or in bondage, most had learned how to read and practice a trade or profession such as teacher or minister, however poorly compensated. Few had participated in the abolitionist movement. The "gospel of prosperity" appealed strongly because it promised swift and steady improvements both for them and for their constituents, as long as they worked hard and were allowed to reap the fruits of their labor. As the historian Eric Foner writes, "Many black officials . . . saw individual initiative in the 'race of life,' not public assistance, as the route to upward mobility." They also knew that a movement for confiscation would enrage white Southerners already seething at the authority of black troops and black lawmakers. Attacks by vigilantes, many of whom belonged to semisecret gangs like the Ku Klux Klan, could well mushroom into a full-scale war between the races.[37]

The meteoric career of Aaron Bradley illustrates how difficult it was for a Southern radical to defy the fears and challenge the ideology of his fellow black politicians, as well as the animosity of former Confederates. Bradley was born in 1815, the property of a planter who became South Carolina's governor during the Civil War. As a young man, he had escaped from slavery and made his way to Boston, where he became a lawyer and worked with local abolitionists. After the war, Bradley, like many other ambitious African Americans who had tasted freedom, returned to the South with great hopes for himself and his people. He moved to Savannah and earned his keep doing legal work for poor farmers in the surrounding Georgia low country where blacks formed a majority.[38]

A charismatic orator, Bradley could have gained influence as an apostle of individual uplift, as did many of his counterparts. But, even more strongly than Thaddeus Stevens, he believed that only a collective uprising of the poor could gain equality for black Americans. Soon after settling in Savannah, Bradley organized meetings to protest Andrew Johnson's order to surrender the fertile acres which General Sherman had given during the war to blacks in the lowlands. Even soldiers' bayonets, Bradley declared, would not prevent freedmen and -women from fighting for their moral due. Arrested for using "seditious and insurrectionary language," he was found guilty and sentenced to a year in jail. Pressure from his supporters won him release on parole. Soon, Bradley was again denouncing the Reconstruction authorities for betraying black people. This time, they retaliated by forcing him to leave the state.

When Aaron Bradley returned to Georgia several months later, he had transformed himself from a freelance agitator into a skillful leader. He helped Savannah's black longshoremen strike for higher wages and condemned the city's white mayor, a former Confederate officer, for taxing workers unfairly. He became the spokesman for hundreds of plantation laborers, armed with rifles, who demanded some kind of confiscation. In one corner of Dixie, Bradley seemed to be emerging as the head of an embryonic alliance of black farmers and workers.

He sported a flamboyant style to match his politics. Bradley's all-weather couture featured a beaver hat and kid gloves, and he routinely moved through the streets of Savannah with "a retinue of lackeys and bodyguards," as much for effect as for protection. In 1867, black voters elected "their Apostle Bradley" to a seat in the Georgia Senate and also chose him to represent them at the state's constitutional convention. During one campaign, he rode through the streets of black Savannah on a "well-fed steed," accompanied by a brass band. The radical was on the rise.[39]

But so were his enemies. At the convention, Bradley got embroiled in a nasty battle with white delegates over accusations of sexual misdeeds and was expelled from his seat. His fellow state senators then barred him from serving in the legislature as well. In 1868, Bradley broke with the Republican Party and ran an independent race for Congress. Weeks after his defeat, he helped lead a strike by rice workers near the Ogeechee River. They held out for over a month before police and troops intervened, jailing over a hundred participants. Bradley retained a core of loyalists until the end of Reconstruction in the mid-1870s. But the flicker of a mass insurgency from below had gone out.

The source of his failure lay in the hostility of authorities of both races. Bradley's talk of insurrection and recovery of land for the tiller threatened to destroy the unprecedented, yet tenuous, influence law-abiding African Americans had gained in the halls of government. Savannah's black middle class shunned him and made no protest when the city's mayor clapped him in jail and curbed his organizing. Unlike most black leaders, radical or not, Bradley belonged to no church and never seems to have quoted the Bible to legitimate his calls for the not-so-meek to inherit their fair share of the earth. Lacking a base in any institution— religious, economic, or political—the Apostle could not hold on to his flock for long. In the late 1870s, Bradley retreated from the struggle and left for Missouri, part of a movement of black "Exodusters" who hoped they could find in the West a more durable kind of freedom. In 1882, he collapsed and died on a street in St. Louis. Local friends had to raise the funds to give him a proper burial.

Half a century later, W. E. B. DuBois wrote *Black Reconstruction*, an eloquent Marxian analysis of what Stevens, Bradley, and their like-minded contemporaries had tried to accomplish. DuBois claimed slaves who fled their plantations in the hundreds of thousands were waging "a general strike" that played a decisive part in winning the war. Reconstruction, he wrote, was but one phase of the "modern labor problem . . . the kernel of the problem of Religion and Democracy," its defeat an equally weighty, but hardly final, setback in the war of classes that could end only with the "emancipation of that basic majority of workers who are yellow, brown and black."[40]

DuBois's book provided a powerful counternarrative to the prevailing myth about Reconstruction: that it had been a "tragedy" in which vindictive white Republicans and ignorant, licentious Negroes ravaged the South and fattened their own wallets. But he was wrong to read the history of the era through a class-conscious lens. While DuBois chronicled, in arresting prose, the defeat of his radical forerunners, he did not appreciate how unradical were the aspirations of most of the black people they had hoped to liberate.

The true failure of Reconstruction lay not in the defeat of a black proletariat but in the unfulfilled promises of the American Revolution itself: the denial to individual black men and women of the freedom to pursue happiness in their own ways, aided by the strength of their own communities and a color-blind government. Only their assumption of racial superiority kept white Southerners from seeing that what one Mississippian called the freedpeople's "wild notions of right and freedom" were really no differ-

A Union Army infantryman with a black man,
perhaps his servant, c. 1863. Although close to
200,000 African-Americans served in the U.S. Army
during the Civil War, the racial hierarchy endured.

ent from their own. Confiscation might have helped black farmers escape
their dependence on white employers and landowners, although they still
would have lacked the easy access to credit on which a prosperous agrarian
economy depends. But without such an economic base, African Americans
were unable to stop ex-Confederates from taking over the governments of
every Southern state by the mid-1870s. The new conservative rulers, who
called themselves "Redeemers," consolidated the rule of Jim Crow—that
quaintly innocent name for the system of statutes, informal exclusions,
and officially sanctioned terrorism that kept most African Americans poor
and forced them to live and work in ways and places no prominent white
Southerner would tolerate. The Fourteenth and Fifteenth amendments
were repealed, in effect if not in law.[41]

Few abolitionists in the middle years of the nineteenth century had
ever embraced the vision of labor solidarity that DuBois saw as the hope
of the world. Wendell Phillips and Benjamin Wade were exceptional

figures. Most activists on the left remained faithful to the romantic individualism that had bloomed during the first half of the nineteenth century. They worshipped the caring but self-reliant man and woman and
condemned slave owners and Confederates for preventing black people
from being able to emulate that ideal. For all its shortcomings, the party
of Lincoln seemed an indispensable means of defending and advancing
that end. With Democrats openly courting white racists in the North
and Klansmen in the South, it was easy to take sides. As Frederick Douglass put it, "The Republican Party is the ship and all else is the sea."[42]

But the captains of the partisan vessel were not about to steer toward
social equality. After Lincoln's death, in fact, his party rapidly became
the favored party of most industrial employers. It was increasingly difficult to be both a GOP loyalist and a champion of working-class demands
for the eight-hour day and a measure of democracy on the job. Radical Republicanism "was admirably suited for the task of erecting the
equality of all citizens before the law," observes historian David Montgomery, "but beyond equality lay the insistence of labor's spokesmen
that . . . propertyless wage earners were effectively denied meaningful
participation in the republic." Neither labor activists nor most of the

Thomas Nast celebrates emancipation, 1863. In this rich image, the old evils
of the lash and the auction block give way to education, free labor, and a reunited
black family free to gather around its own hearth.

white people they tried to organize had ever joined with black Americans in a common movement or regarded blacks, free or slave, as their equals. So workers of the two races would struggle on, in mostly separate ways, to realize their own definitions of freedom.[43]

Meanwhile, for most abolitionists, the Civil War quieted any serious questioning of an economic and political system that, in contrast with that of the Slave South, appeared to be a model of fairness and opportunity. On the wings of Union victory, the Constitution was altered in ways only radicals on the Garrisonian fringe had dared to advocate before the war with Mexico. The republic now stood, in law if not yet in practice, as a beacon of individual freedom and voting rights for all men. To point out serious flaws in this new order would have cast doubt on lives spent defining what a moral republic should look like and toiling, with great skill and courage, to realize it. After the savage, exhilarating era that began with the American 1848, aging white radicals could justly celebrate their part in cleansing the nation of its greatest sin and helping to nudge the South onto a more enlightened path. It was a halfway revolution that nevertheless gave great satisfaction—and access to power—to the more pragmatic among them.

But the abolitionists had done little to alert Americans to the growing problem of economic inequality. Among his former comrades, Wendell Phillips stood practically alone when he demanded in 1868: "Let the passengers and the employees own the railway. Let the operatives own the mill . . . Make the interests of Capital and the Community identical." This was the only way, he had come to believe, to "have free, self-government in this country." Soon, those mills and railways would fill up with plebeian migrants from all corners of Europe and the coasts of East Asia—men and women who had not participated in the drama of slavery, anti-slavery, and Civil War. The next generation on the left would have to construct a new kind of oppositional culture for a new kind of working class.[44]

*Chapter Three*

# THE SALVATION OF LABOR,
## 1870s–1890s

The question that forces itself upon us, and imperatively demands an immediate answer, is this: In the great strife of classes, in the life and death struggle that is rending society to its foundations, where do I belong?
—Florence Kelley, 1887[1]

A map of the world that does not include Utopia is not worth even glancing at, for it leaves out the one country at which Humanity is always landing.
—Oscar Wilde, 1891[2]

### TURNING POINT?

ONE EVENING in the fall of 1886, New Yorkers crowded into the Great Hall of Cooper Union to hear the labor candidate for mayor who, it appeared, had a splendid chance to win. All nine hundred seats were occupied, as was every spot onstage, the aisles, and the surrounding streets. Henry George did not disappoint. "Working-men of New York," he declared in a loud, steady voice, "I am your candidate . . . In your name I solicit the suffrages of all citizens, rich or poor, white or black, native or foreign-born."

George bristled with contempt for the unscrupulous politicians who ran the metropolis of over two million: "This government of New York City—our whole political system—is rotten to the core." Officeholders engorged themselves on privileges and bribes, while "we have hordes of citizens living in want and in vice born of want, existing under conditions that would appall a heathen." George concluded with words of hope: "We are building a movement for the abolition of industrial slavery, and what we do on this side of the water will send its impulse across the land

and over the sea, and give courage to all men to think and act."[3]

Such self-confidence, bordering on arrogance, was typical of the man. With the energy of a self-taught evangelist, George had made himself the most popular radical in America. Raised in genteel poverty in Philadelphia, he had left school in his midteens to experience the world. George shipped out on merchant voyages to Asia, set type for a master printer, then moved west to San Francisco, where he became a crack journalist who set out not simply to report the news but to change it. George first made his name by predicting the rapid fall in living standards that accompanied the coming of the transcontinental railroad to California in 1869. Then he made an intensive study

Henry George, c. 1880s. Author of *Progress and Poverty*, George called for doing away with speculative landholding and every other form of monopoly. In 1886, he came close to being elected mayor of New York City on the Union Labor ticket.

of economic thought and emerged with a stirring, simple answer to the age-old problem of inequality: use the power of taxation to make land the property of all.

"The land is the source of all wealth," he declared in *Progress and Poverty*, his 1879 book, which outsold every other economic treatise in U.S. history. The fortunes being made in speculating on that land—which was, after all, a divine creation—were the main source of the problem. Speculation choked off opportunity for individuals with no capital, forcing the great majority to compete for scarce wages in crowded cities full of disease and prey to all manner of immoral pursuits. But institute a "single tax" on the value of that land, and the barriers to a new golden age would soon fall away. In place of unending misery, mankind would achieve nothing less than "the City of God on earth, with its walls of jasper and its gates of pearl . . . the reign of the Prince of Peace!"[4]

*Progress and Poverty*, and a series of lecture tours George made to promote the book in the U.S. and the British Isles, made him an international celebrity. In 1880, he moved to New York to take full advantage of his transatlantic esteem. But what won George the affection of most of those packed into Cooper Union was neither the single tax nor the volume thick with historical reflections and a theoretical argument that justified it. To his audience that night in Manhattan, George was a fellow workingman, one armed with the eloquence of a great revivalist. George was indeed a pious man, but his cause was the salvation of all wage earners, whose fear of the pitiless marketplace had grown along with their numbers.

The New York that Henry George hoped to govern was America's unrivaled metropole, home to hundreds of thousands of immigrants from all over Europe and Latin America as well as to migrants from the rural South and Midwest. Its residents included José Martí, the revolutionary from Cuba (then under Spanish rule), as well as exiles from other autocratic regimes. To wage and win a class-conscious campaign in New York could begin to transform the nation's political culture. It might be one of those events, like the battle of Valley Forge or the attack on Fort Sumter, on which history turns. The gospel of laissez-faire might give way to a state committed to the public welfare, one imbued with the egalitarian ideal of socialism, even when advanced by thinkers like George who denied he had any affinity with Marxist ideas.[5]

George's mayoral candidacy benefited greatly from his warm identification with one of the more prominent ethnic groups in urban America as well as with a rising social class. One of every three New Yorkers was Irish, whether by birth or parentage. They dominated the local labor movement, the Catholic Church, and the Democratic Party, which was ruled by the sachems of Tammany Hall. In the past, most Irish Americans had spurned radical overtures of every kind; they smacked of evangelical purism, a conversion through secular means.

While George was a Protestant, he had long voiced the hopes and defended the interests of Hibernian Catholics on both sides of the ocean. Since the 1860s, he had written knowingly and passionately about the plight of landless Irish tenants. He cursed their absentee landlords and supported the nationalists who sought to break the grip of the British Empire. In New York, George worked closely with Patrick Ford, a famine emigrant who edited the *Irish World and Industrial Liberator*, the leading voice of the Irish-American left. Ford also headed the U.S. branch of the Land League, a massive though short-lived lobby for radical change in the agrarian economy of his homeland. While visiting with Land Leaguers in Ireland in 1882, George's reputation even got him arrested "as a suspicious stranger."

George could also claim an influential disciple from among the Catholic clergy: Father Edward McGlynn, pastor of the largest and poorest parish in the city. Known to his mostly Irish-born flock as *soggarth aroon* or "precious priest," McGlynn found in *Progress and Poverty* the answer to a question that had long plagued him: "Is this God's order that the poor shall be constantly becoming poorer in all our large cities, the world over?" In the face of hostility from his conservative archbishop, McGlynn campaigned tirelessly for the insurgent author alongside Irish-American unionists.[6]

But the coalition supporting George in 1886 stretched far beyond the ranks of Irish workers, critical though they were to his chances of winning. Samuel Gompers, the Jewish immigrant from London who was a leader of the new American Federation of Labor, organized Henry George Clubs all over Manhattan. Terence Powderly, leader of the Knights of Labor, gave speeches for the campaign. So did the popular novelist William Dean Howells, the charity reformer Josephine Shaw Lowell, the economist E. R. A. Seligman, the great British naturalist Alfred Russel Wallace, the Episcopalian theologian Heber Newton, and Robert Ingersoll, the flamboyant agnostic who normally campaigned for Republicans. Visiting from England, Karl Marx's daughter Eleanor and her lover, Edward Aveling, worked to persuade their fellow Socialists that a George victory would be a great boon to their cause.

The Saturday night before the election, thirty thousand people marched for labor's candidate through a steady downpour, despite lacking funds for the customary signs, uniforms, and torches. "The hope of the fathers is about to be realized," declared William McCabe, grand marshal of the parade. "The political rights of the first American revolution are now to be the peaceable instruments of achieving industrial and social rights in the second and greater revolution."[7]

Yet for the American left, the 1886 campaign was a potential turning point that did not turn. On election day, George won over sixty-eight thousand votes but lost to the candidate of Tammany Hall, Abram Hewitt, an iron manufacturer and congressman. Hewitt had warned darkly that "Anarchists, Nihilists, Communists, and Socialists" were attempting "to organize one class of our citizens against all other classes . . ." If the contest had been waged solely between Hewitt and George, the working-class hero might have triumphed. But the Republicans also fielded a candidate—twenty-eight-year-old Theodore Roosevelt, fresh from herding cattle and catching thieves in the Dakota

Territory. Roosevelt drew some sixty thousand votes, almost three times the margin that separated George and Hewitt. Tammany had a precinct network its rivals could not match, and the machine's men stuffed an untold number of ballots and short-counted others.

To the end of his life, George believed that "a square vote" would have elected him. But unionists would never again mount a serious effort to take control of the nation's largest city. The best opportunity to launch an American labor party probably died when the polls closed in Manhattan that November evening in 1886.

### ANSWERING THE LABOR QUESTION

For the European left, the 1880s turned out quite differently. At the beginning of the decade, radical organizations on the continent were small, fragile entities, submerged within the plebeian millions crowding into the largest cities. But by the early 1890s, mass parties dedicated to achieving a classless world had sprouted in nearly every nation west of the czarist empire. The once marginal movement had become a established force in both politics and culture. In 1889, the burgeoning parties of the left created the new Socialist International, which gave comrades from many lands a forum for debating ideas and strategy. The International's very existence signaled the hope that national identities, which socialists believed profited no one but the rich and the bloodthirsty, would soon wither and die.

Most European socialist parties did not peak in membership or votes until the eve of World War I, but their upward trajectory was already clear by the time George took the podium at Cooper Union. Socialists were increasingly dominant in most European labor unions and had gained the sympathy of such prominent intellectuals as George Bernard Shaw, Émile Zola, and Henrik Ibsen. The "Reds" had quickly become the main political opposition, a goad to states and employers who mixed reform and repression to block their march toward power.

By the turn of the century, a factory hand or office clerk could spend his or, in a few enlightened nations, *her* leisure time in a party milieu dedicated, at least officially, to the goal of world revolution. In Germany and Austria-Hungary, there were socialist hiking clubs, socialist singing societies, socialist chess and soccer clubs, and, of course, socialist reading circles. All strived to construct a new world while waiting for the collapse

Soldiers attack a Chicago crowd during the railroad strike
of 1877. The "Great Upheaval" shut down the nation's
most important industry and signaled the onset of an age
of fierce battles between capital and labor.

of the old. As the Austrian Workers Funeral Association put it: "A proletarian life, a proletarian death, and cremation in the spirit of cultural
progress."[8]

In Gilded Age America, labor radicals were never able to establish
so large or varied a cultural network or to maintain a party capable of
winning seats in Congress. Henry George's 1886 campaign was the closest they came to winning the top office in any major American city or
state. Yet, in an era of galloping industrialization, they did achieve something of lasting significance: they persuaded Americans of all classes to
confront the peril that "the labor question" posed to the survival of the

braided ideals of a democratic government and a society of free individuals, both anchored by a pragmatic Christian credo.

The labor question began with an indictment. Radicals charged that the Civil War had done nothing to redistribute power in America. In its aftermath, a new band of oppressors had seized control—armed with wealth, technology, and allies in the counting houses of Europe. This was a Goliath richer, larger, and more potent than the antebellum lords of either lash or loom. As George asked at Cooper Union: "Work is the producer of all wealth. How does it happen that the working class is always the poorer class? Because," he answered, "some men have devised schemes by which they thrive on the work others do for them."[9]

In New York and across the country, the source of popular discontent crystallized into a single, terrifying word: monopoly. The American economy was booming in the late nineteenth century, but the fruits of that boom were doled out in grossly unequal shares. International banks and stock speculators helped keep interest rates high and the prices of commodities low, forcing millions of farmers into a deep well of debt. The unprecedented size, market dominance, and flagrant union-busting and price-gouging actions of Standard Oil, Carnegie Steel, Southern Pacific Railroad, and their ilk led many citizens to revise the free-market gospel that had once seemed the best way to assure that hard work would receive its just reward.

Monopoly, critics charged, also corrupted politics. Although most Americans were loyal to one of the two major parties and voter participation had never been higher, radicals and many reformers viewed the whole process as an elaborate ruse. "Until economic equality shall give a basis to political equality, the latter is but a sham," charged the radical writer Edward Bellamy. Whether the tariff was high or low or the dollar pegged to the supply of gold or silver, big businesses and speculative landowners seemed firmly in control. They kept politicians on a short leash by financing their campaigns and, whenever necessary, slipping them a stock tip, a railroad pass, or a thick roll of cash.[10]

Monopoly's greatest alleged sin was its exploitation of the productive majority for its own selfish ends. In response, millions of workers waged the most violent mass strikes in American history. Most strikes took place in the great workshops of "carboniferous capitalism," where small armies, mostly of European ethnicities, manipulated coal, iron, crude oil, and steel to make products that lifted the U.S. to global economic supremacy. In 1877 and 1894, workers shut down most of the nation's railroads; it took thousands of state militiamen and federal troops—and dozens of deaths—to quash the uprisings. In 1886, a strike for the eight-hour day closed factories and workshops throughout the Midwest. In 1892, a lockout of union employees at Carnegie Steel in Homestead, Pennsylvania—then the largest metalworks in the world—climaxed in a pitched battle on the shore of the Monongahela River between workers, their families, and mercenaries from the Pinkerton Detective Agency, who fired at the crowd from a floating barge. After the outnumbered Pinkertons surrendered, they had to walk through a gauntlet of angry citizens who spat at and beat them. Strikers were motivated not only by immediate self-interest but by a fear that society was rapidly dividing into two antagonistic classes: ill-paid laborers on one side and millionaires on the other. The class violence frightened Americans and stirred the conscience of many.[11]

How to resolve "the labor question" was the paramount issue facing radicals during the final third of the nineteenth century. The urgency of the problem galvanized movements of wage earners and farmers that seeded national organizations on the broad left, most of which survived, in one form or another, into the next century: the Knights of Labor, the American Railway Union, the American Federation of Labor, the Socialist Labor Party and the anarchist International Workingmen's Association, the Women's Christian Temperance Union and the National American Woman Suffrage Association, the Farmers' Alliance and the People's Party. Both Henry George and Edward Bellamy, author of the utopian novel *Looking Backward, 2000–1887*, proposed sweeping changes that they promised would civilize a brutal society. The moral failings of monopolists inspired the creation of a Social Gospel dedicated to helping the meek vanquish the money changers. The inequity of the profit system propelled socialists and anarchists into the maelstrom of political debate, though they got shackled with a reputation as bomb throwers and atheists.

Above all, the collective pain made many Americans receptive for the first time to a collective solution. Antebellum radical movements had been inspired by the drama of individual salvation: one by one or in tiny, planned communities, citizens would shed their ignorance and cleanse their souls of racial prejudice, the arrogance of male tradition and the timidity of women, and the brutality of market competition. The Civil War and the failures of Reconstruction demolished the rosy spirit of romanticism. It took a new understanding of the roots of injustice to produce a new paradigm of social rebellion.

For radical activists in the late nineteenth century, economics was the key both to understanding the problem and to resolving it. The grip of industrialists and financiers over a national market with transoceanic connections created a new world in which there was little room for the old visions of artisanal independence and individual redemption. The "incorporation of America" made it seem imperative to unravel the mysteries of currency, taxation, the ownership of land, and authority at the workplace. Reform-minded sociologists like Lester Ward, philosophers like William James, and theologians like Washington Gladden agreed that one could not confront the materialist challenges of an incorporated age with the old faith in personal autonomy. Society is an interdependent organism, they argued. To embrace that fact was to take the first step toward transforming it. As Ward wrote in 1892, "individual freedom can only come through social regulation."[12]

Jane Addams, whose father was a founder of the Illinois Republican Party, translated this new wisdom into a vision of social democracy:

> It is difficult to see how the notion of a higher civic life can be fostered save through common intercourse . . . the blessings which we associate with a life of refinement and cultivation can be made universal, and must be made universal if they are to be permanent. The good we secure for ourselves is precarious and uncertain, is floating in mid-air, until it is secured for all of us and incorporated into our common life.[13]

At Chicago's Hull House, the pioneering settlement Addams helped found, well-educated young people taught English and history to immigrants, agitated for labor unions and cleaner streets, and battled ward bosses who ridiculed their efforts as those of mere "petticoat politicians."

Anyone who worked alongside Addams or simply admired her work viewed the emphasis on individual liberation that had fueled the antebellum insurgencies as outmoded. Evangelical fervor still burned on the left, but now it was dedicated to serving "the working masses"—whether they welcomed that aid or not. Like George, Bellamy, and Addams, most left activists during the Gilded Age still sprang, as before the Civil War, from white, native-born, and Protestant roots. But their definition of social evil had changed. The personal was no longer so political. The collective salvation of wage earners and the poor now took priority over freedom for the self.

The cooperative commonwealth leftists dreamed about remained as elusive as it had for socialists before the Civil War. But its Gilded Age apostles taught reformers to think seriously about curbing the power of capital and the state and to recognize that interdependence was the inescapable reality of modern life. Early in the next century, a cross-class progressivism would embrace that wisdom. Henry George and his fellow prophets gained honor without power, but they were most certainly heard.

Edward Bellamy, c. 1880s. A soft-spoken journalist from Massachusetts, Bellamy was the author of *Looking Backward*, the most influential argument for socialism ever written by an American.

## PROPHETS AND PANACEAS

Unlike the European left, which socialists dominated, how collective liberation should occur was a source of endless internal conflict in the U.S. There was neither a dominant organization on the American left, nor agreement about how best to combat the monopolists and, one day, depose them. Some radicals stressed the power of workers on the job or in the polling booth; others the influence of virtuous women to cleanse the body politic; others the potential of a broad alliance between farmers and wage earners. Only in the 1890s did a third party on the left, the People's Party, gain enough votes to throw a real scare into the business and political establishment. But the Populists' moment in the sun was brief.[14]

Despite the frequency of bloody strikes, only a small minority of radicals advocated a violent revolution. Most left activists took the Sermon on the Mount to heart, whether or not they quoted from the Beatitudes. They would not turn back evil with arms, which would soil the purity of their spirit and risk hurling the nation into another civil war. Instead, they would espouse the new Social Gospel of cooperation and brother-hood. While blaming big business for creating social misery, in the spirit of Christian optimism, they barred no one from helping to end it. The left, in theory, could attract and benefit all classes. A messianic panacea seemed both the most humane and the most practical way to achieve worldly salvation.

Unlike in antebellum days, few activists felt it necessary to leave their congregations in order to preach the new gospel. Most could speak out freely against the exploitation of the poor within major denominations, although they did have to rebut ministers and parishioners who feared the loss of revenue and support from employers and the pro-business press.[15]

Americans who preached and applied the Social Gospel ran the gamut from those who dedicated their lives to charity to those who looked for-ward to a working-class revolution, albeit a peaceful one. However, sol-diers in the Salvation Army and members of the Society for Christian Socialists did agree on one big thing: to follow Jesus meant to dedicate your life to collective uplift. Radicals had an alternative system in mind and were willing to collaborate with anyone who shared their vision. That included Catholics, Jews, devotees of such new spiritual enthusi-asms as Theosophy—even "freethinkers" like Ingersoll. The dividing line was one of political sympathy, not theology.

Thus, the Social Gospel ushered in a new kind of American religion, one that was immersed in worldly events and in the world of modern thought. Individuals who looked to preachers and scripture primarily to help them endure the long night of the soul recoiled from this turn; some even denounced it as a rejection of Christianity itself. But Social Gospelers lodged a moral claim that was difficult to ignore and has been echoed by left-wing Christians ever since.

While the new gospel had many apostles, only George and Bellamy built mass followings in the U.S. and around the world and continued to inspire reformers and radicals long after their deaths at the end of the nineteenth century. As personalities, they had almost nothing in common. George was a robust traveler and magnetic speaker who had earned his keep with his muscles as well as his pen. Bellamy was often ill and spent most of his adult life in the same house in Chicopee Falls, Massachusetts, where he had been raised; he communicated with his many admirers almost entirely through the written word. Their cures for the cancer of monopoly differed markedly as well: George's ideal state would enforce the single tax but otherwise wield little more power than in Jefferson's day; in the future order described in *Looking Backward*, a benevolent government runs the entire economy, ensuring that no one has more wealth or privileges than anyone else.

The two would-be prophets did share an evangelical Protestant background: Bellamy's father was a Baptist minister; George's had owned a religious bookstore in Philadelphia. Each son retained a faith in God's beneficence while departing from the biblical literalism of their youths. Their writings profess a strain of Christianity that transcended the realm of individual piety and called on readers to commit themselves to millenarian projects. George swore by "a God whose judgments wait not another world for execution, but whose immutable decrees will, in this life, give happiness to the people that heed them and bring misery upon the people who forget them."[16] Bellamy put his faith in a "religion of solidarity" that would usher in a new world of selfless service.

Of course, each man assumed his utopia would be graced with plenty. In George's case, the relentless energies of what Americans at the time called "the productive classes" would wrest abundance on lands the single tax had liberated from lazy speculators. Once these artificial fetters were removed, honest men would gain the "liberty to avail themselves of the opportunities and means of life" and "stand on equal terms with reference to the bounty of nature."[17]

In contrast, the animating spirit of Bellamy's panacea was avowedly collectivist. In *Looking Backward*, a great tract in the awkward masquerade of a romantic novel, a wealthy, selfish young Bostonian named Julian West falls asleep during the class warfare of the Gilded Age. He awakens in 2000 to a marvelous new America whose inhabitants live an idyll both efficient and harmonious. Every man and woman between the ages of twenty-one and forty-five is a member of the industrial army. As in any well-run military force, they receive instruction in "habits of obedience, subordination, and devotion to duty." Whether retired or active, all Americans now live in blissful dependence on one another. They do their wash in communal laundries, eat in communal restaurants, and shop with debit cards at vast communal stores. When it rains, they stroll along sidewalks sheltered by an unbroken covering that replaces the ridiculous single-person umbrellas of old.

Bellamy understood that most Americans mistrusted the very idea of socialism and sought to persuade them of its merits in other ingenious ways. He called his good society nationalist, not socialist. His future Americans are motivated by patriotism and altruism, not class consciousness. As Dr. Leete, Julian West's omniscient guide, explains, "The worker is not a citizen because he works, but works because he is a citizen." The industrial army evoked the Civil War, which, as remembered by most white Americans, was a glorious, albeit bloody, event that had called on the better angels of their nature.

Claiming patriotism for the left was something of a Bellamy family tradition. In 1891, Francis Bellamy, Edward's first cousin and an avowed Christian socialist, wrote a short pledge to the Stars and Stripes that he hoped would bind American children to a shared set of progressive convictions. Francis Bellamy admired the French Revolution and so considered including "equality and fraternity" in the pledge, before deciding those words might prove too controversial in a society riven by differences of race and ideology. So he restricted himself to a single phrase, "one nation indivisible, with liberty and justice for all," that would succinctly define the republic during the next century and beyond.[18]

Meanwhile, cousin Edward knew he had to rebut those who worried that incentive would wither in a society where everyone earned the same income. So the new America depicted in *Looking Backward* features abundant opportunities for workers to rise to higher ranks, where they practice advanced skills and compete for medals and other types of (non-pecuniary) prizes. Talented writers and artists in this imagined future easily find readers and audiences, free of censorship. And all citizens have a standard of living that, during the Gilded Age, was enjoyed only by the comfortable and well-educated. In *Looking Backward*, everyone dresses for dinner.[19]

For Bellamy and George, the grim facts of monopoly rule were no reason to doubt the superior virtues of their homeland and its white majority. In *Looking Backward*, "the more advanced nations, ours surely first of all," achieve the good society and then "reaching strong brotherly hands downward, help up" such "laggards" as Turkey, then a declining Islamic state. For his part, George casually referred to the U.S. as "the most advanced of all the great nations" and cursed Chinese immigrants as "treacherous, sensual, cowardly and cruel." He claimed that Americans, unlike Europeans, were born to govern themselves and had no desire to "substitute for the calm and august figure of Liberty the petroleuse and the guillotine!"[20]

Despite such chauvinistic views, both would-be prophets had a considerable influence on radicals in other lands. George's *Progress and Poverty* sold over a million copies outside the United States and was translated into eleven languages during its author's lifetime. Leo Tolstoy read the book to his peasants, and the hunger for land reform helped popularize his ideas among other discontented Russians in the twilight of the czarist regime. The governments of Australia and New Zealand adopted tax policies inspired by George. Labor unionists in Britain and Ireland flocked to his lectures, captivated by George's proud identity as a workingman who had unlocked the secret of economic injustice.

Not every member of the socialist movement struggling to be born in the United Kingdom at the end of the nineteenth century embraced George's ideas. Some comrades echoed Marx's sneer, "Theoretically the man is utterly backward," because George focused so resolutely on the question of land and all but ignored the factory system. But abridged editions of George's work outsold any book written by the author of *Capital.* "When I was . . . swept into the great Socialist revival of 1883," wrote George Bernard Shaw, "I found that five-sixths of those who were swept in with me had been converted by Henry George."[21]

Bellamy's vision had an even greater reach. His didactic romance was easier to digest than George's repetitive, rather turgid tome. More important, its vision dovetailed with one that radicals were already preaching in cultures less wedded to individualism than the United States. In Russia, urban workers snapped up translations of *Looking Backward;* one union leader thrilled two thousand striking weavers in 1895 with the tale of the great future he "had learned by heart and was carrying everywhere in my pockets." In Britain and the Netherlands, Bellamy was most popular among reformist Socialists, who were slowly gaining leverage over their more militant, revolutionary brethren. His novel met "every sneer, every objection, every argument I had ever read against socialism," recalled Alfred Russel Wallace, exposing them "to be absolutely trivial or altogether baseless." Admirers of Bellamy also launched the socialist movement in Canada; in Germany, the Social Democratic Party (SPD) published several editions of the novel, all of which sold well. Party leader August Bebel did add a cautionary preface in which he warned that Bellamy was "a well-meaning bourgeois . . . a Utopian and no socialist."[22]

Bebel's swipe unintentionally suggested what made *Looking Backward* and, for that matter, the writings of Henry George so meaningful to the growing international left. Few ordinary people on either side of the Atlantic were converted to radicalism by reading the works of such learned contemporary Marxists as Karl Kautsky in Germany and Georgi Plekhanov in Russia, both of whom couched their arguments in theoretical jargon. But the amalgam of futuristic fantasy, applied Christianity, moralistic economics, and a dollop of romance could do wonders for the anti-capitalist cause. It also smoothed the reception of Bellamy's and George's "utopian" ideas that, unlike Fanny Wright and John Humphrey Noyes, they did not defy the sexual mores of their fellow Victorians.[23]

George and Bellamy had their greatest influence on their fellow Americans, who, in an age awash in inexpensive tracts and periodicals, turned them into radical celebrities. Organizational skill had nothing to do with it. In 1887, the United Labor Party put up candidates for statewide office in New York, including George, who ran for secretary of state. All did poorly. In the aftermath, the party split into pro-George and Marxist factions, both of which soon went out of business.

In 1888, a group of fervent Bellamyites in Boston founded the Nationalist Club and soon began publishing a monthly magazine. At the outset, the movement seemed to have a promising future: In 1890, *The Nationalist* listed 127 separate clubs in twenty-six states and the District of Columbia. The numbers, however, were deceiving. Most clubs did little more than encourage the reading of Bellamy's works, and the core of their membership was composed of older men and women who hailed from the same intellectual and professional background as the author himself. In Boston, a group of retired Civil War officers signed up, hoping perhaps to staff the high command of the future industrial army. The clubs' shared aim, wrote one skeptic, was to bring "Socialism up from the workshops and beer-gardens into the libraries and drawing rooms." No radical body could long sustain itself on such a narrow, genteel basis. For his part, Bellamy gave little encouragement to the clubs and began publishing a weekly journal of his own. In 1892, he threw his support to the Peoples Party—and the Nationalist Club movement effectively dissolved.[24]

However, both George and Bellamy made significant contributions to the emerging culture of opposition to the corporate order. George brought the Jeffersonian vision of a nation of contented smallholders into the industrial age. His panacea inspired workers to imagine themselves as homeowners, farmers to hope for more and cheaper land, and urban dwellers of all classes to envision their cities free from corruption and speculation.

A good many Populists were devotees of the single tax, as was a group of young reformers from the Midwest who would be mainstays of urban progressivism in the early twentieth century, including Tom Johnson, the mayor of Cleveland; Brand Whitlock, the mayor of Toledo; and Newton Baker, secretary of war under Woodrow Wilson. Before World War I, labor unionists and their middle-class allies waged numerous campaigns to enact the single tax in several western states and cities. As Herman Guttstadt, a leader of the Cigarmakers' Union in California, argued in 1912, "indolence and not industry should bear the burden of taxation."[25]

George merely wanted to remove the artificial fetters on what would otherwise be a naturally prosperous market economy. But many admirers adapted his economic theories, crusading language, and fierce empathy with the working classes to different and broader purposes. A young lawyer from rural Ohio declared himself to be "a pronounced disciple" of Henry George and joined a Single Tax Club soon after he moved to Chicago in the 1890s. Soon that idealistic attorney, Clarence Darrow, would become the most celebrated scourge of "legal injustice" in American history—and a famous agnostic who spoke kindly about socialism. In the 1920s, the philosopher John Dewey ranked George with Plato as "one of the great names among the world's social philosophers." Dewey, the foremost exponent of democratic pragmatism, lauded *Progress and Poverty* for giving readers a concrete way to resist "the force of tremendous vested interests" without sacrificing either eloquence or erudition. George's power to inspire imposed no ideological limits on the devoted.[26]

Edward Bellamy had an even more profound impact on American political culture. The worldly paradise he described in *Looking Backward* now appears, in some aspects, like an authoritarian nightmare: the entire society is run by a small group of retired "officers," and any citizen who refuses to work is considered to be mentally defective. But Bellamy's contemporaries did not have the examples of Stalin's USSR or Hitler's Germany before them as they read. Instead, many contrasted his efficient, caring, egalitarian vision with the messy brutalities of their capitalist nation and allowed themselves to dream of what might be. *Looking Backward* sold over a million copies in the decade after its publication, more than any American novel since its prophetic precursor, *Uncle Tom's Cabin*.

Moreover, Bellamy, like Harriet Beecher Stowe, appealed strongly to both genders. Unlike George, who proudly wore the image of a self-made man who wrote and fought for others who aspired to that status, the author of *Looking Backward* inveighed just as passionately against the oppression of women. "The broad shoulders of the nation," Doctor Leete tells Julian West, "bear now like a feather the burden that broke the backs of the women of your day."[27] In Bellamy's utopia, women return to work about a year after giving birth and have all the help they need in raising their children. They also elect their own "officers," albeit to staff a separate female army of labor. What is more, in a society that has abolished want, there is no reason but love to choose a mate.

No wonder so many feminists hailed *Looking Backward*. Activists of the Seneca Falls generation like Lucy Stone, Julia Ward Howe, and Mary Livermore and such younger leaders as Charlotte Perkins Gilman and Frances Willard found in Bellamy's tract the apotheosis of the womanly, millenarian ethic that had propelled them into politics in the first place. Given to the teenaged Elizabeth Gurley Flynn by her mother, the book launched the "rebel girl" on a lifelong career with the labor left. Willard, president of the massive Women's Christian Temperance Union (WCTU), remarked that Bellamy's real first name must be "Edwardina," because only "a great-hearted, big-brained woman" could have written such a book.[28]

That the leader of the WCTU, the largest female organization in Gilded Age America, was a Christian socialist suggests the breadth of the emerging Social Gospel. By the publication of *Looking Backward*, the idea that a Christian could only bring about the Kingdom of God by healing the ills of society—the labor question, in particular—was swiftly gaining influence among Protestants all over the country. "What else is the conflict between the employed and the employing classes, the combination of the one in labor unions and the other in monopolies," asked George Herron, a Congregationalist minister and the first chair of

Applied Christianity at Iowa College (now Grinnell), "but a stumbling of the world unawares into the brotherhood of Christ?"[29]

At the beginning of *Looking Backward*, Bellamy compares capitalist society to "a prodigious coach which the masses of humanity were harnessed to and dragged toilsomely along a very hilly and sandy road." While those seated on top had "breezy and comfortable" seats, they were at perpetual risk of falling to the ground, where they would share the miserable lot of "their brothers and sisters in harness." Bellamy was certain this intolerable arrangement could not last. It bred envy and hostility among the masses and a mix of condescension and fear among elites. Surely, working together across the class divide, men and women armed with reason and faith could find a more humane way to organize the world.[30]

## A CLASS BY ITSELF

For the comrades of the Socialist Labor Party (SLP), founded in 1877, Bellamy's inclusive vision was nothing but a fantasy, and a dangerous one at that. As Marxists, they were certain the conflict between labor and capital was *the* engine of modern history and that any attempt to deny or qualify that fact only played into the hands of the employing class. On occasion, a branch of the SLP might ally with a "bourgeois" figure like Henry George against a common enemy. But the defeat of George's mayoral campaign convinced most comrades to return to the true, if lonely, path. At their 1888 convention, SLPers resolved "that faithful allegiance" to the party and "severance of all connections with other political parties be a condition of membership . . . all other parties being considered as forming one reactionary mass."[31]

Why did the first Marxist party in the U.S. preach separation from the only political terrain American-born workers knew? Most SLP members fatefully regarded themselves as Germans who were only sojourning in America. Reich Chancellor Otto Van Bismarck's virtual ban on the Social Democrats from 1878 to 1890 had produced a small wave of radical emigrants to the U.S. Most of the German newcomers were craftsmen or their spouses; they were experienced at organizing unions, editing newspapers, creating progressive kindergartens, theatrical troupes, and book circles. To them, the dominant culture of the native American left—from Bellamy's well-dressed utopia to Willard's cold-water army to the notion that one could topple capitalism by quoting Jesus—seemed naïve, irrational, and puritanical.

The Germans set about building institutions like those in the old country that might bring the truth of "scientific socialism" to the benighted Americans in their midst. They created trade unions of carpenters, brewery workers, machinists, and cigarmakers, sponsored concerts and picnics, lectured about compassionate methods of raising children. They organized vigorously—especially within the working-class populations of major industrial cities like Chicago, New York, and Milwaukee. Hatred of the bosses and the state authorities who safeguarded their property ran deep in their souls. By 1890, close to a hundred locals of the SLP were agitating throughout the industrial North and West.

But their reluctance to abandon their native tongue ensured that the purity of doctrine would be preserved. Only seventeen locals routinely held meetings in English, and no one even bothered to translate most writings by leading German Socialists or, for that matter, major articles in the SLP's own press. "I tell you, study, and learn English above all else," William Liebknecht, a leader of the German Social Democrats, instructed his *genossen* (comrades) when he visited the U.S. in 1886. Engels himself scoffed that the SLP's platform, while "theoretically correct," was "useless . . . if it is unable to get into contact with the actual needs of the people." When Florence Kelley, daughter of a leading Republican congressman, rendered *The Condition of the Working Class in England* into English, SLP leaders expelled her, their most talented U.S.-born member, for "incessant slander." Her translation included a preface by Engels which admonished them "to become out and out Americans."[32]

Ideological correctness proved a political disaster. In 1888, the SLP ran its first slate of presidential electors; they received exactly 2,068 votes. Few of its candidates for local office did any better. When party stalwarts in Manhattan set up socialist academies for children receiving a poor education in the public schools, fewer than three hundred students signed up in five years.[33]

The SLP succumbed to the temptation that often plagues fundamentalist movements, whether in politics or religion. The *genossen* were "trapped by the unhappy problem of living '*in* but not *of* the world,' " as Daniel Bell later put it, quoting Martin Luther's motto for his new church. To embrace the strangeness of their new land, the German Marxists would have had to compromise with Americans they considered philistines and God-addled fools. How, they protested, would such craven behavior speed the day when "the wretched of the earth" would become "the human race," as a veteran of the 1871 Paris Commune famously predicted in "The Internationale"?

Perhaps surprisingly, the anarchist movement which emerged in the political hothouse of the 1880s took a more flexible attitude toward native-born Americans than did the SLP. Anarchists were, after all, revolutionaries who proclaimed their right, even their desire, to use bullets and dynamite against the police. They believed capital, the state, and the church all conspired to rob and enslave the masses. Urban dailies routinely depicted the archetypal anarchist as a swarthy immigrant with beady eyes and a fuse sticking out of his pocket. The very term in English was coined by a critic; only in the early 1880s did anarchists in the U.S. start using it to describe themselves.[34]

Yet, in Chicago, the International Working People's Association (IWPA) enjoyed a brief heyday among skilled workers and day laborers alike. The five thousand local anarchists who belonged to the group with the grandiose name conducted their business mostly in English and drew large, supportive crowds to their street rallies. They built a counterculture more extensive than that of the SLP. In 1886, they helped lead the massive strike for the eight-hour day. Many IWPA stalwarts had begun their political lives as Socialists, either in the U.S. or Europe; they shared the SLP's hatred of the current system and belief that a proletarian rebellion would overthrow it. Yet, as anarchists, they saw no point in running candidates for office. Men and women could organize their affairs quite well, they believed, without the aid of any boss or master, even that of a workers' state.[35]

A group of talented young orators promoted the anarchist cause. There was August Spies, a handsome German-born upholsterer, who employed sarcasm and exposés of corruption on high to thrill audiences in both his native and adopted tongues. There was Johann Most, who packed halls throughout the urban East and Midwest with speeches that threatened an armed uprising against the state while sketching the vision of a future free from coercion of every kind. "He seemed transformed into some primitive power," recalled a fellow anarchist, "radiating hatred and love, strength

Albert Parsons, c. 1880s. The fiery Parsons routinely drew crowds in the thousands, and his anarchist, pro-union speeches helped him and his comrades to rise to prominence in Chicago's labor movement, the largest in any U.S. city at the time.

and inspiration." There was Lucy Parsons, a stunning light-skinned mulatto from Texas who had probably been born a slave. She spoke out for both women's rights and the liberation of the working class, sometimes with her two young children sitting nearby. A Chicago police official claimed that she was "more dangerous than a thousand rioters." And there was her husband, Albert Parsons, a former Confederate cavalryman turned Radical Republican who spent the rest of his life agitating for revolution.[36]

What Albert Parsons said and how he said it illustrates both the attraction and the limits of labor anarchism in the late nineteenth century. A slight man with a big black mustache, Parsons denounced all manner of oppression in an urgent, melodic tone. He welcomed every race and both sexes to participate in building the new society. Neither Bellamy, nor George, nor the Socialist Laborites wove the plight of blacks in the post-Reconstruction South or the conquest of Indian lands into their writings and speeches as he did. A "typical" American in a movement filled with immigrants, Parsons could spin a powerful narrative about his conversion from ignorant "wage-slave" to apostle of freedom. It was one thing for Most or Spies, who had grown up in the aristocratic Old World, to scoff at the idealistic claims of the U.S. republic. It was more convincing when Parsons, who still spoke with a Texas drawl, declared that "America is *not* a free country . . . Our American rulers differ not one whit from the despots of other lands. They all fatten upon the miseries of the people, they all live by despoiling the laborers." Parsons routinely drew crowds in the thousands, and his speeches and those of his comrades helped the anarchists rise to prominence in Chicago's labor movement, the largest in any U.S. city at the time.[37]

Yet their eloquence persuaded few Americans who were not already outraged at big employers and the police. Anarchists' defiance of the dominant order and threats of violence against it scared far more people than they cheered. Their unbridled rebelliousness prevented them from helping to build an anti-monopoly coalition across class lines that might have made the left a durable force for change.

In March 1885, Parsons took part in a debate about socialism sponsored by the West Side Philosophical Society, a group of stuffy, prosperous, mildly reformist Chicagoans. The militant began, disarmingly, by introducing himself as "the notorious Parsons, the fellow with the long horns, as you know him from the daily press." Soon, however, he was lashing his comfortable audience for living off the sweat of hovel dwellers and warning them of the bloodletting to come: "Listen now to the voice of hunger when I tell you that unless you heed the cry of the people, unless you hearken to the voice of reason, you will be awakened by the thunders of dynamite!"[38]

In their zeal to level and crush, the anarchists failed to appreciate that most American workers did not equate tyrannical employers with either

MRS. LUCY PARSONS.
From a Photograph.

Lucy Parsons, c. 1886.
A light-skinned mulatto from Texas, she spoke out both for women's rights and for the liberation of the working class, sometimes with her two young children sitting nearby. A Chicago police official claimed she was "more dangerous than a thousand rioters."

the nation or organized religion. All white men had won the right to vote decades before the 1880s. Neither they nor their wives and sisters were likely to reject a political system that, despite its flaws, was more democratic than any in Europe at the time. A rich variety of Christian denominations flourished in the U.S., and none received a subsidy from the state. Thus, Social Gospelers like Bellamy and George had more credibility when they denounced monopoly than did their freethinking and atheist counterparts.

Still, anarchists might have had a chance to build a durable movement in the United States if they had eschewed the rhetoric and practice of violence. Americans in the nineteenth century were leery both of strong central governments and of big corporations that abused their workers. The vision of a society governed through autonomous institutions of ordinary citizens might have been appealing, if the anarchists had committed themselves to patiently organizing toward that end. But a reputation for revolutionary terrorism sentenced the anarchist movement to an early death—although the gifted anarchist orator Emma Goldman would still provoke large audiences in the early years of the next century. "Your agitation inspires fear," a labor activist told Lucy Parsons, "it shocks the public mind and conscience and inevitably calls forth strong and brutal men to meet force with force."[39]

Proof of those words arrived on the morning of November 11, 1887, when Albert Parsons, August Spies, and two other leaders of the IWPA died on the gallows at Chicago's Cook County Jail. They had been found guilty, along with four other comrades, of conspiring to bomb a protest rally on May 4, 1886, in which eight policemen died. The nation's pro-business press immediately accused every labor militant of abetting the crime. The prosecuting attorney, Julius Grinnell, readily acknowledged that no direct evidence linked any of the defendants to the crime. But he reminded the jury that anarchists were "organized assassins" and "loathsome murderers," as well as "godless foreigners" and "traitors."[40]

The Socialist Labor Party and the IWPA both looked upon their marginality with resolute indifference. As revolutionaries, they were convinced they held the sole key to the labor question, and it required a sharp break with hallowed American traditions of politics and religion. The homegrown proletariat would simply have to learn that only by organizing as what Marx called a "class for itself" could it defeat its enemies and win its liberation. Believing that history was on their side, the unbending rebels ignored the burdens and the possibilities of the nation's past.

## IN UNION, THERE IS LIMITED STRENGTH

Marxists and anarchists were correct about one thing: millions of American working people were moving aggressively to resolve "the labor question" for themselves. During the 1880s, wage earners surged, in unprecedented numbers, into two different union organizations, each led by self-conscious radicals. Largest was the Noble and Holy Order of the Knights of Labor, headed by Terence Powderly, a charismatic Irish American. The smaller one proved far more durable: the American Federation of Labor, headed by Samuel Gompers, a secular Jewish cigarmaker who had immigrated from London. Neither group advocated proletarian revolution, although individual Marxists and anarchists took part in both efforts, "boring-from-within" in pursuit of their ultimate end.

The Knights were a unique phenomenon in U.S. history. Despite a name befitting a band of lodge brothers, they welcomed female members, whether they earned wages or were only raising a family. The Knights signed up black workers as well as white ones and even opened their rolls to professionals and the owners of small businesses—if they treated their employees well. At the height of their strength, roughly a tenth of the membership was female and a tenth African American, and both women and blacks served as local officials and organizers. The Knights preached that "no pride of craft, no caste of trade should separate" those who believed that hard work for moral ends should receive its just reward.[41]

Terence Powderly, 1886. Powderly was the leader of the Knights of Labor during its heyday in the 1880s, when it swelled to a million members and briefly became a power to be reckoned with both in the workplace and in the polling booth.

The morality of labor was central to the self-image of the Order. Unlike the SLP and the anarchists, most Knights did not view the economy as divided sharply between toilers without property and the capitalists who hired and fired them, often at will. In the rhetoric of the Order, "producer" was a more frequent term of identity than "worker," and the only Americans ineligible for membership were those deemed to be social parasites: bankers, speculators, gamblers, liquor dealers—and lawyers. The exclusion of saloon keepers did not mean the Knights favored a legal ban on the traffic in beer and spirits. That was the demand of a mostly middle-class and almost entirely Protestant and evangelical movement that often viewed Catholics and recent immigrants as a dangerous lot. It was, instead, a warning that bondage could come in the form of a whiskey bottle as well as a profit-hungry boss. "The firmest link in the chain of oppression is the one I forge when I drown manhood and reason in drink" read a pledge signed by tens of thousands of Knights in 1886 alone.[42]

The Order grew slowly through the 1870s and early 1880s. Powderly, who held the top post of Grand Master Workman, lectured about the need to transcend the wage system and to build a new economy based on cooperative enterprises. He envisioned a market system without capitalists. This had a particular appeal to craft workers who despised new-rich industrialists such as the steel baron Andrew Carnegie and meatpacker Gustavus Swift for driving their wages down, their hours up, and trying to eliminate as many skilled jobs as possible.

Like George and Bellamy, Powderly frowned on strikes as counterproductive; they often turned violent and ended up costing strikers their jobs, their health, and their will to fight on. Instead, he and other leaders of the Knights hoped to inspire an "army of the discontented" to build an egalitarian commonwealth that would make class hostility a thing of the past.

But in 1885, several thousand Knights who worked on Jay Gould's Great Southwest line, which snaked over four thousand miles from southern Illinois into Texas, did go on strike—and they won a surprising victory. Gould, whose shrewd investments had made him one of the richest men in America, had vowed never to deal with unions. So forcing him to sign a contract was particularly sweet, and over the next year "producers" of every variety flooded into the newly potent Order. Suddenly, the Knights could claim over seven hundred thousand members in local assemblies that sprouted in nearly every city, factory, and mining town in America. There were some four hundred assemblies in New York City alone. The labor movement was moving more quickly and brashly than ever before in U.S. history. One sympathetic editor reported:

> The time was, and not so long ago, when an artisan in the presence of his employer or overseer scarcely dared say that his soul was his own, or speak above a whisper; but the Order of the Knights of Labor has changed all this. There is an atmosphere of independence on all sides. It is felt in the workshop, the mill, the cars, on the street; even the boys and girls show a spirit that they lacked before.[43]

Yet, as often occurs in the history of social movements, rapid growth outpaced the ability to convert it into lasting gain. Early in 1886, Knights on the Great Southwest struck again, this time to win a minimum wage for unskilled laborers and to protest the firing of union militants. The railroad workers sought to press the advantage of a surging national movement. They had broken their contract with Gould, however, and the "Wizard of Wall Street" quickly took the offensive. He hired thousands of strikebreakers and encouraged the press to report that "Czar Powderly" had ordered his servile members to leave their jobs "without knowing why" (in reality, the Grand Master Workman was struggling to raise funds and gain some supportive publicity for his members). Exhausted, Powderly offered to resign. By April, the strike was lost, and most of its ringleaders were blacklisted or in prison. Powderly moaned that it was "one of the worst managed affairs I ever saw."[44]

The defeat emboldened labor's enemies all over the nation. In New York City, judges upheld the arrests of hundreds of union officials for leading boycotts against firms that refused to negotiate with their workers. As 1886 ended, the membership of the Knights was plummeting, as employers used lockouts, private detectives, the courts, and the revulsion of the comfortable classes to regain sway over their businesses. "The Great Upheaval" had ended in a great reversal for organized labor.

But if democratic rights were denied at the workplace, they could still be exercised with gusto on election day. That fall, in close to two hundred places as diverse as the "marble city" of Rutland, Vermont, and the cotton port of Mobile, Alabama, local labor parties mounted spirited and competitive campaigns. Insurgents typically demanded that city police stop breaking strikes and that private utilities and municipal agencies provide the same level of service to working-class neighborhoods as they did to wealthy citizens. Many of these parties elected a mayor, several council members, or both. In Rutland, Irish Catholic craftsmen and laborers took control of the town meeting. In Kansas City, Kansas—headquarters of the Great Southwest line—the votes of black, Irish American, and German American workers brought to power a new mayor, who immediately raised the wages of city workers and fought utility barons to a standstill.[45]

Yet the Knights' political offensive rested on a fragile base. Rhetoric about what all "producers" had in common could not sustain tenuous bonds between people who had long mistrusted one another on racial, occupational, or religious grounds. The heyday of what its friends called "workingmen's democracy" lasted only as long as skilled and unskilled, black and white, native and immigrant, Protestant and Catholic, were able to submerge their defensive loyalties. Meanwhile, local Democrats and Republicans lured many a working-class hero onto their own tickets and co-opted or sanitized their demands for social redress. For millions of workers, the Knights' rousing call to solidarity had meant little more than a one-time protest against overweening employers. By 1890, the

Holy and Noble Order had dwindled to a hundred thousand members, and its power was all but gone.

The fate of the Knights did not surprise Samuel Gompers. The cigar-maker and a group of like-minded craftsmen had launched the American Federation of Labor (AFL) in 1886 as an alternative to the large but fragile movement over which Powderly presided. They were determined to establish an organization workers could count on instead of an insurgency that could not last. Unions funded by high dues and bonded by the particular skills of their members would, they believed, be able to weather a losing strike or an economic downturn. AFL leaders did not denounce the state and electoral politics; they had no sympathy for anarchism. Gompers worked hard for Henry George's mayoralty campaign and did not oppose attempts to form labor parties in individual cities. But neither he nor his allies expected to gain significant or lasting changes at the ballot box. Only "the trades-union movement," Gompers told a government commission in 1894, could save "the young and innocent, the weak and the unfortunate . . . from the horrible consequences of our industrial disorder."[46]

It was a conviction initially grounded in Marxist orthodoxy. Gompers, who served as president of the AFL during all but one year from the group's founding to his death in 1924, increasingly viewed socialism as a dangerous illusion for American workers, a threat to the fragile economic gains and cultural legitimacy of union members. Yet this wasn't always the case: soon after arriving in the U.S. in the 1860s from London's impoverished East End, Gompers had joined a tight community of well-read, mostly immigrant craftsmen that has been dubbed "a who's who of socialist New York." An older Swedish shopmate named Ferdinand Laurrell translated *The Communist Manifesto* for Gompers and then explained it "paragraph by paragraph." Nothing in the document impressed Gompers more than the famous declaration that "the emancipation of the working class must be the act of the working class itself."[47]

By the 1880s, following this logic, Gompers was attacking the Knights for hoping to build a multi-class coalition on nothing but sheer desire. He argued that unions should be instruments of combat, not mere vehicles for education or springboards for cooperative businesses. The AFL pledged to unite North American workers into "one solid phalanx powerful [enough] to resist the aggressions of the opponents of the emancipation of our class." In 1891, Gompers tried to enlist the aid of Frederick Engels in a dispute with unionists who belonged to the SLP. The union chieftain appealed to Marx's aged collaborator "in the interest of *our* great cause."[48]

A decade later, Gompers would damn socialism as "un-American" and "an impossibility." Yet his class consciousness never flagged. He always despised the temperance crusade as the work of evangelical meddlers from comfortable backgrounds and resented Powderly for supporting it. Gompers was also a freethinker; although he had attended Jewish schools as a child in London, as an adult he adhered to no faith other than Freemasonry and feared religious zeal could only divide the rank-and-file.

While local unionists often chafed at the AFL's reluctance to engage in politics, Gompers and his fellow leaders stuck to their conviction that labor's strength depended on the muscle workers could exert on the job. Whatever favors some politicians might do for wage earners could always be repealed by other officeholders seduced by corporate ideology or cash. Working people everywhere, AFL officials believed, were just as skeptical about the motives of their social "betters."[49]

Unionists in most other industrializing nations did not share the AFL's hostility toward a powerful state. Across western and central Europe, socialists and labor organizers were linking up for mutual advantage: party members helped build unions, and most unionists voted Red. Nowhere did this partnership achieve a parliamentary majority, but it did produce a larger and more influential working-class movement than in the United States. The fruits of this arrangement included social insurance, public housing, and employer liability for accidents—none of which yet existed on the other side of the Atlantic.

The disdain of AFL leaders for political partisanship was hardly the only reason for the comparative weakness of American labor. No workforce in industrial Europe was so deeply split by differences of region, race, ethnicity, and religion; no other working-class movement had to struggle for its very existence against courts and large employers whose definition of "freedom" excluded picket lines and boycotts. But the ironic effect of Gompers's mistrust of any alliance unionists did not control was to limit the potential strength of laboring Americans. In Europe, writes the historian Geoff Eley, "working people acquired compelling reasons for seeing themselves as a class, because their patent powerlessness in society made the ballot box hugely valuable." In contrast, American unionists who viewed the ballot box as the coffin of class consciousness were only encouraging employers who wanted to push them into an early grave.[50]

The left's focus on the oppression and potential might of white working-men, on the job and at the polls, created a dilemma for radicals whose race and/or gender left them on the margins of the great drama of labor conflict. Hardly any black people or women of either race toiled in the northern citadels of carboniferous capitalism. And when the textile industry began to move from New England to the southern Piedmont in the 1880s, mill owners refused at first to hire non-whites or to allow white females to operate the dirty, dangerous machinery lest they be accused of imperiling the future of "the race." Activist women and African Americans, groups which had been in the forefront of the antebellum left, now had to make their way in a political debate that tended to ignore or minimize their particular grievances.

Prominent male labor leaders did *hope* to assemble a more inclusive movement. The AFL, at its founding, endorsed woman suffrage and welcomed unions of waitresses, seamstresses, and other female-dominated trades. Gompers insisted that excluding black workers from unions was both unjust and self-defeating. It violated the principle of class solidarity and risked creating a race of potential strikebreakers. Yet by century's end, he had decided that, at least in the South, segregated unions might be the only feasible way to lure every wage earner into the fold. At a time when lynchings were on the rise and state legislatures were enacting Jim Crow laws, white union officials would have had to be moral giants to resist the tide. Instead, they were merely practical men, concerned more about the sensitivities of their fellow white craftsmen than about the fading quest for racial justice.

Befitting their visionary self-image, the Knights of Labor officially welcomed black members as equals. In the banner year of 1886, the Order held its annual convention in Richmond, which was barely twenty years removed from its status as the capital of the Confederacy. Terence Powderly asked Frank Ferrell, a black socialist from New York City, to introduce him and then defended Ferrell's right to share the same accommodations as his white brethren. "Rather than separate from that brother," Powderly announced, the delegates from New York "stood by the principles of our organization, which recognizes no color or creed in the division of men." Yet the event provoked such an uproar from local whites that the Grand Master Workman, like Gompers, soon withdrew his support for "social equality."[51]

Many African Americans were still eager to join the only labor body that had ever humbled a mighty corporation. In Texas, black railroadmen served on the Knights' executive board, and cotton pickers organized their own local assemblies. In Louisiana, the Knights led a 1887 strike by thousands of black sugar workers whose wages had been slashed.

Henry George's writings helped stir some radical thinking among people who toiled on lands they had little hope of possessing. "Parcel out . . . your large estates among your laborers," a black newspaper editor in Louisiana recommended, "lease a portion to each on reasonable terms and periods long enough to teach them to look upon the place as their home . . . The large plantations," he concluded, "have had their day."[52]

The planters disagreed, of course, and backed up their dissent with savage force. With the aid of the Louisiana state militia and private vigilantes, they evicted strikers from their homes and imported strikebreakers from Mississippi. At least fifty black workers who had sought refuge in the town of Thibodaux, seventy miles west of New Orleans, were murdered in cold blood. One planter, who had been a Republican during Reconstruction, cursed the Knights as "a secret oath-bound association of ignorant and degraded barbarians."[53] Up north, the order was beginning its gradual decline; down south, the Black Knights were being destroyed. Bosses in Dixie would not allow a race of "barbarians" to imagine that the promise of American liberty applied to them.

Whatever their differences, nearly all black and white activists singled out one group of foreign-born workers as deserving neither the benefits of union organization nor citizenship: the Chinese. The immigrants from a crumbling Asian empire were maligned as servile "parasites" willing to labor for subpar wages while living in disease-ridden tenements any self-respecting Christian would spurn. Both the Knights and the AFL explicitly barred Chinese from joining. Only a tiny number of leftists considered the hounding of this—or any—ethnic group a betrayal of their common humanity. In 1885, San Francisco seaman Sigismund Danielewicz pleaded with his fellow unionists to consider whether their slurs against the Chinese were any "more justifiable" than the "persecution" of the Irish, Germans, or his fellow Jews. The audience shouted him down before he could finish his speech. As the novelist Jack London would later bark during an argument with fellow radicals, "What the devil! I am first of all a white man and only then a Socialist!"[54]

Unionists strained to make their case against the Chinese in anti-monopolist terms. The cheap labor of "coolies," they charged, made white workers into paupers and capitalists into tycoons. "The rich have ruled us until they ruined us," declared Denis Kearney, a small businessman from San Francisco with a talent for igneous rhetoric. "The republic must and shall be preserved, and only workingmen will do it." In the late 1870s, Kearney led his new Workingmen's Party of California to win control of the state government and its two largest cities. The party soon dissolved in factional squabbles, having failed to enact any significant bills to aid its plebeian constituents. But its momentary success emboldened white workers to construct a nativist movement larger and more powerful than the unions themselves. In 1882, Congress affirmed the stand taken by western labor: it enacted the Chinese Exclusion Act, the first law in U.S. history to restrict immigrants from a particular nation. Its passage should have taught labor activists a sobering lesson: in politics, the cry of self-defense for the white race easily trumped a solidarity based on class.[55]

## TO MAKE THE WORLD MORE LIKE A HOME

Feminists who made their mark during the Gilded Age also did so by softening or abandoning brave, if unpopular, stances taken by the founding mothers of their movement. Outside of anarchist circles, few activists still entered into "free marriages" or publicly doubted the virtues of sexual monogamy. Victoria Woodhull became a national celebrity in the 1870s by using her beauty and the funds of steamship and railroad magnate Cornelius Vanderbilt, an occasional lover, to publish a radical weekly which endorsed "the rights of adult individuals to pursue happiness as they may choose." Hers was also the first U.S. periodical to print *The Communist Manifesto* in English. But participants at a woman suffrage convention in 1872 refused to put Woodhull's free love proposal up for a vote and kept their distance from her quixotic campaign for president that year on the Equal Rights ticket; any votes she received went unrecorded. Among prominent feminists, only Elizabeth Cady Stanton stood by her side. Woodhull's tiny party nominated Frederick Douglass for vice president, but he rejected the honor and remained loyal to the GOP. In 1877, realizing her notoriety was damaging her cause, Woodhull moved to Britain, married a wealthy banker, and became an ardent eugenicist.[56]

Advocates of women's rights, like men in the labor movement, made heroic efforts but won few durable victories. The two national suffrage groups waged energetic campaigns for the vote in a number of states; they circulated countless petitions, held hundreds of rallies, collared thousands of male legislators. Yet after the Utah Territory awarded the franchise to women in 1870, the only victory suffragists achieved over the next two decades came in the Washington Territory in 1883—and the territorial supreme court invalidated the law six years later. In 1890, feminist campaigners finally put old squabbles behind them and united to form the National American Woman Suffrage Association (NAWSA). But their predictions of rapid gains were dashed: NAWSA attracted no more than ten thousand members until early in the next century. "The size of our membership is not at all commensurate with the sentiment for woman suffrage," lamented Carrie Chapman Catt, a rising leader, in 1895. Our "chief work" for decades, she said, "has been education and agitation, and not organization." That would have to change.[57]

The content of the agitation may have been part of the problem. During the Gilded Age, most suffragists continued to make the same individualist argument they had been articulating since the 1848 gathering at Seneca Falls: every female citizen was entitled to the same rights and privileges as every adult male. All laws—whether about the franchise, divorce, property, or employment—that discriminated against women violated that principle and should be repealed.

The same year that Catt was lamenting the size of her movement, Elizabeth Cady Stanton extended the logic of women's rights one radical step further when she issued a feminist revision of the Bible. "Why is it more ridiculous for woman to protest against her present status in the Old and New Testament, in the ordinances and discipline of the church, than in the statutes and constitutions of the state?" she asked. Stanton repeated the gospel of total freedom she had been preaching for nearly half a century: "The object of an individual life is not to carry one fragmentary measure in human progress, but to utter the highest truth clearly seen in all directions, and thus to round out and perfect a well balanced character."[58]

Catt and other young NAWSA leaders regarded *The Woman's Bible* as a step too far and openly condemned the book. Stanton denounced their "religious bigotry" and vowed to spend the remainder of her days trying "to lift women out of all these dangerous and degrading superstitions."[59]

Still, few suffragists were prepared to break with the individualist creed, which was rooted in the anti-slavery tradition from which most middle-class Protestant radicals and reformers had sprung. As we have seen, that worldview had little to offer poorly paid workers and immigrant city dwellers in the industrial age. The aged veterans of the struggle for women's rights were not necessarily hostile to collective uplift. While in her eighties, Susan B. Anthony attended a lecture by the Socialist leader Eugene V. Debs and, with a laugh, chided him about his priorities. "Give us suffrage," she said, "and we'll give you socialism." Debs responded, "Give us socialism and we'll give you suffrage." But overshadowed by the labor question and voices demanding relief from untrammeled monopoly, most middle-class suffragists held themselves apart from the fray and asked mainly that women gain access to the same jobs that were oppressing men.[60]

The Women's Christian Temperance Union (WCTU) offered a more far-reaching, if less confrontational, alternative. With a huge membership of over 150,000, the WCTU crusaded, in the words of its leader, Frances Willard, "to make the whole world HOMELIKE." A remarkably ambitious program lurked within this anodyne phrase. Motivated by Willard's view that "women as a class have been the world's chief toilers," WCTU members endorsed the demand for "equal pay for equal work." They also denounced "rich corporations" for opposing safety regulations in factories and set up separate departments to help miners and timber workers; WCTU officials even addressed a convention of the Knights of Labor. Under Willard's charismatic leadership, the group became a crossroads of organized discontent, though most of its members were white Protestants with comfortable homes and a servant or two. Temperance women worked to reform prisons, establish municipal ownership of utilities, set up shelters for ex-prostitutes, and organize unions for female wage earners, as well as to aid suffrage cam-

paigns. The WCTU abounded with enthusiasts of the moralistic utopia described in
*Looking Backward*.[61]

As a consequence of its "Do Everything"
philosophy, the WCTU became a major
force in American culture at the end of the
nineteenth century. It helped pass prohibition laws in a number of midwestern states
and encouraged activists of both genders to
blame poverty and the amoral, laissez-faire
state for causing intemperance. The organization also extended its presence overseas, crusading for prohibition and woman
suffrage in the British colonies and Japan.
The WCTU had a respectable, somewhat
patronizing image: prosperous women urging sinners to do the right thing. But, under
Willard's leadership, the group pursued a
vision more radical than that of most Gilded
Age suffragists. The WCTU sought, in the

Frances Willard, sometime in the
1880s. Eloquent and charismatic,
Willard turned the Women's
Christian Temperance Union into
an advocate for woman suffrage and
labor unions, and declared herself a
Christian socialist.

words of one socialist minister, "to keep alive . . . the spirit of essential
religion, which will make the State the conscience of the people."[62]

At the same time, Willard carefully avoided taking the kind of pro-
vocative stands that had isolated Victoria Woodhull and Elizabeth Cady
Stanton. When she advocated suffrage, she did so in a sentimental, patriotic key. In one popular address, Willard remembered, as a teenager,
watching her father and older brother leave their house to vote: "as I
looked I felt a strange ache in my heart, and tears sprang to my eyes.
Turning to my sister Mary, . . . I said, 'Don't you wish we could go with
them when we are old enough? Don't we love our country just as well
as they do?' " Willard wrote her own feminist critique of the Bible and
led her intimate life solely with other women. But in public she insisted
only that churches allow women to become ministers and scolded men
for imperiling the "purity" of society by visiting brothels and consuming
pornography.[63]

On occasion, Willard's pleas for sexual self-control revealed her
own racial prejudices. The WCTU held integrated conventions and
appointed black women to positions of authority in several of its depart-

ments. But Willard declined to join the embryonic campaign against lynching and, instead, spoke out against "the unspeakable outrages [of rape] which have so often provoked such lawlessness." In anger and some surprise, both the elderly Frederick Douglass and the young Ida B. Wells, foremost publicist of the anti-lynching campaign, denounced her. In the grim wake of Reconstruction, the beloved leader of the WCTU was no more able to imagine the home or the world from a black perspective than were most white radicals.[64]

## CRUCIBLE OF THE 1890s

Events in the waning years of the nineteenth century held out the promise of another potential turning point for the American left—one that would have had greater consequences than capture of the mayor's office in one big city. By itself, no labor organization had been able to defeat the monopolists. But the multiple, overlapping movements of working-class rebels, temperance crusaders, suffrage agitators, and Social Gospelers continued to gather into a force that, while disorganized, had an undeniable power to raise hopes and generate fear. "The present assault upon capital is but the beginning," warned Supreme Court Justice Stephen Field in voting to strike down a small progressive income tax passed by Congress in 1894. "It will be but the stepping stone to others, larger and more sweeping, till our political conditions will become a war of the poor against the rich; a war growing in intensity and bitterness."[65]

From 1892 to 1894, battlers for "the poor" were cheered by several events occurring in fairly rapid succession. First, anti-corporate activists from around the nation launched the People's Party; in 1892, its presidential ticket won close to 10 percent of the popular tally and twenty-two electoral votes—the best showing by any left party in American history. Two years later, as the nation suffered from a depression, Jacob Coxey's army of unemployed men—who styled themselves the Commonweal of Christ—staged a cross-country march that ended on the steps of the U.S. Capitol; along the route, WCTU chapters fed the marchers and local churches housed them.

That summer, the young American Railway Union (ARU) voted to support a strike by the men and women who built the plush Pullman sleeping cars that were coupled onto most interstate passenger trains. In a burst of solidarity, union members refused to work on any train that had a Pullman car attached to it. President Grover Cleveland quickly seized on the opportunity to douse the fires of labor militancy. His attorney general, Richard Olney, obtained an injunction against the strike on the grounds that it was impeding delivery of the mail. Thousands of soldiers and federal marshals rushed in to enforce the ruling, handcuffing the union's top officials and sending them off to prison.

But Eugene Debs, the ARU's charismatic leader, emerged from his jail cell in Woodstock, Illinois, a national hero to every foe of big business. Before the crowd of over a hundred thousand which greeted him in Chicago, Debs declared, "Manifestly the spirit of '76 still lives. The fires of liberty and noble aspirations are not yet extinguished."[66]

Then in December 1894, John McBride, a Populist who was president of the mine workers' union, dethroned Samuel Gompers as head of the AFL; a political alliance between organized farmers and organized labor had never seemed closer to fruition. Amid the worst depression in U.S. history, radicals allowed themselves to imagine that their fellow Americans were also rejecting the monopolists and the major-party politicians who shilled for them. The People's Party would begin to contend for power all over the map. *This* would be a turning point to celebrate.

The Populists did signify a leap beyond what the anti-monopolist left had achieved before. They brought together, if only briefly, a coalition for radical change that crawled over barriers as old as the nation itself. Most significant was the joining of farmer and worker activists from both North and South, the older of whom had been trying to exterminate one another on the battlefield less than three decades earlier. The Populists were rooted in an agrarian class of modest means from the cotton-growing South and the wheat-growing Great Plains. Most of the party's rank-and-file belonged to the Farmers Alliance, a nonpartisan group that had grown to some two million members since its birth in Texas during the early 1880s; it had spawned hundreds of insurgent newspapers and a network of lecturers who stumped through much of rural America. But the party preached that "the interests of rural and civil labor are the same; their enemies are identical" and backed it up with demands for an eight-hour day for public workers and abolition of the Pinkerton Agency that were guaranteed to please most wage earners.

As a result, Populists won the votes of large numbers of miners in the Rocky Mountains and urban craftsmen in the cities of the Mississippi Valley and the Far West. The new party elected governors and a majority of state legislators in Colorado and Kansas, a mayor in San Francisco, and forty-five congressmen and six senators. Through 1896, Populist candidates were competitive nearly everywhere outside the industrial Northeast.

The involvement of women in the growing movement put the older parties to shame. Female Populists organized camp meetings on the prairies and in the fields, spoke widely at rallies and wrote for the movement press, and extended networks first established in the Farmers' Alliance, the Knights of Labor, and the WCTU. The fame that descended on Mary Elizabeth Lease for (allegedly) advising Kansans in 1890 to "raise less corn and more hell" was no coincidence. Lease had earlier been a paid organizer for both the Knights and an Irish nationalist group and had run for local office in Wichita on the Prohibition Party ticket. When Populists took charge in Colorado in 1892, one of their first acts was to place a referendum on woman suffrage before the voters. It passed easily, with big majorities coming from the same counties that had recently delivered the state to the insurgent party.[67]

The Populists also moved, in halting steps, from their white core to the black periphery. They welcomed the formation of a separate Colored Farmers Alliance, only to shun it in 1891 when thousands of black cotton pickers staged a strike at harvest time against employers who included members of the white alliance. Still, blacks joined the People's Party in states from North Carolina to Kansas, and their ability to persuade black men to switch away from the GOP was crucial to electing scores of third-party candidates, all of them white, in the former Confederacy. During the 1892 campaign in Georgia, two thousand white supporters rushed to stop the lynching of the Reverend Henry S. Doyle, a black Populist leader. "We propose to wipe the Mason and Dixon line out of geography," stated Ignatius Donnelly, one of the party's most powerful writers and orators, "to wipe the color-line out of politics." For a few exhilarating years, it did not seem impossible.[68]

As the Populists demonstrated their appeal to ordinary producers, they picked up allies from across the spectrum of the Gilded Age left. Florence Kelley, who was then working at Hull House with Jane Addams, hoped to use the party as the springboard for a new organization of "*American* Socialists." Terence Powderly donated whatever support his dwindling Knights could muster to the new party. After his release from prison, Debs gave numerous speeches urging workers to vote Populist; at the third party's 1896 convention, opponents of fusion with the Democrats clamored to nominate him for president—before Debs wired that he was supporting William Jennings Bryan. Frances Willard backed the People's Party in 1892, despite the refusal of its leaders to include prohibition and woman suffrage in their platform, lest they alienate workingmen who didn't share the affection of evangelical women and men for these "intelligent, virtuous, and temperate" measures. Following Edward Bellamy's lead, many Nationalists joined up as well; they staffed several of the party's lonely outposts in Massachusetts and New York. Among prominent radicals, only Henry George, protective of his panacea, expressed his "indifference, even hostility" to Populism. Plenty of single-taxers still campaigned for the People's Party.[69]

Inevitably, Populists wrapped their aspirations in the Social Gospel. Given the size and range of the movement, quite different versions of the worldly faith commingled within it. Southerners of both races, reared in biblical literalism, tended to believe that "God has promised to hear the cry of the oppressed," and insisted that "no man in this nation can live a consistent Christian life" unless he threw himself into the agrarian insurgency. Most black Populists were deeply involved in their churches, usually Baptist ones, where illiterate laborers could hear newspapers and pamphlets read aloud. Ordained ministers became the most trusted and eloquent leaders of the "colored" insurgency. But no one attempted to bar believers in evolution, spiritualism, or freethinking from taking part in the smaller Populist parties that sprouted in the urban West and Northeast.

In 1894, a sympathetic journalist, Henry Vincent, inadvertently captured the ecumenism of the entire movement. Describing the religiosity of Jacob Coxey, the Ohio businessman who commanded his own tramping "army," Vincent wrote that Coxey longed "to uplift humanity, relieve the oppressed, and 'let my people go free.' " His church was "the big one . . . irrespective of sect divisions." For Populists, the virtue of one's motivation eclipsed the details of one's theology. Such pluralism was notable at a time when the Supreme Court unanimously hailed the U.S. as "a Christian nation" that respected the Sabbath and financed "Christian missions in every quarter of the globe."[70]

Yet despite their breadth of support, the Populists found it difficult to balance the demands of radical exhortation and reformist necessity. Their spokesmen often sounded as if they were declaiming phrases lifted, in translation, from the Paris Commune. Thomas Watson, leader of the People's Party in Georgia, subtitled the official 1892 campaign book, "Not a Revolt, It Is a Revolution." Ignatius Donnelly opened the party's founding convention in Omaha with the charge, "A vast conspiracy against mankind has been organized on two continents and is rapidly taking possession of the world." Threatening that his state would secede if not allowed to coin silver, Davis Waite, the Populist governor of Colorado, declared in 1893, "It is better, infinitely better that blood should flow to the horses' bridles rather than our national liberties should be destroyed." No wonder the prospect of the third party gaining power, alone or in fusion with a major party, horrified conservatives.

Yet such apocalytic anger was absent from the Omaha platform Donnelly helped draft for the Populists in 1892. There, one could find only a series of ways to restrain and regulate corporate America so that "the plain people" would once again believe the government was standing up for their interests: a graduated income tax, a "flexible" currency based on silver as well as gold, the nationalization of the railroads and the telegraph, the initiative and referendum, and a ban on aliens owning land whose main target was wealthy European investors. The Populists' most radical idea was the subtreasury program, which would have replaced bank loans to farmers with a new federal agency that extended credit secured by staple crops held in storage. But the Omaha platform did not mention it.

Thus, Populists described the struggle for a limited welfare state that would restrain the greediest capitalists in the land as an ultimate conflict between good and evil that might require another civil war. Edward Bellamy, despite his aversion to violence, was left in awe: "It is not so much their specific propositions, however radical," he wrote, "as the tone and language of their papers, their campaign orators and their campaign songs, which give an adequate idea of the thoroughly revolutionary spirit of these men."[71]

In the end, the People's Party suffered the same fate as the local workingmen's parties of the preceding decade, writ very large. In 1896, the Populists endorsed William Jennings Bryan for president, largely because the Democratic nominee's rhetoric seemed to promise that deliverance from corporate rule could be just an election victory away. The former congressman from Nebraska was just thirty-six years old; he had defended the Pullman strikers and was a more eloquent champion of an income tax on the rich and a flexible money supply than any Populist.

Bryan began his celebrated speech at the Democratic convention in Chicago with "I come to speak to you in defense of a cause as holy as the cause of liberty—the cause of humanity." Reading his words, a remarkable number of Americans believed Bryan was the only man who could bring the monopolists to heel. A furniture salesman from Pittsburgh wrote to him, "God has brought you forth, and ordaind [*sic*] you, to lead the people out of this state of oppression and despondency into the Canaan of peace and prosperity." Bryan received tens of thousands of letters in the same spirit. Two decades of organizing motivated by the Social Gospel had culminated in a politician who vowed, "You shall not press down upon the brow of labor this crown of thorns; you shall not crucify mankind upon a cross of gold."[72]

But Bryan was a reform-minded Democrat, not a radical. He wanted to cleanse the system of the corrupting influence of big money, not destroy it and create a new one. A month after the Democrats met, the Populists also endorsed "the boy orator from the Platte," but only after an angry debate which left them irrevocably divided. The ensuing campaign, one of the most dramatic in U.S. history, convinced the business establishment and most big-city newspapers that victory for the "Popocrats" would lead to "anarchy" and bankrupt the nation. Bryan's loss to William McKinley doomed the third party to a slow but certain demise. The embryonic grand alliance of the producing classes seemed to expire along with it.

The Democrat from Nebraska did achieve one lasting success: he effectively remade his party, formerly a bastion of economic laissez-faire, into a strong supporter of union rights and the strict regulation of corporations. On Labor Day 1896, Bryan offered a crowd of fifteen thousand workers and their families a metaphor for what would become the progressive approach to business from his campaign to Harry Truman's more than half a century later. Bryan recalled that during his youth in southern Illinois he had been in charge of tethering the family swine so they would not tear up the land. "And then it occurred to me that one of the most important duties of government is to put rings in the noses of hogs."[73]

So the defeat of Populism opened the way for a different kind of triumph. The powerful critiques of monopoly and the labor question voiced by radicals like George and Bellamy and bolstered by the splintered insurgencies of workers and farmers persuaded the major-party nominees Bryan, Theodore Roosevelt, Woodrow Wilson, and thousands of candidates who followed their lead to put an end to the freebooting capitalism of the nineteenth century. Some did so because they feared that a failure to act could lead to a homegrown edition of the Paris Commune or a terrorist campaign whose scale would dwarf the Haymarket bombing. Others sympathized strongly with the protesting masses and believed a benevolent state would be the best protector of their welfare.

As president, Wilson proclaimed that his goal was to steer a middle course between socialism and laissez-faire. "The question which stands at the front of all others . . . is the question of labor," he declared, ". . . how are the men and women who do the daily labor of the world to obtain progressive improvement in the conditions of their labor, to be made happier, and to be served better by the communities and the industries which their labor sustains and advances?" For him, the answer was found in such reforms as the income tax amendment, the Federal Reserve System, and the granting of an eight-hour day to railroad workers. Thus was born an enduring truism of twentieth-century American politics: the disruptive potential and moral critique of the left helped powerful liberals reform the nation.[74]

*Chapter Four*

# A TALE OF THREE SOCIALISMS, 1890s–1920s

Permeate our souls with divine discontent and righteous rebellion. Strengthen within us the spirit of revolt; and may we continue to favor that which is fair and to rise in anger against the wrong, until the Great Revolution shall come to free men and women from their fetters and enable them to be good and kind and noble and human!

—A Socialist prayer, Oklahoma, 1913[1]

I do not expect to work wonders in Congress. I shall, however . . . accomplish one thing that is not in the platform of the Socialist Party. I hope that my presence will represent an entirely different type of Jew from the kind that Congress is accustomed to see.

—Meyer London, upon election to the House of Representatives, 1914[2]

The most cruel of all denials is to deprive a human being of joyous activity.

—Walter Lippmann, 1914[3]

## DAWN OF THE MARXIST ERA

WITH THE ECLIPSE of the People's Party, Americans who longed for a collective and radical solution to the ills of the economic order were left with just one real choice: socialism. During the nineteenth century, the idea of a world run by and for the working class had been an utterly marginal creed, preached in a smattering of immigrant neighborhoods and practiced in a handful of communal outposts. But during the first half of the twentieth century, socialism as Marxists defined it became the official doctrine of the largest and most influential battalions on the American left: the Socialist Party (SP), from its founding in 1901 to 1920, and then the Communists (CPUSA), who split from the Socialists in 1919, surged to prominence during the 1930s, and swiftly declined during the first decade of the Cold War.

Although Marxism had never wielded great influence among American leftists before and, except during the height of the Vietnam War, would never be dominant again, it fundamentally altered what it meant to be a radical—both for activists and for their enemies. To be a Socialist or Communist was to belong to a movement that spanned the globe and promised to free humanity from exploitation and want. During the Gilded Age, most radicals had relied on moral outrage and a grab bag of panaceas; they benefited from fears that the industrial capitalist order was destroying older, supposedly egalitarian ways of life. But Marxian socialists celebrated the progress of industry, technology, and theoretical knowledge; they girded themselves with a "scientific" certainty that history was moving their way.

With its faith in the future and its grounding in learned texts, socialism in the early twentieth century appealed more strongly to intellectuals and artists than had any previous American left. The roster of such figures who, before 1920, either belonged to the Socialist Party or gave aid and sympathy to its cause was a long and distinguished one. At various times, it included Walter Lippmann, John Dewey, Charles and Mary Beard, W. E. B. DuBois, Jack London, Carl Sandburg, Upton Sinclair, Theodore Dreiser, Helen Keller, John Reed, Eugene O'Neill, Randolph Bourne, Florence Kelley, Isadora Duncan, Thorstein Veblen, Walter Rauschenbusch, Clarence Darrow, Max Eastman, George Bellows, John Sloan, and Charlie Chaplin. High-circulation newspapers and magazines ran features about the movement whose respectful tone contrasted sharply with the vitriol they had dumped on the Populists. Moreover, their columns were open to nearly all the figures named above. Chapters of the Intercollegiate Socialist Society sprouted on dozens of campuses, although few sons and daughters of the working class could afford to attend college.

The threat of socialism, added to that of populism, helped convince prominent politicians from both major parties to make a decisive break with the gospel of laissez-faire. Progressivism in the early twentieth century was a tree with multiple roots: the Social Gospel, pragmatic philosophy, a desire for efficiency and honesty in government. But the socialist challenge stretched across the Atlantic, posing the threat or promise of an upheaval that would, to paraphrase Leon Trotsky, hurl every old order into the dustbin of history.

In the United States, perceptive politicians understood that in a democracy a rising opposition force that aims to replace the entire system has to be co-opted, not simply repressed. On trips to Europe in between his campaigns for the presidency, William Jennings Bryan praised the public ownership of utilities and railroads and marveled that the German Socialists "have educated the working classes to a very high standard of political intelligence and a strong sense of their independence and of their social mission." Theodore Roosevelt, who despised class-conscious radicals, nevertheless worked hard to steal their thunder. He declared that "property shall be the servant and not the master of the commonwealth" and promoted corporate regulation and craft unions. As governor of New Jersey, Woodrow Wilson told his fellow Democrats that "the service rendered the people by the national government must be of a more extended sort and of a kind not only to protect it against monopoly, but also to facilitate its life." In the White House, he struck up an alliance with organized labor that frustrated Marxists who had believed such a cross-class partnership was impossible.[4]

Despite all this attention, the SP did not win many votes or significant offices. Before 1920, every one of its comrade parties in Europe that was allowed to compete in open elections gained at least a fifth of the ballots; those in France, Germany, Finland, and the settler nation of Australia came close to achieving parliamentary majorities. But in only one of his five presidential campaigns, that of 1912, did Eugene Victor Debs, the SP's charismatic standard-bearer, win as much as 6 percent of the vote.

Around the nation, hundreds of party members did capture a share of local power, from the mayor of Milwaukee to the mayor of Antlers, Oklahoma. Yet only two Socialists became members of the House of Representatives, and none came close to winning a seat in the U.S. Senate or a high executive post in any state. The SP did better in the smaller universe of organized labor; before World War I, Socialists led the machinists, mine workers, clothing workers, and several smaller unions, although Gompers easily parried their attempts to capture the AFL itself. At its zenith in 1912, the socialist movement had been able, observed the critic and historian Irving Howe, to escape "the isolation of the left-wing sect" without becoming a durable mass movement. In the end, the "working class party" was unable to woo more than a small minority of workers away from voting for politicians beholden to the "capitalist class."[5]

For over a century, scholars and activists have been arguing about why it failed. Serious debate began in 1906 with a short book, *Why Is There No Socialism in the United States?*, by the German academic Werner Sombart. At the time, anyone who visited the hungry coal towns of Appalachia or the fire-prone sweatshops of the Lower East Side could have refuted Sombart's contention that incomparable prosperity—what he called "reefs of roast beef and apple pie"—prevented American workers from emulating their European counterparts. So the question remained alive through the twentieth century, even as the program of most socialist and labor parties on the continent came to resemble that of liberal Democrats in the United States and vice versa.

Influential commentators tended either to blame American socialists for their own marginality or to view their cause as doomed by conditions particular to the nation's history. Thus, Daniel Bell contended that socialists "could not relate to the specific problems" of the "give-and-take, political world." And Aileen Kraditor claimed they spoke to working people as if they were the ignorant dupes of capitalism, with no ideas or cultures of their own. On the other hand, Louis Hartz maintained that the hegemony of liberal thought, with its vaunting of the classless individual, made Marxists politically superfluous. Other writers focused on the absence of a feudal past, with its deep class feelings, or on ethnic and racial and religious divisions in the U.S., or on the ideological flexibility of the two-party system.[6]

In recent years, left-wing scholars have tried to alter the terms of discussion. They defend the achievements of socialists, however modest, as deeds of prophets in an unjust society. Nick Salvatore portrayed Debs as a union leader who gradually came to believe that monopoly capitalism was betraying the American Dream. Mari Jo Buhle paid tribute to "the tens of thousands of rank-and-file women who formed the Socialist women's movement . . . the defeated and now forgotten warriors against triumphant capitalism." Such views echo a remark by Mr. Dooley, the fictional Irish-American bartender created by Finley Peter Dunne, who delighted newspaper readers at the turn of the twentieth century. Dooley disdained the kind of historians who, like physicians, "are always lookin' f'r symptoms" and making "a post-mortem examination." "It tells ye what a counthry died iv," he complained. "But I'd like to know what it lived iv."[7]

For all their insights, few of the participants in this unending debate appreciate that three different kinds of socialisms coexisted, somewhat uneasily, during the Progressive Era, and they suffered different fates. The largest one was anchored among skilled workers in midwestern cities and tenant farmers on the Great Plains. Most of these radicals were white Protestants who, like the Populists before them, mistrusted East Coast cities as dens of immorality as well as plutocracy. This plain-folks socialist movement produced most of the votes the party received and the local candidates it was able to elect. Its most popular organ was *The Appeal to Reason*, a weekly magazine edited in Kansas that at times reached close to a million readers. Like their antecedents in the Gilded Age, these socialists viewed radical change through a messianic lens. They anticipated a glorious future in a "cooperative commonwealth" that would do away with class distinctions but leave the roles of women and men, whites and racial minorities, essentially intact.

Secular Jewish immigrants composed the second wing of American socialism. Based in the garment unions and a rich variety of self-help institutions and periodicals, they nurtured a powerful ethnic left, one whose influence would, in time, ripple far out from its origins in the Yiddish-speaking neighborhoods of lower Manhattan and a handful of other cities. Jews are the only American ethnic group with an unbroken history of radicalism, and that tradition began with the rise of the socialist movement at the turn of the twentieth century.

The third socialism was far smaller than the other two; it existed mainly in New York and a scattering of neighborhoods in Chicago and a few other metropolises. This was the modernist left, home to young intellectuals and artists for whom socialism, tinctured with anarchist notions, was the means to a liberation that transcended a politics bounded by election campaigns and labor conflict. Their favorite publication was *The Masses*, an icon-smashing monthly whose masthead boasted, in capital letters, "A SENSE OF HUMOR AND NO RESPECT FOR THE RESPECTABLE" and vowed to print "WHAT IS TOO NAKED OR TRUE FOR A MONEY-MAKING PRESS: A MAGAZINE WHOSE FINAL POLICY IS TO DO AS IT PLEASES AND CONCILIATE NOBODY, NOT EVEN ITS READERS."[8]

Modernist radicals sympathized ardently with the plight of labor and aided strikes by Jews and other recent immigrants from eastern and southern Europe. But their true passion was cultural revolution. They advocated birth control and sexual freedom for both men and women, civil rights for black people and a new transnational identity to replace the "100 percent Americanism" espoused by Teddy Roosevelt and conservative nativists alike. For modernists, organized religion was a nightmare from which they had happily awakened. Not since the political spotlight briefly shined on Frances Wright and her supporters had a significant group on the left rejected Christianity as a guide to moral behavior.

Plain-folks socialists and working-class Jewish ones both detested the bosses for stealing the fruits of their labor; modernist radicals condemned the culture of big money for stifling free spirits. The first two socialisms feared capitalism was invading and degrading personal life. The third firmly believed that "the personal is political," as feminists would put it half a century later. "The older rebels claimed to be more orthodox than the Church," Walter Lippmann reflected in 1914. "The radicals of recent times proclaim that there is no orthodoxy, no doctrine that men must accept without question. Without doubt," he added, "they deceive themselves mightily."[9]

Of course, no group of socialists bent the nation to their will. But the modernists, despite their tiny numbers, did advance a cultural agenda whose appeal would grow in the years to come. Peering out at America from their bohemian enclaves, they may have deceived themselves less than did their fellow radicals who dreamed about a peaceful, cooperative society. In the crucible of World War I, enthusiasm for that vision would gradually burn away, leaving a harder and more cynical type of leftism in its place.

## CRUSADERS ON THE PRAIRIE

On a rainy night in the spring of 1907, Oscar Ameringer traveled to a one-room schoolhouse in the village of Harrah, Oklahoma, to tell a group of farmers about socialism. The German-born activist considered himself a "missionary," and it is easy to understand why. Since arriving in the U.S. as a teenager in the 1880s, the stocky, rumpled Ameringer had mostly kept to cities like Milwaukee and Cincinnati where immigrant radicals were a familiar presence. He wielded the baton for a

German band, edited the journal of the Brewery Workers' Union, and thrilled to the works of Henry George and Edward Bellamy, as well as those of Marx and Engels. Before he arrived in Oklahoma, Ameringer had regarded farmers as "capitalists, exploiting wage labor . . . they had a great deal more to lose than their chains."[10]

The meeting in Harrah confounded him. Water sloshed around the floor, affording no relief to men and women dressed in old, threadbare clothing who had made their way to the school in open wagons or on horseback. The chairman was thoroughly caked with mud; the storm had washed out the road between his home and the village, and so he swam into town. Ameringer learned that most members of the audience worked land owned by others and were perpetually in debt. Expecting a gathering of the diligent and prosperous, he instead saw before him an "indescribable aggregation of moisture, steam, dirt, rags, unshaven men, slatternly women and fretting children." Ameringer "had come upon another America!"[11]

Oklahoma was granted statehood that same year, and such hard-luck residents would make it as strong a citadel of socialism as existed anywhere in the union. In state and federal elections from 1908 to 1916, the party won an average of 12 percent of the vote. In 1914, the six Socialists elected to the Oklahoma legislature outnumbered those from every other state but Wisconsin, a bastion of German immigrants with sturdy class-conscious traditions. More than three thousand Sooners paid dues to the party in 1914 (about one of every three hundred adults in the state). They published dozens of weekly papers with such names as the *Constructive Socialist* and the *Sword of Truth*. Indeed, a century ago, Oklahoma, now a bastion of conservative or "Red America," was home to a remarkable number of genuine Reds.

To accomplish that feat, Sooner Socialists had to bend their ideology to suit agrarian realities. While the Oklahoma party dutifully swore its solidarity with the international working class, it took particular care to appeal to the kind of people who had greeted Ameringer inside the saturated schoolhouse. The SP's "Renter's and Farmer's Program" included a plan for the state to purchase arable land for the use and occupancy of those willing to cultivate it. The party also vowed to remove all taxes from farms worth less than $1,000 and to develop cooperatives for the purchase of tools and the marketing of produce. State banks and warehouses would help small farmers stay in business and, perhaps, make a modest profit. The echo of Henry George's attack on land speculation was unmistakable, although the state party never advocated the single tax. Ameringer later wrote, "I still regard a social arrangement in which some possess thousands of acres of life-giving earth, while millions of children are born without earth to plant their little pink bottoms on, a black betrayal of democracy, and an insult to Christianity."[12]

It would have been difficult to find an Oklahoma radical who did not routinely invoke the carpenter of Nazareth. Ordained preachers proclaimed "Christ's church was a working class church . . . grafters were not eligible for membership in it" and cited the verse in Ecclesiastes that decrees "the Profit of the Earth is for all." On the Great Plains, many Socialists were former Populists, and they saw no reason why joining a Marxist organization should cause them to question their religious beliefs or confine them to private life. Party meetings were routinely held in schoolhouses that doubled as churches.[13]

At least once a year, prairie Reds held massive encampments that blended a faith in Christ with a belief in socialism. For a week or more after harvest season, thousands of families would park their wagons in an open field and spend their days and evenings listening to Socialist orators and authors and singing radical lyrics set to popular and religious melodies. Anyone weary of instruction could ride a Ferris wheel or play carnival games. At least once, the prairie Marxists even put on a rodeo. Everyone understood that a sort of revival meeting was under way, even when the roster of speakers did not include a Socialist clergyman. "To these people radicalism was not an intellectual plaything," recalled Ameringer. "Many of their homesteads were already under mortgage. Some had actually been lost by foreclosure. They were looking for deliverance from the eastern monster whose lair they saw in Wall Street. They took their socialism like a new religion."[14]

It was not, however, a particularly tolerant faith. Anti-Catholic sentiment ran high in Oklahoma and neighboring states, where a hate-filled journal, *The Menace*, outsold most weekly publications in the region. Some radicals stoked the flames, even as others warned against setting one sect of working people against another. Socialist journalists accused nuns and priests of forcing their flock to vote a straight Democratic ticket and were not above using epithets normally aimed at land barons and financiers. In 1913, the SP organ in Oklahoma City charged local Catholics with hurling the nation's flag into the street, "where the automobiles of the parasites passed over and crushed Old Glory in the dirt, while they speeded on their way to Romanize our public schools."[15]

Since the eighteenth century, radicals in America and elsewhere had considered the pope and his minions a fount of privilege, ignorance, and reaction. Debs called the Catholic church "the rottenest political machine that ever stole the livery of heaven." This animus persuaded most Catholics in Oklahoma—and their co-religionists elsewhere in the country—that socialism was not a hope but a hazard.[16]

Race posed a different sort of dilemma for Sooner Socialists. Officially, the SP hewed to a position that was both color-blind and remarkably naïve: "the only line of division which exists . . . is that between the producers and owners of the world." Black people were urged to join the party but should not expect it to help them fight against lynching, Jim Crow laws, or the prejudices of their fellow workers. African Americans made up about 10 percent of Oklahoma's population and faced hostility rivaling that in the Deep South, from which most white Sooners hailed. Party activists could not ignore the problem, but a firm stand on anti-racist principle would surely have alienated the people they most wanted to reach.

As politicians in a difficult spot, Oklahoma Reds mostly straddled the issue. In 1910, the Democrats who dominated the legislature placed on the ballot an amendment to the state constitution that became known as "the grandfather clause." It required voters to pass a literacy test but exempted anyone whose ancestors had been eligible to cast a ballot before the start of Reconstruction. Oscar Ameringer and other leaders of the Oklahoma party campaigned against the amendment and urged black residents to insist on their rights, even after the change was enacted and the state supreme court upheld it. But a large minority of rank-and-file Socialists voted for the measure, fearing that equal rights at the polls might slip into race mixing in more intimate arenas. The *Sword of Truth* warned, all too truthfully, that the SP's principled stand was "a sweet morsel for some of our opponents"; another weekly mocked Democrats for preaching racial purity while fathering biracial children. So socialism in Oklahoma, and elsewhere in the nation's heartland, remained a virtually all-white affair. Thaddeus Stevens still had no successor on the grassroots left.[17]

In 1912, the state party expelled Ameringer, together with a fellow German-American official who was his good friend. Native-born members resented them as outsiders who had sought to enforce party doctrine on the perilous matter of black rights and a range of other controversial issues. To retain southern as well as socialist beliefs fit both the convictions and the short-run political needs of most Oklahoma radicals. So the witty band leader turned organizer returned to Milwaukee, where he had always kept a home.

### THE SEWER SOCIALISTS' DILEMMA

Oklahoma was not the only part of the rural hinterland where the SP mounted a serious, if short-lived, challenge to the political establishment. From Winn Parish in northern Louisiana (the birthplace of the great populist demagogue Huey Long) through the coalfields of eastern Kansas to the silver mines of Colorado and the lumber camps of the Pacific Northwest, Socialist candidates drew on the discontent of small farmers and manual workers to win a healthy minority of votes and a sprinkling of local offices.

The *Appeal to Reason*, published in the hamlet of Girard, Kansas, was the main voice of this far-flung constituency. A sales force of thousands fueled the paper's huge circulation. Staffing the *"Appeal* Army" were at least fifty thousand craftsmen and farmers, nine-tenths of them native-born, who talked up the cause while peddling discount subscriptions to their neighbors and workmates. Reading George and Bellamy had converted many of the salesmen to socialism. But, being salesmen, they were not about to give up the dream of becoming self-made men. In the *Appeal*, alongside stirring tales of strikes and electoral triumphs ran ads touting investments in gold mines, courses in public speaking, and schemes for selling eggs and novels door to door. While waiting for the revolution to begin, why not take advantage of a good business opportunity?[18]

Practical Socialists achieved a measure of success in a few dozen small and midsized cities where the gap between the manufacturing elite and wage earners had widened alarmingly during the Gilded Age. In St. Mary's, Ohio, SP candidates swept to victory in 1911 with the votes of native-born workers disheartened at how their town of six thousand residents had changed. New sewer lines and gas and electric service were provided only to the "better" neighborhoods, and the children of workers did not feel welcome in the newly opened high school.

Socialist journalist Frank Bohn visited St. Mary's soon after the 1911 election and reported that "the old time American workman is very much embittered" as "men he has known from boyhood" drove off in new automobiles, leaving him to do all the hard labor. "In the small town the worker is bred to be both religious and patriotic," wrote Bohn. "When his living conditions have deteriorated, when he sees his children denied the opportunities that would make their life easier than his, and after he has seen local politicians grow rich through town and country graft— then he is ready for a larger view of life." St. Mary's was not alone. Ohio had the distinction of electing more SP members to local office than any other state in the country.[19]

For short periods before 1920, Socialists governed thirty-three American municipalities, from Berkeley in the West to Schenectady in the East. In most cases, they owed their triumphs, as in St. Mary's, to the ballots of skilled workers who had either been born in the U.S. or had emigrated from industrializing nations like Britain and Germany where class consciousness was taken for granted. These were votes for fair treatment and a caring, honest government—not for revolution. Socialist administrations tried to deliver with factory inspections, public hospitals and new schools in working-class neighborhoods, and a police force that remained neutral during strikes. Comrades impatient for a proletarian uprising scoffed that this was merely "sewer socialism," a mess of palliatives that would only delay the demise of an evil system. As it happens, few Reds stayed in local office long enough to rebut their critics. In St. Mary's, Berkeley, and Schenectady, the Socialist mandate lasted for just a single term.

Even those sewer socialists who managed a longer tenure were unable to resolve the fundamental dilemma of ends and means that faced any radical in a democratic society. As Marxists, they desired and expected that workers, with the help of allies from other classes, would capture the state and bring to birth a new world of equality and harmony. But to win elections, they had to make "immediate demands," most of which progressives in the major parties could applaud and adopt. To compete for the mantle of reform, American socialists, like their "revisionist" comrades in Europe, had to put their ultimate aims aside, lest they appear manipulative and insincere. Yet doing so irked their more radical brothers and sisters. How, they wondered, would a strategy of "slowcialism" ever lead them to the promised land?

Victor Berger, c. 1900.
Born in Austria, Berger was a
leader of the reformist wing of
the Socialist Party of America
and one of two congressmen
elected on an SP ticket.

In no place did reformist socialism undergo so lengthy a test as in Milwaukee, the only major city where Marxists held control for more than a few years. In 1910, the industrial metropolis beside Lake Michigan had close to 375,000 residents, making it the twelfth largest city in the nation. Almost half the population was composed of either German immigrants or their children. Predictably, the local left was cast in the mold of the *Sozialdemokratische Partei Deutschlands* (SPD), the Berlin-based citadel of the Second International. Milwaukee radicals named their first paper *Vorwärts* (Forward) after the organ of the SPD and kept the name "Social-Democrat" for their local party although comrades elsewhere in the U.S. simply called themselves Socialists.

The pragmatic, "revisionist" approach taken by the German parliamentary left seemed as well suited to cautious midwesterners as to the authoritarian milieu of Kaiser Wilhelm's Second Reich. Milwaukee Social-Democrats organized unions of skilled workers, taking care not to insist that local labor bodies endorse their nominees for city or state office, a step that would have alienated many rank-and-filers as well as Samuel Gompers. The radicals inveighed against corporate monopolies—the hated "trusts." As dutiful partisans, they drew up an elaborate platform of feasible measures ranging from public slaughterhouses and hospitals to "care for the trees" that bloomed on the streets of the city. Just one caveat stayed the rush to reform: "Socialism will some day entirely remove the causes" of "the evil" in the world. But much like liberal Christians and the Second Coming, the platform makers did not dwell on the future. We "ought not let out of [our] sight even for a moment the real sentiment of the masses," wrote Victor Berger, architect and unrivaled leader of the Milwaukee movement. "Nothing more ought to be demanded than is attainable at a given time and under given circumstances." Socialism would advance one small victory at a time.[20]

In 1910, Berger's wisdom seemed borne out at the polls. That spring, the Social-Democrats, whose vote had steadily increased since the turn of the century, defeated both "capitalist" parties to place woodworker Emil Seidel in the mayor's office. They also elected their candidates to such executive positions as city attorney and treasurer, and a majority on the city's Common Council. In November, Berger completed the triumph when he won a seat in Congress and became the first Socialist ever elected to that body.

But during the Seidel administration, the party faithful learned how modest the attainable could be. Soon after the Social-Democrats took power, Berger delivered an uncharacteristic warning to his followers: Do not forget our ultimate end. He would "wish the victory had never been won . . . ," he said, "if [it] should in the least interfere with the revolutionary spirit of the Milwaukee movement." In that spirit, Social-Democrats aimed to turn Milwaukee into a model of municipal ownership their counterparts elsewhere in the nation could emulate. But the government of Wisconsin, run by progressives, resisted the changes, citing various laws that prohibited them. So Seidel and his comrades had to be satisfied with enacting less ambitious reforms: improving city services, cutting down on wasteful spending and graft, and winning an eight-hour day for municipal workers. In the next election, a fusion ticket of Democrats and Republicans again relegated the Milwaukee Reds to minority status.

Their defeat was only temporary. In 1916, city attorney Daniel Webster Hoan took back the office for the Social-Democrats. He remained in that post continuously until 1940, although Milwaukee voters sent a dwindling number of comrades to join him in City Hall. Under Hoan, Milwaukee erected the nation's first public housing project, and the city took ownership of the water and sewage system. But the animating vision of Marxism all but expired, along with the ranks of German-born radicals. Modern sewers were quite proficient at flushing the old dream of socialism deep underground.[21]

In Congress, Victor Berger did his best to avoid a similar fate. The dignified, erudite son of Austrian monarchists was determined to show the entire country what a socialist in high office could accomplish. On the one hand, he introduced quixotic measures to nationalize basic industries. He also demanded the withdrawal of U.S. troops from the border with Mexico, where they were poised to intervene in the revolution that had just broken out in that country. At the same time, Berger proposed a variety of welfare measures. The most significant would have provided a pension of $4 a week to every "impoverished" worker over the age of sixty who was a longtime citizen and had never been convicted of a felony. He borrowed the idea from the German system of social insurance. But it irritated Berger's more radical comrades. They accused him of discriminating against fellow workers who happened to be new immigrants or had fallen afoul of capitalist justice. The congressman from Milwaukee had an impossible task: to champion socialist principles while acting as a lawmaker able to make deals. Perhaps a brilliant orator could have squared the circle, but Berger had neither the voice nor the charm to carry it off.

### BEAUTIFUL LOSERS

Eugene Debs did not worry much about the dilemma of means and ends. Although the eloquent campaigner refused to engage in intraparty conflicts between the "revisionist" right and the insurrectionary "left," he left no doubt about his true convictions. To a heckler along the trail who shouted that a vote for the Socialist Party was a wasted ballot, Debs responded, "That's right. Don't vote for freedom—you might not get it. Vote for slavery—you have a cinch on that." The five-time candidate for president drew huge crowds by making as genuine and emotional an appeal for human solidarity as was ever expressed by an American politician. But unlike his brethren from Milwaukee, Debs kept his vision fixed on the dream of proletarian revolution.[22]

Born in 1855, Debs had come rather late to the cause. Until he was almost forty, the Indiana native had traced the arc of a self-made man, albeit one making his way largely within the humble orbit of organized labor. As a teenager, Debs dropped out of school to work on the railroads. At the age of twenty, he founded a local lodge of the Brotherhood of Locomotive Firemen, the conservative union that represented some of the most highly skilled and well-paid tradesmen in America. Five years later, the firemen named him their grand secretary, or top leader, as well as the editor of the union's journal. Debs intended to keep peace between the classes. "The mission of the Brotherhood . . . ," Debs wrote in 1884, "is not to antagonize capital. Strikes do that; hence we oppose strikes as a remedy for the ills of which labor complains." That same year, the talented young man, running as a Democrat, won a seat in the Indiana legislature.[23]

But his fidelity to unionism would soon override his political ambitions. In 1888, firemen on the Burlington Railroad stopped work in sympathy with a strike begun by fellow employees who belonged to the Knights of Labor. Debs, despite his misgivings about such tactics, tried to convince the railroad bosses to bargain with their employees. Instead, the company secured court injunctions against the unions and fired most of the strikers. To his alarm, Debs learned that capital was interested only in a peace of the victor. He now declared, "The strike is the weapon of the oppressed, of men capable of appreciating justice and having the courage to resist wrong and contend for principle. The Nation had for its cornerstone a strike."[24]

Class-conscious anger led Debs to take actions which completed his ideological transformation. In the early 1890s, he assumed the helm of the new American Railway Union (ARU), a brave attempt to transcend the complex differences of craft and region (although not race) which frequently had workers in the nation's most important industry fighting more with one another than with their anti-union employers. The Pullman strike made him a hero to radicals everywhere, but the government's brutal victory shattered the ARU before it could fulfill its promise.

While the defeat did not immediately persuade Debs of the need to destroy capitalism, it did convince him that by themselves unions could never reverse the hostility of a state dominated by the allies and ideology of their bosses. Armed with this logic, he first joined the Populists and then campaigned for Bryan. After the 1896 election, Debs finally announced that he had become a socialist. "We have been cursed with the reign of gold long enough," he wrote in an open letter to the beleaguered members of the American Railway Union. "Money constitutes no proper basis of civilization. The time has come to regenerate society—we are on the eve of universal change."[25] The millenarian roar was an echo of radical prophets from the Puritan John Winthrop to Wendell Phillips and Ignatius Donnelly.

Debs, who lived until 1925, became the most popular messenger American socialism has ever known. He crisscrossed the nation for more than twenty years, stretching out his long arms as if to touch the crowds, urging them to use their votes to destroy "the foul and decaying system" and erect a free, cooperative order in its place. Often, Debs would pace back and forth on the stage, sweat pouring down from his balding head.

His inspirations were eclectic: he praised Christ as "a pure communist" and described socialism as the fulfillment of shared American ideals instead of an alien creed. But nothing in the meat of his speeches departed from the orthodox Marxism of his day. Debs insisted that the reforms advocated by Roosevelt, Wilson, and other progressives would do little to improve the lives of workers in an economy that was "no longer adapted to the needs of modern society." The capitalist order would inevitably collapse, just as the fathers of "scientific socialism" had predicted. Still, Debs's romantic, hopeful, utterly sincere protests against the daily outrages of capitalism made the dogma ring like poetry. "He was a tall shamblefooted man," wrote the novelist John Dos Passos, who "had a sort of gusty rhetoric that set on fire the railroad workers in their pine-boarded halls . . . made them want the world he wanted, a world brothers might own where everybody would split even . . ."[26]

Although the messenger was beloved, his message left most Americans cold. Debs preached that socialists had to reach beyond what was to what ought to be. "Only Socialism will save . . . the nation"; the SP would "not fuse with any other party and it would rather die than compromise." The more radical the creed, the greater was the need for a rhetoric of transcendence. But the major parties offered more tangible rewards: patronage jobs, money for roads and schools and defense of the expanding realm, and a fellowship that flowed from local and ethnic traditions. Why vote Socialist when powerful progressives were also denouncing the big money and putting forth serious, if less than radical, remedies of their own? Debs's great spirit could not obscure the futility of his cause.[27]

Debs's confidence about the future was buoyed by the existence of a revolutionary organization of labor: the Industrial Workers of the World. The IWW was founded in the early summer of 1905, at a conference in Chicago where freelance radicals outnumbered delegates from existing unions. The worldview of the IWW expressed a rigorous militancy in the simple prose of a grade-school primer: "The working class and the employing class have nothing in common. There can be no peace so long as hunger and want are found among millions of the working people and the few, who make up the employing class, have all the good things of life." At its zenith in the years just before World War I, the IWW signed up tens of thousands of blue-collar workers, most of them native-born, with the promise that they could, as Ralph Chaplin wrote in

A poster produced by the Industrial Workers
of the World, c. 1910. At its zenith in the years
just before World War I, the revolutionary
IWW signed up tens of thousands of blue-
collar workers with the promise that they could,
according to "Solidarity Forever," America's only
great labor hymn, "bring to birth a new world
from the ashes of the old."

"Solidarity Forever," America's only great labor hymn, "bring to birth a new world from the ashes of the old."

Most "Wobblies" (a nickname of obscure origin) occupied the lowest rungs of the labor force: harvest hands, lumberjacks, textile workers, stevedores, denizens of hobo jungles and flophouses. The craft unionists who dominated the AFL rarely tried to organize such workers, whom they saw as lacking in organizational know-how and self-confidence. The IWW returned the insult, cursing Gompers and his associates as "labor lieutenants of capitalism."

The Wobblies had a rough idea of how the salvation of the proletariat should come about—and it didn't involve politicians (even socialist ones), armies, or check-writing reformers. By engaging in frequent strikes and constant agitation, the IWW would gradually persuade wage earners of every race and immigrant group to stop competing against each other and join the "One Big Union." Then, some glorious day, workers would usher their bosses out the door, take possession of every factory, mine, warehouse, and office, and run the economy for the benefit of all. The analysis was Marxian, but the vision was anarcho-syndicalist: the state would be replaced by the revolutionary union. In the catchy phrase of IWW leader William D. "Big Bill" Haywood, it would be "socialism with its working clothes on."

Haywood, a veteran leader of hard-rock miners in the West who often engaged in gun battles with company police and state militias, knew the revolution was unlikely to be peaceful. Under his guidance, Wobbly publications advised unhappy wage earners to try a bit of sabotage whenever their foremen or bosses tried to lengthen their hours or decrease their pay. A claw-brandishing "sab cat," in either tabby or black hue, appeared on countless leaflets and stickers, gently prodding workers to snarl up a machine or dump a cargo overboard. "The class struggle is a physical struggle and depends on physical force," announced one IWW editor. In 1913, the SP expelled Haywood from its executive committee for advocating sabotage. He offered no defense.[28]

In fact, rank-and-file Wobblies rarely initiated violence, even during strikes; they knew the heavily armed state could easily squash their embryonic movement. Instead, they resorted to civil disobedience as a way of highlighting the repressive nature of the system. Wobblies swarmed into the downtown streets of Spokane, Fresno, and other anti-union cities, They stood up to agitate, got arrested for disturbing the peace, and filled up the local jails. The campaigns embarrassed the authorities and earned sympathy from citizens who quaked at the thought of revolution but cherished free speech.

Aside from defending the First Amendment, the Wobblies also did a service for American culture: they abandoned the stiff pieties of the Victorian left. Like the sab cat, most IWW propaganda was fresh and playful, unlike that of most electoral Socialists who imitated their earnest mentors on the continent. The labor insurgents ambled toward the day of class judgment with a joke on their lips and a melody in their hearts. IWW papers published cartoons about a self-deceiving worker named "Mr. Block" and clever takeoffs on corporate ads and government recruiting posters. Unique in the history of radicalism, the union sold more copies of a songbook—palm-sized, with a cover of blazing crimson that vowed "to fan the flames of discontent"—than anything else it produced.[29]

Indeed, one can still chuckle at such tunes as "Hallelujah, I'm a Bum" ("Oh, I like my boss, / He's a good friend of mine, / That's why I'm starving / Out on the breadline") or Joe Hill's "The Preacher and the Slave": "Work and pray, live on hay, / You'll get pie in the sky when you die / (That's a lie)." Hill, an itinerant songwriter and illustrator who was born in Sweden and whose life ended in 1915 before a Utah firing squad, became a model of sorts for brash modernists like Carl Sandburg, Allen Ginsberg, and Jack Kerouac who gamboled in the spirit of the radical hobo. We will never know whether Hill actually murdered a Salt Lake City grocer and his son, the crimes for which he was executed. But thanks to a knack for such epigrams as "Don't mourn for me, boys, organize," a gauntly handsome face, and a catchy postmortem tribute song, he almost does seem "alive as you and me"—or at least as vital as any proletarian martyr in America can be.[30]

That outlaw style should not obscure the IWW's heroic efforts, fleeting though they were, to mobilize some of the poorest workers in America to help themselves. Wobblies agitated among lumberjacks in the Pacific Northwest who lived in lice-infested bunkhouses and worked as many hours as their fiercely competitive bosses demanded. They stirred up a revolt among migrant wheat and hop pickers in the Central Valley of California, who dodged shotgun fire when they demanded clean water on summer days when the temperature topped 100 degrees.

Wobblies also refused to toe the color line, in contrast to AFL leaders who quietly allowed any member union to bar blacks from joining. On the docks of Philadelphia in 1913, the IWW convinced Irish and black longshoremen to go on strike together; then they built an island of interracial cooperation which lasted until the onrush of wartime migration from the South made such comity impossible. In the piney woods of northern Louisiana, Wobblies helped black and white mill workers battle for higher wages against strikebreakers and gun-wielding company thugs—before they succumbed to the might of their employers and the poisonous ideology of Jim Crow. The story was repeated in dozens of other venues: IWW organizers would arrive on the scene, inspire working people who earned little and owned nothing, and then prove unable to counter the multiple weapons arrayed against them.

At first, the 1912 IWW-led strike in the textile town of Lawrence, Massachusetts, appeared to be a bright exception to this dismal pattern. In midwinter, fourteen thousand operatives walked out into the grimy snow to protest a pay cut at a string of woolen mills that stretched along the Merrimack River. The workers hailed from dozens of nations and spoke some forty-five languages; they were led by Joseph Ettor, a young Italian-American radical who was fluent in five tongues and his charismatic friend Arturo Giovannitti, a seasoned organizer and a decent poet. Elizabeth Gurley Flynn, the twenty-one-year-old daughter of radical Irish immigrants, gave dozens of the sort of anti-capitalist speeches that led Theodore Dreiser to call her "the East Side Joan of Arc."[31]

The Lawrence workers held out until spring, thanks to a strike committee as clever as it was energetic. Each large ethnic group sprouted its own relief brigade, providing food and medicine and clothing to working-class families. The committee diligently raised funds from supporters in eastern cities where compassion for the underdog ran strong.

From that sentiment sprang the initiative that forced employers to agree to a rapid settlement of the strike. In February, friends of the union arranged for hundreds of children whose parents were busy on the picket lines to stay with middle-class families in New York and Philadelphia. They also gave their young charges what may have been the first medical checkups of their lives. The same tactic had been used in several European strikes—and it enraged the owners of the textile companies and the city fathers of Lawrence who did their bidding.

Two weeks after the "children's crusade" began, local police blocked a large group of children who gathered at the train station with their mothers and sponsors to travel to Philadelphia. According to eyewitnesses, "The police . . . closed in on us with clubs, beating right and left . . . The mothers and children were thus hurled in a mass and bodily dragged to a military truck, and even then clubbed, irrespective of the cries of the panic-stricken women and children."[32] Three weeks later, the company essentially surrendered: it offered a big wage increase and agreed not to discriminate against any employee who had walked off the job. "The strikers of Lawrence," declared Big Bill Haywood, "have won the most signal victory of any organized body of workers in the world."[33]

The euphoria did not last long. Just a year after their triumph, the polyglot proletariat of Lawrence was once more at the mercy of its employers. The firms temporarily closed down several mills and encouraged each immigrant group to compete with the others for the jobs that remained. Radical workers drifted away, leaving less able and more conservative unionists to maneuver on unfavorable terrain. Haywood and other Wobblies of national prominence had left earlier to fan the flames of revolt elsewhere in America. Abjuring any truce in the class war, Wobblies refused to sign contracts or build durable locals, and their beachheads of militancy soon disappeared.

The Lawrence uprising had been a thing of beauty for the textile workers and their revolutionary spokesmen. Upton Sinclair later dubbed it "the Bread and Roses" strike, after a contemporary poem in which picketing women remark, "Hearts starve as well as bodies; give us bread, but give us roses." But the aftermath of the big strike revealed that, for all its romantic élan, the IWW was an organization of beautiful losers.

### THE JEWISH EXCEPTION

The Wobblies' inability to sustain their support among recent immigrants pointed to a larger problem that crippled radicals in industrial America. During the early twentieth century, wage earners from Europe and their U.S.-born offspring formed a majority in every sector of the manufacturing economy, from textiles to steel to electrical products to clothing. If socialism, with or without its working clothes on, failed to reach the "new immigrants," most of whose roots lay in eastern and southern Europe, it would never become a mass movement in the biggest and fastest-growing metropolises in the land. Welcoming locales like Oklahoma and Milwaukee could never supply the numbers or strategic influence a radical movement needed to force changes in either the state or the workplace.

Most newcomers from abroad were either untouched by or indifferent to the existing culture of the American left. While they warmed to any union that could wrest more money and free time from the boss, their politics seldom strayed far from ideas and institutions that valued ethnic consciousness over class solidarity. Southern Italians, the largest group of new immigrants, were slow to shed their adherence to *campanilismo*, a defensive loyalty to one's ancestral village or province. Away from the sight of the bell tower—the *campanile*—was alien terrain. At least half of these migrants ended up returning to Italy; as long as they viewed themselves as sojourners, there was little reason to join a political party or even to vote.

There did exist a lively clan of Italian-American radicals, including Ettor and Giovannitti from the IWW, the dashing anarchist Carlo

Tresca, and militant Sicilian cigarmakers in the "Latin" enclave of Ybor City, Florida. But it was perpetually at odds with the tight network of church, small business, and family that reigned in Little Italys from San Francisco to East Boston. A similar isolation was the lot of would-be revolutionaries from Greece, Poland, Hungary, and Japan.[34]

Just two sizeable ethnic groups departed from the norm. Finnish-American socialists eager to emulate the mighty Social Democrats back home (who routinely drew 40 percent of the national vote) created an impressive counterculture. Their newspaper, *Tyomies* (Workingman), boasted a larger circulation than any other Finnish-language periodical published in the U.S.; it helped promote a welter of consumer cooperatives and the Work People's College, which was located outside of Duluth. In 1913, the Finnish Socialist Federation, tethered to the larger SP, claimed over twelve thousand members, roughly 10 percent of all Finnish immigrants in the country at the time. Yet for all their diligence, the Red Finns left only a slight impression on the larger radical movement. Most Finns lived and agitated in the frigid ports and mining towns of the northern Great Lakes and argued about politics in a language few Americans elsewhere encountered or understood.[35]

The two million Jews who fled eastern Europe for the U.S. from the 1880s until the early 1920s became the great exception to the immigrant narrative. Hundreds of national and ethnic groups streamed into the country between the Gilded Age and World War I, but only Jews chose socialists to lead and teach them, about both culture and politics. What emerged from the more permeable ghettos of the New World was one of the few local lefts that could do more than protest and wage electoral campaigns devoted more to spreading the light than winning votes.

Jewish Marxists established and directed unions—particularly the International Ladies Garment Workers (the ILGWU) and the Amalgamated Clothing Workers—which organized tens of thousands of Jewish men and women who cut fabric and toiled at sewing machines. They created the Workman's Circle, the immigrant community's largest mutual aid society, which provided funds to succor the ill and needy and bury the dead. Jewish socialists operated schools and summer camps, choirs and bookstores, restaurants and masquerade balls. They published newspapers read by most Yiddish-speaking immigrants, whatever their ideological preference. The circulation of the daily *Forverts* (Forward) reached a quarter of a million soon after World War I. With advice columns, humor, and well-crafted features on community life, the *Forward* made clear that Jewish socialists championed the progress of their people as well as the salvation of humanity. The achievement of Jewish-American leftists rivaled that of the largest socialist parties across the Atlantic, and dwarfed the activities radical Jews in Russia and Poland were able to carry on in spite of the czar's censors and police.[36]

Why were secular Jews so drawn to the left? In part, they found in socialism a new faith as idealistic and messianic as that of the Torah they no longer regarded as holy. Abraham Cahan, longtime editor of the *Forward*, reflected, "Well, the rich man has his worldly pleasures; he eats well, he goes to the theater, he travels in automobiles, he has his worldly delights. The worker does not have all this. For the worker the socialist ideal is a necessity. It sweetens his sad life. It gives him a spiritual pleasure which is higher than all." Socialism allowed Jews to condemn the existing order by adapting the injunction of Isaiah: "Give counsel, Grant justice; make your shade like night at the height of noon; Hide the outcasts, Betray not the fugitive . . ."[37]

Many of the Jews who migrated to the United States already had an economic foothold in the modern world. They tended to be young men and women from urban areas who were literate and who practiced a trade essential to any industrial society, such as tailoring, teaching, or bookkeeping. While such Jews had an advantage over immigrants who only knew how to till a field or carry a load, they still had to endure the common indignities of working-class life. So they marshaled their skills as writers and organizers to build a movement that both cursed American capitalism and offered a collective way to prosper within it.

Although their new nation gave no official sanction to anti-Semitism, the memory of persecution also enhanced the allure of socialism. In western and central Europe, Jews unwilling to accept pariah status had welcomed a variety of ideologies, each of which promised escape and a degree of transcendence. Liberalism and Zionism appealed strongly to many of the Jews who had emigrated earlier to the U.S. from Germany or Austria and who by the early twentieth century were prospering in small businesses and the professions.

But young immigrants with fresh memories of pogroms in the realm of the czar were more likely to favor the radical alternative. Socialism encouraged such Jews to make common cause with other oppressed outsiders, in the U.S. and around the world. The clothing workers' unions signed up Italians and other Christians, while the *Forward* campaigned strenuously for Debs and other SP candidates. Looking down from the façade of its ornate building in lower Manhattan, completed in 1912, were portraits of Marx and Engels and two other sages of German Social Democracy. "The emancipation of the workers will be the task of the workers themselves," the paper declared on its front page. A Jew who became a radical was no longer simply a Jew; she or he was an American willing, like other Americans, to stand up for their rights and accept nothing less than equal treatment.

Armed with that dual identity, the Jewish left scored a number of triumphs, industrial and political. In 1909 and 1910, general strikes in the garment trades ended in agreements that boosted wages and guaranteed a form of union recognition for thousands of workers in New York City and Chicago. "In my mind," wrote Abraham Rosenberg, president of the ILGWU, "I could only picture to myself such a scene taking place when the Jews were led out of Egypt." Unlike in the mills of Lawrence, this victory endured.[38]

At the polling booth, Socialists drew support from the hundreds of thousands of Jews who lived in New York City. Between 1911 and 1920, they elected more than twenty candidates to the New York state legislature. The local SP's signal victory occurred in 1914, when the voters of the Lower East Side elected to Congress Meyer London, a Lithuanian immigrant with a law degree from NYU who had risen to fame as the attorney for striking garment workers. In and out of political office, London, who spoke English with a thick Yiddish accent, kept faith with his people. He donated part of his earnings back to his union and his party and never moved away from the old neighborhood, as did most Jewish professionals who did well. London also opposed restrictions on immigration, which many of his SP comrades endorsed in the desire to protect the jobs of American workers. And he persuaded his fellow congressmen to hold the first hearing on a program that later became known as Social Security. Grateful East Siders twice re-elected him to the House.

Yet the appeal of socialism to Jewish New Yorkers only underlined its weakness in the nation as a whole. The strength of Marxist parties in Berlin, Paris, and Helsinki (in which Jews were a small minority) reverberated out to the provinces, inspiring comrades to build working-class organizations to emulate and buttress those which thrived in the metro-

Young marchers in the New York City May Day parade, 1909.
Hundreds of national and ethnic groups streamed into the country between
the Gilded Age and World War I, but only Jews chose socialists to lead
and teach them, about both culture and politics.

poles. But New York was neither a capital nor a city whose culture and politics most Americans, radical or not, wished to emulate. That Jewish immigrants were the core of its left only added to its alien identity. Some Christian members of AFL unions even thought of socialism as "a specifically Jewish trait." In both Milwaukee and New York, Marxists depended on support from a single ethnic group and adopted the political strategy and the name of their most popular newspaper from the largest socialist party in Europe. While one can understand their fraternal pride, this was not the best way to build a mass movement among Americans who believed their nation, whatever its flaws, was a paragon of virtue compared to the bad Old World.[39]

Jewish radicals in the Progressive Era did, however, begin to leave a durable imprint on American culture, one that would grow larger as the twentieth century wore on. They became the foremost advocates of what might be called "altruistic modernism." This combined the hallmarks of cultural modernism: the freedom to choose one's religion and sexual partners, fluidity of class and ethnic lines, and a desire to live in a society filled with other newcomers and strangers. But that modernism was paired with and defined by altruism: Jewish leftists believed they had a mission to help the oppressed, to bring about social equality, to practice a secular version of the commandment to love your neighbor as yourself.

The absence of deep-seated anti-Semitism in the United States freed Jews from the need to seek protection from friendly rulers against hordes of ordinary people who despised them. Eastern European Jews in America thought of themselves, quite accurately, as outsiders—the memory of persecution ensured as much, as did the fact that most Americans were Christians who had their own kind of messianism. But, in their reasonably tolerant new nation, Jews were able to rally fellow outsiders and to combine their Jewishness with other identities—worker, socialist, anarchist—without a serious concern that an anti-Semitic campaign would brand them hypocrites or traitors to the more inclusive group and cause. Jewish radicals, writes Irving Howe, created "a new type of person: combative, worldly, spirited, and intent upon sharing the future of industrial society with the rest of the world." The grandest of ambitions required no less.[40]

## MILITANT MODERNS

Emma Goldman's life was studded with crises. When she was a child in Russia, a sadistic uncle kicked her down the stairs for refusing to do an errand for him. At the age of sixteen, in 1885, she was raped by a friend in a St. Petersburg hotel; in shame, she fled to the United States with an older sister. By the time she was twenty, Goldman had already been married and divorced and was devoting all her free time to the anarchist movement in New York City. In 1892, her lover, Alexander Berkman, tried to murder the steel magnate Henry Clay Frick at his Pittsburgh office and began serving a long jail term for the crime. In 1901, she became the most notorious woman in America after Leon Czolgosz, a jobless, deranged man inspired by her speeches, assassinated President William McKinley.

For nearly a decade, beginning in 1906, Goldman lectured all over the country to big crowds, although her talks were often disrupted by local police and vigilantes. She fell passionately in love with her handsome, younger manager, fellow anarchist Ben Reitman, who made no attempt to stay faithful to her. During World War I, the government jailed her for opposing the draft. In 1919, a few weeks after her release, Goldman and Berkman were deported together to Soviet Russia. Until her death two decades later, Goldman remained in exile, against her will. As the female embodiment of "a new type" of Jew, she encountered hatred and fascination at every turn.

A cascade of such experiences would have persuaded some leftists to retreat from politics or, at least, to find comfort in more anonymous pursuits. But Emma Goldman seemed to flourish amid the tempests, public and intimate. She accepted them as the price for speaking the truth about the powerful and leading a life of absolute freedom—from all manner of authorities, including her family and Jewish tradition. Every woman, Goldman believed, should follow her example, by "asserting herself as a personality, and not as a sex commodity." She should refuse "the right to anyone over her body," refuse "to bear children unless she wants them," refuse "to be a servant to God, the State, society, the husband, the family, et cetera." Individuals who did so would become "a force hitherto unknown in the world, a force for real love, for peace, harmony: a force of divine fire, . . . a creator of free men and women."[41]

No prominent American radical had used language like this since the "utopian" socialists of the antebellum era, and most of them had mingled their defiance of worldly authorities with a respect for the religious and moral beliefs of their contemporaries. Goldman was thus blazing a new kind of movement—one that linked social change with personal liberation and that viewed Victor Berger and the evangelical Reds of Oklahoma as uncertain allies in the modern world struggling to be born. "If I can't dance," Emma Goldman once said, "it's not my revolution."[42]

The movement was small, as intellectual lefts always are. But the militant modernists who lived in Greenwich Village and a scattering of other bohemian outposts had a remarkably broad conception of human needs and capabilities. They learned from Freud, Nietzsche, and Ibsen as well as Marx and saw no reason to draw sharp distinctions between socialism and anarchism when both were committed, in theory, to doing away with an unjust order. Goldman lectured about "The Failure of Christianity," "Man: Monogamist or Varietist?" and "Sex: The Great Element for Creative Work," as well as the Mexican Revolution, modern drama and dance, the IWW, Irish Republicanism, and birth control. Older anarchists grumbled that she was linking their creed with sexual license. But after the Haymarket debacle, they no longer had more than a hand-

Emma Goldman, c. 1890s. The most prominent
anarchist in America, the Russian-born Goldman
spoke widely and passionately against all manner
of authorities and urged listeners to lead a life
of absolute freedom, as she tried to do. Every
woman, she believed, should follow her example—
by "asserting herself as a personality, and not
as a sex commodity."

ful of beer shops and crude magazines to sustain them. Goldman may
have been the only anarchist whom Americans did not suspect of having
a bomb concealed in her coat pocket.[43]

Her expansive philosophy also differed sharply from how mainstream
socialists understood the world. In 1909, Oscar Ameringer wrote a little
historical pamphlet, *The Life and Deeds of Uncle Sam.* It begins with an
unabashed brief for "economic determinism": "Way down at the bottom
of every human movement are the selfish material interests of classes
which strive against other classes in an endeavor to make an easier living. Now the easiest way to get a living is to get someone to get it for
you . . . When somebody talks about carrying the cross, the flag, freedom or civilization to some heathen nation you bet your bottom boots
that that heathen nation has got something the other fellow wants."[44]

Ameringer was a clever and witty man, and his palm-sized primer sold half a million copies. But neither he nor most of his readers recognized that his analysis straitjacketed his purpose: if motivation could be reduced to narrow self-interest, why would anyone transcend the quotidian struggle for cash and goods to invest time and hope in forging a new world of cooperation, equality, and brotherly love?

Modernist radicals were more realistic as well as more romantic. They scoffed that "sewer socialists" like Ameringer could never hope to alleviate human misery with their timid campaigns and cautious programs. What was needed were acts of will, on a mass scale, to bring about a revolution that would not simply transfer power from one social group to another. It had to be a revolution in daily life, one that would give individuals of every class the freedom to pursue what Walter Lippmann, when he was still a young man on the left, called "joyous activity." That spirit would, they hoped, transform relationships between the sexes and ethnic groups and spark a style of journalism that fit the playful, mongrel energy of the modern city. To realize the dream of a liberating culture, Americans would have to topple a social system based on wage slavery.

No one embodied this dual vision more fully than Margaret Sanger. Emma Goldman earned fame as an orator, and amplified her words and those of a few friends and allies in a monthly magazine, which she self-importantly named *Mother Earth*, that circulated mainly among other militant romantics. But Sanger was a trained nurse, and she applied her knowledge and empathy to a practical problem that faced working-class women more frequently than their privileged sisters: unwanted pregnancies. Sanger did not just declare, "Women must learn to know their own bodies." She wrote clear, unpolemical guides to women's reproductive systems and to devices and drugs that might prevent conception. In a Brooklyn immigrant neighborhood, Sanger also established the nation's first birth control clinic where she aided prostitutes as well as housewives.[45]

Most of her activities violated the laws of either New York state or the nation. Sanger therefore had to spend nearly as much time in court or avoiding the police as on her work. Her efforts did, however, succeed in turning birth control—a term which she invented—from a furtive, underground pursuit into a growing political movement with international connections. Sanger's genius was to marry an overarching purpose to a desperate human need. "I am the mother of six children," wrote one of her anonymous correspondents in 1914. "I am not well enough

Margaret Sanger, c. 1910. As a radical in the years before World War I, Sanger, a trained nurse, broke the law by distributing information about contraceptive devices. Her efforts helped turn birth control—a term which she invented—from a furtive, underground pursuit into a growing movement with international connections.

to have any more, and hardly strong enough to work for these . . . Your [sic] doing a noble work for women."[46]

Until the aftermath of World War I, Sanger was in the forefront of those who battled simultaneously for the rights of women and the emancipation of the working class. The key men in her young life encouraged this fusion of causes. Her Irish Catholic father belonged to the Knights of Labor and named one of his sons after Father Edward McGlynn, the apostle of Henry George. She married a German-Jewish architect who ran for New York City alderman on the Socialist ticket and took primary responsibility for the care and education of their offspring.

Sanger's baptism of class-conscious fire occurred during the Lawrence uprising of 1912. In early February that year, she helped lead one of the evacuations of strikers' children. No violence occurred, but Sanger was shocked to discover that only 4 of her 119 young charges wore underpants. "It was the most bitter weather," she testified to a congressional investigating committee. "We had to run all the way from the [union] hall to the station in order to keep warm . . ."[47]

Like Goldman, Sanger didn't hesitate to act in heterodox ways. In 1914, she traveled to England on a false passport in order to escape prosecution. One of her first stops was the London flat of Havelock Ellis, the author of works that analyzed all manner of sexual practices in sympathetic detail. They quickly became friends, and Sanger embraced the older man's view that sex should be understood as an effort to fashion "man's own paradise" rather than merely a biological need. She had just taken a lover—the Catalan anarchist Lorenzo Portet—and told her husband, by mail, that their relationship was over.[48]

Since the decline of the utopians in the 1850s, most socialists had opposed turning sex into a political issue. To do so, they warned, would alienate prudish workers and seduce activists into thinking that what took place in the bedroom mattered as much as what occurred on the factory floor and in the halls of state. In the 1960s, the eminent Marxist historian Eric Hobsbawm still held that view: "Conventions about what sexual behaviour is permissible in public," he wrote, "have no specific connection with systems of political rule or social and economic exploitation." Hobsbawm allowed a partial exception for the "rule of men over women."[49]

His last phrase unintentionally suggests why sexual modernism contained the seed of a great upheaval. In the opening years of the twentieth century, women, for the first time, took an equal part in defining what it meant to be a radical and what type of changes would be necessary for any society to become truly free. It was no accident that "feminism" and "birth control" both entered the American lexicon around 1910. For Goldman, Sanger, and their cosmopolitan comrades—of both sexes— to abolish mandatory motherhood was to open up a limitless future for women, and thus for all of humanity. Decades earlier, Engels had asserted that, in the family, "the man is the bourgeois, the woman represents the proletarian." Yet he insisted that only a workers' revolution would do away with this onerous reality, and most socialists repeated his argument, while retaining in their own homes the division of labor Engels deplored. The modern generation of self-declared feminists— educated, articulate, and sexually confident—was not willing to wait.[50]

Their candor about personal matters was a departure from the previous two generations of left-wing activists. Since the Civil War, leading radicals of both sexes had kept their personal lives almost exclusively private concerns. Thaddeus Stevens, Frances Willard, Terence Powderly, Eugene Debs, even Albert and Lucy Parsons did not consider their erotic desires or their intimate behavior to have political significance—and the press, whether friendly or hostile, usually agreed. But the bohemian feminists revived Marx and Engels's dictum about the "free development of each" and applied it in ways that may have horrified its authors, whose reticence about private life paralleled that of the typical bourgeois Victorian.

Where many of the radical modernists chose to live made it easier for them to slip the bonds of the recent past. Since the mid-nineteenth century, artists and writers had given Greenwich Village and the crowded neighborhoods adjoining it the reputation of a bohemian colony. In the 1850s, Walt Whitman caroused at Pfaff's beer hall on lower Broadway; after the Civil War, painters and sculptors set up dozens of studios near

Washington Square; by the end of the century, popular novelists and journalists had turned "the Village" into the American counterpart of the Latin Quarter. Although some refugees from the Paris Commune found cheap lodging there, the area was known more for raucous fetes and nude models than for insurgent movements. Anonymous Irish, Italian, and black families filled "the streets that meandered around until they ran at times almost into themselves"; for déclassé intellectuals, they gave the place an air of plebeian legitimacy.[51]

The young leftists who moved into the Village in the early twentieth century certainly threw their share of good parties. But as much as they believed that passion between equal partners was a political matter, they were equally passionate about other radical causes. Sanger's participation in the Lawrence strike revealed whom the Village modernists sided with in the labor movement. Only the IWW promised to break the chains that bound workers to the profit system—and it favored street protests, strong women, and a rebellious counterculture. The garment unions that belonged to the AFL had far more members in New York City than did the Wobblies, but they courted respectability, and their leaders preferred legal reform over romantic gestures. On the other hand, the key figure in the IWW was Big Bill Haywood, whom Max Eastman admired as "the arch rebel, the one-eyed gigantic satan . . . prepared to storm the fortress of Capitalism with a proletarian army as soon as he could get one together."[52]

Eastman's opinions were often shared by his fellow Village intellectuals. But it would be a mistake to view them as privileged dilettantes, dispatching love letters to besieged workers from the comfort of their bohemian salons. In stern yet colorful prose, Eastman reported on the massacre of striking miners in Ludlow, Colorado. John Reed staged a massive pageant in Madison Square Garden to dramatize the walkout of silk workers in nearby Paterson, New Jersey—before traveling down to Mexico to ride with and write about Pancho Villa's rebel army. Margaret Sanger was just one of several Manhattan modernists who helped ferry children away from frigid Lawrence. Crystal Eastman, an attorney and Max's older sister, conducted a pioneering study of industrial accidents which spurred passage of early workers' compensation laws. She was also a militant suffragist, an anti-war organizer, and a gifted journalist who chronicled the revolutions which broke out in Europe at the end of the Great War. Like Frances Willard, the Eastmans and their comrades were not content unless they could "do every-thing" for radical change—which often meant using their pens to gain sympathy for people with neither the resources nor the skill to do so for themselves.

*The Masses* became justly famous for its sty-listic ingenuity and antinomian élan. It featured what Max Eastman called "a clean and clear make-up": articles were neither interrupted by ads nor pinched by tight margins, and the magazine routinely published full-page illustra-tions by such emerging realists as John Sloan, George Bellows, and Boardman Robinson, who elevated political advocacy into fine art. Instead of idealized proletarians lifting torches of freedom from sculptured chests, *Masses* con-tributors drew fleshy men in cloth caps sell-ing flowers and one slack-jawed shopgirl in a floppy hat telling another, "Gee, Mag. Think of us bein' on a magazine cover!" Rather than wave a rhetorical fist at class enemies, the journal's writers and artists skewered them with satire. "We would give anything for a good laugh except our principles," Eastman later reflected.[53]

Max Eastman, c. 1910. Eastman was editor of *The Masses*, journalistic avatar of the modernist left in Greenwich Village. Rather than wave a rhetorical fist at class enemies, the magazine skewered them with satire. "We would give anything for a good laugh except our principles," Eastman reflected.

That spirit helped the editor and his journalistic comrades bring cover-age of labor and the poor down to earth. For the first time, middle-class, native-born readers could appreciate people who lived in "foreign" neighborhoods like the Lower East Side and Hell's Kitchen, and in the mining camps of the West, as articulate, witty individuals. They lost their noble veneer and gained relaxed and credible personalities.

This new view of the American worker was not confined to the pro-vocative columns of *The Masses*. In the previous decade, the radical journalist Hutchins Hapgood wrote two popular books, *The Spirit of the Ghetto* (1903) and *The Spirit of Labor* (1907). The first admiringly depicted Jewish immigrants in New York; the second, a German-born anarchist union organizer in Chicago. Hapgood, one of the first report-ers to insert himself routinely into his stories, flattered the labor activist, Anton Johannsen, and his friends: "It is the man-in-street, the common

*The Masses* portrays the bloody miners' strike in Ludlow,
Colorado, 1914. Illustration by John Sloan.

man, the working man who is giving tone to all the rest of society . . . It
is your sentiment that is gradually affecting all classes. It is your philosophy that is affecting the old philosophy, broadening it, giving it a larger
human basis."[54]

Coming from Hapgood, a Harvard graduate and a businessman's
son, this sentiment represented a literary sea change from middle-class
radicals in the Gilded Age like Edward Bellamy for whom "the masses"
were interchangeable, often invisible victims of a cruel system. It also
departed from *The Jungle*, the 1906 muckraking novel by Upton Sinclair,
an avid socialist. Sinclair could only imagine his hero Jurgis, a Lithuanian immigrant who loses his health and family in the hellish maw of
the Chicago stockyards, finding deliverance from his plight by hearing
a messianic orator modeled after Debs. In contrast, Hapgood's gritty,
often erotic reportage may have erred on the side of romance, but he and
his modernist contemporaries were handling what one historian aptly

calls "cultural dynamite." From novels like *The Grapes of Wrath* to TV dramas like *The Wire*, the blast effects of this streetwise prose are with us still.[55]

No less explosive was the bohemians' embrace of ethnic identities that repelled most of their fellow native-born Christians. In between his trips to cover, and take part in, revolutions abroad, John Reed looked out from Washington Square and reflected, "Within a block of my house was all the adventure in the world; within a mile was every foreign country."[56]

Radical modernists shared that cosmopolitan thrill. At the Ferrer Center—named after a martyred Spanish anarchist and educator—they attended lectures, plays, and political meetings alongside freethinking Jews, Italians, and an occasional Greek, Pole, and African American. In Madison Square Garden, they mounted the pageant conceived by Reed in which immigrant workers acted out roles inspired by the strike they were waging across the Hudson River in Paterson. "Certainly nothing like it had been known before in the history of labor agitation," observed a mainstream magazine. They argued about the Irishness of the desperate characters in O'Neill's plays and debated whether Zionism was an escape from class conflict or a sign that a long-persecuted race was at last forging its own destiny.[57]

This empathetic sensibility inspired one gifted Village intellectual to produce an elegant manifesto. In 1916, as President Wilson and a bevy of militarists demanded that ethnics drop their hyphens as the nation prepared for war, Randolph Bourne wrote an article for the *Atlantic Monthly* entitled "Trans-National America." It has always been tempting to view Bourne, who died at the age of thirty-two in the great flu epidemic of 1918, as a prophet of darkness. A hunchback with a disfigured face, his very appearance seemed, in retrospect, like an augury of calamities to come. But his now-famous essay actually saw a roseate future for the nation, if its people embraced what the "plastic next generation may become in the light of a new cosmopolitan ideal."[58]

Bourne was not just asking his countrymen and -women to respect the pluralism of what was then one of the most culturally diverse societies on earth. Such prominent progressives as Jane Addams and Horace Kallen—and ethnic radicals like Abraham Cahan—had already written powerful critiques of the coercive fist hidden within the "melting pot" ideal and of the official crusade to "Americanize" all immigrants. For Bourne, these pluralists were speaking self-evident truths.

But Bourne dared to leap beyond mere tolerance to a vision of the United States as the embryo of a better world. "The failure of the melting-pot, far from closing the great American democratic experiment, means that it has only just begun," he wrote. ". . . In a world which has dreamed of internationalism, we find that we have all unawares been building up the first international nation." For that new nation to emerge, the old institutions built on the myth of Anglo-Saxon superiority had to be destroyed. "The Anglo-Saxon element is guilty of just what every dominant race is guilty of in every European country," wrote Bourne; "the imposition of its own culture upon the minority peoples." The defeat of such arrogance would produce the first truly democratic society on earth—one "in which all can participate, the good life of personality lived in the environment of the Beloved Community."

This was a breathtaking departure from the reigning Marxist orthodoxy, on both sides of the Atlantic, which held that ethnicity was a superficial attribute that would vanish come the revolution. Bourne announced that a self-conscious multicultural left was being born, even if, before his early death, only his fellow intellectuals heard the news. A system based on ethnic supremacy, he argued, was anathema to freedom. Worse than the damage done by capitalism alone, the ruling elite wanted to squelch immigrant voices who together could turn the world away from an endless cycle of nationalist carnage.[59]

Of course, the dreams of any prophet are limited by his own history. Though he rebelled against his wealthy Presbyterian family, Bourne still felt the need to issue sweeping judgments about the traits of foreign races. Ironically, his hostility to the tyranny of the melting pot led him to adopt a mirror image of ethnic condescension. Bourne disdained those immigrants who were struggling to become "American" by shedding their inherited beliefs and practices. He praised both Zionists and orthodox Jews but disparaged "the Jew who has lost the Jewish fire and become a mere elementary grasping animal." And Bourne said nothing at all about how black people would fare in the new transnational America. In his silence, he may have assumed, like many of the pro-war politicians he detested, that they would go wherever the enlightened majority was heading.[60]

Not every white radical was similarly myopic. In 1909, several prominent white socialists—Mary White Ovington, William English Walling, and Charles Edward Russell—signaled their hatred of racial supremacy when they helped to found the National Association for the Advancement of Colored People (NAACP). Ovington, a wealthy social worker, idolized W. E. B. DuBois, who became editor of the NAACP's journal, as "the master builder, whose work will speak to men as long as there is an oppressed race on the earth"; later, she sided with him when political conflicts riddled the organization. After 1915, migrants from the rural South began streaming into Harlem seeking good jobs and personal freedom. Emilie Hapgood, the journalist's sister-in-law, produced plays with an all-black cast in a downtown theater. The white modernist Carl Van Vechten began promoting gifted black writers, artists, and performers.[61]

Most radical modernists, however, took little more interest in what African Americans thought about their own lives and problems than did those socialists who focused on winning the hearts and votes of white workers. Not many black thinkers made their homes in lower Manhattan, and informal segregation was still the rule in the big city. Before the U.S. entered World War I, only a handful of African Americans joined the local Socialist Party, and they seldom stayed in it long. Hubert Harrison, a recent immigrant from the Virgin Islands, wrote a few pieces for *The Masses* and frequented the Ferrer Center. But, in 1915, he denounced the SP for putting whites first and became an ardent black nationalist.[62]

In the end, the bohemian rebels stumbled more out of naïveté than prejudice. They hailed the IWW for its color-blind creed and condemned Victor Berger for declaring that the U.S. should remain "a white man's country." But they failed to grasp why activists of a darker race rejected their earnest tutelage. Hutchins Hapgood once asked W. E. B. DuBois to help him research a book about black people; the result would presumably resemble those Hapgood had already written about other sorts of plebeian Americans. The offer was immediately rejected. "The Negroes," explained DuBois, "do not wish to be written about by white men, even when they know that they will be treated sympathetically. Perhaps, especially then, they do not desire it."[63]

Hapgood was discovering the limits of what any small group, no matter how radical, could change. He and his fellow modernists, writes historian Christine Stansell, "created the first full-bodied alternative to an established cultural elite, a milieu that brought outsiders and their energies into the very heart of the American intelligentsia." As feminists, sexual adventurers, and the eloquent allies of radical labor and new immigrants, they shocked the defenders of Victorian America in their most vulnerable places. Enviably perched in the nation's center of publishing and art, their cultural politics was a fitting expression of the lines from "The Internationale": "No more tradition's chains shall bind us . . . A better world's in birth."[64]

Yet a cluster of free individuals drawn mainly from the middle classes could not reach the promised land alone. Like the antebellum utopians, Village radicals erased class and racial lines more in words than in movement. For all its brilliance, *The Masses* was not much read by the masses; it survived only with donations from a series of wealthy patrons. As Max Eastman put it, his magazine was "a luxurious gift to the working-class movement from the most imaginative artists, the most imaginative writers, and the most imaginative millionaires in the Adolescence of the Twentieth Century."[65]

In a country where few mill workers could afford underwear for their children, a politics of the self drew more controversy than recruits. On the road, Emma Goldman packed houses with the curious, but she did not have many followers on the Lower East Side. Intensely involved with one another, the young modernists seldom gave a thought to how bizarre they seemed to most Americans of their day. Socialist organizers in Oklahoma had to rebut persistent charges that they belonged to a party of "free love" and atheism. Artists can make a revolt that is liberating and joyful; they cannot make a revolution.[66]

## RESUMING HISTORY'S BLOODY COURSE

The springtime of the left ended abruptly in the spring of 1917 when Congress, by decisive majorities, declared war on Imperial Germany. Despite their differences, champions of the three socialisms had always opposed armed conflict between modern nations with equal vehemence and the same reasoning. They shared the conviction, announced by the Second International in 1907, that "the proletariat, which contributes most of the soldiers and makes most of the material sacrifices, is a natural opponent of war." Alas, seven years later, many of the same European socialists who had cheered that statement betrayed it when they backed their nations' plunge into what soon became known as the Great War. "We were children reared in a kindergarten," wrote Max Eastman years later, "and now the real thing was coming. History was resuming its bloody course."[67]

Yet, across the Atlantic, most Reds still believed workers had nothing to gain from killing other workers in the name of a patriotism that benefited no one but their bloody-minded rulers. In 1916, *The Masses* published a cartoon by Robert Minor that made this case with elegant simplicity: the medical officer for an unnamed army smiles up at a massive, male body who stands ready for action. The recruit is missing his head. "At last a perfect soldier," beams the doctor.[68]

The U.S. declaration of war caused few American radicals to change their minds. One day after Congress voted, the SP met in an emergency convention in St. Louis and easily passed a resolution denouncing the government's act as "a crime against the people of the United States." At this climactic moment, Kate Richards O'Hare, an engaging orator from the Great Plains, revealed that Christianity remained vital to her part of the left: "I am a socialist, a labor unionist and a believer in the Prince of Peace *first*, and an American second." The delegates named O'Hare to head a new committee entrusted with running a vigorous campaign against "War and Militarism." In May, the SP helped create a broader group, the People's Council of America for Democracy and Peace, which signed up an impressive number of liberal ministers, rabbis, and social workers, as well as unionists based in the upper Midwest and the New York garment trades. Months before any U.S. soldier went into combat, an anti-war movement was gathering strength, with radicals in the lead.[69]

Meanwhile, the IWW, in its decentralized fashion, took no official stand against either going to war or cooperating with the draft that soon followed. But neither did the Wobblies refrain from calling on workers to keep up the class struggle, regardless of what impact their actions might have on the war effort. "The masters are undoubtedly looking for an opportunity to close down some of our halls," wrote an organizer from the state of Washington, ". . . and if we do give them an excuse we should be sure to give them a damn good one."[70]

No real excuse was necessary. Congress quickly enacted the Espionage Act of 1917, which made it a felony to "promote the success of its enemies . . . when the United States is at war" or to "wilfully obstruct" the draft. The lawmakers later imposed censorship on disloyal statements whether made out loud or in print. What followed was the most sweeping crackdown on dissent in U.S. history. *The Masses* and hundreds of other left-wing magazines were banned from the mails, and thousands of socialists and Wobblies were thrown into prison. Emboldened by such acts, local vigilantes around the country set after radicals with fists, fire, tar and feathers, and, on several occasions, a tightly coiled noose.

As part of the crackdown, the government indicted Big Bill Haywood, Eugene Debs, and Victor Berger—the three most prominent radicals in America. The first two served time in prison, a fate Berger escaped on a technicality three years after the war ended. Before that, however, he endured a punishment rare in the annals of politics: the House of Representatives twice refused to let him take the seat to which the voters of his district had elected him. The repression, official and otherwise, devastated an organized left whose institutions were already underfunded and on the defensive. Neither the SP nor the IWW ever recovered from the blows.[71]

Courageous though they were, most American radicals might have found it harder to stick to their internationalist principles if they had not been so isolated from the centers of power. By rallying to their respective flags, European socialists hoped to gain popularity and pro-worker reforms in nations where they already held dozens of political offices. One German radical who volunteered for combat exulted, "We are defending the fatherland in order to conquer it!" Upton Sinclair, Charles Edward Russell, and a few other Socialist intellectuals broke with their party and endorsed Woodrow Wilson's war. But they did so because they agreed with the president that the future of democracy was at stake. They did not imagine their decision could bring a divided and embattled left to power.[72]

But the declaration of war briefly halted the SP's retreat to the far side of American politics. In the local elections of 1917, Socialists benefited from their status as the only peace candidates on the ballot. Many Americans with working-class jobs and ties to nations like Ireland, Germany, and Russia were furious at the prospect of crossing the ocean to fight for King George V or Czar Nicholas II and against their former countrymen. The SP vote increased markedly in communities from the Great Lakes to the Hudson River. Socialists came close to electing mayors in Dayton, Toledo, Cleveland, and Buffalo.

In New York City, Morris Hillquit made headlines for refusing to buy war bonds and then ran the most competitive race for mayor by any radical since Henry George back in 1886. Theodore Roosevelt sneered that the Latvian-born attorney was "worse than the Hun," and a leading New York daily depicted him as a hook-nosed "Hillkowitz or Hillquitter." The slurs may have boosted Hillquit's popularity among his fellow Jews and other ethnic minorities. He received 22 percent of the vote in a four-way race, far outpacing the party's total in any previous race for the office. The large turnout also helped to elect ten Socialist candidates to the state assembly and seven to the board of aldermen.[73]

Hillquit won a surprising 25 percent of the votes in Harlem, crowded mecca of African Americans fleeing the poverty and prejudice of Dixie. W. E. B. DuBois and other leaders of his race had endorsed the war, hoping that thousands of black men battling in the trenches of Europe would help win civil rights for millions back home. But draft resistance was rampant in Harlem, fueled by anger toward Wilson's sympathy for Jim Crow and a reluctance to help white Belgians "after what King Leopold and his gang had done to the Congolese." Leading Hillquit's campaign in the district were Chandler Owen and A. Philip Randolph, two young black Socialists who had studied Marxism together at the left-wing Rand School and had just begun to edit a new radical magazine they called the *Messenger*. The pro-worker, anti-war Hillquit, they wrote, "was the only candidate any self-respecting Negro could vote for." Their vigorous effort signaled that black people would no longer dwell on the outer fringes of the Marxist left. A biracial radicalism, anchored partly in Harlem, would blossom during the coming decades.[74]

In Oklahoma, however, hatred of the war drove some Socialists to commit political suicide. In 1916, a new interracial group called the Working Class Union sprang up to defend tenant farmers against high interest rates and foreclosures. That defense sometimes took the form of red-shirted night riders attacking the property of bankers and landlords. A year later, the group added to its grievances the new draft law many young men in Oklahoma were trying to evade. Crude posters appeared on rural fenceposts urging a rebellion against "Rich mans war. Poor mans fight. If you dont go J. P. Morgan is lost." In one county, Working Class Unionists were arrested for trying to blow up a waterworks, and black farmers exchanged rifle fire with a sheriff and his deputies.

That summer, bands of armed tenants announced they would trek all the way to Washington, D.C., to stop the draft, end the war, and perhaps topple the federal government in the bargain. The long-marchers vowed they would subsist on green (unharvested) corn and barbecued beef. One leader of the Green Corn Rebellion, "Captain" Bill Benefield, commanded his men while wearing a crimson sash and wielding a saber. The authorities easily quelled the undermanned and undisciplined insurgents before they could reach the state's eastern border.[75]

The fiasco made every radical in Oklahoma vulnerable to repression. While no local Wobblies had joined Benefield and his group, they still got blamed for various acts of individual terrorism. "Kill 'em just as you would any other kind of snake," editorialized a local daily. "It is no time to waste money on trials and continuances and things like that." Some rural socialists did join the Green Corn Rebellion, and its ignominious fate left the party reeling. By 1918, the Oklahoma SP could muster less than a third of the members and only a sixth of the popular votes it had won in 1916, when the nation was at peace. Mr. Wilson's war remained unpopular in the state, but Sooner socialists had become outlaws to many of their fellow citizens. Never again would a Marxist party be more than a cipher in Oklahoma or anywhere else on the prairies.

Throughout their history, most American radicals had been reluctant to endorse the use of violence to defend or spread their ideals. They denounced the professional armies that crushed the untrained, poorly equipped revolutionaries of 1848 and the Paris Communards of 1871 and showed little inclination to create forces of their own. In the U.S., it took John Brown's raid and the attack on Fort Sumter for William Lloyd Garrison and most of his fellow abolitionists to abandon their faith in "non-resistance." Calls to assassinate powerful men, whether acted upon or not, had devastated the anarchist movement in the 1880s. In 1915, the Texas Rangers crushed a band of armed Mexican-American anarchists who sought to carry out "the Plan of San Diego," which promised to win back control of the territories the U.S. had conquered in the 1840s as well as to carve out land for both a black republic and a reborn Indian nation. Such episodes seemed to confirm the old wisdom that radicals should never challenge the state to a bloody fight they could not win.[76]

But the Bolshevik victory in Russia was a conversion experience. Lenin and his comrades went beyond denouncing the socialist parties of Europe for sending workers off to kill their brothers in neighboring lands. The Bolsheviks campaigned to "turn the imperialist war into a civil war" and then cleverly exploited the collapse of the czarist order to do just that. With astonishing speed and ease, Marxists had seized power in the largest nation on the planet. All over the world, socialists who had cursed the appalling waste of life on the battlefields of Europe hailed the Bolshevik triumph; many embraced the idea that a violent revolution led by a disciplined party would hasten the liberation of humanity. In 1919, the new leaders of Russia launched the Communist International (Comintern), dedicated to "combat without mercy" against the old "right-wing" socialists and which called on the proletariat of every nation to seize state power. Early that year, from a cell in Leavenworth Prison, Big Bill Haywood wrote feverishly to Margaret Sanger:

> Margaret all my dreams are coming true my work is being fulfilled. Millions of workers are seeing the light, Russia Poland, Germany France Great Britain, Australia South America, we have lived to see the breaking of the glorious Red Dawn. While you and I and others were doing a little in this country other men and women were doing much in other countries. The world revolution is born, the change is here, we will of course not live to see it in its perfection. But it is good to have been living at this period.[77]

But for American radicals, 1919 was an annus mirabilis whose miracles turned quickly into calamities. That year, over four million workers engaged in the greatest strike wave in U.S. history. Steelmakers, textile operatives, and coal miners closed down their industries all across the nation; general strikers ruled Seattle for four days. The whiff of revolution was in the air: some unionists in the Pacific Northwest proclaimed "the Seattle Soviet," while striking San Francisco longshoremen demanded part ownership of the shipping firms that employed them as well as several seats on their boards of directors. Even the Boston police—icons of Irish Catholic conservatism—walked off the job. But by year's end, nearly all the strikes had been lost, with many of their leaders blacklisted for life. The combined might of bosses, politicians, and the pro-business press—and mistrust between workers of different ethnic backgrounds who had not gone on strike together before—were impossible to overcome.

That did not stop a growing number of radicals in the U.S. from imagining that they could capture their own equivalent of the Winter Palace. Since the onset of the Great War, immigrants from the czar's crumbling regime had been flocking to the Socialist Party. Most joined through one of the foreign-language federations—Russians, Letts, Finns, and others—that gave them a sense of solidarity with the upheaval under way back in their old countries. By 1919, with the collapse of plain-folks socialism in Oklahoma and elsewhere, the federations, at fifty-seven thousand strong, constituted a narrow majority of the party's membership. Few of the new members were eligible to vote or could deliver a speech in good English. They had contempt for the meager gains Berger, Hillquit, and other "slowcialists" had been able to achieve. Hadn't Leon Trotsky himself, on one of his sojourns in the U.S., sneered that the SP was a "party of dentists"? With revolutions on the Bolshevik model apparently breaking out all over, shouldn't the main organization on the U.S. left prepare to do its part?

An ugly split was all but inevitable. Leaders of the party's old guard were also excited by the revolution in Russia. Berger wrote, "Here is a government of the people and by the people in actual fact." But they understood how little the capitalist republic in which they lived had in common with the near-feudal order the Bolsheviks had overthrown. In order to preserve their viability in a democratic nation, Berger, Hillquit, and their allies resorted to blatantly undemocratic means. In May, the National Executive Committee, the party's leadership body, met in Chicago where it suspended the largest foreign-language federations and expelled the state party of Michigan, which had forbidden its members to advocate immediate reforms. In August, after a furious round of emergency meetings, internal fights, and constant fulminations, the left-wingers gave up the effort to Leninize the SP.[78]

The would-be revolutionaries cherished ideological rigor over the need to assemble a unified front. Proclaiming their undying fealty to the Bolsheviks, the foreign-language groups launched a new Communist Party. According to Max Eastman, they cared more about "expelling heretics than winning converts." John Reed and other radicals with a background in the IWW founded a separate Communist Labor Party on the grounds that their immigrant rivals were insufficiently committed to industrial unionism and did not know how to talk to American-born workers. Both groups proclaimed themselves the only true apostles of Bolshevism. They would compete for two long years, as their numbers and insurgent élan steadily dwindled. All these maneuvers led many an unaffiliated leftist to despair. "I did not leave a party of crooks to join a party of lunatics," lamented the theorist Louis Boudin.[79]

Thus the dream of a joyful march to socialist democracy was buried in the mire of government crackdowns and internal conflict. In retrospect, radicals of all sorts had been captive to grand illusions. Socialists and Wobblies both lived within an ideological cocoon from which the world seemed garbed in absolute categories: workers had no reason to love their country, the triumph of the proletariat was inevitable, electoral coalitions with other parties just delayed the revolution. In a national environment already inhospitable to Marxism, this dogma could only bind leftists into a subculture that looked more and more like a doctrinal ghetto. For their part, the radical modernists assumed they were the vanguard of new ways of thinking and loving, only to discover that the culture of steel and gunpowder had smothered their idylls of freedom.

In 1920, Eugene Debs received more votes for president than he had received in any of his previous campaigns. But the great orator could not deliver a single speech on his own behalf. As Convict #9653, he ran for president from the bottom bunk of a cell in Atlanta's federal penitentiary. "I was in the midst of what are called the lowest type of criminals," he wrote, "flanked by Negro murderers, and yet, I never felt myself more perfectly at one with my fellow beings. We were all on a dead level there and I felt my heart beat in unison with the heartbeats of those brothers of mine."[80] Debs remained in jail until Christmas morning in 1921, when he received clemency from the new conservative Republican president, Warren G. Harding.

While he sat behind bars, the Socialist tribune had become the prime symbol of a movement to win amnesty for anti-war prisoners. The most influential section of the movement was the National Civil Liberties Bureau, led by Roger Baldwin, a Harvard-educated social worker from St. Louis. Baldwin had himself served nine months in jail for resisting the draft and, on his release, made his radical convictions clear: "I am going to do what a so-called intellectual can do . . . [to] aid in the struggle of the workers to control society in the interest of the masses." That Debs was a "class war prisoner" linked his fate to other martyrs around the world who had resisted the "imperialist" debacle in which millions of working people had perished.[81]

The amnesty campaign had an ironic consequence. In 1920, Baldwin's bureau changed its name to the American Civil Liberties Union. Ever

Eugene V. Debs, on his release from the Atlanta
penitentiary, 1921. Debs, a former union leader,
ran five times for president on the Socialist ticket,
the last time from federal prison.

since, the ACLU has been the main organization that is committed to
upholding the rights of individuals, as defined by the Founding Fathers
at the end of the eighteenth century. The group whose original mission
was to aid believers in a collective commonwealth is now best known for
defending erotic artists, physicians who perform abortions, and citizens
who protest religious displays on public property. Somewhere, perhaps,
Emma Goldman is dancing.

# Chapter Five

# THE PARADOX OF
# AMERICAN COMMUNISM, 1920s–1950s

The young workers and toilers of the capitalist countries who are groaning
under the yoke of capitalism look with great love and hope to Comrade
Stalin, the leader of the world proletariat . . .
—*Clarity*, organ of the Young Communist League, 1940[1]

We are against people who push other people around, just for the fun of
pushing, whether they flourish in this country or abroad.
—Motto of *PM*, a left-wing daily published
in New York City during the 1940s[2]

The test of a first-rate intelligence is the ability to hold two opposed ideas
in mind at the same time, and still retain the ability to function.
—F. Scott Fitzgerald, 1936

## ON BEYOND STALIN

TO UNDERSTAND THE FORTUNES of the American Communist Party
during its heyday in the 1930s and '40s requires a healthy taste for irony.
On the one hand, the apostles of Lenin and Stalin yoked themselves to
one of the bloodiest, most repressive regimes in history and the first one
whose dictatorial nature mocked its own vision of a world run by working people. Millions died or were unjustly imprisoned in the name of
"building socialism" in the USSR and the client states the Soviets erected
in the wake of the Second World War. But for decades, Communists in
the U.S.—along with their counterparts everywhere else—consistently
denied their patrons in Moscow had done anything wrong. Only in
1956, when Soviet premier Nikita Khrushchev acknowledged that Stalin

had ordered the murder of thousands of his comrades, did members of the CP begin to reflect on their complicity in one of the biggest, most resilient lies ever told.

Yet, during the previous quarter century, most American Communists had devoted their lives to fighting for many of the same causes as had their radical predecessors. And their efforts helped advance reforms any contemporary liberal would favor. The Party—the shorthand term used by friend and foe alike—mobilized jobless men and women to demand immediate aid from the government; organized low-paid workers into unions; battled discrimination by race and religion and national origin; and advocated a good education, health care, and access to cultural resources for every American. (Communists were also the most vigorous foes of fascism, except for twenty-two notorious months beginning in late August 1939, when the USSR signed a non-aggression pact with Nazi Germany and the CP declared a plague on all "imperialist" powers.) Knowing that the tyrants in the Kremlin approved all these activities does not diminish their positive impact on American society. Rank-and-file Communists helped make the U.S. a more tolerant, more democratic society—and put pressure on Franklin D. Roosevelt and other New Deal liberals to dismantle barriers between people who were deemed worthy of government help and those who were not.

At the same time, the Party's dominance in radical circles essentially brought to a close the left's century of close engagement with religious Americans. From the perfectionism of the abolitionists to Edward Bellamy's utopian revelations to the evangelical socialists who stoked divine discontent on the Great Plains, every sizable radical movement in the past had articulated a version of social Christianity. Communists paid tribute to all wage earners. But, as doctrinal atheists, they had a distaste for piety. Only one conversion experience was legitimate in their eyes: to see the light of Marxism-Leninism. Thus, even those ministers who shared a socialist vision—like Reinhold Niebuhr, a Lutheran and prominent intellectual—seldom felt comfortable working with the CP.[3]

The Party's fealty to a foreign power also helped make it anathema to voters. In contrast to the Socialists in the era of Debs and Berger, the Communists elected no member to Congress and just two to any significant local office—both as members of the New York City council. Never did the Party top a hundred thousand members; due to constant turnover, its loyal core was always less than half of that. The CP's presidential campaigns were never more than perfunctory affairs; the most successful one, in 1932, drew far less than 1 percent of the total vote.[4]

Before it imploded in 1919, the Socialist Party had members, friends, and a smattering of elected officials in most regions of the country. Millions of Americans had a neighbor or a union brother or sister who proudly belonged to the SP. But only a small minority of citizens ever met an open member of the Communist Party. The CP began its life with the image as a band of aliens and outsiders; despite a long and mighty effort, it never managed to lose that crippling reputation.

During the Party's heyday, public opinion polling was a primitive craft, and few surveys included questions about radical groups. Still, when Gallup reported, in the spring of 1941, that 70 percent of Americans wanted to outlaw the CP and endorsed "repressive measures" against it, few Party members could have been surprised. The new House Committee on Un-American Activities (known as HUAC) was already in the business of exposing "Reds," real or imagined, who operated inside and outside the federal government. During the early years of the Cold War, most Americans believed that some Communists were spying for the Soviet Union or had done so in the past—a suspicion that, at least in the case of several hundred Party members, later turned out to be true.[5]

The prospects for building a large and durable socialist movement in America were never bright. Even a charismatic leader like Debs and a healthy membership in both the tenements of lower Manhattan and the dirt farms of Oklahoma did not save the SP from rapid decline. But the ascendancy of the Communists and the fear and loathing directed toward them destroyed the possibility that Marxists of any stripe would ever be more than bit players in the nation's political life. By 1950, Daniel Bell could announce, "American socialism as a political and social fact [has] become simply a notation in the archives of history." That judgment stands.[6]

Yet the despised CP had a striking influence on American culture, although seldom in its own name. Around the Party's small but disciplined core grew a vigorously democratic and multiracial movement in the arts and daily life—Popular Front culture. Its themes endured long after the Party had been banished to the crumbling margins of American politics. The number of renowned writers, filmmakers, entertainers, and artists who traveled with the Communists during the 1930s and often into the '40s was quite remarkable, given the Party's modest size and electoral inconsequence. CP members wrote "Ballad for Americans," "Strange Fruit," "This Land Is Your Land," *Native Son*, *The Little Foxes*, and *Mr. Smith Goes to Washington*. Artists who, while not members, had spent many evenings in the party's milieu; created *Citizen Kane*, *Death of a Salesman*, "Fanfare for the Common Man," *For Whom the Bell Tolls*, *Yertle the Turtle*, *Invisible Man*; and wrote the screenplay for *Casablanca* and the lyrics for *The Wizard of Oz*. Less celebrated, pro-Communist authors popularized the "ethnic pastoral" in novels and films which led directly to *The Godfather*. Novelists in or close to the Party had nine books at or near the top of the best-seller list from 1929 to 1945.[7]

The popularity of Popular Front culture owed much to a tradition of democratic radicalism which flowered long before the 1930s. Walt Whitman and Mark Twain celebrated the wisdom and art of working people, and Twain warned against the temptations of empire; Frederick Douglass and Sojourner Truth preached that "to understand, one must stand under"; Randolph Bourne and W. E. B. DuBois argued that to realize its democratic promise the United States had to celebrate its multi-ethnic character.

But spurred by the outrageous misery of the Depression, figures like Richard Wright, Orson Welles, Arthur Miller, and Lillian Hellman refreshed familiar tropes of virtuous common folk beset by the greedy, intolerant few with a sensitivity to ethnic differences and international context. Their realistic narratives made the Victorian pieties espoused by such figures as Edward Bellamy and Upton Sinclair seem stiff and superficial. In their candor and racial variety, their delight in rebelling against "bourgeois" authority, younger Popular Frontists took after the Village modernists of the previous generation. But in their paeans to the wisdom of workers and dreams of a collectivist future, they owed more to the likes of Oscar Ameringer and Big Bill Haywood (who jumped bail to Moscow and was buried in the Kremlin wall).

Later, such critics as Lionel Trilling, Irving Howe, and James Baldwin scorned most of the output of the Popular Front as bathetic and simplistic. Richard Rovere, a former Communist turned *New Yorker* pundit, blasted the left-wing "tone" in the thirties as "cheap and vulgar and corny." But, whatever its flaws, this unashamedly demotic art did much to re-infuse the national culture with an anti-authoritarian, pluralist spirit that soon became ubiquitous.[8]

To become icons of Americana, their creators had to work in venues where the largest number of Americans could be found. Talented left-wing artists usually began their careers writing and performing for fellow radicals. But many soon moved on to Hollywood studios, major publishing houses, big-city orchestras, and the Broadway stage. Their radical predecessors had generally regarded the emerging mass culture with ambivalence. In a land ruled by dollars, they suspected that guardians of the profit-making status quo would always be hostile to the arts of the left; at best, a strong message would get diluted in apolitical broth. Back in the 1840s, the Hutchinson Singers had resisted this logic, but even those abolitionist celebrities chafed against the anodyne expectations of congressmen and other temporary fans of their music.

However, the pro-CP left was growing at a time when mass culture was both more powerful and more ideologically diverse than ever before. Increasingly, decisions about what millions of people could see, hear, and read were being made by urban entrepreneurs and managers who, either out of conviction or calculation, were eager to sell what bright young engaged minds were producing and who viewed political censorship as the vestige of a provincial, rural order. There were limits of doctrine as well as taste; only during World War II, when the USSR and the U.S. were allies, did Hollywood studios make films about the "heroic" Russian people. But certain leftists who understood what the market would welcome attained an audience larger than any previous Marxist had found. The fact that Stalin was, at the same time, sending freethinking artists in his country to the Gulag or to death added a harsh irony to this episode in the history of the American left.

The little CP was able to wield so large a cultural influence, in part, because of where and among whom it found its main strength. The party's biggest and most loyal contingent lived in and near New York City; at least half that number were Jews. By the mid-1930s, the Yiddish-speaking immigrants who had created the *Forward* and lifted Meyer London into Congress were aging and losing their ardor for transforming the world. But their children, raised in the United States and fluent in its language and customs, were not about to confine their ambitions within an ethnic enclave. By the Great Depression, many were flocking to public colleges, writing for major newspapers and radio programs and such left-leaning magazines as *The New Republic* and *The Nation*, and publishing books with established Manhattan houses. They were struggling into the middle class and taking their radical ideas along with them.

The ideas and style they expressed in the capital of culture had a way of rippling out to the borders of the nation. Jews in or close to the CP were more effective as producers than performers: gentiles like Woody Guthrie and the scriptwriter Dalton Trumbo could convey the same messages without awakening the sleeping hounds of anti-Semitism. But what was popular about the Popular Front owed a great deal to Jews who were beginning to gain acceptance in a nation whose political and economic structures the Party eventually hoped to destroy.[9]

At the same time, an organization whose membership differed greatly from the demographic norm was unlikely to have much political success, even without its blind loyalty to a foreign dictator. To avoid the alien taint, Jewish leaders in the CPUSA often changed their names to ones that harked back to colonial Boston instead of to modern Bialystok: Israel Regenstreif became Johnny Gates, longtime editor of the *Daily Worker*, while Sol Auerbach became James S. Allen, one of the Party's leading authorities on race and American history. But they could not disguise their looks or lose their accents. The CP never ran a Jewish candidate for U.S. president or vice president or, in its heyday, chose a Jewish general secretary to lead it. From 1930 to 1956, the highest offices in the Party were occupied by Earl Browder from Protestant Kansas, William Z. Foster from Irish Catholic Philadelphia, and Eugene Dennis, a lapsed Catholic from polyethnic Seattle.

Communists were not the only Americans who sought to nudge the nation further leftward than Franklin Roosevelt and his fellow liberals were willing to go. The Socialist Party, led by Norman Thomas, an eloquent former Presbyterian minister, continued to stump for a collectively owned and run economy and retained its old base in the garment workers' unions. In the Midwest and the Rocky Mountain states, shifting groups of left-wing but non-Marxist politicians and intellectuals sought to establish a new farmer-labor party or one rooted among consumers. In some of the nation's worst slums, the pious anarchists of the Catholic Worker movement doled out pacifist homilies along with free soup and a bed for the night. Yet none of these groups rivaled the CP's influence in social movements or its ability to inspire thousands of creative men and women to envision an America run by and for all the common people.

## TO RUSSIA WITH FAITH

Before they could bloom in the sunlight of a New Deal majority, the Communists endured a dark decade of myopia and division. The landslide victory of Warren G. Harding in the presidential election of 1920 should have made American revolutionaries realize how foolish it was to think they had a decent chance of emulating their Russian comrades. But the two Communist parties that formed in 1919 did not unite until 1921, and the fused organization did not dissolve its underground component until two years later. Even then, it took an order from the Communist International to persuade America's would-be Bolsheviks to cease preparing for armed insurrection. At the time of the stock market crash in 1929, the CPUSA claimed fewer than seven thousand members.

Part of the problem was that most Communists in the U.S. did not yet regard themselves as Americans. Throughout the twenties, close to 90 percent of Party members had been born abroad; a majority may have spoken so little English that they had trouble conversing with workers who knew no other language. In these early years, Finns formed the party's largest ethnic detachment—over two-fifths of the entire membership in 1923. Their counterinstitutions, many established under socialist aegis at the turn of the century, were flourishing: in dozens of towns along the upper Great Lakes, one could eat, attend a play, and attend adult classes inside an elaborate Finn Hall. The Red Finns even operated a consumer cooperative that annually sold products worth $6 million—most proudly stamped with a hammer and sickle. But their network could have been located in the environs of Helsinki, for all the impression it made on other Americans.[10]

The extended birth pangs of the Communist movement did accomplish one vital task: its loyalists gradually became "cadre," a name borrowed from military parlance that left no doubt about the rigorous discipline required by a party bent on taking and holding state power. Unlike the Socialists, who still believed patient organizing in workplaces and election campaigns would eventually turn Americans their way, Communists aspired to live up to Trotsky's description of themselves as belonging to "the general staff of the world revolution"—even after the former head of the Red Army had been banished, condemned, and assassinated.

Thanks to the Bolshevik triumph, American Communists shared the élan of belonging to an international fighting force, one composed of comrades from every race and continent, and headquartered in the largest nation on the globe. They thrilled at the effectiveness of the Leninist method, which combined sharp theoretical debate with the authority of a crusading army. By following the Bolshevik way, the Party could become the collective engineer on the locomotive of history. To be sure, the voyage would be rough and dangerous; the train would rattle, careen, occasionally catch fire, and throw the weak and unseated onto the tracks. But the pace and direction of the trip were clear: The revolutionary party, a godless messiah, would lead the proletariat and, in the fullness of time, dissolve itself into a perfected human race.

This conviction and method instilled many a cadre with the devotion of a would-be saint. The historian Eric Hobsbawm recalls a fellow British Communist who was badly wounded by a German bomb that fell on London in 1940. In what she thought were her last words, his friend exclaimed, "Long live the Party, long live Stalin . . ." Even in Auschwitz, Hobsbawm reports, good Communists kept up their party dues, "paid in the inconceivably precious currency of cigarettes."[11]

Such dedication helped the American party survive the 1920s. In Moscow during that decade, steely-minded Bolshevik leaders were exhibiting the competitive ruthlessness of precinct captains from Tammany Hall—if the urban bosses had been steeped in Marxist theory. Lenin's death early in 1924 touched off a complex, five-year-long contest for leadership that featured the intellectual titans Trotsky and Nikolai Bukharin and the organizational masterminds Grigori Zinoviev and Joseph Stalin. Aside from brute ambition, the conflict concerned how best and how quickly to transform a backward agrarian nation into an industrial power. Stalin emerged on top by wresting control of the party apparatus and promising "a determined *offensive* of socialism against the capitalist elements in town and country."[12] The result was the first Five-Year Plan. Under it, millions of citizens built heavy industry at a dizzying pace, while millions of peasants lost their land, their homes, and their lives.

Naturally, Communists in the U.S., many of whom had emigrated from Russia or one of its neighbors, followed the debate with intense concern. On frequent trips to Moscow, Party leaders had come to know

the principal combatants, and their personal alliances inevitably mingled with their ideological preferences. But they managed to avoid the
vicious fratricide consuming their older and mightier brethren in the
USSR.

In 1928, the CPUSA expelled James Cannon for defending Trotsky,
who was heading into exile in Turkey. Just a hundred comrades gathered
behind the lanky Cannon in his new Communist League of America.
A year later, CP general secretary Jay Lovestone, a Jewish immigrant
and popular leader, suffered the same fate after he made the mistake of
declaring that the American economic order was too robust and stable to
be toppled anytime soon. His personal and political closeness to Bukharin, who also believed capitalism could stabilize itself, made his defeat
inevitable.

Stalin, who at the moment was contending that world revolution
was nigh, ordered the Russian-born Lovestone and his allies to a meeting in the Kremlin. The only reason they were in power, he informed
them, was that "the Party regarded you as the friend of the Comintern.
But what will happen if the American workers learn that you intend to
break the unity of the ranks of the Comintern . . . —that is the question,
dear comrades?" Lovestone, who could guess the answer, left Russia in
haste. A month later, the American party expelled him as well. Only two
hundred comrades joined *his* new sect. The "capitalist" press alternated
between ignoring these battles and implying they were arcane theologi-
cal disputes that pit "heretics" against "the official catechism."[13]

The rush to please the Kremlin may seem absurd in retrospect, but
given its birthright the CP had no real choice in the matter. If the American Reds had declared their independence from Moscow, they would
have been just another group of immigrant radicals with little to offer
the great majority of American workers—another Socialist Labor Party,
hurling defiant jargon in several foreign languages at a heedless nation.
But as members of the Comintern, they could dream of someday marching in step with their comrades in Shanghai, Berlin, Prague, and Mexico
City where revolution was more than a slogan in the party press. At the
end of the twenties, loyalty to Stalin gave American Communists the
confidence to stand at the barricades until reinforcements arrived—or
until their attacks on the capitalist system began to sound like common
sense.

## INTO THE STREETS, MAY FIRST

The depression thus provided the Marxist left with an unmatched opportunity. Economic slumps in the late nineteenth century had certainly caused their share of pain, but they occurred at a time when only a minority of Americans lived in urban areas and worked for wages. The depression of the thirties was "great" because it affected nearly everyone in the country—whether as workers, consumers, or investors—and because it lasted for an entire decade. The self-confident, "scientific" way in which Marxists analyzed the crisis appealed to many of the metropolitan journalists and intellectuals who had to explain the debacle to a bewildered public. This made a stark contrast with the 1890s, when most big-city writers scorned the Populists for blaming that depression on a conspiracy by haughty goldbugs and greedy foreign bankers.

Radicals in the 1930s focused as much on the evils of the system as on the malefactors in charge of it. Following Marx, they argued that capitalism had done its historical duty by developing the means of production, but that era of necessity had now passed. The system, wrote the CP's Michael Gold, who had a knack for inflammatory prose, "has broken down, it can no longer feed the multitudes; it . . . must be executed before it murders another ten million young men in another war." Only an organized working class could save humanity.[14]

Communists and socialists made the same case, and both gained in membership and self-confidence during the frenzied period of job losses and bank failures between the Wall Street crash in 1929 and Franklin Roosevelt's inauguration forty months later. Running for president in 1932, Norman Thomas almost matched Debs's highest vote total, which fooled many of his followers into believing that the best days of the Socialist Party still lay ahead. Communists never did that well at the polls, but they soon outpaced their main rivals on the left in every other way. Only the CP could boast of its allegiance to the one industrial nation on earth that was not depressed but booming, where the future worked, as the muckraker Lincoln Steffens famously put it after a hasty visit. And it was the Communists, not the legatees of Debs, who used the depression to play an aggressive, if always controversial role, in the limelight of social protest and cultural ferment.[15]

The Party's rise to prominence on the left was hindered by Soviet policy and the Communists' own penchant for rhetorical bravado. In

1928, the Communist International announced an end to all illusions about gradual change. Launching the "Third Period" of Comintern policy, Stalin declared "the era of capitalism's downfall has come." To hasten its demise, every member party was required to organize militant strikes and protests, break off ties with other groups on the left, and steel its cadre for the revolutionary tumult ahead. Socialists, once viewed as fraternal competitors for the affections of the proletariat, were now officially dubbed "social fascists"—an enemy from within that had to be wiped out.

In Germany, this sharp turn to the left had a disastrous result. Unemployed young Communists staged fights with Social Democrats in the streets of Berlin, while the Nazis gained votes in the country at large and made plans to outlaw both parties once Hitler seized power. "Seldom in history," wrote two critics of this extremist lurch, "has so transparent an intellectual absurdity had so tragic an impact upon the lives of millions of people."[16]

The CPUSA was far too small to wreak that kind of havoc. The party's fierce, sectarian rhetoric merely limited the gains it could make among the millions of people whose joblessness and hunger left them potentially open to taking aid and political direction from unorthodox sources.

In 1932, William Z. Foster, the Communist candidate for president, published *Toward a Soviet America*, perhaps the least welcoming campaign book in the history of that genre. Once a brilliant labor organizer, Foster now seemed intent on shocking voters into immediately ditching all their "bourgeois" ideas and traditions. He mocked religion as "a monstrous system of dupery" clung to by "superstitious dolts"; vowed that Communism would "liquidate" all other political parties and anyone who engaged in a "socially useless" occupation such as law or advertising, and promised that a workers' state would nationalize the press and radio and transform them into "institutions of real education." With such talk, it's no wonder Foster's comrades had trouble winning votes among the uninitiated. As one Chicago militant put it, "We had not only to teach the principles of Communism, but we had to create a dictionary. The workers did not know what we were talking about."[17]

Still, those CP rank-and-filers who eschewed esoteric jargon and quotations from Stalin were often able to build a reputation as tireless organizers, devoted to building a movement from below. In March of 1930, they mounted large demonstrations of jobless workers in several northern cities. Then they quickly set up interracial councils of the unemployed which helped urban dwellers demand relief payments, resist foreclosure and eviction, and engage in other types of "reformist" behavior. The councils had few active members; not many unemployed people were eager to spend their days handing out leaflets or their evenings attending meetings. But the cadres in charge earned respect when they persuaded neighbors to move an evicted family's furniture back into its apartment or reconnected the electricity to residents who could not pay their utility bills. Unafraid to stand up to city bureaucrats or go to jail, the Communists slowly gained the confidence of people who had no taste for revolution and whose votes helped put Franklin D. Roosevelt in the White House.

The Party particularly appealed to a small but growing number of African Americans. Communists were determined to become the new abolitionists. This required a rather swift makeover. In 1919, not a single black person had helped organize either of the two new Communist factions. The largest political group in black communities during the 1920s was the million-strong Universal Negro Improvement Association. The UNIA's leader, the charismatic Jamaican immigrant Marcus Garvey, preached a message of racial solidarity and the liberation of Africa from European rule.

Since the Civil War, no national radical group led by whites had dedicated itself to eradicating racial inequality both in theory and practice. By the late twenties, however, the CP had taken that decisive step. In New York and Chicago, Communists boycotted stores that refused to hire blacks and landlords who would not rent to them. They also encouraged racial pride, wooing followers of Garvey whose UNIA was collapsing due to bad investments, personal scandals, and harassment by federal authorities.

The Party also offered selected black radicals lengthy, free trips to the Soviet Union. Some who accepted the invitation lectured the Comintern about how to handle "the race question" in the U.S.; most returned with tales of ordinary Russians who rushed to give them a coveted place in line or invited them to dance. It helped, too, that Foster's running mate in 1932 was James Ford, a dark-skinned World War I veteran from Alabama. The mere sight of Ford's face on a campaign poster was a welcome shock to black people, even if few were inclined to vote for a Soviet America.

In 1931, the Communists guaranteed themselves years of goodwill by hiring experienced criminal attorneys to defend the Scottsboro Boys, eight young black men falsely accused of raping two white women on a freight train as it rolled through the Deep South. The years of litigation that followed enabled the Party and its sympathizers to make the case a cause célèbre—one of the first legal defenses to train a national spotlight on the routine outrages of Jim Crow. Meanwhile, CP officials made a point of punishing white cadre who insulted African Americans, even if the slight was unintentional. One Party member in Chicago had to apologize to a "jury" of a hundred peers and endure a two-month suspension after he accidentally slapped a black man during a street-corner argument.[18]

Such anti-racist rigor, like any noteworthy stance the Party adopted, was stamped with the imprimatur of Moscow. Stalin maintained that blacks in the United States constituted "an oppressed nation" with a right to secede from the union and form their own government in the Deep South, if necessary, to gain their freedom. His American disciples did little to promote this implausible idea, which the Soviet leader had awkwardly adapted from the grim history of the czarist empire, that "charnel house of nations." Yet Stalin's special concern with the exploitation of blacks did fix the minds of his American followers on race, in personal relationships as well as in society at large. One former black Communist recalled that the Party had more "day-to-day alertness on the issue" than any other group on the left. In 1933, alarmed that the *Daily Worker* had no African Americans on staff (though it did have black contributors), the CP's "Negro Department" quickly remedied the problem. Sensitivity could reap its own rewards.[19]

Beyond the black ghettos in the early thirties, Communists appealed most strongly to intellectuals. The USSR's image as the tough-minded apotheosis of progress was part of the reason. "For the first time, a great people has embarked upon a consciously organized effort to plan its entire economic life," marveled a prominent political scientist in *The New Republic*. Moreover, the CP seemed to pose the most muscular and lucid alternative to "the earthquake," as literary critic Edmund Wilson called it, that was devastating a land ruled by heartless corporations and feckless Republicans. "The whole structure of American society seemed actually to be going to pieces," wrote Wilson. In a series of eloquent reports from the urban front, he contrasted "the deadened civilization of industry, where people are kept just alive enough to see that the machines are running" with a well-fed clergyman, his "round, pink, bald boyish head so shiny that it might be buttered," who assured the rich they would be safe in the arms of the Savior. Wilson ended one of his pieces with a line of graffiti he saw scrawled on a shuttered factory wall: VOTE RED. THE PEOPLE ARE GOOFY.[20]

In a nation riddled with social extremities, only extreme protests would do. So in 1932, Wilson and fifty-one other prominent writers signed an open letter endorsing the ticket of Foster and Ford. Few members of the group—which included Sherwood Anderson, Malcolm Cowley, John Dos Passos, Sidney Hook, Langston Hughes, and Lincoln Steffens—had joined the CP or had any real intention of doing so. At the time, Communist organs, in tune with Foster's manifesto, were criticizing novels or reportage that did not describe "the flesh and blood reality" of working-class life and make clear that revolution was the only salvation. This was a standard for propagandists, not serious artists. The "proletarian" novels and poems that clattered out of small presses in the 1930s prided themselves on a studied gracelessness; most concluded on a redemptive note they had done little to earn.

Still, Wilson and his colleagues, like radical modernists of the previous generation, felt the need to declare, without qualification, which side they were on. The choice for "trained intellectuals and professionals," they wrote, "is between serving either as the cultural lieutenants of the capitalist class or as allies and fellow travelers of the working class." Their statement was distributed by *The New Masses*, a journal open to writers friendly to the CP's worldview. Contributors to the old *Masses*, by then fifteen years in its grave, would have used a rapier instead of a hammer. But the moral obligation of the talented few to stand with the exploited many was the same.[21]

Some notable sprouts of creativity did manage to break through the concrete of the CP's hyper-radical line. Richard Wright published his first reflections about black life, a series of poems, in magazines published by the John Reed Clubs, the CP's earnest attempt to nurture "proletarian" writers. Dashiell Hammett composed all his "hard-boiled" detective novels during the depression, when he was warmly sympathetic to the Party; the anti-heroes in such classics as *The Maltese Falcon*, *Red Harvest*, and *The Glass Key* wade through bottomless swamps of capitalist sleaze for uncertain ends. "Most things in San Francisco can be bought, or taken," snaps Sam Spade in the book that defined the genre. After Hammett joined the CP in 1936, he spent a good deal of time on politics and never published another novel.[22]

When James Farrell wrote *Studs Lonigan* and John Dos Passos completed the bulk of *USA*, fictional trilogies whose brutal portraits of urban America in the early twentieth century still shock and inform, both were regular contributors to Party periodicals. In fact, the only false note in Farrell's great saga of an Irish Catholic family comes near its end, when Communism suddenly appears as the crimson hope of a hopeless world. Paddy Lonigan, father of Studs, the dying protagonist, accidentally comes upon a throng of "Reds" marching through downtown Chicago. Seeing their fists stretched high and hearing them belt out "The Internationale," Paddy realizes he is "just an unhappy old man . . . those people in the parade, they were happy, happier than he was."[23]

On occasion, fine art did mingle fruitfully with dogmatic politics. The abstract qualities of music could enable a gifted composer like Aaron Copland to soar above the leaden clichés of Leninism. In 1934, Copland composed a short song that was performed at the City College of New York by a "revolutionary workers' chorus," eight hundred voices strong. His music won a contest *The New Masses* had sponsored to accompany the poem, "Into the Streets May First," written by the young Communist Alfred Hayes. A typical stanza exults: "Up with the sickle and hammer, / Comrades, these are our tools, / A song and a banner! / Roll song, from the sea of our hearts, / Banner, leap and be free; / Song and banner together, / Down with the bourgeoisie!" Copland crafted a simple, folklike melody for flutes and harp. During World War II, its tone of swelling optimism would animate his famous "Fanfare for the Common Man" and "Lincoln Portrait." In 1934, Copland's desire to march along with the proletariat did not prevent him from composing a fresh and quite distinctive piece of music, one that was indebted to the neoclassicism of Stravinsky and Poulenc as well as to traditional ballads from the British Isles. Seldom has such beautiful music adorned such dreadful verse.[24]

### THE PRO-ROOSEVELT FRONT

Even as the Communists strutted their desire for a final conflict with capital, events abroad and at home were encouraging a shift toward more sober aims. Hitler's seizure of power in Germany emboldened right-wing parties across the continent. Declaring war on "Reds," they sanctioned violent attacks on the offices of left-wing groups and banned or restricted them whenever possible. Meanwhile, Franklin Roosevelt's vigorous efforts to generate jobs and his avuncular empathy for Americans in trouble were negating the best argument for a radical alternative: that there was no real difference between the major parties. The revolution would have to be postponed. In 1934, chastened Soviet leaders shelved all talk of "social fascism" and blessed ties between Communists elsewhere and fellow parties on the left.

The following summer, delegates to the Seventh Congress of the Comintern gathered in Moscow and announced a head-twisting change in strategy that was both shrewd and cynical. Fascism, declared Georgi Dimitrov, the charismatic Bulgarian Communist who had recently emerged from one of Hitler's jails, was "the open, terrorist dictatorship of the most reactionary elements of finance capital." To combat this ruthless enemy, Communists everywhere were now instructed to work with *any* individual or group willing to defend democracy, "bourgeois" though it and they might be. These new "popular fronts" could include all sorts of small businesses and unions, churches and synagogues, liberal and moderate newspapers, professional organizations, even elected leaders like FDR. The *Daily Worker* had recently called the president "the leading organizer and inspirer of Fascism in this country." But such counterproductive, as well as absurd, charges would now have to stop. Communists around the world were under siege, and the security of the USSR was itself in doubt.[25]

Although there were never enough genuine fascists to build a true movement in the United States, the CP embraced the Popular Front as a politics and a culture with a zeal unmatched by comrades in other nations. The new strategy allowed rank-and-file radicals to make America's ideals and culture their own. For men and women who had either been raised in another country or in an ethnic neighborhood, the Popular Front was an opportunity to abandon a kind of rebellion that had deepened their alienation from the citizenry. Harsh mistrust of any figure who departed from the party line was now replaced with a willingness to cooperate with a variety of other Americans in big battles for undeniably important and feasible ends: building industrial unions, demanding civil rights, combating right-wing tyrants abroad. While engaged in mass movements, Party members now avoided drawing attention to their ultimate ends. "I . . . discovered that those of us on the left have certain duties to perform," recalled Louis Goldblatt, a leader of the West Coast longshoremen's union. "Among them is to learn the technique of doing 99 percent of the work and taking one percent of the credit."[26]

By pursuing this approach with diligence and skill, Communists achieved a certain acceptance in parts of the industrial North and West, as well as in Hawaii, where they formed the core of a sizable labor left. At least a thousand Party members proved their anti-fascist credentials by shedding their blood in the Spanish Civil War, as part of the Abraham Lincoln Brigade, which endured a horrific casualty rate of over 50 percent. It helped, too, that a good many non-radical Americans believed the tale of a Soviet Union that had conquered unemployment and racism. Perhaps, one could muse, Communists were just a more disciplined group struggling for the same ends as left-wing New Dealers.

Irving Howe later labeled the CP's tilt toward reformism during the Popular Front "a brilliant masquerade." "The party as an institution," he scoffed, "gave itself a remarkable paint job, changing from bright red to a lively red, white, and blue." The makeover, Howe pointed out, coincided with the Great Terror, when the Soviet state murdered millions of its citizens for a variety of thought crimes. Thus, at the pinnacle of Stalin's savagery, the Comintern was hailing its American cadres for their dedication to advancing workplace democracy and racial equality.[27]

The Party's newfound patriotism did result in several flights of incongruous rhetoric. In 1937, the Young Communist League chided the Daughters of the American Revolution for neglecting to celebrate the anniversary of Paul Revere's ride. Hundreds of demonstrators marched up Broadway behind a sign that read "The DAR forgets but the YCL remembers." A year later, Communists at the University of Wisconsin issued a leaflet to their fellow students:

> Some people have the idea that a YCLer is politically minded, that nothing outside of politics means anything. Gosh no. They have a few simple problems. There is the problem of getting good men on the baseball team this spring, of opposition from ping-pong teams, of dating girls, etc. We go to shows, parties, dances and all that. In short, the YCL and its members are no different from other people except that we believe in dialectical materialism as a solution to all problems.[28]

While some Popular Frontists were masking their true intentions, the disguise quickly came to seem quite natural to many others. For the strategy helped Communists achieve the zenith of their status in capitalist America. From 1933 to 1939, the CP's membership tripled, reaching a height of about seventy-five thousand—as many as five thousand of whom were on the party's payroll.

The numbers had less significance than did the tasks the cadre set for themselves. Communists like Louis Goldblatt proved indispensable to the success of industrial unionism, the largest social movement of the 1930s. They formed the busy nucleus of such mass organizations as the National Negro Congress, the League of American Writers, the American League Against War and Fascism, and the American Student Union—each of which gained respectful coverage in the press and an occasional greeting from either Franklin or Eleanor Roosevelt. Individual Communists also occupied prominent positions in the Democratic parties of Washington, California, and Minnesota. And they controlled New York's American Labor Party, whose endorsement was critical to the victories of liberal Democrats in what was then the most populous state in the union. Although the CP entirely lost its proximity to power during the Cold War, it would never return to the revolutionary defiance of the early depression years. Having experienced the joys as well as the travails of normal American politics, there was no going back.[29]

But the price of that engagement was high. On every important domestic issue save racial equality, the CP from the mid-1930s on was every bit as "slowcialist" as Victor Berger and Morris Hillquit had been in the years before World War I, except Communists never came close to winning control of a single city government. Until Roosevelt's re-election in 1936, the Party flirted with the idea of forming a farmer-labor party "to unite all of those who want to stop reaction and fascism." But Earl Browder, the party's general secretary, was a bland figure, more effective at administering a bureaucracy than at public speaking or coalition building. No other left spokesman in the 1930s enjoyed the kind of personal appeal with which Garrison, Douglass, Powderly, and Debs had charmed a good many Americans who did not agree with most of their ideas.

Thus, by default, the real leader of the Popular Front in America was Franklin D. Roosevelt. This underscored the fragility of the CP's politi-

Communist Party election poster, 1936. The CP was the first party
to run a black man for national office, but its influence was far stronger
in cultural affairs than in electoral politics.

cal gains. For any true Stalinist, the president could only be an ally of
convenience, not conviction.[30]

Whatever political clout reform-minded Reds commanded was due
largely to their work in unions belonging to the CIO, the Congress of
Industrial Organizations. That relationship took a while to develop.
During the "Third Period," from 1929 to 1934, the CP had set up its
own revolutionary unions. Much like the Wobblies before the Great
War, these bold, if scattered, attempts to mobilize migrant and long-
shore workers in California and factory hands in the Midwest succeeded
at training cadre in the ordeal of industrial combat but failed to create
organizations that could survive a losing strike.

So, in 1935, when the heads of eight AFL unions broke away from the
stodgy old federation to form the CIO, Communist officials were fear-
ful of isolating themselves again from the main body of organized labor.
They also nursed a deep mistrust of John L. Lewis, the CIO's gruffly
charismatic leader. As longtime president of the United Mine Workers,
Lewis had often battled Communists and other radicals who opposed his
blatantly undemocratic, if pragmatic, ways.

But the Comintern's practical turn soon obliged its American contingent to become partners instead of rivals: Lewis needed organizers willing to devote their lives to the working class, and the party was able and eager to provide them. Lewis also hired a general counsel for the CIO, Lee Pressman, who secretly reported back to CP officials, and a publicity director, English immigrant Len DeCaux, who was a Party member. By the early 1940s, Communists wielded influence in as many as two-fifths of CIO unions, including its largest affiliates in the steel, automobile, maritime, and electrical industries. The Socialists had never enjoyed such sway during Samuel Gompers's reign at the AFL.[31]

But, unlike radicals in the era of World War I, Communists during the Popular Front years aimed to be little more than good unionists. During the winter of 1936–37, CP worker-activists such as Wyndham Mortimer and Bob Travis planned the sit-down strike in Flint, Michigan, that forced General Motors to recognize the United Auto Workers. But only a handful of their fellow union sparkplugs were even aware that Mortimer and Travis belonged to the Party. As editor of the *CIO News*, Len DeCaux kept his columns scrupulously free of any references to the achievements of the USSR or the policies of the CP. John L. Lewis once told reporters that he refused to turn his organizers upside down "to see what kind of literature falls from their pockets." If he had, it is unlikely that any of it would have been emblazoned with the hammer and sickle.[32]

How reliant the CPUSA had become on powerful, if temporary, allies became clear when Stalin stunned the world in August 1939 by signing a non-aggression pact with Nazi Germany and then dispatched the Red Army to occupy eastern Poland. After American Party leaders recovered from the shock, they called for a new "democratic front" to struggle for both peace and socialism. But most Communists had to spend the next two years defending what their erstwhile allies believed was indefensible. Several thousand members deserted the Party, though most Jewish comrades remained; previously supportive intellectuals like Ernest Hemingway and the exile Thomas Mann turned into hardened critics. Scores of unions and liberal groups passed "Communazi" resolutions which excluded any member of a "totalitarian" group, whether of the far right or far left. The jewels in the crown of the Popular Front—the League of American Writers, the National Negro Congress, and the American Student Union—all cracked apart, leaving a rump of party-liners to pass toothless anti-imperialist declarations. The federal government tried and convicted Earl Browder of passport fraud; he spent over a year in prison. For most of that time, hardly anyone who was not close to the party voiced a protest, although Browder's punishment far exceeded the norm for his offense.[33]

Given their party's swift decline, some Communists felt almost cheerful one late June day in 1941 when they heard the news that Germany had invaded the Soviet Union. "This is Our War," declared *The New Masses*, whose editors had to remake an entire issue that had already gone to press: "Never did writing come easier. You get a special kick writing when every word is, in effect, a shovelful of earth over the grave which Hitler and his crowd dug for themselves this weekend." Now CPers could return to the halcyon days when, with Stalin's blessing, they had embraced what they took to be the core beliefs and best interests of the American people.[34]

But six months later, when America too went to war, it became even more difficult than during the Popular Front years for the left to offer a clear alternative to the new liberal status quo. Radical pacifists who resisted the draft and went to jail barely got noticed. Communists continued to demand equal rights for blacks and Latinos—and to define those rights as requiring economic security as well as individual freedom. However, the Party opposed any action—including strikes—that might lengthen the war or make trouble for the Soviet Union, whose casualty rate dwarfed that of the U.S.

"To hold the home front line," asserted Browder in 1943, who was out of prison and back in charge, "is now of equal importance to holding the battle line." Later that year, after Churchill, Stalin, and Roosevelt met together for the first time, in Teheran, Browder was moved to write, "If J. P. Morgan supports this coalition and goes down the line for it, I as a Communist am prepared to clasp his hand."[35] The prospect of a truce with forward-looking capitalists led the general secretary, in early January 1944, to announce a shocking departure from the Leninist creed. The Party would now become the Communist Political Association—a "non-partisan association of Americans" that would neither run its own candidates nor talk about overthrowing the state.[36]

The CPA seems to have been entirely Browder's idea, but most Reds probably sympathized with him, whether they were officials elaborating doctrine from national headquarters on the Lower East Side, housewives campaigning for pro-labor Democrats, or GIs fighting for their lives on the beaches of France and the South Pacific. Al Richmond, editor of the

CP's West Coast paper, recalled, "The [Communist] Left, in the name of its valid commitment to defeat the Nazis, was subordinated so completely to the Commander-in-Chief . . . that its independent identity was increasingly smothered." Some members hoped that, after the war, the worldwide class struggle would resume. Certainly such comrades as Julius Rosenberg, who passed military secrets to Soviet spies, were prepared for that to happen. But as long as the war continued, a Communist could be both a sincere patriot and a follower of Stalin, without tripping over the contradiction. My in-laws and most of their siblings joined the Party just before the attack on Pearl Harbor. On the spring day in 1945 when FDR died, they wept as if they had lost a father, both wise and kind.[37]

## THIS LAND IS *OUR* LAND

A different kind of sorrow clings to the words and images of the Great Depression that remain icons more than eighty years after the long slump began. "Once I built a railroad, / Made it run / Made it race against time / Once I built a railroad / Now it's done / Brother, can you spare a dime?": In Yip Harburg's lyric, set to a Russian-Jewish lullaby, a beggar talks back to the system that stole his job. The man seeking a handout is everyman—at once a farmer and a combat veteran, as well as a construction worker. Then there is Dorothea Lange's "Migrant Mother" (whose name was Florence Owens Thompson). Framed by two shy children, she reflects while she suffers, hinting that poverty can ennoble, even strengthen one who bears no responsibility for her plight. In *The Grapes of Wrath*, John Steinbeck crafted an epic about such figures, documenting the same dialectic between oppression and fighting back. "We're the people that live. Can't nobody wipe us out," asserts Ma Joad in the prizewinning film John Ford made from Steinbeck's best-selling book. "Can't nobody lick us. We'll go on forever, Pa. We're the people."[38]

All these works were created by individuals who were active in the culture of the Popular Front. Harburg was a leading member of pro-Soviet groups in Hollywood and penned dozens of songs that satirized racist lawmakers and Cold Warriors—which helped earn him a blacklisting in 1950, though no one could take away the Oscar he had won a decade earlier for writing "Over the Rainbow" for *The Wizard of Oz*. In 1935, Lange left a fairly comfortable life as a portrait photographer to join

Yip Harburg, standing next to his 1935 Chevy roadster,
Beverly Hills, late 1930s. Harburg wrote, "Brother,
Can You Spare a Dime?" as well as "Over the Rainbow"
in *The Wizard of Oz*, for which he won an Oscar.
He was a leading member of pro-Soviet groups in
Hollywood and penned dozens of songs that satirized
racist lawmakers and Cold Warriors.

other artists of the Farm Security Administration (FSA), most of whom
were on the left fringe of New Deal opinion. Her pictures of farmworkers from all regions and races appeared in *Life* and other mainstream
outlets. The photos, according to her biographer, "not only challenged
an entire agricultural political economy, but tried also to illustrate the
racial system in which they operated—a system it also reinforced." Steinbeck, who occasionally wrote words to accompany Lange's images, had
worked closely with the CP-led union of agricultural and packing workers, known as UCAPAWA, in its valiant, vain attempt to bring democracy to the bountiful fields of California. His wife at the time, Carol
Henning, was a Party member. When the state's agribusinessmen and
favored lawmakers tried to get *The Grapes of Wrath* banned from public libraries, Communist periodicals helped organize an anti-censorship
campaign to stop them.[39]

For most Americans, these documents—together with FDR's "nothing to fear but fear itself" and his fireside chats—are the primary way in which the depression is remembered. Few realize that the political projects which inspired them ended largely in frustration, due in part to decisions Roosevelt made or, at least, acquiesced in: the New Deal never did create enough jobs, public or private, to end the chronic joblessness. Only the industrial boom stimulated by World War II accomplished that. Meanwhile the votes of congressional Democrats from the rural South and West kept agricultural workers—a large number of whom were black, Latino, or Asian—from enjoying the protections of the Wagner Act, the landmark labor law passed in 1935 that enabled industrial unions to gain a sturdy foothold in factories and mines and on the docks.

That we see the depression largely through such images suggests that the left was more influential working through aesthetics than organization. Lasting political changes did occur under Franklin D. Roosevelt's long tenure: a limited welfare state, a governing coalition rooted among wage earners and urban dwellers, the triumph of secular thinking among intellectuals and policy makers. These were liberal achievements, which most leftists applauded, albeit not uncritically. But radicals achieved their only lasting triumphs during the FDR years by advancing a new common sense about larger social and moral questions: Who were the people? How did they want the nation to change? What did a commitment to equal rights require? As a young left-wing critic observed in 1942, "It was the depression of the mind that from the first gave significance to the depression of society, for the impact of the crisis on culture was far more violent than its transformation of the social order."[40]

When breadlines and Hoovervilles were spreading across the land, this writer and his fellow intellectuals saw solidarity with the tormented working class as a moral necessity; a good many had risen from the working class themselves. But with FDR in power, most of these radicals switched to more optimistic, but no less aggressive, thoughts about transforming the nation through mass, largely nonviolent actions and abundant goodwill. In place of tough talk about a proletarian revolution, one now heard praise for hardy pioneers who had settled the West and for the folkways of humble people from every race and national background.

This new spirit transcended the requirements of the Popular Front line, which was intended mainly to counter the threat of fascism. It brashly claimed the left's desire and need to claim America—its polyglot culture, its history, its productive might—for an expanded definition of the common people. Unofficially, the New Deal encouraged this move; such agencies as the Works Progress Administration and Federal Theater Project signed up leftists to write pro-labor plays and regional guidebooks and to paint populist murals on post office walls.

A Mexican migrant worker and his child, photographed by Dorothea Lange in California, 1935. Lange's images of the Great Depression continue to shape the way Americans view that calamitous era.

But those who paid the piper could not dictate the melody and seldom even tried. Either implicitly or directly, Popular Front artists took up subjects and themes that went beyond the limits of New Deal politics. Neither the Nazi-Soviet pact nor the forced unity of wartime kept such artists from flourishing. They hailed the creativity and progressive impulses of traditional folk and blues musicians, reinterpreted the American past as an ongoing struggle between an economic elite and a loose coalition of working people of all races, made films that paid tribute to populist mass movements, and fertilized a campaign against segregationist laws and practices that would reach its full flowering a generation later.

As Harburg, Lange, and Steinbeck demonstrated, most Popular Frontists did not hesitate to engage in the venues of what other radicals disparaged as "bourgeois" or mass culture. From time to time, a radical writer or cartoonist might contribute to *The New Masses* or another periodical that adhered to the CP line. But the makers of Popular Front culture were determined to be popular, and that meant going directly to the venues—from Tin Pan Alley to radio networks to Hollywood to big-city dailies, to *Life* and the best-seller list—where ordinary Americans were reading, watching, and listening.

This could have ironic consequences for those who lauded the unsullied music of "the common people." A prime mover of the folk revival was the musicologist Charles Seeger. He and his friend Aaron Copland had been active during the hyper-revolutionary days of the early thirties in a small, CP-sponsored group named after Pierre Degeyter, composer of "The Internationale." At the time, Seeger disparaged folk songs as "complacent, melancholy, [and] defeatist." But the Popular Front transformed him into a promoter of all that was homegrown and authentic—and uncommercial. From his office at the WPA, Seeger wrote, "The folk music of America [has] embodied . . . the tonal and rhythmic expression of untold millions of rural and even urban Americans . . . the American people at large has had plenty to say and ability to say it."[41]

However, most left-wingers who made a name for themselves performing folk tunes had little interest in keeping their art pure from the seductions of commerce or the influence of other styles of music. The singer Josh White, for example, seemed to have the perfect background for a man from the downtrodden masses. He grew up in South Carolina, the son of a black Baptist minister who was locked away in an insane asylum for refusing to pay his bills. As a boy, White made a few dollars guiding blind bluesmen around the streets of southern towns. "It was a life that no child should know," he remembered, "roaming the roads, never certain where I'd sleep, and almost always hungry. . . . But the music—and the songs and the guitar—somehow made up for everything." While still in his teens, White began recording blues and gospel for labels that catered mainly to black people.[42]

White's first "crossover" hits wore his political commitments on their covers. In 1940, he recorded *Chain Gang*, an album of songs like those performed by black men in southern prisons. His backup group included Bayard Rustin, a young Communist who soon broke with the party and became the right-hand man to A. Philip Randolph. The next year, White came out with a three-disk set, *Southern Exposure: An Album of Jim Crow Blues*. In the liner notes, Richard Wright dubbed the music "fighting blues." White went on to perform songs that touted CIO organizers and ones that blasted the segregated armed forces: "Airplanes flying 'cross the land and sea, / Everybody flying but a Negro like me." By the end of World War II, Josh White had become "the best-known black songster in the country."[43]

But he achieved that fame with a style better suited to a nightclub stage than a rural juke joint or storefront church. White's voice was sly and sophisticated, almost completely free of the intonations of the black South. He played acoustic guitar with what his biographer describes as an "unmatched vibrato and clear, singing tone" and appealed more to white, "progressive" audiences than to black ones. During the 1940s,

White performed regularly, as did Billie Holiday and Lena Horne, at Café Society, a club in Greenwich Village that was a mecca for white middle-class New Yorkers with left-wing sympathies.[44]

Adopting a smooth, hip style did not have to mean dulling one's political edge. The owner of Café Society, Barney Josephson, hired left-wing muralists to decorate the walls of his establishment and hired such emcees as the comedian Zero Mostel, who did savage impersonations of Hitler and an archetypal racist lawmaker he dubbed "Senator Pellagra." Billie Holiday closed most of her performances at Café Society with "Strange Fruit," the anti-lynching ballad written by Communist Lewis Allan (whose real name was Abel Meeropol). In 1938 and 1939, *The New Masses* sponsored "Spirituals to Swing" concerts at Carnegie Hall featuring a variety of African-American musicians, most of whom were previously unknown to white audiences. The message was unmistakable: Americans of all races should understand that the most meaningful art was produced by those who stood under. As CP composer Earl Robinson (who had studied with Aaron Copland) put it, black "songs have everything, tremendous strength and power of image and purpose and longing, soft beauty, subtlety of idea, humor—sometimes all these elements in the same song."[45]

Then there was Woody Guthrie. The folksinger from Oklahoma, who died in 1967 after a long illness, would certainly have enjoyed the vaunted place he now holds in American musical culture. He was a prime inspiration for both Bob Dylan and Bruce Springsteen, and "This Land Is Your Land" has become almost an alternative national anthem. But Guthrie was a dedicated ally of the CP during and after the heyday of the Popular Front; for a time, he even wrote a regular, unpaid column, "Woody Sez'" for the *People's World*, the West Coast version of the *Daily Worker*. "If he wasn't a member of the party," recalled Dorothy Healey, a leading Communist in California, "he was the closest thing to it." More important, Guthrie was an engaging radical voice from the rural, Christian heartland that a movement full of Jews and big-city dwellers badly needed.[46]

Indeed, most images of "the people" expressed in Popular Front culture were of Americans who were white and presumably native-born. Two Jewish CIO cartoonists drew a series of strips featuring "Joe Worker," whose muscular face and straight hair made him resemble Superman (himself the creation of a pair of Jewish socialists). Although Lange's

"Migrant Mother" was actually a Native American who had been born in a tepee, the photographer and most of her audience assumed she was as white as most Dust Bowl refugees. "We ain't foreign," one Joad says to another in *Grapes of Wrath*. "Seven generations back Americans, and beyond that Irish, Scotch, English, German. One of our folks was in the Revolution, an' they was lots of our folks in the Civil War—both sides. Americans."[47]

The Joads were only fictional creations, but Woody Guthrie seemed to be the real thing. He was born and raised in a tough oil town, often traveled in boxcars, and sounded much like any musician on a country-and-western station. And unlike most entertainers at Café Society, Guthrie unashamedly drew on religious themes that had once been familiar fare on the left: "Jesus Christ was a man who traveled / through the land / A hard-working man and brave / He said to the rich, 'Give your money to the poor,' / But they landed Jesus Christ in His grave." Guthrie also brought to the CP left a folksy sense of humor. "There are a lot of good ideas in a pint of whiskey, but not too many in a quart," he reflected; his *People's World* column was stuffed with such one-liners as "I ain't a communist necessarily, but I been in the red all my life."[48]

Yet Guthrie's art transcended his cultural roots. In 1940, he moved to New York City and recorded several albums of songs with political undertones for Victor Records, a major label. He also made a pilot for a one-man radio show on CBS, "Back Where I Come From." Although it did not attract a sponsor, the pilot landed Guthrie dozens of appearances on national networks and on the stages of New York nightclubs. "They are giving me money so fast I'm using it to sleep under," he marveled to the folklorist Alan Lomax. Dust Bowl radicalism turned out to be as marketable as any other cultural commodity.[49]

Just before he began to make a decent living with his art, Guthrie wrote the song that would make him immortal. In February 1940, a month after arriving in Manhattan, he sat in a dingy hotel room and quickly scratched out some lines meant as a protest of Irving Berlin's sunny "God Bless America." They began, "This land is your land, this land is my land / From California to New York Island / From the Redwood Forest, to the Gulf Stream waters / God Blessed America for me." Half the verses rang out with an anger born of a decade of depression: "One bright morning in the shadow of the steeple / By the relief office I

Woody Guthrie during World War II. Author of
"This Land Is Your Land," the Oklahoma-born
Guthrie was an engaging radical voice from the rural
Christian heartland that a radical movement full of
Jews and big-city dwellers badly needed.

saw my people— / As they stood hungry, / I stood there wondering if /
God Blessed America for me." Guthrie did not get around to recording
the song until 1945; by then, the spirit of wartime unity—and the end of
mass unemployment—had made the latter verse sound obsolete.[50]

That Woody Guthrie was a real proletarian from white, Protestant
roots illustrated how far the CP left had traveled since the awkward days
of "proletarian realism" in the early thirties. Back then Charles Seeger
had advised his fellow archivists, "The main question . . . should not
be, 'is it good music?' but 'what is the music good for?' "[51] In reducing
usable art to agitprop, Seeger was blind to what cultural radicals could
actually accomplish.

Left-wing artists did not have to choose between Seeger's two
options—as Aaron Copland, Josh White, and Woody Guthrie made
clear. A number of Joe Hills were thriving in the 1930s and '40s, but
most had either stopped riding the rails or, like Charles's son Pete—
Guthrie's close friend and collaborator—had never had that dubious
pleasure. Instead of singing at strike rallies and hobo jungles, they were
performing in concert halls and over national radio networks for audi-

ences drawn from a variety of social classes. The left-wing cult of the common worker had shed its dour, alienated trappings and was gradually becoming a romantic staple of mass culture.

Americans could also indulge in a few hours of vicarious rebellion on the big screen. During the depression and world war, the popularity of motion pictures dwarfed that of radio and the press. At least 40 percent of the populace took in a movie every week. And much of what they saw had an earnestness and sentimental vigor that dovetailed with the ethos of the Popular Front. Feature films, writes the historian David Thomson, "were the most telling, deeply felt impression of who we were and might be . . . For the movies needed an America like that of the thirties and the forties, where passion was respectable and being moved was an everyday thing."[52]

But a great passion is not, by itself, a politics. Scholars disagree about whether the pro-Communists who worked in Hollywood during its golden age were involved in making pictures that challenged the powers-that-be in fresh and memorable ways or sought merely to earn a handsome income by stirring Americans with easily marketable fare. In Europe between the world wars, most prominent filmmakers were on the left—but then so were most of the leading artists and writers in cities from London to Berlin to Moscow. On the other hand, to know that certain American radicals had a big hand in shaping such profitable and now iconic movies as *The Public Enemy, Frankenstein, Casablanca, The Wizard of Oz, Woman of the Year,* and *Mr. Smith Goes to Washington* does not mean that audiences were consuming a left-wing sensibility along with their sodas and popcorn.[53]

Judging solely by their numbers, Reds in the film industry should not have left much of a mark at all. Roughly three hundred studio employees belonged to the CP at some time between the mid-1930s and the end of the 1940s; most kept their membership secret. This group, a majority of whom were screenwriters, represented only about 1 percent of all workers in the industry.[54]

However, as elsewhere, Communists in Hollywood had a particular talent for making themselves useful and tilting the opinions of others their way. CPers and their close allies took the lead in forming the first independent unions of writers, actors, and craftsmen—and sponsored

Pete Seeger, then a member of the Communist Party, leading a
crowd singing, "When We March into Berlin." Photographed at
a canteen sponsored by a left-wing CIO union, 1944.

such groups as the Hollywood Anti-Nazi League, whose events drew
thousands of participants and widespread media attention. Appearing
under the aegis of Popular Front groups, such liberals as Katharine
Hepburn, Humphrey Bogart, Orson Welles, and James Cagney spoke
out for Republican Spain and the CIO, and helped earn legitimacy for
Party members like John Howard Lawson, a leader of the Screenwriters
Guild and the closest thing to an ideological commissar the Hollywood
CP ever had. Even Ronald Reagan, then a confirmed supporter of FDR,
attended the occasional left-wing meeting.[55]

The presence of such a broad alliance gave the political culture of the
film world an unmistakable tinge of pink. No one in Hollywood objected
when Howard Koch, the principal screenwriter of *Casablanca*, described
Rick, the hero played by Humphrey Bogart, as someone who "ran guns
to Ethiopia" (which Mussolini's armies invaded in 1935) and fought
for the Spanish Republic or when Ginger Rogers, in a script for *Tender
Comrade* written by CP member Dalton Trumbo, asserted, "Share and
share alike, that's democracy." Later, the House Un-American Activities Committee would blast that line as unpatriotic. HUAC also branded
*Mission to Moscow*, a warm portrayal of Stalin and his regime produced in

1943, as undiluted Communist propaganda. But it was Jack Warner, a wealthy Republican, who hired Koch to write that film and eagerly promoted it as a boon to the war effort.[56]

In their textual literalism, the Red hunters missed the more lasting influence of certain radical screenwriters. A stray line or two and a ham-handed brief for Stalin (in a film that bombed at the box office) could not convince Americans to admire the USSR. But as with the folk revival, films that embodied a spirit of left populism became a prime way to identify "the people" with the aims of the left.

There is no better example of that than *Mr. Smith Goes to Washington*, directed by Frank Capra in 1939. The story adapted, in a controversial fashion, the traditional genre of a virtuous innocent who comes into conflict with a corrupt urban elite. Jefferson Smith, played by James Stewart, is a new appointee to the U.S. Senate from a rural western state. When he learns he is only a "stooge" in an influence-peddling scheme run by a party boss, his venal colleague, played by Claude Rains, pressures him to resign. Instead, Smith mounts a solitary, twenty-three-hour filibuster to salvage his reputation and ends up exposing the plot to drive him from office. Near the end of the marathon, which naturally rivets the nation's attention, the exhausted senator evokes the statue of Liberty on the Capitol dome:

> Get up there with that lady . . . Take a look at this country through her eyes if you really want to see somethin'. And you won't just see scenery. You'll see the whole parade of what man's carved out for himself after centuries of fighting. And fighting for something better than just jungle law. Fighting so as he can stand on his own two feet free and decent, like he was created no matter what his race, color, or creed. That's what you'd see. There's no place out there for graft or greed or lies! Or compromise with human liberties!

Capra made other films with a populist flavor: *Mr. Deeds Goes to Town*, *Meet John Doe*, and *It's a Wonderful Life*. But *Mr. Smith* is the only one that challenged the probity of a hallowed government institution. And it incensed the keepers of the institutional flame. "The thing was outrageous," declared James Byrnes, a powerful Democrat from South Carolina who attended the Washington premiere, "exactly the kind of picture that totalitarian governments would like to have their subjects believe exists in a democracy." Senate majority leader Alben Barkley called the

In a scene from the 1939 film *Mr. Smith Goes to Washington*, Jimmy Stewart clutches letters opposing his filibuster. Sidney Buchman, then a member of the Communist Party, wrote the screenplay for the movie, which was directed by Frank Capra.

film "as grotesque as anything I have ever seen." Lawmakers from both parties united in disgust, as did many newspapers, which echoed the charge that *Mr. Smith* echoed the propaganda against America spewed out by Hitler, Mussolini, and Stalin. Joseph P. Kennedy, then U.S. ambassador to Great Britain, offered to purchase all negatives of the film from Columbia Pictures for $2 million, in order to destroy them.[57]

Capra was fortunate that his critics didn't know the film's main scriptwriter was a member of the Communist Party. Sidney Buchman, although still in his thirties, already had several popular comedies to his credit, the most recent of which was *Holiday*, starring Cary Grant and Katharine Hepburn. But *Mr. Smith* was his first serious film, and he had to persuade the director to accept its strong Popular Front message. Capra knew Buchman had joined the Party and, as a result, "mistrusted me terribly." The scriptwriter argued that, with fascism on the march, they needed to emphasize "the spirit of vigilance which is necessary if one believes in democracy, the refusal to surrender even before small things." Capra responded, "Go fuck yourself with your theme." But he altered few of Buchman's lines, and the film made Capra one of the most popular directors in the country. The left-wing Americanism expressed by *Mr. Smith*—sentimental, combative, and implicitly interracial—was little different from that sung about by Woody Guthrie and Josh White. But the film's huge audience and numerous Oscar nominations helped make its species of patriotism the most ubiquitous legacy of Popular Front culture.[58]

That didn't save Buchman from suffering the same fate as most Hollywood Reds. In the early 1950s, he was blacklisted after appearing before the self-appointed arbiters in Congress of who was and was not an "un-American." Buchman admitted his former membership in the CP (he had resigned in 1945) but refused to name anyone else. Days later, underneath the dome of the Capitol, the House of Representatives found him in contempt of Congress. There was not a single dissenting vote.

Among the many intellectuals radicalized by the Great Depression, few were teaching history in American colleges. Sociologists and economists had fervent arguments about the cogency of Marxism and whether it could be applied to current affairs; disciples of Marx insisted they possessed the ultimate social science and relished debates with defenders of the status quo, theoretical or otherwise. Moreover, the relative newness of these disciplines allowed talented Jews and recent immigrants from Europe to find teaching positions, albeit mostly in large, urban schools.

But history was still largely a profession of gentlemen, well-born, white, and Christian. In the 1930s, just one prominent historian, Fred Shannon at Kansas State, had grown up in a working-class family. Shannon also happened to be an active Socialist, one of a tiny group of radicals who were tenured professors in the field. Not until the 1950s did the American Historical Association include more than a small number of black or Jewish members. Most academic historians between the world wars tended to shy away from political disputes. They suspected grand interpretations of being tainted by ideology and so preferred to stick doggedly to narrative detail.[59]

Meanwhile, popular history was thriving, and left-wing authors were among its leading practitioners. Charles and Mary Beard's *The Rise of American Civilization*, published in 1927, was a perennial best-seller and one of the most significant surveys of U.S. history ever written. The Beards combined a materialist interpretation of the nation's past with a floridly romantic style. They viewed both the American Revolution and the Civil War as episodes of conflict between competing elites; first, colonial merchants and landowners grabbed power from George III and his court; then, the rising capitalists of the North shattered the power of the slaveholding plantocracy. The Beards considered ideas mere rationalizations and wrote little about the lives of working people, free or enslaved. Neither believed class struggle was either beneficial or inevitable, although they had taught adult classes in a New York school set up by the Socialist Party. Still they passed on their jaundiced view of the powerful to millions of sympathetic readers.

Outside academia, a number of other historians prospered with an explicitly Marxist analysis and a vigorous, demotic style. Leo Huberman's *We, the People*, a brisk survey of America from the Jamestown colony to the New Deal, was distinguished by the labor reporter's sharp anti-racist perspective: "Negroes fresh from Africa were slow to learn the white man's ways . . . Because Negroes were given no opportunity to learn, their masters mistakenly believed they could not learn." CP members Herbert Aptheker and Philip Foner wrote dozens of sympathetic works on both black and working-class history. Like Huberman, they took the kind of ardently supportive view toward movements for class and racial equality that would become the norm among scholars three decades later.

Such views about the American past also made their way into the most public of venues. Beginning in 1940, the Russian-born artist Anton Refregier created a huge, lushly colored mural inside the main San Francisco post office. The images, which covered every wall in the building, depicted the city's history as a series of stark battles between workers of different races and their pitiless exploiters. When the murals were finally completed in 1948, protests by the Veterans of Foreign Wars (VFW), the American Legion, and the local Chamber of Commerce forced the artist to remove some features, such as a veteran's cap worn by a longshoreman during the San Francisco General Strike of 1934. Otherwise, the murals remained intact, educating and/or shocking patrons and tourists for decades to come.[60]

No historian on the CP left during the 1930s sold as many books or received as much praise as Matthew Josephson (who was unrelated to the owner of Café Society). Remarkably, he did so by writing about the late nineteenth century, a period which had not previously kindled the public's imagination. His 1934 work, *The Robber Barons*, elbowed its title into the permanent vernacular; *The Politicos*, published four years later, gave a rich, convincing account of government and party corruption on a grand scale. Josephson mastered the repertoire of journalistic history, pioneered by the dyspeptic conservative H. L. Mencken. *The Politicos* is ripe with mocking anecdotes, suggestive physical traits, and statistics that both shock and inform. But unlike Mencken, Josephson emulated Marx by conveying the idea that all politicians were captive to class interests and conflicts and "do not mean what they say." Taken together, his books established a view of industrializing America that journalists today still conjure up when they refer to the Gilded Age.[61]

Josephson's narratives appeared at a time when big business had become a synonym for arrogant failure. *The Robber Barons* outsold every other nonfiction book that year and made its thirty-five-year-old author a literary star. Josephson was able to convince readers living through the Great Depression that the roots of the calamity could be traced to the power and greed ascendant at the end of the last century. During the Gilded Age, the U.S. was a swiftly developing country, and the men who rose to the top seemed hostile to the interests of everyone but themselves.

Josephson often relied on elegant, if vituperative, caricatures and quotations to make his points. He described John D. Rockefeller as having "small bird-like eyes set wide apart" while "his mouth was slit like a shark's." Jay Gould was "small, dark, of a somewhat furtive and melancholy cast." According to Josephson, when a reporter asked J. P. Morgan during a Wall Street panic if the investment wizard wanted to make a public statement, the response was "I owe the public nothing."[62]

*The Robber Barons* is dedicated to Charles and Mary Beard, who were friends and neighbors of the author. Unlike them, however, Josephson was an orthodox Marxist. He had helped draft the 1932 statement by writers endorsing the ticket of Foster and Ford, and his wife, Hannah, was a member of the Party. Josephson never joined the CP himself; he prized his freedom to write however and whatever he pleased. But he rarely dissented from the Party line on any major issue. When *The Robber Barons* came out, Josephson was not around to bask in his new celebrity. He was midway through an extended tour of the Soviet Union. "Before people pass judgment on Comrade Stalin," he wrote to his wife from

Moscow, "they ought to come here and see his Works, his Opus Major, in many volumes with their own eyes. It is very impressive; and few other statesmen in all history have so much to show."[63]

In his youth, Josephson had been a different kind of rebel. While a student at Columbia, Josephson lived, inevitably if briefly, in Greenwich Village. He then joined the herd of rebellious minds in Paris, where he grew close to such surrealists as Louis Aragon, Max Ernst, and Tristan Tzara and helped edit a series of little magazines that practiced the ludic anti-gospel of Dadaism.[64]

Not until the early thirties did Josephson become a man of the left. But that commitment endured: When he died almost half a century later, Josephson was struggling to complete a lengthy defense of Alger Hiss, the former diplomat imprisoned for lying about his Communist past. To the end, the historian kept battling with "noble indignation" against the injustices of bourgeois society.[65]

The central thrust of the Popular Front was always the kind of left Americanism that made the works of Josephson, Guthrie, Steinbeck, and Lange so compelling. Its main ideas filtered through many institutions in society—from film to press to government. During World War II, the anti-fascist message also became a radically democratic one: defeating Hitler and his Axis allies would usher in a new dawn for the common man and woman. This wasn't socialism, but neither was it an endorsement of whatever policies liberals might favor.

The long reach of such thinking could be glimpsed in unexpected places, such as the official military handbook for U.S. soldiers in occupied France, distributed to the troops in 1944. In a vignette about workingmen's cafés, the anonymous author promised, "The workman will welcome you; he is a regular fellow. In his velveteen pantaloons and beret he will look more picturesque than his opposite number back home in the United States. He is what the French call *le peuple*—The People. They have more sense, resistance and pride than any other class in France." GIs were then reminded to tip the waiter exactly 10 percent of the bill.[66]

## THE HOUSE WE SHOULD BE LIVING IN

Previous lefts had shared such populist sentiments, although never with so warm and routine an embrace of solidarity across national borders. But no white-led radical movement since the Civil War had staked so much on a commitment to racial equality. For the CP, a victory for the working class would not just include full rights for Americans of African, Latin, and Asian backgrounds. It could not be achieved *unless* the color barrier was dismantled in the course of the struggle.

The party never attracted many non-white members and had trouble holding on to those it did. But its constant assaults on racist laws and politicians earned the respect of prominent black figures who had no intention of joining. "I don't mind being called a Communist," the president of Howard University, Mordecai Johnson, told a gathering of churchmen in 1933. "The day will come when being called a Communist will be the highest honor that can be paid to any individual; that day is soon coming." In 1945, two black sociologists observed, "The Reds won the admiration of the Negro masses by default. They were the only white people who seemed to really care about what happened to the Negro."[67]

However, the Party's courageous rhetoric on race was not always a guide to its actions. Communists fought for civil rights the same way they fought for industrial unions and intellectual freedom: with one eye fixed steadily on the needs of the USSR. Thus, in 1936, black CP stalwart John P. Davis initiated the National Negro Congress and put together an impressive, biracial coalition of activists from labor, the Urban League, black churches, and the Socialist Party as well as his own to fight Jim Crow laws and hiring practices. But four years later, a majority of Congress delegates endorsed the Nazi-Soviet pact and denounced the New Deal. This led A. Philip Randolph, the group's president, to resign and charge the Party with "serv[ing] an alien master . . . a dictatorship with no concern" for democratic rights. After the U.S. went to war, Communists railed against segregation in both industries and unions but opposed any protests that might slow production. Party members even refrained from criticizing the government's forced removal of Japanese Americans to prison camps until the war was almost over. While interned at the camp in Manzanar, east of the Sierra Nevada, the veteran Communist Karl Yoneda gushed that "the workings of democracy are clearly demonstrated before our eyes . . . Those of us who are American citizens of Japanese ancestry are grateful to our government for the way this grave question of evacuation is being handled."[68]

What did remain consistent from the start of the depression was the Party's vision of a society that would encourage both racial equality and expressions of racial pride. This marked a step beyond the attacks on discrimination that such white liberals as Eleanor Roosevelt were pressing on government officials and employers alike. It meant grappling with the pain of history by forging a multiculturalism in embryo which appealed to Americans who wanted to transcend race by acknowledging its painful presence. A mass, sustainable civil rights movement would not emerge until the 1950s, when the Party had all but vanished from political life. But during the Popular Front and after, Communists helped put forth a new way of understanding race in America, and it was on such an understanding that the marriage of pluralism and equality depends.[69]

That dual ambition—for rights and identity—motivated comrades in the barrios of the Southwest as much as on the streets of Harlem. By the 1930s, Mexican Americans could draw on a rich, continuous narrative of radical activism on both sides of what was then a largely unguarded border. The social revolution that broke out in Mexico in 1910 followed battles in the nineteenth century to win and then secure independence from European powers. Before World War I, the anarchist Partido Liberal Mexicano (PLM) and its leaders, the brothers Ricardo and Enrique Flores Magón, had gained mass support among their compatriots in both California and northern Mexico—and forged close ties in Los Angeles with the IWW and the Socialist Party. A generation later, refugees from the bloody revolution kept its memory fresh, although neither Emiliano Zapata's demand for *"Tierra y Libertad"* nor Pancho Villa's desire to expropriate *Yanqui* holdings had been achieved back home.[70]

Keeping faith with their forebears, Mexican-American radicals during the 1930s rejected the assimilationist dreams of reformers like those in the League of United Latin American Citizens (LULAC), who hoped to blend into the larger white republic. They pursued the traditional aims of the socialist left while vaunting a separate ethnic heritage as activists in CIO unions, legal defense campaigns, and Popular Front organizations like the broad Congress of Spanish-Speaking People (El Congreso) and the smaller Asociación Nacional México-Americana (ANMA).

The leaders of this dual venture were often young women and CP members. Josefina Fierro was born in 1914 in Mexico to a mother who had worked with the PLM and a father who had fought with Pancho Villa. Raised in Los Angeles, she organized boycotts against businesses that catered to her people but refused to hire them. Luisa Moreno, a native Guatemalan who was the main organizer of El Congreso, asserted that "the American people, all of them, owe an enormous cultural and physical debt to the Spanish-speaking people." She also pointed out that Mexican immigrant laborers paid more taxes than did the California agribusinesses for which they toiled. Emma Tenayuca, a young organizer from Texas, called for bilingual education and making Spanish an official language in those parts of the United States where Mexicans formed a majority.[71]

Tenayuca was the most famous of the three, and the only one to articulate her multicultural politics at length. In 1938, already a veteran activist at the age of twenty-one, she led a strike by thousands of San Antonio pecan shellers whose employer had suddenly slashed their wages. *Time* called her "slim, vivacious . . . with black eyes and a Red philosophy" and chuckled at her local nickname, "La Pasionaria de Texas," a reference to a celebrated Communist firebrand in the Spanish Civil War. A year later, Tenayuca wrote, with her husband, Homer Brooks, an article for a CP magazine which offered a bracing analysis of "The Mexican Question in the Southwest." They began by stating flatly, "The treatment meted out to the Mexicans as a whole has from the earliest days of the sovereignty of the United States been that of a conquered people." Then they detailed the consequences: abysmal living and working conditions, white "land-grabbing," and language discrimination in the land of their birth. The couple took care to deny that Mexican Americans constituted a separate nation within a nation. They did not, after all, fit "Comrade Stalin's classic definition" of a group with territory to call their own. Yet they were still a self-conscious "people" who deserved power and respect on their own terms.[72]

As a Marxist, Tenayuca could not espouse the ethnic nationalism that would later inspire allegiance to "la Raza" and spawn Chicano studies departments. Moreover, both she and Fierro married white, native-born American Communists, challenging the Southwest's informal color bar separating Anglos and dark-skinned Mexicanos. As it happens, Homer Brooks completely lacked his wife's common touch. He would spend hours lecturing strikers in San Antonio about the fine points of Party doctrine and the glories of the USSR but never get around to union business. A few months after absorbing the shock of the Nazi-Soviet pact, "La Pasionaria de Texas" left both her husband and the Party. El Congreso dissolved soon after as well, another casualty of Stalin's abrupt turn in foreign policy. Tenayuca found work as a secretary and

Emma Tenayuca, on her release from a San Antonio jail,
c. 1938. A young radical labor organizer from Texas,
Tenayuca led a strike by thousands of pecan shellers and
advocated both bilingual education and making Spanish an
official language in those parts of the United States where
Mexican Americans formed a majority.

later taught the children of migrant farmworkers to read. Her life as a
radical activist was over.[73]

The Party's tangible gains among Mexican Americans were slim as
well. Spanish-speaking Communists worked diligently in the CIO and in
a variety of Popular Front groups. But UCAPAWA, the union in which
they invested most of their time and hopes, was unable to force employers to sign more than a few contracts and dissolved during the Red scare
of the late 1940s. Neither El Congreso nor ANMA endured long enough
to achieve the acceptance among their people which the National Negro
Congress had gained among black Americans before World War II. In
the cities and fields of the Southwest, Communists could never escape
their deeply alien reputation, thanks in part to the hostility of the Catholic Church and the Anglo middle class. There were fewer than fifty Party
members in San Antonio; until Tenayuca joined, they had usually conducted their meetings in Yiddish.[74]

Yet her small cohort of radicals created a legacy for Mexican Americans who would elbow their way into the mainstream of political culture

two decades later. When Cesar Chavez organized a new farmworkers' union in the early 1960s, he and his *compañeros* adopted the emblem of an Aztec eagle to symbolize the marriage of Mexican history with labor militancy, although many members belonged to other ethnic groups. At the same time, young people who began to call themselves "Chicanos" were self-consciously adopting a term that had long been a slur against lower-class migrants from Mexico, the people Communists referred to as "*el pueblo olvidado*" (the forgotten people). Mass campaigns against media stereotypes of lazy, ever-grinning Mexicans had their origins in the modest efforts of ANMA during the early 1950s to boycott radio stations, films, and advertisements that featured comic characters who rattled on in such broken English phrases as "I am a leetle hongry por Weber's Bread." Once such unthinking prejudices are challenged in an organized way, they seldom regain legitimacy.

The Party's main goal in racial matters was to be the vanguard of the movement for black freedom. It had many competitors. The NAACP spearheaded most legal battles against Jim Crow, Randolph's Brotherhood of Sleeping Car Porters pressured lily-white unions to integrate their ranks, and black nationalists warned their people to rely on their own efforts instead of putting faith in any group led by white radicals.

But during the late 1930s and again from 1941 to 1945, the CP burnished the reputation it had built during the early years of the depression, and expanded its organizational clout. The Party sponsored broad ad hoc coalitions on a variety of issues, from a federal anti-lynching law to voting rights to battling against fascism as a system of explicit race hatred.

These efforts attracted, if only temporarily, an extraordinary group of African Americans from the realms of politics and entertainment. The roster included W. E. B. DuBois, Richard Wright, Paul Robeson, James Weldon Johnson, Josh White, Billie Holiday, Duke Ellington, Lionel Hampton, Ella Fitzgerald, Lena Horne, and Adam Clayton Powell Jr.— who was not just Harlem's first black city councilman and later its first black member of Congress but also the minister of one of its largest churches, Abyssinian Baptist. According to one Communist organizer who knew the scene well, "75% of black cultural figures had Party membership or maintained regular meaningful contact with the Party."[75] A. Philip Randolph was still the most famous civil rights activist in the country, but his Socialists were an insignificant presence in the black urban communities where the CP was thriving.

The Popular Front's appeal to black people, as to Mexican Americans, combined both civil rights and ethnic pride. The latter was stoked by such enterprises as the Negro People's Theater, Spirituals to Swing concerts, and the mass campaign to oppose the Italian conquest of Ethiopia—the largest independent nation in Africa. Former Garveyites appreciated these efforts, and some, like the powerful orator Audley "Queen Mother" Moore, actually joined the Party. But most black nationalists harbored an abiding discomfort with a movement that, as Moore later put it, saw the world "in a European way" and seemed to encourage interracial sex.[76]

The CP's mighty efforts were marked by an exaggerated optimism. The Communists rarely acknowledged that the racism of working-class whites might pose a serious problem. The labor slogan "Black and white, unite and fight" became, in effect, the Party's grand strategy to attack Jim Crow. But an organization led and financed by white Marxists could have taken no other stand.[77]

The Party's militant anti-racism had its prophetic moments, particularly in the area of mass culture. In 1939, in New York and other big cities, the CP launched a boycott of the movie *Gone with the Wind*, whose rosy depiction of the Confederacy clashed with histories of the Civil War era by W. E. B. DuBois and other radicals. A writer for *The New Masses* declared he "should like to take" the film's producer, David O. Selznick, "out of his chartered skysleeper and rub his nose in the South of pellagra, of Jim Crow, of illiteracy, . . . of sharecroppers, of the modern Ku Klux Klan riding down unionists." Although the boycott's effect on the box office was minimal, it was the first major salvo in a conflict over media images of black people that would rage for decades to come.[78]

Communists had more success when they protested against the Jim Crow barrier in a form of entertainment older than film: major league baseball. Since the beginning of the century, the sport had truly become the "national pastime"; no other athletic pursuit drew as large crowds or as much space in the daily press and as much time on the radio. But due to an unofficial agreement among team owners, no black player had taken the field with white ones since the mid-1880s. When he became sports editor of the *Daily Worker* in 1936, Lester Rodney resolved to do away with that tradition.

Before the Popular Front, Rodney's fellow Reds would have disdained his purpose as trivial. "It is unquestionably true that American workers are greatly interested in professional sports," wrote one ideologue in 1934, "far too much, in fact, for their own class interest." But when the Party decided it needed to convince the public "that Communism is nothing strange and foreign," it quickly blessed Rodney's mission.[79]

Cleverly, the young editor framed the campaign in the language of muckraking as well as principle: "the *Sunday Worker* will rip the veil from the 'Crime of the Big Leagues'—mentioning names, giving facts, sparing none of the most sacred figures in baseball officialdom." The strategy gained new readers for his paper as well as lavish praise from the black press. In return, Rodney reprinted similar features from such black weeklies as the *Pittsburgh Courier*, which further enhanced the credibility of his stand.[80]

Over the next decade, the Party made its case in a variety of venues. May Day paraders carried banners demanding integration of the sport; Young Communists picketed Yankee Stadium before a game. In interviews with Rodney, various major league managers stated their support for abolishing the color bar. Finally, in the fall of 1945, the Brooklyn Dodgers signed Jackie Robinson, a college graduate and army veteran, to a contract. The Party rushed to point out that it had long been the only significant white-led organization in the fight. "I hope this lesson will teach America that the Communists are useful citizens who form the core of a healthy democracy," crowed Mike Gold.[81]

A few months later, the immensely popular Frank Sinatra lent his own fame and talent to the multicultural cause. In a ten-minute film, Sinatra sang "The House I Live In" to a group of white street kids, after he stops them from beating up a Jewish boy their own age. "What is America to me?" the lyric asks. The answer is a small-town version of social equality: "The house I live in, . . . / The faces that I see, / All races and religions, That's America to me . . . / The house I live in, My neighbors white and black . . . / A land of wealth and beauty, / With enough for all to share." The film won a special Academy Award for "tolerance short subject." But the studio's tolerance went only so far. Sinatra was not allowed to sing the line about "neighbors white and black" on-screen. The lyricist, Lewis Allan (Abel Meeropol), protested the decision but failed to alter it. Both he and the composer, Earl Robinson, were Party members.

Such hopeful, inclusive Americanism did not always satisfy some of the CP's most prominent black "influentials." As enlightened as their racial views were, the Communists answered to a higher calling and to a foreign ruler for whom African Americans were just one group of proletarians to be wooed and managed. A glimpse at how Richard Wright and Paul Robeson struggled to be both Red and black reveals the lure and limits of that marriage of identities.

Only Wright actually joined the CP, and the experience turned him from a grateful comrade into a bitter critic. In 1934, the Mississippi native signed up in Chicago after writing numerous pieces and poems for *The New Masses* and several smaller magazines affiliated with the Party. "Racial hate had been the bane of my life," he wrote in his memoirs, "and here before my eyes was concrete proof that it could be abolished." But, from the first, he rebelled at demands that he spend less time writing and more time organizing his fellow workers. The expectation that a good Party member would turn out literature that parroted the correct line rankled him even more. "God, I love these people," he wrote, "but I'm glad that they're not in power, or they'd shoot me ... I had fled men who did not like the color of my skin, and now I was among men who did not like the tone of my thoughts."[82]

Although Wright quietly dropped out of the Party in 1940, he continued to support its policies and write for its publications as his literary reputation soared. That same year, the Book-of-the-Month Club selected his novel *Native Son*. Its protagonist, Bigger Thomas, is a poor black man who gets involved with well-heeled white Communists, one of whom, a beautiful young woman, he accidentally murders. Back then, the club's choices inevitably became best sellers, and *Native Son* sold close to a quarter million copies in its first year of publication. No black writer had enjoyed such fame or fortune before.

Publicly, his former comrades seemed pleased. Mike Gold compared the novel favorably to *Uncle Tom's Cabin*, and Ralph Ellison, whom Wright had mentored, was just as effusive. But many black Communists cringed at the descriptions of Bigger's violent behavior and the suggestion that interracial comradeship was sexual at its core. Some leaders of the Harlem branch considered whether to tell Wright that "you should be forced to attend meetings and do party work, so that you would learn how not to make such a mistake as *Native Son*."[83]

Such attitudes convinced the author to cut all ties with his first political home. A devout realist, he believed that "no theory of life can take the place of life." How could an honest writer about race in America deny that oppression was capable of producing "thwarted and twisted" individuals like Bigger Thomas? Wright also maintained that organized Christianity gave black people an emotional balm no political group could match: "Our going to church of a Sunday is like placing one's ear to another's chest to hear the unquenchable murmur of the human heart." By 1944, he decided to expose how the ideological blinders worn by Party members and their followers were holding back the struggle for black freedom. "I Tried to Be a Communist," Wright's two-part article in *Atlantic Monthly*, was an early example of the genre of disenchanted essays by former Communists that would later be published in the anthology *The God That Failed*. It remains one of the best. But the disappointed idealist never found a better way to advance the well-being of African Americans. In 1947, he and his family left the country whose racial practices he considered beyond repair, and Wright spent the rest of his life in Europe.[84]

Paul Robeson was not always happy with the Party's views on race, but unlike Wright, he never let a qualm slip into the public record. As a result, during the 1930s and most of the 1940s, he provided the CP with an asset of unrivaled worth. With the possible exception of heavyweight champion Joe Louis, Robeson was the most celebrated black person in the country—and the best-known and most traveled black American in the world. In a voice of great range and power, he sang in every genre and dozens of languages. He starred as Othello on Broadway, the first black man ever to play that role in the U.S., and was the lead in several films. Whatever their politics, most white people considered the charismatic, articulate Robeson a "credit to his race" and did not object that he frequently lent his talents to radical politics. As one admirer recalled, "He strode onto the crowded stage with a combination of dignity, grace and responsive enthusiasm . . . It was as though each person there had been struck by the lightning of that smile, the grandeur of that presence."[85]

The CP relied on Robeson to promote their most important causes.

He sang for the troops in Republican Spain, demanded the release of Earl Browder from jail, and campaigned successfully to elect black Communist Ben Davis Jr. to the New York City Council. Robeson also routinely praised the USSR for having conquered both unemployment and racial discrimination. After the attack on Pearl Harbor, he was able to balance statements that "the war is ours" with protests against the continued segregation of the armed forces. "I like to feel that my work has a farther reach than its artistic appeal," he said at the height of his fame in 1944. "I consider art a social weapon."[86]

Paul Robeson, photographed by Gordon Parks, 1942. World-renowned singer and actor, Robeson was also an activist for black freedom both in the U.S. and Africa—and a reliable ally of the Communist Party.

Yet that "farther reach" was always teth-ered to the limits of the Popular Front. Robeson was a boon to the CP left as long as he stuck to attacking such brittle customs as Jim Crow in sports and the military. But when the Cold War began, he refused to conceal his deepest, most radical convictions. The United States, he believed, had succeeded the British and French as the chief sponsors of colonial rule over non-white peoples. Only the USSR stood in its way. Speaking in April 1949 at a pro-Soviet peace conference in Paris, Robeson thundered that America's wealth had been built "on the backs of white workers from Europe . . . and on the backs of millions of blacks . . . and we are resolved to share it equally among our children." Then he declared, "We shall not make war on anyone. We shall not make war on the Soviet Union." An Associated Press dispatch quoted him, erroneously, as saying it was "unthinkable" that "American Negroes" would go to war against "a country which in one generation has raised our people to the full dignity of mankind." But Robeson did believe that and so made only a slight attempt to correct the record.[87]

At a time of rising fear and anger about Communism at home, Robe-son's words quickly transformed him from a well-liked celebrity with questionable views into the most hated black man in America. "It was an accident unfortunate for America that Robeson was born here," blared an editorial on the front page of every Hearst paper. A. Philip Randolph convened a meeting of black leaders who denounced Robeson's statement, as did Jackie Robinson in testimony before the House Un-American Activities Committee. The State Department revoked Robeson's passport.

In August, the embattled singer traveled to the Hudson River town of Peekskill, New York, to give a benefit concert for the Civil Rights Congress, a Party front in which Dashiell Hammett was a leading official. Hundreds of protesters from local veterans' and Catholic groups attacked the audience with rocks and fists as well as with slurs against "Commies" and "kikes." Eleanor Roosevelt and the ACLU both condemned the violence, but they also repudiated the views of the man whom they accused of provoking it. In 1952, midway through the Korean War, which Robeson fiercely opposed, he accepted the dubious honor of a Stalin Peace Prize from the USSR. Until his death a quarter century later, he would bear the crippling reputation, inside his own country, of a Soviet hack.[88]

Richard Wright abandoned Communism because he was convinced it stifled his creative freedom and that of any other blacks who wished to think for themselves. Robeson believed black people could win their rights only by adhering to the one movement whose rising world power countered that of racists and exploiters. As great artists, each, for a time, brought luster to the CP and helped convince other African Americans that the Party was on their side. But in his own way, each man also failed to overcome the limits of an ideology rooted in foreign terrain and of a political culture still hostile to the idea of racial justice. Contrary to the sanguine lyric, the house they lived in was not yet ready to become a house for all.

## LOSING THE PEOPLE

The Cold War began early for the American Communist movement. In the summer of 1945, the Party was reconstituted, as its members officially rededicated themselves to fighting for a socialist future and an end to the illusion that coexistence with capitalism was possible. The impetus for the abrupt change came from an article by a top French Communist, Jacques Duclos, who harshly criticized Earl Browder for believing in "class peace" and "liquidating" the political arm of the American working class. Believing Duclos was voicing the sentiments of most European

Reds, as well as of the Kremlin hierarchy, the men and women who had followed Browder's lead for over a decade quickly turned him out of office. They even refused to give the fifty-five-year-old a paying job of any kind in the organization he had loyally served since 1921.[89]

Despite this sudden shift at the top, most comrades did not alter their political behavior in any fundamental way. CP unionists continued to organize new members and to campaign for higher wages; civil rights activists kept demanding an end to segregation in law and practice; artists and writers still produced bottom-up, egalitarian images and stories. Even as the U.S. and the USSR divided Europe into armed camps, Party rank-and-filers kept talking much as they had since the dawn of the Popular Front. While defending every Soviet action, they sought, in the words of the screenwriter John Howard Lawson, to "serv[e] democracy and the interests of the American people" in fidelity to the "country's most sacred principles."[90]

But Lawson, who had once been the leader of his own union, made that statement in 1947 before the hostile members of HUAC and a mainstream media that shared the committee's opinion that "subversives" had to be fingered and ostracized, if not placed behind bars. Lawson was convicted of contempt of Congress, spent a year in prison, and never wrote a film under his own name again. The Red Scare did not just damage or destroy the careers of such cultural figures like Lawson and Robeson. It induced the CIO to expel eleven unions that usually adhered to the CP line, the largest of which was the United Electrical Workers (UE). Before waning in the mid-1950s, the great fear was responsible for the firing of thousands of scientists, factory and office workers, and teachers, most of whom had never been Communists or had left the Party years before investigators accused them of subverting the republic.

The last, best opportunity to reverse this assault came in 1948 when former vice president Henry Wallace ran for the White House under the aegis of the new Progressive Party. A left-wing New Dealer, Wallace hoped to win enough votes to pressure the winner to restore the wartime alliance with the USSR, establish a more generous welfare state, and enact a sweeping civil rights law. But he reluctantly depended on Communist activists to staff his campaign and drew just over a million votes, almost half of which came from New York state. The Party would never again play a significant role in American politics or culture.

However, before Wallace's campaign disintegrated, it helped persuade liberal Democrats to take a step they had dithered about for decades. In 1948, they finally became unqualified supporters of racial equality under law. Galvanized by the oratory of Hubert Humphrey, then mayor of Minneapolis, the Democrats at their convention in Philadelphia endorsed a tough civil rights plank for the first time in their history. Soon President Harry Truman ordered the military desegregated, and several northern states and cities passed equal housing laws. These were milestones on the way to the enactment of national legislation in the 1960s. But it was no coincidence that they occurred as Wallace was denouncing Jim Crow and insisting on speaking only before integrated audiences—or when millions of Asians and Africans were battling, with Communist support, to free themselves from the rule of white Europeans.

The downfall of the CP cannot be blamed primarily on the wave of legal and extralegal repression that began in the Truman era and ended during the Eisenhower presidency. Elsewhere in the world, Communists had endured far more brutal treatment and emerged from the ordeal swelling in strength and numbers. From the 1920s to the mid-forties, thousands of Reds in Italy, France, Germany, Czechoslovakia, and China were imprisoned, tortured, and slaughtered. Yet their parties mobilized armed resistance against their enemies and recruited millions of followers. After the defeat of fascism, Communists in Italy and France became the main political opposition; from East Berlin to Beijing, they governed millions of people.

In the United States, the Red Scare killed nobody, unless one counts victims of blacklisting, like the actor Philip Loeb, whose anguish drove him to suicide. But in 1951, fear of a brutal crackdown drove many leaders of the CPUSA underground for a year or more, preparing for a fascist takeover that never came. In 1956, after the dual blows of Khrushchev's revelations about Stalin and the Red Army's crushing of the Hungarian Revolution, the American CP retained only about five thousand members, perhaps a third of whom were secret agents of the FBI.

Throughout its history, the Party was ensnared in a fateful dilemma: either work toward a Bolshevik uprising and remain an impotent sect or behave like "liberals in a hurry" and survive only as long as real liberals tolerate your presence. The actor Gary Cooper's 1947 statement to HUAC that he "didn't like" Communism because it was "not on the level" probably captured a sentiment shared by most of his fellow citizens. The only notable dissent came from black Americans—at least those in the nation's largest city. A graduate student who interviewed over five hundred Harlemites at the time found that over three-fifths were still sympathetic to Communism; his more educated informants were the most avid supporters.[91]

Away from the hot lights of congressional hearings, several artistic shoots of the Popular Front continued to bloom. Dr. Seuss was just one of the progressive authors of best-selling books for children which lampooned racial discrimination and rendered American history as a saga of hardworking people who get the better of the pompous and the mean— like the tyrannical Yertle, who orders his fellow turtles to lift him up to the sky but falls from the heights and ends up as "King of the Mud." Arthur Miller, who as a college journalist had reported enthusiastically on the Flint sit-down strike, in the late 1940s wrote *Death of a Salesman* and *All My Sons*, plays which dissected the greed of the prosperous and the desperation of ordinary people who failed to steel their emotions in a culture ruled by money. Such popular films as *Home of the Brave* and *Pinky* also attacked prejudice with plots about blacks passing as whites. Gradually, the anti-racist position once found primarily on the left was spreading out to the liberal mainstream.[92]

None of the people who created these works had belonged to the Party, which made it easier for them to deflect authorities who suspected their motives. In the 1950s, HUAC did get around to questioning Aaron Copland and Arthur Miller. But by then, the composer's works had become staples of Americana, while the playwright was able to rely on an unimpeachable defender: his wife, Marilyn Monroe. "Is there a red-blooded American boy from six to sixty who does not hope some day to marry Marilyn Monroe?" joked radical journalist I. F. Stone. "Surely, as at Lexington, there is a point at which America will stand and fight."[93]

Red-minded feminists were beginning to stand up too. By the end of World War II, women made up half the CP's membership. Swept into activism through unions, community groups, and the mood of wartime idealism, many of these new recruits also voiced their discontent with the place of women in U.S. society. They demanded equal pay and child-care centers—and complained about the patronizing outlook of men. In 1946, Susan B. Anthony II equated the causes of blacks

Dr. Seuss attacks big business racism during World War II in a
cartoon for *PM*, the left-wing daily published in New York City.

and women in the same way her great-aunt had done a century before:
"Just as the white race likes to raise its own prestige by detracting from
and minimizing the abilities of the Negro race, so men in general like
to build up their superiority by minimizing all women . . . this process
begins in the home, and is nurtured by textbooks, press, movies, radio
and theater . . ."[94]

With the Party reeling from attack, Anthony and her fellow activists
were not able to build a mass movement to embody their views. They
did launch a Congress of American Women in 1946. But the group with
the unfortunate acronym had fewer than twenty chapters and spent more
time supporting strikes and protesting Jim Crow than trying to change
the "culture of women's subjugation" before it collapsed in 1950. Male
comrades did correct their "chauvinist" behavior, at least a little. CP
publications stopped running photos of pretty girls in bathing suits, and
Philip Foner started teaching readers of the *Daily Worker* about women's
history.

But the real import of this embryonic consciousness was to revive a
tradition of radical feminist ideas that had been largely neglected since
the split in the Socialist Party thirty years before. CAW leader Eleanor
Flexner would go on to write *Century of Struggle*, the first comprehensive history of the movement for women's emancipation, published in

1959. A decade later it became required reading for every woman on the left. Betty Friedan, who drew close to the Party while at Smith College during World War II, reported on working women's issues from 1946 to 1952 for the *UE News*. In search of a better income and a measure of fame, she then switched to writing articles about unhappy suburban housewives for such high-circulation magazines as *McCall's* and *Ladies' Home Journal*.

Neither in the latter pieces nor in her best-selling manifesto, *The Feminine Mystique*, published in 1963, did Friedan reveal her pro-Communist past. But there was a definite Marxist flavor to her charge that big businesses peddling cosmetics and household cleaners did much to keep women in their "underused, nameless yearning, energy-to-get-rid-of" place. Gradually, the Popular Front's focus on the plight and might of the common man was widening to include the common woman. One could no longer assume she would be content to remain in a left dominated by men.[95]

Historians continue to battle over how to define the essential nature of the Party and the fronts it spawned. One camp argues that the Communists were, in FBI director J. Edgar Hoover's famous phrase, "masters of deceit." Nothing they did mattered as much as their allegiance to a foreign power, and when that allegiance became a serious handicap, the CP was finished. The other side protests that the brave and honest labors of thousands of rank-and-file organizers should not be reduced to their fealty to a dictatorial regime; we should focus instead on what the comrades did to further democracy and equal rights in their own land.[96]

Both groups might reflect on the line by F. Scott Fitzgerald that appears at the head of this chapter. American Communists doggedly followed the lead of tyrants and found reasons to rationalize their crimes. They should have listened to Orwell's warning that "the central problem—how to prevent power from being abused—remains unsolved." Yet it is also myopic to dismiss the beneficial achievements, more in culture than in politics, of CPers and "fellow travelers." These accomplishments were too essential to the history of their time to be written off as crowd-pleasing banalities or Stalinist apologetics.[97]

Reflecting on the Communists in Harlem, the historian Mark Naison concludes, "The story of the Party . . . is in some measure the story of the rise and fall of a dream of human betterment. To scrutinize the dream, while respecting the dreamer, is the historian's special challenge." That ambivalence does not capture the full tragedy or romance of American Communism. But it does suggest a more sober verdict on its meaning. The only way the Reds could win, could help to change America in ways most Americans would welcome, was to conceal or abandon their desire to imitate Lenin and Stalin. The more they delayed and diluted their ultimate ends, the better they did. Their success was also their failure.[98]

*Chapter Six*

# NOT WITH MY LIFE, YOU DON'T,
## 1950s–1980s

If we appear to seek the unattainable, as it has been said, then let it be
known that we do so to avoid the unimaginable.
>—Final words of the Port Huron Statement, 1962[1]

When I think of revolution I want to make love.
>—French slogan, May 1968[2]

We realize that the only people who care enough about us to work consistently for our liberation is us.
>—Black feminist statement from the
>Combahee River Collective, 1977[3]

American leftism was revived in the 1960s by calls for revolution which,
fortunately, were not successful.
>—Richard Rorty, philosopher, 1998[4]

### 1956: GOING AWAY AND COMING BACK

UNLIKE WARS or election campaigns, American radical movements
do not begin or end on a particular day or even during a single year.
They tend to grow slowly and fitfully, picking up adherents while gaining strength and confidence. Then, aided by fortune and, sometimes,
by gifted leaders, they quickly swell in numbers and influence before
descending into a swamp of internal disputes and public hostility or,
worse, indifference. On occasion, a group staggers on for decades after
the movement it belonged to has died. You can still join the Socialist
Labor Party, although you will first have to answer such questions as

"Do you recognize the irreconcilable class antagonism between workers and capitalists that exists under the present economic system?"[5]

So one cannot say precisely when the Old Left died and a new one got busy being born. But a series of events that occurred in 1956 made it virtually impossible for the CP to revive and hinted that a different kind of radicalism was beginning to flower. First, the Party was devastated by Nikita Khrushchev's acknowledgment that Josef Stalin had, in fact, been a brutal murderer. Then, a few months later, Khrushchev directed the bloody suppression of a democratic revolution in "socialist" Hungary. As Red Army tanks blasted through the streets of Budapest, black people were again riding buses in Montgomery, Alabama; their yearlong boy-cott against segregated seating had ended in triumph.

The Montgomery boycott was the first mass action of a crusade for racial equality that would change U.S. society as profoundly as had any movement on the left since the one that helped to end slavery. Like the abolitionists, activists in the black freedom movement aimed to trans-form not just the racial order in their own nation but the social hierarchy of an unjust world. "The struggle of the [American] Negro," announced Martin Luther King Jr. on the eve of victory in Montgomery, was part of an international struggle of non-white peoples to throw off the colonial yoke. While the twenty-seven-year-old minister condemned both Com-munism and its doctrine of class struggle, he was also sharply critical of the "abuses" of his own nation's capitalist system. That same year, King told a convention of his fellow black Baptists that the United States had a responsibility to deploy its vast wealth "to wipe poverty from the face of the earth."[6]

Also in 1956, two white radicals rushed into print with quite different but equally bold ideas about what ailed American society; their notions about what might cure it, however, were somewhat vaguer. In *The Power Elite*, Columbia University sociologist C. Wright Mills, a lapsed Catho-lic raised in Texas, indicted an interlocking group of businessmen, politi-cians, and top military officers for practicing "a higher immorality" that corrupted public life and brought the world to the brink of nuclear war. Mills saw little difference between the American elite and its counterpart in the Kremlin: the rulers of both superpowers "monopolized . . . the material and cultural means by which history is now powerfully being made." The motorcycle-riding professor argued that it would take an uprising of "ordinary men," led by intellectuals with a democratic vision, to set things right.[7]

On the other side of the continent, a small San Francisco publishing house was distributing a different sort of printed rebellion: *Howl and Other Poems*, by Allen Ginsberg. In the title selection, Ginsberg swirled together candid glimpses of his own life on the road with laments about the damage America was doing to maverick souls. His name for that culture was Moloch, a Semitic deity who gobbled up innocent children. Ginsberg drew no distinction between rebels who fought Moloch by letting "themselves be fucked in the ass by saintly motorcyclists" and that other breed of heretics who handed out "Supercommunist pamphlets in Union Square." Resisting on one's own terms was enough. The professor and the poet had little in common, although the (heterosexual) Mills did love to ride and repair his German-built motorcycle. But, in 1956, both their books gained large audiences and earned them fame as radical voices in an era marked by political moderation and an uneasy kind of cultural conformity.[8]

The arc of a New Left inspired in equal measure by an eloquent Baptist preacher, a blunt-spoken Ivy League academic, and a euphoric gay poet—all of whom were then under forty—was inevitably going to diverge from that of its Marxist predecessors. Politics, as conventionally defined, was of only secondary importance to the historical achievements of this "movement of movements," as one historian calls it. Unlike every previous left, the New Left built neither a national party nor a durable membership body. It even lacked a mutual gathering point, aside from national anti-war marches. Few radicals seemed to care. They belonged to "the Movement," and that was enough. After all, sturdy organizations, with their bureaucracies and fixed doctrines, were part of the System they were trying to dismantle.

The lack of structures made it easier to join the Movement but often made the act of joining a rather casual thing, defined along a broad continuum from attendance at a couple of demonstrations to abandoning any life outside the community of permanent struggle. Radicals who grew up in the age of television also depended as much on media owned by big corporations to disseminate their ideas and images as they did on their own "underground" newspapers, documentaries, and low-frequency radio stations. It seemed quite natural—and thrilling—to rush home from a demonstration to see how you and your friends looked and sounded on the evening news.[9]

That the New Left also heralded itself as a *young* left was critical to its growth—and to its ultimate political failure. Radical movements everywhere have nearly always depended on the zealous energies of people who need little sleep and do not have to worry about the feeding and clothing of children. The average age of the Bolshevik leaders who took power in Petrograd in 1917 was all of twenty-six. But never before had an American left made youth itself a badge of rebellion—or prided itself on breaking away from its older predecessors. Jack Weinberg, the Berkeley radical who popularized the famous line "We don't trust anyone over 30" meant it as a rebuttal to the charge that subversive, perhaps Communist, adults were pulling the strings. But few people outside the movement got the joke.[10]

The notion of a "revolution" made almost exclusively by the young was both brilliant and absurd. On the one hand, it expressed the self-confidence of activists from a generation that was both larger and better educated than any in U.S. history. College enrollment tripled during the 1960s to nearly ten million, and few students had experienced the privations of the Great Depression. The radicals among them had little respect for established political groups on the left which had failed to achieve their stated ends, whether a workers' state or an end to racial discrimination. Many New Leftists admired the revolutionary societies of Cuba, North Vietnam, and China. But few regarded any of these peasant nations as models for an overdeveloped America; the New Left would not emulate the Socialists before World War I who had viewed the German SPD as a model party or the Communists who imagined the USSR as a paradise in the making. And for Americans who believed that one can always remake one's life, the plain-spoken brashness of the young radicals was often appealing, even if they disagreed with the point of their protests.[11]

Yet age has no intrinsic political merit, and the arrogance and impatience of the young radicals also led them astray. Contemptuous of liberals, they failed to build durable interclass, interracial coalitions that might have sustained the new age of reform led by John Kennedy and Lyndon Johnson and prevented or delayed the rise of the New Right. Disenchanted with old formulas for remaking American society, they gave little thought to devising new ones. In the late 1960s and early

1970s, frustration at the lack of an alternative led an aggressive minority in the movement to take up one variety of Leninist dogma or another, while other activists sought to refashion a liberalism cleansed of Cold War hypocrisies. Neither project was successful. Soon, for the first time in over 150 years, no American radical movement survived that was worthy of the name.

But before it expired, the New Left helped cause a mighty dislocation in the national culture—one which nudged Americans to change some deep-seated ideas about themselves and their society, even as the young radicals did little to change structures of power in the workplace or the halls of government. The New Left articulated a critique of everyday life, which was, in time, taken up by millions of people who had little regard for those who had originated the ideas.

Indeed, by the late 1980s, many citizens welcomed expanded notions of individual freedom, of self-expression, and identity—despite two landslide elections of a conservative president who defined freedom mainly as a defense of property and the market, and hostility to Communism. During the darkest days of Ronald Reagan's presidency, there was more radical dissent in the United States than was present at any time in the 1950s. Tens of millions of Americans, perhaps even a majority, had come to reject racial and sexual discrimination, to question the need for and morality of military intervention abroad, and to worry that industrial growth might be imperiling the future of life on earth. Neither the power nor the influence of the radicals who had helped promote these changes were what they had desired. But their message had certainly been received.[12]

In part, what made the New Left new was its deep sense of alienation from the old. In the fall of 1956, the narrator of *Going Away*, an autobiographical novel by Clancy Sigal, takes a long drive across the American continent. The erstwhile labor activist and screenwriter travels from Los Angeles to Manhattan in a gaudy, red and white De Soto convertible, looking up old comrades and lovers along the way. News of the doomed revolt in Hungary accompanies him on the radio like a Greek chorus, exploding the myth of socialism by and for the workers that had already died at home. "None of the boys talk Red any more," an official of a union once run by Communists tells him. "All they talk about is sex, baseball, cars and the lousy Company." By the end of the novel, the narrator suffers a nervous breakdown and moves to England. "The thirties had been my time, and I had been fourteen in 1940," writes Sigal. "The historic agencies of change are collapsed; and with them I. Why? I must find out."[13] He ends the book, which was published in 1961, without an answer.

The New Left he did not stay around to witness was indeed abandoning the belief that the American working class would someday "bring to birth a new world from the ashes of the old," as a Wobbly songwriter prophesied in 1915. Half a century later, millions of American wage earners were living in a society far superior to the one their parents and grandparents had known: they enjoyed the highest incomes and most secure jobs in history, thanks to the postwar boom, the GI Bill, and strong, no longer radical, unions like the one Sigal's character encountered on his painful trek across the continent. Martin Luther King and C. Wright Mills both retained a sympathy for the ideals of the labor movement: in his first book, the sociologist had criticized the timidity of union chieftains; a local leader of A. Philip Randolph's union helped organize the Montgomery bus boycott; and the liberal United Auto Workers contributed funds and prestige to the cause of civil rights. But the UAW had also expelled its own radicals and become a pillar of the Democratic Party; its president, Walter Reuther, worked closely with employers to build and sell as many cars and trucks as the market could stand. "The new men of power," Mills dubbed Reuther and his counterparts in other unions; neither the social critic, the visionary preacher, nor other fresh voices on the left trusted whom that power would serve.

The sharp discontent with the liberal order—at once self-satisfied, anxious, and unequal—brought about a momentous shift in the ideology of American radicalism. Since the rise of militant unions and small Marxist parties after the Civil War, no man or woman with influence on the left had questioned the desire of ordinary people to acquire the good things of life, from clean underpants to a six-seat sedan, twinkling with chrome. For all their differences, Bellamy, Willard, Debs, and Robeson all believed that freedom for working men and women meant, at minimum, putting the fear of poverty behind them forever.

New Leftists certainly wanted to abolish poverty and encourage workers to join unions, but neither was a primary concern. Instead, many replaced the old struggle against material deprivation with alarm that, for Americans of all classes, a fixation on acquiring more and more had become a kind of self-oppression: it numbed individuals to boring jobs and unhappy marriages and despoiled the natural landscape. The endless pursuit of plenty also kept the power elite in firm control at home and allowed it to exploit peasants and workers in the Third World. Early in the 1970s, Tom Hayden, a leader of the young white left, wrote *The Love of Possession Is a Disease with Them*, a book that rooted the war in Vietnam in a long history of economic aggression that began with the conquest of Native American territories by European settlers. For his title Hayden lifted a phrase from a speech given a century earlier by Sitting Bull, the Lakota chief who fought a desperate battle to keep the U.S. Army from driving his people off their lands.[14]

This critique led in a variety of directions, most of which involved fusing a utopian social vision with the desire for an emancipated self. The quarter century of economic expansion that followed World War II had "allowed masses of people unprecedented latitude in making choices about how to live," wrote the feminist critic Ellen Willis. The young left urged the fortunate millions to break with traditional ideas about race, work, love, and family—and the institutions that promoted and profited from them. "Not With My Life You Don't" was an anti-draft slogan emblazoned on buttons produced by Students for a Democratic Society (SDS), the largest organization on the white New Left. The sentiment was soon taken up by adherents to an ever-expanding variety of causes—black freedom, Chicano rights, women's liberation, gay liberation, the rights of the disabled, and more.

It expressed a brash, ultra-romantic universalism that had not been a major force in radical politics since the days when merchants, artisans, and former slaves worked together for the same ends and occasionally lived together in the same planned communities. When New Leftists named their enemy, they were more likely to indict a System with many faces of evil instead of "capitalism," whose wickedness was tethered to the economic sphere. "If we look into ourselves, we will see how completely our society cuts us off from ourselves, from our deepest feelings and needs and sources of happiness," wrote the young critic Marshall Berman in 1970. "And 'we' here means *everyone*—the upper as well as the underclass, the sultans as well as the slaves. Everyone is being cheated by the system."[15]

Rejecting an "alienated" existence and determined to lead an "authentic" one, college-educated radicals fanned out to many black and several white neighborhoods in both the North and the South, where they attempted to organize a movement that could destroy not just Jim Crow laws and customs but the structures of business and politics that perpetuated inequality. Among these grassroots rebels were young women and homosexuals of both genders who soon began to demand a hearing for their own, individual grievances—ones that had seldom gained a hearing on the labor-centered left of the 1930s and '40s. The attack on consumer excess also helped inspire an environmental movement that rewrote the old script of solidarity to include the fauna, the flora, and the oceans. By the early 1970s, leftists of every racial and ethnic background were enrobing themselves in identities that were at once emblems of protest against white, imperial America and a discovery or revival of cultural traditions: African, Native American, Mexican, Chinese, Jewish, Irish, and more. All these activist passions combined the rage of "Not With My Life You Don't" with the feminist motto "The personal is political."

While rejecting shibboleths about "class struggle" and "the homeland of socialism," the left that emerged in the 1950s and '60s was also turning back, unintentionally, to older impulses that had inspired William Lloyd Garrison, Angelina Grimké, David Walker, and John Brown more than a century before. Both groups of radicals insisted that one had to live one's politics as well as preach them. Both took delight in smashing taboos about interracial sex, about the proper roles of men and women, and about dress and diet. Both experimented with styles of communal living they believed would allow individuals to realize their "true" nature and to find happiness in doing so.

Evangelical Christians were rare in white radical circles, although they were common enough on the black left. But whether pious or secular, most radical activists struggled fiercely to free both minds and bodies from an evil society and to fill the world with perfected individuals. "I had to find out who I am and who I want to be," wrote black militant Eldridge Cleaver in 1968, "what kind of man I should be, and what I could do to become the best of which I was capable." Like Walker and Brown, Cleaver thought only violence could cleanse America of its sins. That temptation, too, was part of the utopian tradition. So the final American left of the industrial age often gestured back, in spirit, to the first.[16]

Every movement, however loosely defined and structured, requires spokespeople, whether formally elected or not. In the absence of traditional kinds of leaders, the ideas of the New Left were articulated most powerfully and prominently by celebrities: the novelist James Baldwin, the actress Jane Fonda, the theorist Herbert Marcuse, the Jesuit pacifist Daniel Berrigan, the Bob Dylan who wrote "Masters of War" and "The Times They Are A-Changin'," the John Lennon who wrote "Imagine" and "Working-Class Hero," as well as Abbie Hoffman, the feminist writer Robin Morgan, Cleaver and Huey Newton of the Black Panther Party, Stokely Carmichael of SNCC—and, of course, Martin Luther King Jr.

Some of these people rose to fame from within the Movement itself; others allied with it only after becoming stars in their own right—and seldom, if ever, attended a radical meeting. But they all straddled the divide between left politics and mass culture—or threatened to obliterate it altogether. In an age when images on film and sounds on vinyl or magnetic tape could rapidly circle the globe, the ability of such people to draw a rapt audience easily overshadowed, while sometimes assisting, the patient organizing done by thousands of local radicals. Certain left celebrities—Frantz Fanon, Che Guevara, Malcolm X, and C. Wright Mills himself (whose skeptical heart gave out in 1962)—probably had more influence dead than alive; each rapidly became a martyr to the cause of total rebellion, proclaiming truths beyond the grave that were hard for any living leftist to challenge.

Of course, celebrities have always had their uses for the left; such notables as Frederick Douglass, Edward Bellamy, Henry George, Frances Willard, and Paul Robeson gave previous radical movements the benefit of their ideas and their ability to attract and hold a crowd. But since the New Left lacked a structure to direct and channel the views of its stars, what they said and did often steered the activist core, instead of vice versa.

All these notables hurled moral barbs at a liberal "establishment" whose crimes lay in being quite cruel in certain venues and too soft in others. The same elites who sent troops and bombers to squash rebellions in the jungles of Vietnam and the ghettos of Harlem and Detroit also sponsored the Peace Corps and the Civil Rights Act, hoping to mollify the discontented before they turned to revolution. New Left activists set out to make history, armed with a moral vision that mixed solidarity with the world's poor with blasts at the inauthentic life led by the majority of people in one of the richest nations in the world. Somewhat remarkably, they did so, but, inevitably, not as they pleased.

## WHAT KIND OF CHANGE IS GONNA COME?

> After the racist statutes are all struck down, after legal equality has been achieved in the schools and the courts, there will yet remain the profound, institutionalized and abiding wrong which white America has worked on the Negro for centuries.
>
> —Michael Harrington, 1961[17]

Whatever their blunders and blind spots, the radicals who came of age in the 1960s made one commitment that has stood up well over time: to achieve, finally, the complete equality of the races. Most participants in this freedom movement were, of course, African Americans, and their example spawned similar, if smaller, radical surges among young Mexican Americans, Puerto Ricans, and Asian Americans in the U.S. But thousands of young whites also worked with the Congress of Racial Equality (CORE) and the Student Non-Violent Coordinating Committee (SNCC), until a mid-decade turn toward black nationalism forced them out. If anything, the sting of that rejection increased the desire of SDSers and other white radicals to aid the black insurgency. This helps explain why the claim of the Black Panther Party to be "the vanguard" of the entire left quickly gained legitimacy among white leftists. They felt that the most militant, self-sacrificing detachment of a moral army had earned the right to lead.

Yet groups like SNCC and the Panthers did not represent the only species of black radicalism in their era. "I believe that the Negro's struggle for equality in America is essentially revolutionary," wrote Bayard Rustin in early 1965. "While most Negroes—in their hearts—unquestionably seek only to enjoy the fruits of American society as it now exists, their quest cannot *objectively* be satisfied within the framework of existing political and economic relations." Rustin had come a long way since his stint as a young Communist who sang backup for Josh White. In 1941, having just broken with the CP, he helped A. Philip Randolph threaten to lead a march on Washington to secure jobs for blacks in defense plants; in the summer of 1963, Rustin was the main organizer of the huge demonstration for jobs and freedom that did descend on the capital city. In between, as a convert to pacifism, he served two years in prison for resisting the World War II draft, traveled to India to learn the techniques of nonviolent resistance from Gandhi and his disciples, and then helped King stage the bus boycott in Montgomery.[18]

By the mid-sixties, the master organizer had come to believe that the only way to liberate black Americans was through a new kind of economic popular front— though as an anti-Communist, he would never have described it that way. "We need to choose our allies on the basis of common political objectives," declared Rustin. This meant strengthening bonds with labor unions, liberal churches, guilt-ridden phi-lanthropists, and sympathetic politicians. With Randolph's backing, Rustin drew up a blueprint for a new, social-democratic order. His "Freedom Budget," unveiled in the fall of 1966, would have guaranteed to every citizen a job, an annual income, health insurance, good schools, and decent housing—all paid for by a progressive

Bayard Rustin, talking to reporters before the March on Washington for Jobs and Freedom, 1963. Rustin, a radical pacifist and democratic socialist, was a key organizer of the modern black freedom movement and a close associate of both A. Philip Randolph and Martin Luther King Jr.

income tax stripped of loopholes for the rich. Rustin counseled his fellow activists not to waste time trying either to soften the hearts of white racists or, like Malcolm X, to scare them "into doing the right thing." Transform the capitalist order, he counseled, and their hearts will eventually follow.[19]

Martin Luther King Jr., the most famous black man in America, had his own vision of racial harmony, but he was just as committed as Rustin to radical structural change. While studying for the pulpit in the late 1940s, King had read *The Communist Manifesto*, *Looking Backward*, and pro-socialist essays by Reinhold Niebuhr. Such texts, bolstered by the young man's firsthand observations of the harsh conditions faced by menial workers, persuaded him that a system which took "necessities from the masses to give luxuries to the classes" was both unjust and un-Christian.[20]

Over the next decade, as he rose to eminence in the freedom move-ment, King forged a bond with such pragmatic socialists as Rustin, Randolph, and Michael Harrington and backed their efforts to build a durable alliance between black insurgents and the AFL-CIO. In 1963, anticipating the Freedom Budget, he argued for policies that would aid

Malcolm X and Martin Luther King Jr. The two met in Washington, D.C., as the Senate debated the landmark civil rights bill in 1964.

working people of all races—"a massive program by the government of special, compensatory measures." Only these, King felt, would make possible a class alliance with poor whites so "confused . . . by prejudice that they have supported their own oppressors."[21]

As a disciple of Gandhi, King continued to endorse anti-imperialist movements in poor nations. At times, he even viewed them as models for black people in the U.S. He also criticized armed interventions abroad long before he delivered his famous 1967 speech against the war in Vietnam, which severed his relationship with President Lyndon Johnson. Rustin, despite his pacifism, avoided the issue entirely—which made it impossible to promote the Freedom Budget to a left consumed by its outrage at the war. King was a skillful political tactician, but his larger purpose was closer to the socialist dream of Debs than to a racially tolerant version of Cold War liberalism. And he articulated that vision in moral terms that merged democratic, patriotic, and biblical themes—all of which he knew most Americans cherished.[22]

Young black organizers in SNCC and CORE did not denounce the idea of an interracial coalition on the left, but they increasingly thought it evaded the root of the problem. The old Popular Front had failed to free black people from their separate and manifestly unequal place in national life. Why would a new version, dependent on aid from the liberal establishment, be more successful?

Long before the summer of 1966, when the cry of "black power" grabbed headlines and TV viewers and divided the movement, young African-American writers had been making their impatience clear. The "mood of Negro writers . . . approaches what can best be described as— *crimson fury* . . . ," playwright Lorraine Hansberry told a group of students in 1959. "If I am asked abroad if I am a free citizen in the United States of America, I must say only what is true—no." Four years later, on the centennial of the Emancipation Proclamation, James Baldwin told his nephew, "You were born into a society which spelled out with brutal clarity, and in as many ways as possible, that you were a worthless human being." In the search for a way out, psychology trumped economics. The novelist John Edgar Wideman later asserted, "The freedom that matters most is how we feel inside about ourselves. Prisons, ghettos, concentration camps . . . can restrict mind and body, kill both, but until the spirit is extinguished, the possibility of freedom lives."[23]

The SNCC organizers who took on violent Jim Crow authorities in the Deep South during the early sixties shared both that anger and that spirit. They were after a greater end than simply registering voters and desegregating public facilities, as difficult and hazardous as those aims were to win. They wanted to demonstrate that black people were finally casting off every shackle that 350 years of American history had fastened on their bodies and minds. In the process, they would also expose the sickness that afflicted the whole nation. "Before the Negro in the South had always looked on the defensive, cringing," recalled Bob Moses, who left a job teaching math in New York City to organize with SNCC in Mississippi. "This time they were taking the initiative. They were kids my age, and I knew this had something to do with my own life . . . for a long time I had been troubled by the problem of being a Negro and at the same time being an American. This was the answer."[24]

Black power flourished in an abundance of forms. When Malcolm X was the leading spokesman for the Nation of Islam (NOI), it meant preaching a pride in one's race and a contempt for "white devils." Then, late in 1963, Malcolm broke with the NOI and began to move toward an embrace of Third World radicalism—before he was silenced by assassins one winter day in 1965. For the Reverend Albert Cleage of Detroit, black power meant rejecting "a total white civilization" by starting a new denomination for Christians who prayed to a dark-skinned Jesus and an ebony Virgin. For the Black Panther Party, it meant brandishing shotguns to stop police brutality, taunting the cops as "pigs," and publishing a ten-point program which included the demand that the government free all blacks held in prison, exempt all black men from the draft, and pay "restitution for [the] slave labor and mass murder of Black people."[25]

As black nationalists who curried white support, the Panthers were an inescapable presence on the sixties left, and they remain the best-known, most controversial radical organization from that era. Politics, in the usual sense of the word, had little to do with it. The party never recruited more than five thousand members scattered across some forty urban chapters and had to spend a good deal of its time and money hiring lawyers and mounting defense campaigns for imprisoned comrades, including Huey Newton and Bobby Seale, two friends who had founded the group and remained its leading spokesmen. On the surface, the Panthers made a fetish of organization, authority, and discipline: their leaders donned such titles as Minister of Defense, Minister of Information, even Field Marshal. In the party's national office in Oakland, a brightly colored poster of Stalin stretched from floor to ceiling. Panther recruits of both sexes were urged to plow through a variety of radical texts, from Mao's Red Book to the lyrics of Bob Dylan's "Ballad of a Thin Man," and appear at public events garbed in a striking uniform of black slacks, beret, powder-blue shirt, and leather jacket.[26]

But Panthers who spent time battling the local police, or recovering from a recent skirmish with them, could not sustain much-touted programs like breakfasts for poor children that were intended to "serve the people" and thus broaden the party's appeal. Newton didn't help the cause by writing *Revolutionary Suicide* and *To Die for the People*, books of praise for armed martyrdom. "We will not die the death of the Jews in Germany," he told a college audience in 1970. "We would rather die the death of the Jews in Warsaw!" Only during the party's final years in the mid-1970s did the Panthers seek to gain a share of urban power through elections. But by then, their influence stretched no farther than their home base in the flatlands of East Oakland.[27]

The group's real power lay in its ability to draw a huge and diverse crowd, which it alternately shocked and inspired. One spring day in 1967, a small band of Panthers marched into the California State Assembly, carrying shotguns to protest a bill that would have banned the carrying of loaded weapons in public. The image of young, sleekly athletic black men and women who would say and do whatever they thought necessary to bring about the liberation of their people set a charge that crackled far beyond the urban ghetto.

The Black Panther Party became a symbol of rebellion that leaped over barriers of race, age, and nation. It enthralled white radicals, in and out of SDS, as well as white liberals like Leonard Bernstein, who hosted a fund-raising soirée for the Panthers at his Park Avenue duplex that Tom Wolfe famously satirized in his essay "These Radical Chic Evenings." In Los Angeles, young Mexican Americans organized the Brown Berets to confront police in the barrio; they copied much of the Panthers' ten-point program as well as their bristling style. Maggie Kuhn, a white Social Gospeler, launched the Gray Panthers for Americans over sixty-five who opposed forced retirement and shoddy health care. The American Indian Movement and the Young Lords, a group of Puerto Ricans living in eastern cities, took their rhetoric and the injunction to "pick up the gun" from the example of Newton and Seale. "Wherever they went, the Americans were the masters," wrote playwright Jean Genet, "so the Panthers would do their best to terrorize the masters by the only means available to them. Spectacle."[28]

Their theatrical potency also led minority activists in other lands to borrow the Panther name—which quickly became international shorthand for militant resistance to every type of discrimination. In Israel, the Black Panthers were Sephardic Jews who demanded equal treatment in a state controlled by richer, better-educated citizens with European roots. In 1971, they confronted Prime Minister Golda Meir, who reported they were "not nice people"; then they staged an unsanctioned rally in Jerusalem which erupted in violence. The British Panthers were created by young people of West Indian background who felt disrespected by the white majority and shut out of good jobs, schools, and housing. Black Panthers also sprang up among Aborigines in Australia and Polynesians in New Zealand, and a group called the Black Berets was organized in Bermuda. The Black Panthers in India belonged to the Dalit—people of the lowest caste who spurned the pejorative term "untouchable." They put together a sizable movement bent on overturning the traditional hierarchy which relegated them to menial labor and social exclusion. None of the other Panther offshoots had a large membership or stayed together for long. But everywhere their uncivil presence, like that of their American namesake, was catnip for the media. In all these nations, the Panther name helped to spur hot, broad debates about the causes of ethnic discontent and the hunger for a proud identity.[29]

Yet the hope that black power could be the pathway to revolution in the United States ignored certain bald realities. Any movement that advocated violence was sure to face attack from state and federal governments whose attempts to preserve order, brutal though they could be, enjoyed the support of most people who didn't share the movement's rage. In the spasmodic history of the armed left in America, only John Brown's raid on Harpers Ferry may have sped the victory of a cause, and that occurred only because its failure helped produce the very end the guerrilla leader desired: a war to abolish slavery. But the Panthers' bravado, like that of the anarchists in the Gilded Age, stirred up a whirlwind of repression that soon finished off both their national organization and their vision of a black-led socialist revolution. Chanting "Free Huey, off the pig" at every rally, Newton's closest followers should not have been surprised that the "pigs" tried either to kill them first or to lock them away for as long as possible. To go down fighting was, by definition, a choice without a future.

The Panthers and their many admirers of all races had no rebuttal to Rustin's critique of a politics based on tough rhetoric and self-sacrifice. The social-democratic coalition needed to enact the Freedom Budget was certainly out of reach by the late 1960s, but the idea that the radical young, led by the poorest among them, could overthrow the power elite by themselves was the sheerest of fantasies. It also helped turn some budding leftists away from the humble tasks essential to any growing movement. "I started as a community organizer for about a week; then I decided I wanted to be a Panther," recalled a former member from Los Angeles. "I was ready to die for the people . . ."[30]

Both the allure and the limits of black power were embodied in the long, ultimately frustrating career of one of its leading spokesmen: Stokely Carmichael. Born in Trinidad in 1941, Carmichael (whose middle name, Churchill, testified to his parents' cognizance of both empire and global war) moved at the age of eleven to New York City, where he began his activist life inside the dwindling but still appealing interracial confines of the Old Left. He lived in a mostly white neighborhood and attended the highly selective Bronx High School of Science. There, he became friends with Eugene Dennis Jr., son of the leader of the Com-

Black Panther Party poster, c. 1971. Artist
unknown. As black nationalists who curried
white support, the Panthers were a major force
on the 1960s left—and remain the best-known
and most controversial radical organization from
that era. Their name and proud, aggressive image
was taken up by minority ethnic groups fighting
for rights in a number of other countries.

munist Party. Dennis lived in Harlem, where he hosted integrated parties
that featured good dance music and vigorous political talk. "I became
identified—completely—with the left," Carmichael recalled. Only his
respect for the black church seems to have kept the talented young immigrant from joining the Communist Party or its youth auxiliary.[31]

Carmichael's decision to attend Howard University altered his perspective forever. He took classes in black history and literature from
such charismatic professors as Rayford Logan, E. Franklin Frazier, and
the future novelist Toni Morrison—whom he remembered as "young,
stylish, and really fine." He joined a campus civil rights group affiliated
with SNCC and, in 1961, took part in one of the Freedom Rides that

braved white mobs to break the grip of Jim Crow in interstate travel. The experience convinced him to drop out of college and become a full-time organizer, based in Mississippi. James Baldwin met Carmichael there, when he "was just another nonviolent kid, marching, talking, and getting his head whipped."[32] The kid was also becoming a speaker with a strong, clear voice and the ability to turn a dramatic phrase.

By the middle of the decade, Carmichael had vowed to turn the whipping around. He played tapes of Malcolm X for voter education classes and helped set up a local rights organization in Lowndes County, Alabama, which called itself the Black Panther Party. Reading about that fiercely named group fired the imaginations of Newton and Seale, two thousand miles away in Oakland. In the summer of 1966, Carmichael, who had just been elected chairman of SNCC, told cheering crowds of black Mississippians, "The only way we gonna stop them white men from whuppin' us is to take over. What we gonna start sayin' now is Black Power!" A large media contingent, on hand to witness a civil rights march that wound through the state, broadcast the new slogan to the world.

It was the zenith of Carmichael's political influence. SNCC was rapidly dissolving in all but name, as its best organizers moved out of the South and into a variety of different pursuits, from running for office to studying for graduate degrees. Carmichael was emerging as "black power's rock star" and a skillful icon of revolutionary bluster. But he had no movement to command.

He did give speeches all over the country, filling auditoriums in Harlem and at Harvard alike. When Lyndon Johnson sent more troops to Vietnam, Carmichael compared him to a rapist and urged black men either to refuse to fight his "racist war" or to use their military training to wage combat in the streets back home. In 1967, he took off on an extended tour of revolutionary capitals—Havana, Hanoi, and Algiers. Fidel Castro embraced him and his cause, as did Ho Chi Minh. The Vietnamese leader, perhaps remembering Marcus Garvey's movement, also inquired when black Americans were "going to repatriate to Africa." The normally self-confident Carmichael could only stammer that it was his "ultimate goal."[33]

Soon, pan-Africanism became his exclusive passion—and a politically barren one. On a trip to Guinea, Carmichael met two charismatic African radicals—President Ahmed Sékou Touré, who had gained the nation's independence from France, and Kwame Nkrumah, exiled from Ghana after a decade of controversial rule. In 1969, the young American firebrand repatriated to Conakry, Guinea's capital, along with his new wife, the world-famous South African singer Miriam Makeba. He took the name Kwame Ture as a tribute to his mentors. Over the next three decades, Ture struggled to build a party of African socialism which might unite black people on both sides of the Atlantic. The group recruited few members and had faded into irrelevance long before its leader died of cancer in 1998. Like other militant American voices, black and white, Ture had, writes the historian Clayborne Carson, "gained almost overnight a fame [he] did not deserve, and gradually . . . fell into an obscurity [he] could not have expected."[34]

But the rhetoric of black power advocates did catalyze a sea change in the lives of African Americans who had no intention of returning to the lands of their ancestors. Under student pressure, hundreds of colleges initiated courses in black studies, whose ideas and texts soon filtered into the curricula of high schools across the country. James Brown's 1968 hit "I'm Black and I'm Proud" signaled the arrival of a new mass art that mocked assimilation and prized racial authenticity—what the hip-hop musicians (including Tupac Shakur, the son of Panther parents) who came to dominate black music would call "keeping it real." *Roots*, the unflinching family narrative of slaves and their descendants by Alex Haley (who earlier had shaped Malcolm X's *Autobiography*), was the most popular television event of the 1970s. In a fury of emulation, champions of other ethnic groups soon launched programs in Chicano studies, Asian-American Studies, Jewish studies, even Irish and Italian studies.[35]

Critics derided all this as "identity politics"—an escape from the real thing, the kind that requires mass movements and electoral clout. In fact, vigorous campaigns inspired by the black freedom movement elected black mayors in the nation's largest cities. But their victories could not stall the industrial decline that stripped away the good jobs and decent housing which had lured millions of African Americans away from the rural South earlier in the century. Still, black radicals like Carmichael and Newton had jolted millions of people to comprehend themselves and their society in assertive and candid ways. Armed with a degree of self-confidence, individual as well as collective, they could reject what Carmichael's "really fine" former professor would call "the policing languages of mastery," which advance "relentlessly toward the bottom line and the bottomed-out mind." Toni Morrison said that in 1993 in Stockholm, where she had just received the Nobel Prize in Literature. This new understanding was an authentic kind of freedom, although without the aid of something more material like the Freedom Budget, it would never be enough.[36]

## STOPPING THE SEVENTH VIETNAM FROM NOW

Young white radicals always tried to keep in close step with the evolution of the black movement. "We are people of this generation, bred in at least modest comfort, housed now in universities, looking uncomfortably to the world we inherit," announced the small gathering of SDS members who ratified the Port Huron Statement in June 1962. The primary cause of that discomfort, they made clear, was "the permeating and victimizing fact of human degradation, symbolized by the Southern struggle against racial bigotry." Tom Hayden, who wrote the first draft of the statement, had been beaten up and jailed in Mississippi while doing civil rights work. His wife, Casey, was part of a band of white southerners who joined the staff of SNCC. Black students, Tom Hayden had written to a close friend the previous year, were already "miles ahead of us . . . chuckling knowingly about the sterility of liberals." In both North and South, "they will be shouting from the bottom of their guts for justice or else. We had better be there."[37]

Whether or not they belonged to SDS, white New Leftists did what they could, gladly if somewhat anxiously, to support their black counterparts. The Free Speech Movement in Berkeley began in the fall of 1964 when university authorities refused to allow students to raise money for civil rights groups from a table they had set up just inside the campus. The mass protests that resulted became the model for hundreds of later "campus uprisings," many of which involved demands for the creation of black studies programs and a halt to university expansion into black neighborhoods. During the 1960s, the walls of white students' dorm rooms probably sported at least as many posters of Huey Newton and Malcolm X as did those of black students, and Carmichael, Eldridge Cleaver, and the scholar-activist Angela Davis could fill a large hall on almost any campus in America with little advance notice. When angry ghetto residents took to the streets to loot and burn white-owned businesses and battle the police, SDS saluted them and criticized liberals for counseling peace. In their rebellions (which the mass media called riots), the poor residents of Watts and Harlem and Newark were declaring, "Not With My Life, You Don't!" in a way more comfortable rebels could appreciate. For white radicals, to endorse whatever black radicals thought was necessary to achieve their freedom was a moral commitment, not a strategic one. The awful burden of America's racist history demanded no less.

This was a big leap beyond what any previous left had either preached or practiced. A century earlier, most abolitionists had assumed that both slaves and free blacks should follow the lead of their white benefactors. Without the latter's verbal skills and access to wealth and political elites, how could emancipation be won? During their heyday, white Communists, despite their respect for black culture, had primarily viewed African Americans—and, by extension, other racial minorities—as victims of capitalists who had brainwashed white workers into shunning their natural allies.

But the white New Left was proud to take its cues from a primarily black movement, singing its freedom songs, chanting its slogans, and adopting its vision as well as its anger. "I see SNCC as the Nile Valley of the New Left," wrote Carl Oglesby, president of SDS, in 1965. "And I honor SDS to call it part of the delta that SNCC created."[38] A sizable contingent of white sympathizers helped change the way Americans spoke about race—and kept opponents of black rights on the defensive well into the 1970s. But from the nonviolent boycotters of Montgomery to the war-ready Panthers of Oakland a decade later, black people would do most of the work of liberating themselves.

However, white radicals played the central role in the second great cause of the left during the long 1960s: opposing the American war in Indochina. The range and ingenuity of their activities were impressive, proof that a movement could flourish despite, or perhaps because, it lacked a central command. Anti-war leftists organized teach-ins on college campuses and staged draft-card burnings at federal buildings and sit-ins in front of draft boards, army bases, military recruiting stands, and even the occasional troop train. They mobilized millions of people in anti-war demonstrations, both local and national, that began with a march on Washington of twenty-five thousand in April 1965, organized by SDS, and reached a crescendo with a week of protests in the capital six years later that attracted nearly a million people. Less visible in the media were the movement's quotidian successes: the draft counselors who helped men slip through loopholes in the Selective Service regulations and the amateur journalists—in and out of uniform—who turned out truly "underground" anti-war papers for soldiers and sailors and found ways to circulate these illegal sheets on navy ships and army bases.

Every major armed conflict in U.S. history has provoked an opposition, often a sizable one. But no dissenters—from the New England Federalists during the War of 1812 to pacifists and Communists during the Korean War—had begun to organize near the start of a war or had grown larger and more powerful as the battles continued. And no previous anti-war movement endured long enough to celebrate the victory of the enemy in what became the most humiliating defeat the United States had ever suffered.

Radicals drew on a tightly woven skein of arguments to condemn America's assault on Vietnam and its neighbors in Southeast Asia: The intervention was undemocratic, since Congress had not declared war, and presidents kept lying about the nature of the conflict in order to secure funding and augment the number of troops sent into the maelstrom. It was racist, since a mostly white and prosperous nation was attempting to force its way of life and politics on masses of Asian peasants. It was counterrevolutionary, since those masses were, with the aid of Communists, engaged in overturning the rule of big landlords and urban merchants. And to sum up the indictment, it was imperialist—the latest, cruelest effort by a profit-seeking system that had to expand its dominion or wither and die. Given the sweeping nature of the diagnosis, most SDSers agreed that putting on yet another big anti-war demonstration would be a waste of time, although they usually attended protests planned by others. The true need was to build a movement that could "stop the seventh Vietnam from now." Until the system was destroyed, it would just keep on killing.[39]

One cannot mistake the legacy of the older, Marxist left in these charges, despite the determination of young radicals to break away from the failed ideology of the past. The white New Left, unlike its black and Latino counterparts, was well stocked with children of Popular Front parents, whether "red-diaper babies" or the offspring of liberals who had never warmed up to the Cold War. "Becoming a radical . . . involves *no fundamental change in core values*," observed one psychologist who conducted a close study of white anti-war activists. Unsurprisingly, as many as half the cohort were Jewish. "Mickey, I've just seen the next Lenin," Dick Flacks, the Jewish son of CP members, exulted to his wife, a fellow child of Jewish Party members, after he first met Tom Hayden—who himself came from a thoroughly unradical Irish Catholic family.[40] Allen Ginsberg also let his Red past hang out: "America I used to be a communist when I was a kid I'm not sorry . . . It's true I don't want to join the Army or turn lathes in precision parts factories, I'm nearsighted and psychopathic anyway. America I'm putting my queer shoulder to the wheel."[41]

A few figures from the Old Left played a significant role in building the anti-war movement: in his eponymous weekly, I. F. Stone, once a pillar at *PM* and then a lonely critic of the Korean War, demolished the shaky tale Lyndon Johnson told in the summer of 1964 about a naval engagement in the Gulf of Tonkin off the coast of North Vietnam, a fib which had convinced Congress to let the president escalate the conflict. Pete Seeger enjoyed a revival of fame at packed concerts featuring a new song that mocked "the big fool" who wanted to "push on" into the "big muddy" of further bloodshed. By the late 1960s, Lenin's writings on imperialism again seemed relevant, as did the writings of such contemporary disciples as Che Guevara and Mao Zedong. Marxism, at least of the anti-imperialist variety, was back in fashion.

Inevitably, radicals of every age began to daub in vivid, romantic hues the people whom the U.S. military was fighting. Tom Hayden was the first of dozens of militant anti-warriors who made a pilgrimage to Hanoi and returned in awe at what he called the "fearlessness, calm determination, pride, even serenity" of the North Vietnamese. "The spiritual loftiness of Ho [Chi Minh] himself—he wrote poems, he looked like a Buddhist sage—was accepted as a given," recalls Paul Berman, a member of SDS at Columbia University. "It became harder and harder to suppose that any virtue at all inhered to the cause of anti-Communism." A knowledgeable few pointed out that, after coming to power in 1946, Ho and his closest comrades had emulated Stalin by murdering their Trotskyist rivals and brutally imposing collectivization on the peasantry. But who cared to bring that up a generation later, when B-52s were massacring many of those same peasant families—as well as pulverizing their land, their livestock, and even their Buddhist temples?[42]

Its blinders notwithstanding, the Movement spawned a culture of opposition to state power that dwarfed anything seen on the left since World War I; and the sexy flamboyance of this culture made the modernist revels of the crowd around *The Masses* seem quaintly cerebral by comparison. By 1968, the radical argument against the war had won over a sizable proportion of students attending colleges in the Northeast, on the West Coast, and along the Great Lakes and in the youth communities that surrounded them. Many of these same young people agreed that the war in Vietnam was a symbol of all that was rotten in America. In such venues, military recruiters felt under siege, "make love, not war" became a cliché, and rock musicians sang about "the revolution" as if it had already begun. Even at the University of Texas, whose administration often barred "subversives" from speaking on campus, the SDS chapter gained a big following by staging "Gentle Thursday," a seasonal festival dedicated to blowing bubbles, dressing up like Indians, dancing to rock music, painting peace symbols, and hearing radical oratory from homegrown rebels. In the fall of 1968, a respected pollster reported that more college students identified with the dead Che Guevara than with any of the living nominees for president. As Todd Gitlin recalls, "All assaults on authority could count on the presumption of innocence; all authority started out with the presumption of guilt."[43]

The fuming culture of disruption also helped force the powerful to alter their plans. Just after the Tet offensive of 1968, in which the Vietcong staged attacks in every city in South Vietnam, officials in the Johnson administration feared the consequences at home of sending more troops into war. They predicted "growing dissatisfaction accompanied as it certainly will be by increased defiance of the draft and growing unrest in the cities . . ." Deputy Defense Secretary Paul Nitze fretted that a whole generation was losing its patriotism and following the lead of those who "were against the whole goddamn show." Soon, LBJ opened peace negotiations and announced he would not run for re-election.[44]

This was not just an American rebellion. Across Europe, Japan, and the urbanized parts of Latin America—whose recent economic growth outpaced that of the U.S.—unprecedented numbers of young adults were also living with their peers in or near colleges and voicing the same disgust towards "the system" and the horrible wars it kept generating. Talk of "alienation" and a hunger for "authenticity" were nearly as common in West Berlin, Prague, and Mexico City as in Berkeley or Cambridge,

Massachusetts—and everywhere led to street marches and building take-overs, accompanied by a rock soundtrack and the scent of marijuana.[45]

While the melodies were familiar, the lyrics diverged. In capital-ist nations outside the U.S., most young leftists remained loyal to the socialist tradition, although they battled fiercely about which tendency—Trotskyist, Maoist, Guevarist, anarchist—should take the lead. In the Soviet bloc, the rebels were, by definition, hostile to what state appa-ratchiks called "Marxism-Leninism." Still, most clung to the dream of a "socialism with a human face" that would protect individual rights—even after the summer of 1968, when the Soviets and their allies crushed the new Czech government that was committed to it. Young radicals in Europe, where recent history had demonstrated how fragile parlia-mentary democracy could be, were also somewhat less cynical about elections than were their counterparts in SNCC and SDS, who scorned the two-party monopoly as rigged against "the people." European New Leftists soon created a variety of new parties, particularly the Greens, who would become a major force in West Germany and a permanent voice for the environment and feminism in several other nations as well. But the few American efforts of this kind fizzled quickly after they failed to attract a major celebrity to run for president.[46]

Into the breach stepped a trio of Democratic politicians who finally understood that the war in Indochina neither could nor should be won. The campaigns of Eugene McCarthy and Robert Kennedy in 1968 and of George McGovern in 1972 did not, of course, result in victory. McGovern lost to Richard Nixon in one of the greatest drubbings in U.S. electoral history.

But together, the trio of anti-war liberals transformed the party of Cold Warriors into a party whose most dedicated members opposed sending troops to fight anywhere in the Third World. Since Woodrow Wilson's administration, liberals had ardently promoted wars to pre-serve and advance democracy. The conflict over Vietnam put an end to that tradition for decades to come. "Within 90 days of my inauguration," promised McGovern in his speech accepting the Democratic nomina-tion, "every American soldier and every American prisoner will be out of the jungle and out of their cells and then home in America where they belong . . . let us resolve that never again will we send the precious young blood of this country to die trying to prop up a corrupt military dictatorship abroad." Exhausted from fighting the system, most radicals applauded the liberals' conversion; thousands took part in McGovern's 1972 campaign and remained more or less faithful Democrats, as their dreams of revolution dissolved along with other whims of youth.[47]

But a zealous, if minute, minority refused to give up either their ultimate ends or their antagonism toward liberalism. One group of American leftists was inspired by Mao and the ongoing "Cultural Revolution" he unleashed in a vain attempt to prevent China from taking "the capitalist road." In the early 1970s, these radicals decided the United States needed a new Communist Party to instill the ideological rigor of "Marxism–Leninism–Mao Zedong Thought" in a movement that had practiced "do your own thing" long before it became a hippie catchphrase. Over in Beijing, the aging chairman knew better than to give his blessing to any start-up by naïve disciples; so impatient American Maoists produced a welter of sects which competed furiously to capture a tiny market for their exotic brand. The names of the new groups were unconscious parodies of past left failures: Revolutionary Communist Party, Communist Labor Party, League of Revolutionary Struggle, Communist Workers Party, and the Proletarian Unity League—which included few proletarians and unified nothing. Even before China's leaders adopted their new, wildly successful creed of market-Leninism in the late 1970s, most of these quixotic grouplets had disbanded.[48]

From another corner of the white radical domain came an even smaller band of aspiring revolutionaries: Weatherman, its name borrowed from a line in a Bob Dylan song. The notoriety of the group quickly surpassed its numbers. Founded as SDS broke apart in the summer of 1969, Weatherman took the young left's adoration of Ho, Che, and Huey Newton to a logical, if wildly impractical, conclusion: If you believed such Third World paragons were the vanguard of the revolution, what were *you* doing without a gun in your hands and a bomb-making manual on your cinderblock shelf? Weatherman never had more than three hundred members scattered in about a dozen collective houses around the country, and that was before it went underground, just nine months after its birth. But Weather leaders were articulate and charismatic; several had already made headlines as local SDS leaders—Mark Rudd and Ted Gold at Columbia, Bernadine Dohrn at the University of Chicago, and Bill Ayers at the University of Michigan. While few of their fellow radicals joined up, many did grant the group a certain measure of respect. Since the first lunch counter sit-ins a decade earlier, "putting your body on the line" had been the acme of left commitment. Even C. Wright Mills, on returning from Cuba in 1960, had told his Columbia students, perhaps in jest: "I don't know what you guys are waiting for. You've got a beautiful set of mountains in those Rockies. I'll show you how to use those pistols. Why don't you get going?" Among white radicals, only Weatherman was willing to go all the way.[49]

It was, of course, a fatal delusion. The Weatherpeople (the name change a bow to the feminist awakening) were perhaps the most inept terrorists on the planet, taking to the shadows in March 1970, after a bomb which Gold was preparing blew up prematurely, killing him and two of his comrades inside a Greenwich Village townhouse. Their most notable attack took place a year later: it blew up an unoccupied men's room in the U.S. Capitol. Along with the tiny number of demonstrators who torched American flags, Weatherman tarnished the anti-war movement with the very image its enemies most preferred: traitors who detested and were willing to destroy their own country. Thus burdened, it is remarkable that other New Leftists were able to affect so many lives beyond their own.[50]

## WHEN ALL POLITICS IS PERSONAL

None had such prodigious influence as the women's liberation movement that greatly expanded the meaning of individual freedom with which the New Left—and its nineteenth-century predecessors—began. "We would replace power rooted in possession, privilege, or circumstance by power and uniqueness rooted in love, reflectiveness, reason, and creativity," the Port Huron Statement had declared. "Politics has the function of bringing people out of isolation and into community, thus being a necessary, though not sufficient, means of finding meaning in personal life." In the early days of SNCC, organizers felt they belonged to a "beloved community," whose empathetic struggles might be the model for a just, caring society. Activists in the women's liberation movement that gathered strength at the end of the 1960s broke away from that "male-dominated left," angry at being valued for their bodies and emotional support rather than for their ideas and leadership. To describe the oppression that all women faced, they invented a new term, "sexism," which rapidly became part of the international vernacular. But in arguing for a politics that would satisfy the needs and respect the rights of every woman, they were recovering a utopian, egalitarian dream as old as the American left itself.[51]

While feminists in the 1960s no longer had to campaign for the right to vote, speak in public, or hold property in their own name, they did express some of the same potent grievances that had rankled Elizabeth Cady Stanton and Angelina Grimké. Most occupations were still confined to one gender or the other, and "women's jobs" typically paid less and allowed little control over how one did the work. Men still dominated the world of ideas—whether religious or secular, in the humanities or sciences—and, more important, they defined what counted as knowledge in every field. And men still expected to make nearly every decision in the realm of sexual matters, from proposing a first date to making love for the first time to naming a first child. These customs were as old as patriarchal civilization itself. In challenging them, American feminists were transcending both politics in the customary sense and the boundaries of the nation itself. Sisterhood might be more powerful and more global than any movement that had come before.

Yet the new feminists were not immune to the kinds of divisions that plagued other sections of the New Left. As in the black movement, older activists who pressured lawmakers to pass reforms quarreled with younger rebels who yearned to dismantle an entire culture of oppression and saw legal changes as a mere sideshow to the real drama. Ironically, many of the foremost "liberal" feminists were veterans of the Old Left: Betty Friedan had written regularly for pro-Communist periodicals in the 1940s; Esther Peterson, head of the Women's Bureau in the Kennedy administration, was a longtime Socialist; Myra Wolfgang, a member of the first presidential Commission on the Status of Women, had belonged to the tiny Proletarian Party in the 1930s before she began to ascend the ladder of officialdom in the hotel and restaurant workers' union. The experience of these women in the labor movement taught them how to form coalitions and make demands that, while far-reaching, did not threaten to defeat liberal officeholders or replace the profit system. The National Organization for Women, born in 1966, initially focused on such issues as sex-segregated want ads and a dearth of child-care centers. With Friedan as its first president, NOW intended to anchor a civil rights movement for half the population, not to bring about the utter transformation of private life.

But for radicals escaping from "the boys' left," only a cultural revo-

lution could strike at the source of the problem. While it was fine to train more female
surgeons and carpenters, such small changes
could never break the grip of patriarchy over
the minds of either women or men. Shocking words and actions, however, might help.
In August 1968, a group of friends organized
as New York Radical Women protested at the
Miss America contest in Atlantic City. They
crowned a sheep, insisted on speaking only
to female reporters, and threw a mélange of
"beauty products"—girdles, false eyelashes,
wigs, and bras—into a huge "freedom trash
can." Critics in the media began sniping at
"bra-burning feminists"; no protester in Atlantic City had set fire to anything, but the militant
image stuck. In 1969, members of WITCH
(Women's International Terrorist Conspiracy
from Hell) went to Madison Square Garden to

Betty Friedan, photographed by
Fred Palumbo, 1960. A radical
labor journalist in her youth,
Friedan went on to write
*The Feminine Mystique* and was
the first president of the National
Organization for Women.

ridicule a bridal fair. They carried signs reading "Always a bride, never a
person" and chanted "Confront the whoremakers." In 1971, Anne Koedt,
another New York radical, argued in her pamphlet *The Myth of the Vaginal Orgasm* that women armed with knowledge of their own anatomy
could get satisfaction from "either men *or* women, thus making hetero-
sexuality not an absolute, but an option." The desire for authenticity had
finally led to the biological core of desire itself.[52]

One of the more prominent figures in this mingling of rage and
self-love was Robin Morgan, and her years in the feminist limelight
revealed how heady, and perilous, that combination could be. Morgan,
who belonged to both Radical Women and WITCH, was also the editor of *Sisterhood Is Powerful*, a pioneering anthology of essays by feminists which sold millions of copies around the world. Unlike most radical
celebrities, Morgan, born in 1941, had first experienced a more conventional sort of fame. Beginning at age four, she worked for over a decade
as a popular and well-paid actress. For most of that time, she played a
perfectly dutiful daughter on *Mama*, a sentimental television drama about
a Norwegian immigrant family in turn-of-the-century San Francisco.
Morgan appeared on the cover of *TV Guide* and hawked dolls based on

her character in department stores across the country. "I cheerfully sat in costume," she recalled, "signing photographs for tongue-tied kids and their gushing mothers, all of us surrounded by eerie, smiling, life-size, stuffed versions of myself." By her midteens, Morgan was disgusted with the whole business and left for school, hoping to become a writer.[53]

During the 1960s, she traced a political path similar to that of thousands of other young women who would become active in women's liberation by the end of the decade. During the Kennedy administration, she campaigned hard for liberal Democrats. Then she threw herself into the civil rights movement; by the midsixties, she was organizing against the war. At one point, Morgan and her husband, the poet Kenneth Pitchford, read translations of Vietnamese verses from flatbed trucks parked in different neighborhoods around New York City. From her involvement with the Yippies, the exhibitionist radical cluster assembled by Abbie Hoffman and Jerry Rubin, Morgan developed the knack of staging media-savvy events like the Miss America protest. Only in the nature of her marriage did Morgan diverge from the activist norm: Pitchford was gay, and their affinity was more intellectual than sexual. Still, they had a son together, and the boy evidently developed a precocious interest in narratives about powerful women.[54]

The strength of Morgan's feminist outlook lay in combining a furious rejection of male revolutionaries with an emulation of their universalist vision. In 1970, as a member of WITCH, she penned a manifesto, "Goodbye to All That," which became as widely known as any document by a woman radical since the 1848 declaration at Seneca Falls: "Let's run it on down. White males are responsible for the destruction of human life and environment on the planet today. Yet who is controlling the supposed revolution to change all that?" Included on Morgan's enemies list were young radicals like Jerry Rubin, older ones like Norman Mailer, and a variety of white radical groups dominated by men. "Women are the real Left," Morgan declared with apocalyptic fury. "We are rising, powerful in our unclean bodies . . . wild hair flying, wild eyes staring, wild voices keening . . . this time we will be free or no one will survive."[55]

At the same time, she published essays in *Sisterhood Is Powerful* that displayed the remarkable breadth, demographically and ideologically, of what was still a very young movement. Morgan included "personal testimonies" by a nurse, a reporter, a navy lieutenant, a secretary, and two factory workers; essays by and about black women and Chicanas;

Robin Morgan with the Freedom Trash Can, Miss America protest, Atlantic City, 1968. Morgan, who abandoned a successful career as an actress, became a leader of the radical feminist movement and editor of the best-selling anthology *Sisterhood Is Powerful*.

articles about women in China, self-defense, the politics of housework, prostitution, old age, lesbianism, and Catholicism. The anthology closed with brief documents and poems, including one by an anonymous "seven-year-old woman." If the book were set to music, one might hear in it an echo of the final line of "The Internationale": "we have been naught, we shall be all."[56]

That ecumenical spirit helped radical feminists avoid the bitter, unproductive splits that drove groups like SDS and the Panthers to early deaths. As that reference to a second-grade "woman" suggests, Morgan and her sisters were occasionally guilty of what one historian calls "purist zeal, impatience with compromise, and [a] doleful view of working with men." One result was that they ceded the slow, patient work of legislative reform to liberals of both sexes. But radical feminists were able to resolve many factional tensions by creating new institutions that translated personal politics into beneficial tasks which appealed to large numbers of women all over the country who had little or no taste for parsing doctrinal lines.[57]

As a result, by the midseventies, women's liberation had grown into a counterculture of impressive size and influence. It included hundreds of women's health clinics, where professionals, most of them female, conducted free or low-cost gynecological exams, gave out birth control information, and sometimes performed abortions. *Our Bodies, Ourselves*, a self-help manual for women written by a feminist collective in Boston, quickly grew from a handbook for the initiated into a best-seller translated into over twenty languages. The movement also generated thousands of periodicals ranging from the gritty tabloid *Off Our Backs* to the slick *Ms.*, whose back pages were festooned with three-color corporate ads. Beginning in 1972 at Sarah Lawrence, women's studies programs mushroomed at colleges, both public and private; budding and established scholars alike reoriented old disciplines to take account of what women had done and thought about every conceivable topic. Seemingly everywhere there sprang up rape crisis lines, take-back-the-night marches, and groups of female workers who met to complain about their male superiors—and sometimes make contact with a labor group like Nine to Five, originally the creation of feminists who did clerical work for Harvard University. NOW boasted chapters in every state but Hawaii, and few affiliates bothered to debate the differences between "liberal" and "radical" feminism. They were too busy suing employers for sex discrimination, battling the right-to-life movement, and baring their emotions in consciousness-raising groups—the seedbed of countless local feminist organizations.[58]

One result of this practical turn was the acceptance, even celebration, of what NOW in 1971 called a woman's "right to define and express her own sexuality and to choose her own lifestyle."[59] Most founders of NOW had feared that embrace of what Betty Friedan called "the lavender menace" would send straight women from Middle America fleeing back to their kitchens and typewriters. But once homosexual women and men began to identify themselves in public and demand the same rights as other minority groups, no serious radical could oppose them.

In fact, "the gay liberation front" was, at its inception, an expressly left-wing project. The first group with that name adapted it from the official title of the Vietcong: the National Liberation Front of South Vietnam. It was organized days after the Stonewall Riot, the now iconic battle in Greenwich Village between police and patrons of a gay bar that took place one hot night in June 1969. The confrontation may have begun when a transvestite escaped arrest by jumping out of a paddy wagon and shouting, "Nobody's gonna fuck with me!" The parallel with the militant spirit that animated black power, draft resistance, and feminism was obvious. Soon, GLF chapters began distributing buttons and posters announcing "Gay is good." Increasing numbers of gay people "came out" to friends, family members, and co-workers. As Allen Ginsberg had understood when he wrote "Howl," coming out was a logical consequence of the urge for personal authenticity that had spurred the young left to action in the first place. By 1976, gay student groups already existed on a quarter of American college campuses, and "gay pride" marches were being staged in major cities on both coasts. A decade later, both would be common all over the Western world.[60]

Radical gay activism proved to be a far greater success than the cautious style of organizing which had preceded it. Starting in 1950, members of a homophile movement had been quietly meeting, usually in single-sex groups, to propose changes in laws that prohibited gay lovemaking and allowed the federal government and other employers to fire homosexuals virtually at will. The Mattachine Society and the Daughters of Bilitis—whose quaint names were derived from medieval and classical sources in part to camouflage their purpose—asked only that "education" dispel "erroneous taboos and prejudices" which prevented those of "variant" sensibilities from full "integration" in American society. They were careful not to demand the freedom to live one's erotic life as one pleased. Neither did Bayard Rustin, whose often furtive homosexual encounters made him and the civil rights movement vulnerable to media exposure.[61]

Some gay liberationists, revealing their origins in the New Left, also made claims that seemed designed to enrage and alienate those who did not share their views. "Feminism is the theory, lesbianism is the practice"—the motto attributed to Ti-Grace Atkinson, a New York City activist—pressured straight women either to break all intimate ties with men or to accept a lesser status in the feminist movement. The gut-checking maneuver was reminiscent of the Black Panther and Weatherman injunction to "pick up the gun," although with no hint of violence.

Such tensions did little to retard the progress of a cause which was, at once, quite simple and breathtakingly radical. Never before had millions of people demanded the freedom to behave in ways that nearly every civilization defined as morally evil and a threat to the future of the race. What is more, they wanted that choice to gain the same respect granted to one's race, nation, and gender. Gay liberation kept growing because, as the critic-historian Paul Berman writes, "it was a movement for the right to love . . . all that was needed was to announce the basic concept of rights for gays—and followers were going to flock to the cause and were going to brush off the nonsense . . ."[62] The movement adopted the most attractive and perhaps most American element in the ideology of the New Left: the expansion of individual liberty into every sphere of private life. In turning defense of the most intimate acts into a political movement, lesbians and gay men gained a measure of cultural power by denying they wanted anything more than to be left alone to love as they pleased.

## EARTH FIRST?

Unlike the other mass movements which bloomed during the 1960s, environmentalism did not emerge from the ideological hothouse of the left. Its forerunners were such upper-class conservationists as John Muir and Harold Ickes who wanted to protect the pristine, natural world from the corrupting forces of humanity. They helped bequeath a legacy of national parks, forests, and hiking trails to the nation. But neither they nor groups like the Sierra Club, which they founded, challenged the gospel of capitalist growth itself. Here and there, individuals crusaded for a different agenda: in the early decades of the twentieth century, Dr. Alice Hamilton, a Hull House veteran and Harvard professor, worked to ban such industrial poisons as lead and phosphorus. But she defined her mission as improving the public health of workers, not cleansing the earth. In her 1962 best-seller, *Silent Spring*, the biologist Rachel Carson forced Americans to recognize the perils of pesticides—and was amazed to hear some critics accuse her of Communist sympathies. After all, she was warning against the destructive effects of believing that "nature exists for the convenience of man"—a delusion as common among Marxists as among free marketeers.[63]

Still, New Leftists who deplored the culture of "materialism" were already environmentalists in spirit; by the end of the 1960s, many explicitly added saving the earth to their protests and their vision. Radical ecology had both a collective and an individualist cast. In solidarity with exploited communities, anti-war activists lambasted the air force for destroying the forests of Vietnam (and injuring the bodies of people on

both sides of the war) with such herbicides as Agent Orange. Local organizers accused big companies of dumping their wastes on neighborhoods
of the poor. At the same time, many young radicals were eager, as always,
to experiment with personal change. Struggling to craft authentic and
socially responsible lives, they took to growing their own food, fixing old
cars instead of buying new ones, and setting up small, nonprofit businesses to build and serve a countercultural market.

For several months in 1970, I lived in a left-wing "collective" of a
dozen people in Portland, Oregon. We raised an organic garden, shared
a single battered Volkswagen bus, and published a radical weekly that
both cheered on armed revolution abroad and condemned Weyer-
hauser, the giant paper company, for destroying the region's forests. We
also volunteered at the People's Food Store, which eschewed corporate
products, and a restaurant, the Stomach, that served neither meat nor
dishes made with white sugar or white flour.[64]

But unlike the future demand for "natural" products, the growth potential of the ecological left was limited by its critique of growth. In urging
everyone to consume less and share what they had, white radicals were
clashing with the needs of most African Americans and other "third world"
people with whom they ardently sympathized. When activists at San Jose
State College burned a new car in protest, they angered the black student
group on campus. George Wiley, black leader of the major welfare rights
organization, worried that curbs on growth would make it even harder for
"the poorest people" to "be able to live decently." Meanwhile, white labor
unionists already wary of what they took to be the unpatriotic tenor of
anti-war marches lashed out at this new movement that seemed willing to
sacrifice high-wage jobs in lumbering, mining, and oil refining to protect
small animals and plants. The slogan "No work, no food—eat an envi-
ronmentalist" sprouted on bumpers in timber towns around the Pacific
Northwest. While young radicals fretted about their anti-labor image,
they had no well-paying, ecologically responsible occupations to offer.[65]

What's more, the direction of the environmental movement was not
theirs to decide. The political flavor of the first Earth Day on April 22,
1970, provided clear evidence of that. Even in a era of mass protests,
it was an extraordinary occasion. As many as twenty million Americans
participated in some way—from singing along with Pete Seeger and Phil
Ochs at a rally next to the Washington Monument, to attending a campus teach-in, passing out flowers on the street, riding horses down a busy

highway, and dumping oil into an elegant pool outside the headquarters of Standard Oil in downtown San Francisco, to rising at dawn to apologize to God for befouling his creation.

But the message of Earth Day was as muted as it was broad. Although many of its organizers came from the anti-war movement, they were careful not to pin blame for the environmental mess on any single nexus of power or group in the population. In its playful insistence, the slogan "Earth—love it or leave it!" neither attacked anyone nor exempted anyone from doing their part. This even included Richard Nixon, archenemy of every liberal and leftist in the land. Earlier that year, the president, in his State of the Union address, had implored Americans to "make our peace with nature" by making "reparations for the damage we have done to our air, to our land and to our water." In July, he created the Environmental Protection Agency.[66]

How did radicals respond to this explosion of good intentions? Some well-known voices on the left refused to applaud any cause Nixon could favor. I. F. Stone dismissed Earth Day as "a gigantic snowjob" that diverted attention from the U.S. assault on Vietnam, while *Ramparts*, the New Left's glossy, mass-circulation magazine, called it "the first step in a con game that will do little more than abuse the environment further." But to call millions of reform-minded people pawns in a grand conspiracy was both an insult and a dead end. More promising were efforts to show how the system encouraged a way of life that bolstered the power and profit of elites *and* imperiled the future of the world. In his 1971 book, *The Lorax*, Dr. Seuss portrayed a factory that ruined a once-idyllic land by producing the "thneed," a ridiculous-looking, if popular, garment that no one really needed. Seuss's concluding advice—"Unless someone like you cares a whole awful lot, nothing is going to get better. It's not"—may have been inspired by Earth Day, but *The Lorax*'s view of big business had a tougher, more confrontational edge.[67]

The most prominent figure to develop this view was the microbiologist Barry Commoner. Dubbed the "Paul Revere of Ecology" by *Time* magazine in a 1970 cover story, the bespectacled, gray-haired, fifty-two-year-old professor seemed, on the surface, a rather unusual leader for a tendency that appealed mainly to the young and iconoclastic. By the first Earth Day, Commoner had spent most of his career teaching science at Washington University in St. Louis, hardly a center of radical activism. His age and appearance undoubtedly made it easier for

Barry Commoner, accepting the Citizens' Party nomination for president, 1980.
As an activist researcher, the biologist helped alert the public to the perils of nuclear
testing and became the Paul Revere of the nascent ecology movement. But the
third party he briefly led was an utter failure.

him to gain attention when he charged that "a phalanx of powerful economic, political, and social forces" had caused the environmental "crisis" and that the only cure lay in "sweeping social change . . . designed in the workshop of rational, informed, collective social action."[68]

Commoner had nurtured that outlook as a young man in the Popular Front. During the late 1930s, the son of Russian-Jewish immigrants had taken part in rallies to support unions and the Spanish Republic and to protest lynchings. As a Harvard graduate student, he had helped establish a chapter of the American Association of Scientific Workers, a small but energetic group that advocated socialized medicine and condemned racist anthropology. Like most other Popular Front groups, this self-described "unifying body for all progressive-minded scientists" fell apart after the Nazi-Soviet pact. But it helped teach Commoner how to use his scientific skills for political ends.[69]

In the 1950s, as a critic of the Cold War, he helped fashion an innovative form of scientific activism. The U.S. military's tests of nuclear weapons in the Nevada desert and the South Pacific had raised public concern about the hazards of radiation. But there was little hard evidence to back up that fear. So in 1958, Commoner led a group of

St. Louis scientists who tested the chemical makeup of thousands of baby teeth. Their research found an alarming buildup of the isotope Strontium 90 in materials consumed by infants and their breast-feeding mothers. The widely publicized study helped spark an anti-nuclear campaign whose size and ideological diversity far outstripped the radical pacifist groups who had been staging lonely protests against the madness of the arms race since the bombing of Hiroshima. In 1963, the larger movement won a partial victory when the U.S. and the USSR signed a treaty that banned all nuclear testing in the atmosphere. Commoner moved on to do research that documented the destructive effects of laundry detergents and mercury on lakes and rivers. By the end of the decade, he was, as *Time* recognized, the best-known ecologist in America, a forceful practitioner of "the subversive science."[70]

But for Commoner, the environmental upsurge was not subversive enough. While thrilled by the massive outpouring on Earth Day, he was also frustrated that no one had advanced a coherent analysis of what had caused the crisis or how it might be solved. So he quickly drafted a manifesto, *The Closing Circle*, for a movement that could liberate humankind while saving the earth: "Suddenly we have discovered what we should have known before: that the ecosphere sustains people and everything that we do; that anything that fails to fit into the ecosphere is a threat to its finely balanced cycles." The only way to survive "assaults on the ecosystem . . . so powerful, so numerous, so finely interconnected" was to abandon "the profit-first mentality of the capitalist economy" that had "driven us down this self-destructive course." Commoner's tone was cooler than that of the New Left; his rhetoric pushed no specific CEO or politician up against a wall of shame. But his plea "to bring the productive system . . . into harmony with the ecosystem" left little doubt about the thrust of his politics.[71]

Published in 1971, *The Closing Circle* sold well but failed to ignite a sizable environmental left. The loose web of outrage at the system that had bound young radical activists together during the height of the Vietnam War had frayed, perhaps beyond repair. While feminists, Maoists, gay liberationists, and advocates of black and Chicano power all agreed that ecology mattered, none thought it mattered enough to alter their rhetoric or their increasingly autonomous strategies for change.

Meanwhile, most Americans shied away from the vision of a new order that would do away with the polluting engines and industries on which their jobs and mobility depended. Encouraged by the mainstream media, lawmakers from both parties, and liberal foundations, a small-scale "fix-it" approach to environmental problems took hold. Recycling garbage and developing more fuel-efficient cars overshadowed larger, structural remedies. Bolstering the theme of the first Earth Day, the mass media and politicians urged everyone to "participate in helping the system work better." Commoner and his supporters kept protesting this retreat to good-neighborliness; by the end of the decade, he was explicitly advocating democratic socialism (along with solar power) as the only way to escape a disastrous energy crisis. But despite a near meltdown at a nuclear plant in Pennsylvania and a spike in oil prices, few Americans thought the hour of doom was near. Unlike Paul Revere, Commoner lacked a people ready to act on his warnings.[72]

Still the eco-socialist was hopeful that, in the fragments that had emerged from the New Left, a fresh version of the Popular Front might be born. In 1980, he ran as the presidential nominee of the new Citizens Party. At its first convention, an unruly affair in which any local group could present its demands, the party cobbled together a platform that Eugene Debs would have been pleased to run on. Under the rubric of "economic democracy," it called for universal health insurance, the nationalization of oil companies and railroads, a huge cut in defense spending, and the right of workers to stop the closing of their factories. Behind Commoner stood a variety of other left figures the media had turned into familiar names: the writer Studs Terkel; Maggie Kuhn of the Gray Panthers; Ed Sadlowski, national leader of dissident steelworkers; and the party's vice presidential candidate, LaDonna Harris, a Comanche activist and the wife of a former Democratic senator from Oklahoma. With funding from a handful of philanthropists, the new party seemed to have an opportunity to demonstrate the electoral clout of a practical left that had abandoned its insurrectionary delusions. The Citizens Party would, vowed Commoner, "provide an alternative for the growing number of dispirited Americans fed up with the major parties."[73]

It proved a different sort of delusion. Frustrated party organizers struggled through the maze of election laws and managed to place Commoner on the ballot in just thirty states. By 1980, liberals had lost any affection they ever had for President Jimmy Carter. But the prospect of Ronald Reagan sitting in the White House with thousands of warheads and the solid backing of the Christian right turned most progressives back, in sorrow, to the lesser evil; others were content to vote for Independent candidate John Anderson, a thoughtful former Republican from Illinois who sounded, at times, like another Adlai Stevenson. These barriers would have been formidable for even an established radical party to surmount. An infant, quasi-socialist group with few loyal followers had no chance to break through. After a strenuous campaign, fewer than 235,000 Americans voted for Barry Commoner—a minuscule .03 percent of the total. Even in "the People's Republic" of Berkeley, he won less than half as many votes as Ronald Reagan, who, as governor of California, had vowed to "clean up the mess" in that city and then dispatched National Guard troops and helicopters to do the job.[74]

The fiasco of the Citizens Party underlined how ill equipped American radicals were to compete in the electoral game, at least under their own name. The switch from calling for revolution by any means necessary in 1970 to struggling to create a third-party coalition a decade later was awkwardly performed and rhetorically unpersuasive. Activists who had once scorned the political system could not, particularly with reduced numbers, revive a strategy that had crested with the Populists and the Socialists in the bygone heyday of industrializing America.

Outside the Soviet bloc, young European leftists had more success in conducting "the long march through the institutions" called for by Rudi Dutschke, a leader of the West German student movement. In the 1970s, some university-trained radicals took blue-collar manufacturing jobs, where they nudged the existing labor left to raise demands for self-management of factories and a shorter working day. Other leftists filtered into the Communist and Socialist parties of many European nations, converting them to feminism, gay rights, and anti-racism. They brought with them a professional brashness and meritocratic attitude that gradually shifted the image of mass parties that had always prided themselves as being of and for the manual-laboring class. In the U.S., something similar occurred in the Democratic Party, especially in large metropolises in the Midwest and on both coasts. But the Democrats had never been a radical party, and an influx of erstwhile protesters from the educated middle class could not make them so. In the U.S., more than in other developed nations, electoral politics remained true to Max Weber's description, "the slow boring of hard boards."[75]

The American New Left had always been a movement dedicated to changing how people thought as much as the structures that employed and governed them. Its impact in that sphere continued to grow, even as the last glimmer of a left-wing third party was extinguished. The injunctions to "question authority" and to challenge "the power elite" attracted millions of people of different classes and regions who never would have considered attending an SDS meeting. The antinomian mood limited what presidents could do abroad. Neither Carter nor Reagan could muster majority support for interventions to topple left-wing revolutions in Central America. Reagan's general popularity did not extend to his view of the Vietnam War as "a noble cause": only a third of the public agreed with that verdict.

Some of Hollywood's most-admired productions helped encourage the skeptics. *M\*A\*S\*H*, the most popular TV show of the late 1970s, conveyed an implicitly anti-war message through characters who mocked the military's mission and discipline and seemed to hold no particular grudge against the Communist enemy. The show was a spinoff of a 1970 movie of the same name, whose screenwriter was Ring Lardner Jr.—a former Communist who had been blacklisted during the early Cold War. *M\*A\*S\*H* was set during the Korean War, but films harshly critical of the Vietnam War itself—such as *Coming Home*, which starred Jane Fonda, and Oliver Stone's *Platoon*, which won the Oscar for Best Picture—attracted large audiences as well.

Meanwhile, the radical vision of personal freedom attracted an increasing number of Americans who had little interest in politics of the conventional kind. In the mid-1970s, the Daniel Yankelovich poll discovered that new attitudes toward authority, sexual morality, and self-fulfillment had spread from elite colleges to much of the younger population. "Indeed," the pollster wrote, "we are amazed by the rapidity with which this process is taking place." These views undergirded the growing acceptance of rights for women, racial minorities, and homosexuals. Baby boomers tended to bequeath their notions of freedom to their children; American culture would never return to its more innocent, or repressive, past.[76]

The most telling examples of this change occurred in the realm of what used to be called "family life." The mass media, initially inclined to dismiss the new feminists with the slur "bra-burners," had made a gradual but dramatic about-face by the end of the 1970s. "Equal pay for equal work" was easily accepted, while young middle-class women routinely expected access to the same education, careers, and compensation as men. Increasingly, women demanded that if men wanted to live and have babies with them, they would have to do their share of the housework and the child-rearing. In 1973, the Supreme Court, in *Roe v. Wade*, ruled that the right to have an abortion was protected by the right to privacy, inflaming a conflict that has never cooled. Other highly charged issues— rape, family violence, incest, sexual harassment—received respectful attention in the media and found their way into the courts, election campaigns, and legislation. The triumphs of the new radicals were thus not simply cultural ones.[77]

But the gender-conscious left also provoked a major backlash and lost some major political battles, among which were the efforts to ratify the Equal Rights Amendment and to use public funds to provide abortions for poor women who wanted them. Meanwhile, the movement for gay liberation that had begun in the U.S. achieved greater political success in Europe, thanks to support from sturdy left parties and the absence of a religious right. By 1990, virtually every non-Communist nation on the continent had decriminalized homosexuality, and many were considering laws to grant full benefits to domestic partners.[78]

In the end, sixties radicals in the U.S. were unable to gain the political clout that might have reinforced their cultural influence and prevented the rise of the political right. More than any left since the Civil War, their movements tried hard to look American society straight in the face and challenge its wrenching injustices of race, sexuality, violence, and egotism—all of which were displayed on an international stage. For New Leftists, politics was everywhere, and the urgency of making the world anew raised a standard that was difficult to live up to and impossible for other Americans to ignore, even if they detested its bearers. The young radicals, writes Paul Berman, spoke "for a tiny fugitive moment" to "the moral quandary that afflicts the reasonably prosperous population everywhere in the democratic world, or ought to afflict it—the feeling of ethical emptiness that now and then descends upon people as they go about their private lives."[79]

But the movement gained few allies in the broad white majority, aside from a few unionists still eager to intensify the "class struggle." Having dismissed patriotism as a smokescreen for imperialist war and the squelching of dissent, the New Left made little headway in the electoral arena, where the promise of America and the need to defend the nation from foreign foes were taken for granted. Worse, the movement's general contempt for national symbols provided Richard Nixon, Ronald Reagan, and like-minded conservatives with an opportunity to brand all foes of military intervention as naïve at best and treasonous at worst. So those who rebelled against an old, alienated society ended up alienating far too many of the people they would need to construct a new one. They never found the new "agencies of change" Clancy Sigal was searching for.

They did, however, succeed in placing themselves at the head of a broad wave of modernist revolt. One day in the spring of 1968, Marshall Berman, who was then a radical student, asked Lionel Trilling his opinion of the SDS-led strike taking place at Columbia—with its furious slogans and colorful banners, its erotic energy and rock music. "It's modernism in the streets," replied the eminent literary scholar. Later, Berman reflected, "It made some ultimate sense for modernism to be alive in the streets; engaging with one's time, putting oneself on the line, was where a modernist should be."[80]

Although the New Left attracted far more recruits than had the Village modernists a half century before, they also raised more hackles. And unlike John Reed and Margaret Sanger, there was no proletarian left to defend them. Most American voters could not sympathize with a rebellion that seemed confined to brash young people, whether they lived in college towns, black ghettos, or rural communes. To champion tearing down all the walls and rules that prevented an individual from expressing his or her authentic being—sexually, racially, or ecologically—ignored the behavior many people from humble backgrounds thought was needed to bring order to disorderly lives. "They say this is a strict school," an assistant principal at a working-class high school told a visiting sociologist in 1969. "That's true, and the reason is that once you start bending and getting permissive . . . so many of these kids [will] come to nothing."[81]

Young radicals had hoped to replace a corrupt, violent system with one dedicated to face-to-face, interracial democracy, one that, as the Port Huron Statement put it, would treat men and women "as infinitely precious and possessed of unfulfilled capacities for reason, freedom, and love." But, notwithstanding some prodigious achievements, they did more to discredit the old liberal order than to lay the foundation for a new one. Conservatives who grasped the opportunity to lead one of the two major political parties would take it from there.[82]

# Chapter Seven

# REBELS WITHOUT A MOVEMENT,
# 1980s–2010

> Oh Karl the world isn't fair
> It isn't and never will be
> They tried out your plan
> It brought misery instead
> If you'd seen how they worked it
> You'd be glad you are dead
> Just like I'm living in the land of the free
> Where the rich just get richer
> And the poor you don't ever have to see
> It would depress us, Karl
> Because we care
> That the world still isn't fair
>
> —Randy Newman, 1999[1]

> Culture is the Ho Chi Minh trail of power; you surrender that province and you lose America.
>
> —Patrick Buchanan, 1993[2]

## NO FAILURE LIKE SUCCESS

ON A COLD DAY in mid-January 2009, Pete Seeger and Bruce Springsteen celebrated the impending inauguration of Barack Obama on the steps of the Lincoln Memorial with a passionate version of "This Land Is Your Land." Although Seeger was eighty-nine and frail, he wore only a flannel shirt and knit cap to protect him against the shining winter chill. Backed by a multiracial youth chorus, the two men sang not just the lines familiar to millions of schoolchildren ("As I was walking a ribbon of highway . . .") but the two "radical" verses Guthrie had written during the Great Depression to protest the immorality of capitalism:

In the squares of the city—In the shadow of the steeple
By the relief office—I saw my people
As they stood there hungry. I stood there whistling
This land was still made for you and me.

A great high wall there that tried to stop me;
A great big sign there said private property;
But on the other side it didn't say nothing;
That side was made for you and me.

Obama and his family tried to sing along, and the vast crowd cheered. Then Tiger Woods strolled out to introduce the next act: the Naval Academy Glee Club. No journalist seems to have remarked on the contrast: Seeger and Springsteen had simply given another performance in a "star-studded" concert entitled "We Are One." Tough lyrics penned by a Communist, sung by his old friend, a former Communist, and accompanied by one of the most popular musicians in the world vanished into the frigid air.[3]

The lack of controversy hinted at both the ubiquity and the weakness of American leftists, most of whom had greeted Obama's election more warmly than that of any president since Franklin Roosevelt in 1936. Seventy years later, such critics as Michael Moore, Barbara Ehrenreich, Noam Chomsky, and Howard Zinn had gained a foothold in popular culture; their undiluted attacks on the nation's health-care system, its job market, its foreign policy, and its image as an authentic democracy sold millions of copies or, in Moore's case, tickets. Meanwhile, in academia, interpretations of history and literature associated with the New Left in the 1960s were so dominant that young conservatives shied away from those disciplines, believing a conspiracy of "tenured radicals" would prevent them from ever landing a teaching job.

What is more, the new radicals and their ideological offshoots—black power, feminism, gay liberation—had left a profound and seemingly permanent imprint on daily life. Few people denied the virtue of equal rights, whether for individuals or for groups with a sizable lobby behind them. As a consequence, by the early twenty-first century most ordinary Americans enjoyed a degree of personal freedom that would have been considered ultra-radical in the 1960s. Women could pursue almost any occupation they chose; increasingly, gays and lesbians no longer had to lie about their sexuality; racial identity posed no legal barrier to full participation in civil society; and the urgency of protecting the environment was taken for granted. Employers and politicians alike accepted the norms of "multiculturalism"; ignoring them or applying them insensitively could damage a profit margin or end a career.

"Making values explicit" should be the central task of politics, declared the drafters of the Port Huron Statement in 1962. "We regard *men* as infinitely precious and possessed of unfulfilled capacities for reason, freedom, and love." That sentence (its gender bias aside) captured, with an aptly romantic tone, how the New Left came to believe a better society would be built: radical democrats would liberate themselves by expanding the definition of freedom itself. That impulse sometimes led to forms of "identity politics" that descended into self-parody. But an expanded and durable meaning of "freedom" did win the day. As the philosopher Richard Rorty wrote, the New Left greatly diminished the amount of sadism in American life. And it drove conservative traditionalists like Patrick Buchanan to shudder that the culture he loved would soon be no more.[4]

Max Eastman and his fellow editors at *The Masses* would probably have been pleased. Their desire for a witty, anti-authoritarian, modernist temperament that showed "no respect for the respectable" had become a dominant strain in the nation's culture. Yet, by the close of the twentieth century, the movement organizations that young radicals created in the 1960s and '70s—SDS, SNCC, the Black Panther Party, the Gay Liberation Front—had all gone out of business and fashion.

Several veterans of the abortive revolution did remake themselves into liberal Democrats who knew how to win elections. Tom Hayden spent eighteen years as a California state legislator, although he failed in races for governor of the state and mayor of Los Angeles. Bobby Rush, once the "deputy minister of defense" of the Illinois Black Panther Party, was elected to Congress in 1992; eight years later, he easily defeated Barack Obama in a Democratic primary to retain his seat in a largely African-American district. As increasingly powerful members of the governing class, Rush and other black officials had no motivation to fire up a fresh insurgency of the inner-city poor. Individual feminists and environmentalists abounded, but the professional lobbyists among them had little time for musing about an ungendered world or a sustainable, postcapitalist one. They were too anxious about preserving abortion rights and stopping humans from smothering the earth in carbon.

Ralph Nader ran three independent campaigns for the presidency, hoping to spur alarm and protest about the "small numbers of large corporations . . . playing roulette with the planet." But he managed only to draw votes away from Democrats, which in 2000 enabled George W. Bush to win Florida and, with it, the White House. As the right took power, leftists who still dreamed about building a new world of equals seemed naïve, if not delusional.[5]

One little-noticed casualty of these diminished expectations was the narrowing and blurring of ideological identities. Americans who had once proudly called themselves "liberals" took refuge in the "progressive" label, unburdened by memories of Henry Wallace's 1948 campaign, most of whose foot soldiers were CP members or fellow travelers. On the offensive, conservatives acquired the pernicious habit of describing the leadership of the Democratic Party simply as "the left." Soon the mainstream media followed along, squeezing everyone from Bill Clinton to Noam Chomsky under the same saggy terminological umbrella. "Radical," once a term of honor for those who sought to extirpate the outmoded and the harmful, now referred primarily to violent actors of any political persuasion—whether inspired by Hitler, Mao, or Osama bin Laden.[6]

All this posed a dilemma for would-be heirs of the historic left. Many of their ideas about how individual Americans should treat one another had become the conventional wisdom of the land; "the free development of each" was hailed and practiced across the ideological spectrum. But as respect for the individual rights of everyone advanced, the advocacy of collective uplift and economic equality receded further. Unions gradually lost both numbers and much of their ability to influence public debate and policy—even as a group of former New Leftists quietly made careers as labor organizers and officials.

Even more than in the 1960s, the left visible to most Americans was composed almost entirely of well-educated professionals and their offspring, with some support from those near the bottom of society, particularly in black and Latino communities. Members of this "new class" had abandoned their fantasies about making a revolution but still found ways to make a decent living by doing good. They staffed environmental organizations, liberal foundations, public health lobbies, and community-organizing networks. The ranks of public-interest lawyers mushroomed, as class-action suits became a central device for challeng-

ing the power of corporations. Meanwhile, left-wing believers tried
to refresh the social gospel in three of the nation's oldest Protestant
denominations—the United Church of Christ (successor to the Congre-
gationalists), the Episcopalians, and the United Methodists—although
adherents to conservative churches rapidly outnumbered them.

As an Ivy League graduate who became a community organizer in a
rust-belt city, Barack Obama was an exemplar of the more sober left that
navigated through the shoals of the 1980s and after. He exchanged his
youthful admiration for Malcolm X for an appreciation of the small-bore
objectives of Saul Alinsky. Then he moved on to Harvard Law School
and a quick ascent through the progressive wing of the Democratic
Party. In his 2008 campaign, Obama frequently placed himself and his
campaign within the tradition of the black freedom movement and other
insurgencies that, often with radicals in the lead, "had pointed the way
to the promised land . . . to justice and equality." But he did so as a man
of the center left in a political universe still dominated by conservative
views about taxes, unions, and the military. To paraphrase a line from
Bob Dylan (who idolized Woody Guthrie), the post-1980 left discovered
there was no success like failure, and failure felt like no success at all.[7]

## SOLIDARITY IS NOT ENOUGH

Radicals were certainly not absent from politics during the Reagan era.
They worked to cut off external funding for the apartheid regime in
South Africa and for counterrevolutionaries in Central America. Students on dozens of campuses organized to ban clothing that bore the
name of their colleges which was made in overseas sweatshops. "Global
justice" became the rallying cry of a transnational insurgency, including a
large detachment of Americans. All these activists thought they belonged
to social *movements;* since the 1960s, the noun itself had become ubiquitous on both the left and the right. But in reality, most leftists were
engaged only in *campaigns.* Each united large numbers of "progressives"
in the hope of achieving a virtuous but limited objective. Each devolved,
after a spurt of well-publicized activity, into a small, dedicated activist
core. Despite dogged efforts, intellectual and practical, no new or strong
political left was born.

Given the historical context, the failure was not really the campaigners' fault. Every past left had been able to make a moral argument

about an inescapable problem, one that touched the conscience and/or self-interest of most Americans. From 1830 to 1975, there was an uninterrupted series of such problems—from slavery to monopoly to mass unemployment to fascism to legal racism to the war in Vietnam and the continuing inequality of women. Each issue, in turn, spawned thousands of leftists and attracted reformist supporters, both inside and outside government. But nothing so big or important emerged during the final quarter of the twentieth century. Meanwhile, conservatives built a powerful, durable movement to deregulate business and protect "family values." With the solid support of several big corporations and hundreds of megachurches, they forced radicals to play defense and to blur their differences with the liberals who were bearing the brunt of attacks from the right.

One progressive campaign in the Reagan era did manage to achieve its goal: South Africa became an interracial democracy. It was a long time in coming. During the late 1940s, black American radicals in the Council on African Affairs began exposing the brutal nature of the Afrikaner regime, which had just won its independence from Great Britain. The council, which was led by W. E. B. DuBois and Paul Robeson, got bullied by Red hunters and was dissolved in 1955. A decade later, SDS organized a mass picket and sit-in at the headquarters of Chase Manhattan bank, which floated major loans to South Africa; both Martin Luther King Jr. and SNCC demanded sanctions against a government whose "barbarism" King compared to that of Nazi Germany. But the urgent need to oppose the war in Vietnam soon eclipsed every other international issue.[8]

Only in the early 1980s did growing revulsion against apartheid crest into a powerful campaign, both in the U.S. and abroad. Thousands of students courted arrest to demand that their universities divest from any company that did business in South Africa. For over a year, waves of demonstrators, including several members of Congress, staged sit-ins at the Pretoria government's elegant embassy on Massachusetts Avenue in Washington, D.C. Popular artists and athletes observed a strict ban on performances in what had become an outlaw country. "It's time to accept our responsibility," sang Steven Van Zandt, a member of Springsteen's band. "Freedom is a privilege nobody rides for free / Look around the world baby it can't be denied / Why are we always on the wrong side?" In 1990, the South African government gave in to enormous worldwide pressure and released Nelson Mandela from jail. Four years later, he was elected president of his nation.[9]

Finding an answer to Van Zandt's anti-imperialist question was never central to the coalition he had joined. Randall Robinson, whose group TransAfrica spearheaded the embassy sit-ins, was a radical who supported "armed struggle" against white rule and demanded that the U.S. pay reparations to its own black citizens. But anti-apartheid quickly turned into a grand liberal cause, an emotional extension of the civil rights consensus forged in the 1960s. The Free South Africa Movement, which organized protests in Washington and twenty-six other cities, had been launched in 1984 at a meeting held inside the Rayburn House Office Building on Capitol Hill. A few months after Mandela was released, he embarked on a speaking tour of the U.S. which included a talk to a joint session of Congress. None of this brought Randall Robinson much satisfaction. In 2001, he moved to the Caribbean island of St. Kitts, explaining, "I was really worn down by an American society that is racist, smugly blind to it, and hugely self-satisfied." Still the campaign he helped organize had translated a demand first raised by black Marxists into one that anyone to the left of Ronald Reagan could happily endorse.[10]

Opponents of U.S. policy toward Central America in the late 1970s and early 1980s faced a more difficult challenge. At a time of renewed intensity in the Cold War, they ardently sympathized with a guerrilla movement in El Salvador and a revolutionary government in Nicaragua, both of which were backed by Communists around the world. As in the case of South Africa, solidarity workers had certain moral advantages: in 1980, a right-wing death squad aligned with the U.S. assassinated Oscar Romero, the archbishop of San Salvador, as he celebrated mass; the prelate had been urging soldiers to refuse orders to kill civilians. In Nicaragua, the Sandinistas overthrew a corrupt dictator and ruled, at first, with the clear support of their people. So a broad, anti-interventionist front akin to that which had helped end the war in Vietnam seemed possible.

Big differences soon became apparent. Reagan was not about to send U.S. troops to battle another guerrilla army or to shed their blood in support of the Contras in Nicaragua, whom he praised as "freedom fighters." Left activists took impressive, novel steps to advance their cause: some churches offered sanctuary to Central American refugees, Witness for Peace volunteers traveled to war zones to shield Nicaraguans from Contra attacks, and campaigners peppered reporters with well-informed rebuttals to administration positions. Left-wing Christians, most of whom were soft-spoken, middle-aged pacifists, were more prominent than during the protests of the the Vietnam era. Their respectability may have helped convince a majority of Americans to oppose Reagan's policy.

But as long as American "boys" stayed out of combat, few of their fellow citizens really cared. In a raging debate between two small, equally vehement camps, the one that held state power would prevail. Through the 1980s, the Republican administration continued to finance the anti-Communist government in El Salvador and, despite mounting opposition in Congress, kept arming the Contras. We "made a big fight out of something that otherwise would have been a non-issue," claimed one anti-interventionist. Others consoled themselves that they had "faithfully acted upon their convictions and principles." Solidarity, no matter how moral and well defended, had not been nearly enough.[11]


The new conservative era did produce one salutary change: economics and class injustice again became vital matters for the left. Hundreds of radicals broke out of their academic, countercultural cocoon and went to work for labor unions, as organizers, publicists, attorneys, and in-house educators. Others, having schooled themselves in the complexities of world trade and manufacturing, accused such U.S.-led bodies as the World Bank, the World Trade Organization, and the International Monetary Fund of exacerbating the very poverty and inequality they were supposed to be healing. This shift to material concerns had multiple causes: the desire of middle-class activists to heal the breach with blue-collar Americans, labor's need for dedicated helpers as its numbers and political clout declined, a yawning gap between wage earners and the rich, and the omnipresence of global corporations.

In truth, the relationship between organized labor and the New Left had rarely been as hostile as the infamous 1970 attack by New York construction workers on anti-war protesters made it seem. The Port Huron Statement was ratified at a summer camp owned by the United Auto Workers. The UAW and other liberal unions then helped finance the grassroots campaigns of both SNCC and SDS during the early 1960s. Later in the decade, radicals who rooted for a Vietcong victory were shunned in white working-class neighborhoods. But they were still welcome to mobilize support for strikes that took place in 1970 at General

Electric and the U.S. Postal Service—and for the national grape boycott which made the United Farm Workers, led by Cesar Chavez, a favorite cause of every progressive in the land.

By the 1980s, the number of talented activist-intellectuals who cast their lot with unions approached a level not seen since the 1930s. The new breed included Paul Booth, a former SDS vice president who became a key leader of AFSCME, the public employees union; Karen Nussbaum, a feminist whose Boston-based group Nine to Five recruited women office workers; and Bill Fletcher Jr., an outspoken black socialist hired as education director of the AFL-CIO. Andrew Stern, who in the midnineties became head of the Service Employees International Union (the SEIU), the largest union in America, had come to college in 1968 expecting to study business but instead joined a series of radical movements. Erstwhile New Leftists approached their union work as they had their earlier political passions: as both an intellectual challenge and a calling.[12]

These activists, together with rank-and-filers frustrated by the old guard's failure to reverse labor's dwindling power in the workplace, brought a new spirit and imagination to organizing. "Put the movement back in the labor movement" was their slogan. They mounted "corporate campaigns" based on intensive research that forced anti-union firms to explain their skirting of environmental, safety, and overtime pay laws. They created "Justice for Janitors," a drive by the SEIU in Los Angeles and other cities, which staged demonstrations at a golf course and a chic restaurant to embarrass employers at play into bargaining with their poorly paid, mostly immigrant workers. And they aligned their unions with opponents of President Reagan's policies in the Third World. One erstwhile New Leftist commented, "Within organized labor, an institution not always known for the richness of its intellectual life, the marketplace for new ideas has greatly expanded even as unions have shrunk."[13]

In 1995, the new labor left helped elect John Sweeney president of the AFL-CIO, hoping the white-haired veteran of union wars and his "New Voice" team could reverse the movement's long slide. Academic allies put on a series of crowded teach-ins where such speakers as Betty Friedan, the philosopher Richard Rorty, and the critic-activist Cornel West hailed the birth of "a movement to transcend the separate interests, the special interests, even the very good interests of identity politics," as Friedan called it. "I have a pretty good Geiger counter," announced the celebrated feminist on returning to what had been her original cause, ". . . and that counter is clicking again, because I think we are on the verge of something new."[14]

But all the fresh energy could not pierce through external barriers that had grown quite solid over time. At the turn of the century, tech entrepreneurs like Bill Gates and Steve Jobs were the face of big capital; in their wonkish style and the dazzling products they brought to market, they were quite unlike the arrogant industrialists whom the CIO had grappled with, often successfully, during the New Deal. Meanwhile, clever corporate managers deployed every means, legal and otherwise, to stymie major organizing drives. In the 1990s, a band of union radicals launched the Labor Party in hopes of pressuring the Clinton administration and perhaps running its own candidates for local office. But with firmly anti-union conservatives at the helm of the GOP, the only course Sweeney and other union leaders could realistically follow was to campaign for and donate to Democrats, even those whose voting records did not match their friendly rhetoric.

It had been half a century since a class-conscious mentality had galvanized the left and spread its spirit through American culture. Despite their steady work, the new breed of union activist did not succeed in changing the popular image of leftists forged in the 1960s: college-educated rebels who had little in common with "ordinary people." In this arena, too, solidarity proved inadequate to the task at hand.

In the 1990s, a new campaign for "global justice" struggled to keep the communitarian, internationalist vision of the left alive. Activists, most of whom were under thirty, announced their resistance to all forces they believed were causing and benefiting from economic misery: multinational businesses, rich states in thrall to the free-market gospel, and a status quo in which "the wealth of the world's 475 billionaires was greater than the combined incomes of the poorest half of humanity." The insurgents' zeal to touch off a mass democratic awakening was matched by the variety of their identities: "ethical shareholders, culture jammers, street reclaimers, McUnion organizers, human-rights activists, school-logo fighters, and Internet corporate watchdogs."[15]

Naomi Klein, the author of that jaunty roll call, had leftism woven deeply into her genes. Two of her Jewish grandparents had been American Communists, her mother was a feminist filmmaker, and her father

Naomi Klein, c. 2008. Photograph by Debra Friedman. Klein is one of the most influential and popular writers in the movement against global capitalism.

was an anti-nuclear activist. Just before Klein's birth in 1970, her parents had emigrated to Montreal to escape the draft.

Klein's ironic wit suited the sensibility of a new generation of North American radicals. In 1999, she published an anti-capitalist manifesto with the deceptively modest title *No Logo: Taking Aim at the Brand Bullies*. Klein was aiming at a grander target than the ubiquitous brand names stitched, printed, or pixeled on everything from skyscrapers to sweatshirts—like the one worn by the adorable blond toddler who appears on the book's cover. She intended "to analyze and document the forces opposing corporate rule, and to lay out the particular set of cultural and economic conditions that made the emergence of that opposition inevitable." As her roll call of resisting groups implied, consumer activists would lead the charge; seldom did Klein mention how workers for those largely non-union corporations might take part. A hip Marxist text for young readers whose entire lives had been saturated in mass culture, *No Logo* sold more than a million copies and was translated into over twenty languages.[16]

The roughly fifty thousand demonstrators who took to the streets of Seattle in the fall of 1999 to shut down a meeting of the World Trade Organization seemed bent on making Klein look like a prophet. They came from grassroots environmental organizations, consumer lobbies, progressive churches, anarchist "affinity groups"—and several industrial unions. Some wore hard hats, while others dressed up in turtle costumes to dramatize the eroding habitat of sea reptiles. The putative anti-corporate alliance of "Teamsters and turtles" briefly caught the imagination of the mass media. If blue-collar militants continued to work closely with middle-class green crusaders, this would become a new left to reckon with. Whatever their differences of ideology and background, all the protesters agreed, as had the Populists in the 1890s, that big business had gained sway over national governments and local communities and that it cherished no value save the bottom line.[17]

But in the U.S., the infant global justice campaign failed to rise out of its cradle. Attempts to repeat the Seattle events at subsequent meetings of the IMF and the World Bank attracted only a few thousand people and hardly any unionists. The media focused on street brawls between police and small bands of black-garbed anarchists rather than on the issues they were shouting about. Even before the terrorist attacks of September 11, 2001, abruptly changed the subject, the new cause had dwindled into a niche concern.[18]

The issues were at the core of the problem. Far more Americans feared losing their jobs to low-wage foreign competitors or their pensions to falling stock prices than were ready to act on behalf of men and women making running shoes in Dacca and polo shirts in Santo Domingo or a species endangered in a place they couldn't even locate on a map. And the alleged misdeeds of international traders, unlike apartheid or the murder of an archbishop, were not self-evident; they required a period of study and argument which only those already inclined to radical activism were likely to undergo. "Economics and politics have been kept falsely separate," explained Kevin Danaher, co-founder of Global Exchange, a center of post-Seattle organizing. "We're just trying to drag capital investment decision-making out into the public realm." He acknowledged "the difficulty of understanding what it is that an institution like the World Bank even does."[19]

Finding a compelling alternative to the unjust global order was no less difficult. Communism had been thoroughly discredited by the collapse of the Soviet bloc and the rise of "market-Leninism" in China, and "socialism" sounded both vague and old-fashioned. "Who wants to be taken for a glassy-eyed sectarian newspaper pusher?" asked one anti-sweatshop journalist. In 2000, two radical theorists, Michael Hardt and Antonio Negri, published a big book called *Empire*, whose rarefied analysis of the current world economy and culture some intemperate enthusiasts likened to *Capital*. But Karl Marx had been certain the international proletariat would soon become the human race; through the middle of the twentieth century, millions of people in dozens of nations, sincerely if erroneously, agreed. Hardt and Negri could only hold out the abstract hope that "*the multitude's ultimate demand for global citizenship*" would be realized. Inevitably, their moment of celebrity was brief.[20]

In the afterglow of the Seattle protests, anarchism became an appealing option to some young radicals. As an impulse, it possessed the same rebellious, antinomian spirit that had animated Albert Parsons and Emma Goldman a century earlier and the New Left in more recent times. Anarchists offered a principled alternative to the collusion between "neo-liberal" governments and rapacious corporations, and they took "direct action" against the rich and the powerful instead of just analyzing their crimes. Black-garbed demonstrators sought to demystify authority by committing civil disobedience, spray-painting large A's on downtown buildings, and occasionally egging on police to attack them. They were proud of their ability to stage events without either permanent organizations or elected leaders.

Yet they forgot or had never learned the first lesson of political strategy: to consider how the changes they desired might come about. "I definitely respect anarchist ways of organizing," Juliette Beck, a thoughtful young activist, told *The New Yorker* in the spring of 2000. "But the real question is: Can this anarchist model that's working so well now for organizing protests be applied on an international scale to create the democratic decision-making structures that we need to eliminate poverty?" Even then, the answer was obvious.[21]

### THE HUMANITIES INTERNATIONAL

While the shouts of Seattle soon faded to whimpers, the fame and influence of one particular anarchist continued to grow. Noam Chomsky would never join a rowdy street march or scrawl defiant slogans on the wall of a corporate headquarters. The means of protest favored by this admirer of Mikhail Bakunin was wholly cerebral: to accumulate details of the lies told and offenses committed by governing and media elites and to present them in print (mostly for small radical presses) and before large audiences all over the world. In the process, the soft-spoken MIT professor, who made his reputation as a pathbreaking linguist, emerged as the one of the best-known, if always controversial, figures on an American left that no longer could muster the ideological coherence or anger at injustice necessary to building a mass movement.[22]

The simultaneous rise of Chomsky and weakness of the left were not coincidental. His withering indictment of American politics and society held out little hope for a revival of grassroots radicalism. Since he became a leading intellectual critic of the Vietnam War in the late 1960s, Chomsky had persistently argued that states act malignly and that the more powerful the state, the more malign will be its actions. "Any form of authority requires justification," he once told a journalist. "It's not self justified. And the justification can rarely be given." Chomsky published exposés of the Indonesian massacre of thousands of people in East Timor in the mid-1970s and of Israel's policies toward the Palestinians, but he turned his fact-filled wrath primarily against the makers of American foreign policy. In Chomsky's eyes, the U.S. was a monstrous power that since World War II had used its military almost exclusively to squelch the freedoms and damage the economies of weaker, mostly non-white peoples. And the American mass media, owned as it is by a wealthy elite, consistently abetted these horrors. "They are the cultural commissars of the system of domination and control," he told an interviewer in 1984. During the Cold War, Chomsky often compared the liberal *New York Times* to *Pravda*, the official organ of the Soviet Communist Party; both believed "the state is noble by definition" and assumed its policies were well intentioned, albeit occasionally criticizing the way they were executed.[23]

Such bold if crude accusations, delivered with calm, prosecutorial authority, lifted Chomsky to international fame. Such popular rock bands as U2 and Radiohead praised his work, and several of his books were best sellers in Europe and Japan. "He is the most cited living person," gushes a biographer, "one who will be for future generations what Galileo, Descartes, Newton, Mozart, or Picasso have been for ours." Hyperbole aside, Chomsky did become, in the decades after the Vietnam War, an articulate, relentless foe of U.S. empire, whose scholarly mien belied the radicalism of his critique. In 2006, when Hugo Chávez, the socialist president of Venezuela, denounced the "devil" George W. Bush in a speech to the United Nations, he held up Chomsky's book, *Hegemony or Survival: America's Quest for Global Dominance*, and praised it for analyzing "the greatest threat looming over our planet."[24]

Yet Chomsky's international renown did not gain him any influence over politics in his own country. In his seventies, he took no part in the anarchist revival on the streets of Seattle, and he disdained electoral organizing, even by radical third parties. While his name and ideas were universally recognized inside the domestic left, they were barely visible outside it. Chomsky's admirers routinely blamed this fact on the collective silence of the "corporate news media," which allegedly refused to give even the smallest platform to one of its sworn enemies. But this charge assumed that millions of Americans were eager to listen to a dour professor who was convinced they lived in a "system" which "has very little to do with people's . . . needs and that . . . therefore has to be imposed by violence and force." Just after the attacks of September 11, 2001, Chomsky dismissed patriotism as the governing elite's way of telling its subjects, "You shut up and be obedient, and I'll relentlessly advance my own interests." The famous anarchist was not just a rebel without a movement; he rejected even the mildest form of patriotism without which, particularly at a time of national crisis, no radical could have gained a sympathetic hearing outside the confines of academia.[25]

But, as Chomsky's fame suggested, those confines had grown quite a bit roomier since the 1960s. A generation of activists who had once protested the "complicity" of their universities with an immoral system gradually became the dominant force in elite humanities departments. Gradually, their ideas about history, literature, and a just society percolated down to secondary schools across the land. Black studies, Chicano studies, women's studies, queer studies, and cultural studies; history which examined America as a nation dominated by white people bent on empire; the so-called "holy trinity" of "race-class-and-gender"; and the virtues of multicultural identity—all were norms of pedagogy and scholarship by the end of the twentieth century.[26]

Since 1990, a majority of the presidents of the Organization of American Historians—the umbrella group in the field—have both sprung from and written out of a commitment to one or more of the movements of the New Left. Moreover, nearly every influential practitioner of American studies—a discipline founded in the 1940s to explore the distinctive qualities of the nation's culture—spent his or her career studying the plight and resistance of racial and sexual minorities. The only thing distinctive about the United States, they now suggested, was its awesome power to oppress. In 1998, Janice Radway, president of the American Studies Association, even dismissed the very "notion of a bonded national territory and a concomitant national identity." She wondered if it still made sense to "perpetuate a specifically 'American' studies" at all.[27]

Predictably, all conservatives and some older liberals sounded the alarm. "The chief issue is this," asserted Roger Kimball, author of *Tenured Radicals*, "should our institutions of higher education be devoted primarily to the education of citizens—or should they be laboratories for social and political experimentation?" The historian Arthur Schlesinger Jr. warned that radical Afrocentrists and their allies were undermining the strength of the nation's shared ideals. "There is surely no reason," he wrote, "for Western civilization to have guilt trips laid on it by champions of cultures based on despotism, superstition, tribalism, and fanaticism." David Horowitz, a former editor of *Ramparts* who had transformed himself into an avenging crusader on the right, published a book that fingered "the 101 most dangerous academics in America."[28]

Under attack, most professors retorted that they were simply cultivating the best kind of citizenship: one which encouraged Americans to acknowledge their nation's flaws and debate how to correct them. By assigning the writings of Toni Morrison alongside or instead of those by Henry James and questioning if there were anything "exceptional" about the U.S. at all, academic radicals—tenured and untenured—sought to redress an imbalance they believed had been weighted in a white, male, elitist direction since the birth of research universities in the late nineteenth century. "The present challenges the past in ways that cannot be denied," wrote the black historian Nathan Huggins. "History, even as national myth, must tell us who we are, how and why we are where we are, and how our destinies have been shaped."[29]

Indeed, scholarship and teaching about the American past had never been transformed so profoundly—or debated so widely. Roger Kimball blasted English departments for turning "the study of literature into a species of political propaganda and virtue-mongering." But the professors he attacked had little power to spread their tastes in fiction and poetry beyond the classroom. Millions of citizens, however, had an opinion about American history, even if they cared only about the Civil War, a particular immigrant saga, the Vietnam debacle, or another discrete segment of the past. So the dominance of multicultural, left history elicited peals of protest from such powerful figures as Lynne Cheney, chair of the National Endowment for the Humanities (NEH) in the early 1990s, and from the Air Force Association, which managed to scuttle an exhibit at the Smithsonian that would have questioned the U.S. decision to drop atomic bombs on Japan in 1945.

In truth, most historians of the U.S. did not view themselves as activists so much as socially responsible pedagogues. By emphasizing what ordinary Americans of all kinds had believed and accomplished, they hoped to make history more relevant to the variety of young people who signed up for their classes. Lawrence Levine, a renowned scholar of black and popular culture who grew up in an immigrant Jewish neighborhood in New York City, declared in 1996 that "the American academic world is doing a more thorough and cosmopolitan job of educating a great diversity of students in a broader and sounder array of courses . . . than ever before in its history." Most students probably agreed with his judgment. They had, after all, grown up during a surge of immigration rivaling that of the early twentieth century and in an age when "diversity" was sacred. As empathetic historians of "the people," Levine and his many ethnic and non-white counterparts were so committed to understanding America's multicultural past, in part, because they represented that cultural pluralism themselves.[30]

This tidal wave of scholarship also washed over the sturdy battlements of public history. Numerous museums featured exhibits on the suffering and contributions of African Americans and Native Americans. With lavish support from big foundations and the NEH (before and after Lynne Cheney), Ken Burns made multipart TV documentaries about the history of wars, baseball, and the West that countered narratives of national triumph and ethnic harmony. Feature films like Edward Zwick's *Glory* (about black soldiers in the Civil War) and Kevin Costner's *Dances with Wolves* (about a white army officer who joins the Sioux instead of fighting them) encouraged mostly white audiences to root for racial underdogs. Such displays and dramatizations attracted large numbers of Americans, even those who viewed classroom history as boring and impractical. Critics of the multicultural turn were correct about one thing, however: no convincing "master" narrative of U.S. history had emerged to replace the old one. The only exception seemed to be among African Americans who, according to a scholar who studied their views, "are sustained by a progressive, enabling historical vision rooted in the story of emancipation and civil rights." As group history thrived, the notion of a shared past withered.[31]

One author did succeed in producing a synthesis of radical history, and its sales and influence were extraordinary. Howard Zinn, in *A People's History of the United States*, first published in 1980, defied what he took to be the received wisdom of the academy: "The mountain of history books under which we all stand leans so heavily in the other direction—so tremblingly

respectful of states and statesmen and so disrespect-
ful, by inattention, to people's movements—that
we need some counterforce to avoid being crushed
into submission."[32]

Born in 1922, Zinn had been a dedicated radical
since his teenage years in the Popular Front. He
became a vocal pacifist after serving as a bombadier
in the European theater during World War II, got
fired from his first teaching job in the early 1960s
(at a black women's college) for civil rights organizing, wrote an eloquent book that argued "the
logic of withdrawal" from Vietnam, and inspired
countless students at Boston University to become
anti-war and community organizers.

*A People's History* is a classic of muckraking
scholarship. From the near genocide of Amerin-
dians by the Spanish and English conquerors to
Ronald Reagan's Cold War belligerence, Zinn
chronicled the crimes of "the most ingenious system of control in world history." The American
elite used its wealth to pit "the 99 percent" of the
people "against one another" and employed war,
patriotism, and the military to "absorb and divert"

Howard Zinn, 2004,
in Havana, Cuba.
A dedicated radical since
his teenage years in the
Popular Front, Zinn helped
organize for civil rights and
against the war in Vietnam.
His *A People's History
of the United States* has
sold more than two
million copies.

the occasional rebellion. But ordinary folks of all races and classes kept
struggling to achieve equality, democracy, and a tolerant society—and
could surely do so again. Understanding the stark realities of an oppres-
sive past would be a necessary step toward building a radical movement
for the future.[33]

Zinn's passionate, pugnacious narrative, sprinkled with hundreds of
quotes from slaves and populists, anonymous wage earners and articulate
radicals, became the most popular work of history an American leftist has
ever written. By his death in 2010, it had sold close to two million copies, gone through five editions and multiple printings, been assigned in
thousands of college and secondary-school courses, and been praised by
such entertainers as Matt Damon, Morgan Freeman, Viggo Mortensen,
and Bruce Springsteen. Zinn's work was hardly as pathbreaking as his
admirers supposed; it depended on the research of hundreds of liberal

and radical scholars. In fact, the "mountain" of texts leaned far more to the left by the early twenty-first century than when Zinn's book was first published. But *A People's History* did reach the people, or at least a politically engaged minority of them. "I can't think of anyone who had such a powerful and benign influence," eulogized his good friend Noam Chomsky. "His historical work changed the way millions of people saw the past."[34]

Unfortunately, like Chomsky's work, Zinn's big book was stronger on polemical passion than historical insight. For all his virtuous intentions, he essentially reduced the past to a Manichean fable and made no serious attempt to address the biggest question a leftist should ask about U.S. history: why have most Americans accepted the legitimacy of the capitalist republic in which they live?

In Zinn's view, the ruling elite was a transhistorical entity, a virtual monolith; neither its interests nor its ideology had changed markedly from the days when its members owned slaves and wore knee breeches to the era of the Internet and Armani. He described the American Revolution as a clever device to defeat "potential rebellions and create a consensus of popular support for the rule of a new, privileged leadership." His Civil War was another elaborate confidence game. Soldiers who fought to preserve the Union got duped by "an aura of moral crusade" against slavery that "worked effectively to dim class resentments against the rich and powerful, and turn much of the anger against 'the enemy.' " Zinn saw nothing remarkable in the 1980 election of Ronald Reagan. It simply "meant that another part of the Establishment," albeit "more crass" than its immediate antecedents, was now in charge.[35]

The ironic effect of such portraits of rulers was to rob "the people" themselves of cultural richness and variety, characteristics that might gain the respect and not just the sympathy of contemporary readers. For Zinn, ordinary Americans seemed to live mostly to fight the rich and haughty and, inevitably, to be fooled by them. They resembled bobble-head dolls in work shirts and overalls, ever sanguine about fighting the power, always about to fall on their earnest faces.

But in a grim era, the book offered many on the American left a certain consolation. They might be on the losing side of history, but they could comprehend the evil of a four-hundred-year-old order, and that knowledge would, to a certain extent, set them free. This was a poor substitute for the power of a social movement.[36]

## A TRULY POPULAR FRONT?

> The common discovery of America was probably that Americans were the first people on earth to live for their humor; nothing was so important to Americans as humor.
> —Norman Mailer, *Armies of the Night*[37]

Radicals were stranded on the margins of political life and had to defend their status in academia, yet they still had something to smile about: they could routinely see and hear their views reflected in products turned out by one of the nation's leading industries: popular entertainment. Bruce Springsteen's fondness for Woody Guthrie's more daring lyrics and Matt Damon's regard for Howard Zinn's prose were among the many examples of the affection many musicians, filmmakers, and creators of television shows expressed for the historical beliefs of the left about class and racial inequality, the demands of bottom-up social movements, and the pieties of traditional family life and churches.

Giant corporations usually had their way in the marketplace and in Congress. Yet in Hollywood, they were nearly always cast as the villains. Oliver Stone's 1987 movie *Wall Street* included the basic elements of what soon became a conventional narrative. The protagonist, an ambitious young stockbroker from a working-class family, engages in insider trading to curry favor with an immoral corporate takeover wizard who declares, "Greed, for lack of a better word, is good." In this and subsequent films, Stone made his leftist opinions clear. But the illegal and sometimes homicidal designs of big business also coursed through a stream of productions whose creators, unlike Stone, were not given to making explicit political statements: Michael Mann's *The Insider* (about tobacco companies), Stephen Gaghan's *Syriana* (the oil industry), and Tony Gilroy's *Michael Clayton* (a pesticide maker), to name just three. In the animated *Wall-E*, polluting industrialists have made the world uninhabitable—but somehow enabled a remnant of several thousand people to circle through space engorging themselves as perpetual consumers served by robots.

In each of these movies, an individual hero emerges to expose the evildoers (or, in *Wall-E*, to restore the earth itself). But it is always a figure who works within the coils of the evil apparatus and understands how to subvert it. On the other hand, a script about a firm's employees uniting against their bosses would have been rejected as the vestige of a bygone time. On American screens at the start of the twenty-first century, robber barons proliferated, while militant labor was nowhere to be found.[38]

Some of the most popular works indebted to anti-authoritarian rebellion were conveyed as satire. *The Simpsons* is a prime example—an extended cartoon that became the most durable situation comedy in the history of television. Debuting at the end of 1989, the show relentlessly mocked the notion of "family values" by portraying a dysfunctional nuclear unit held together by a kind-hearted housewife with bouffant blue hair. Homer worked at a nuclear power plant, then a prime symbol of environmental peril, for a boss as cruel and selfish as anyone imagined by Zinn or Chomsky. The town's mayor, its leading minister, and the anchorman on its local TV station were shallow and venal. Over time, the characters, plots, and taglines grew as familiar to Americans and probably as beloved as those created earlier by Dr. Seuss. The "first family of animation" was even honored on U.S. postage stamps just before the twentieth anniversary episode of the show. By then, conservatives who had railed in the early 1990s against the subversiveness of *The Simpsons* had moved on to other, more profitable causes.[39]

The show's creator had welcomed their attacks. Matt Groening sprang from the same milieu as did many other young radicals who came of age in the long 1960s. As the Nixon administration came to a sorry end, Groening was drawing cartoons for the campus newspaper he edited at Evergreen State College, a "hippie school" in the state of Washington with no grades or requirements that, in his proud memory, attracted "every weirdo in the Northwest." After graduation, Groening launched *Life in Hell*, a syndicated comic strip featuring a bunny named Binky who was alternately threatened, harassed, angered, and bored by advertisers, bosses, teachers, parents, and right-wing Republicans, or "sleazeballs," as he called them. *Life in Hell*, commented one journalist, "was every ex–campus protester's, every Boomer idealist's, conception of what adult existence in the '80s turned out to be." "Your moral authorities don't always have your best interests in mind," the cartoonist explained to *Mother Jones*, a prominent magazine on the left. "They're all goofballs, and I think that's a great message for kids."[40]

The political satires of Michael Moore had a more earnest and polem-

Matt Groening satirizes the Christian right, 1992. The
creator of *The Simpsons* began his career drawing cartoons
for the campus newspaper he edited at Evergreen State
College, a "hippie school" with no grades or requirements.

ical edge. Moore was born in 1954, the same year as Groening, but he
was raised not in a countercultural enclave near the Pacific but in a sub-
urb of Flint, Michigan, a city that grew prosperous during the heyday of
General Motors and swiftly declined along with the quality and sales of
American cars. Flint was also the site of the sit-down strike in the winter of 1936–37 that established the power of the United Auto Workers.
Soon after dropping out of the University of Michigan, Moore began
to publish an alternative weekly that protested the fecklessness of GM
executives and the corruptness of Flint politicians. He discovered his
voice as the ironic champion of a working class few of whose members
either could or would speak up for themselves. By the late 1980s, realizing that most Americans now imbibed their politics on screens of various
sizes rather than in print, Moore began making documentary films.[41]

Surprisingly, they made him the best-known and most controversial radical in America. From *Roger and Me*, released in 1989, to *Capitalism: A Love Story* twenty years later, Moore honed the ability to make the same indictment of big businesses the left had been articulating since the Gilded Age: they exploited or neglected their workers, manipulated politicians, and put profits above human needs. But he did so in the droll persona of an ordinary American, albeit one with a film crew tagging along, who merely wanted to ask rich and powerful men a few innocent questions about how they ran their affairs. Moore employed the same method in a film about gun violence, *Bowling for Columbine* (2002), and one about the U.S. invasion of Afghanistan and Iraq, *Fahrenheit 9/11* (2004)—both of which broke attendance records for documentaries and, to his delight, were shown at multiplexes in places where the left was otherwise invisible. Described as a "baby-faced bear, shambling, down-home and uniformly seen in a baseball cap," Michael Moore became the most familiar brand name of an ideological tendency that saw "consumerism" as a synonym for passivity.[42]

The sly bear did have his limitations as a spokesman for the left. Like most scriptwriters, Moore preferred a simple, dramatic narrative over a truly accurate one: *Fahrenheit 9/11* implied that the U.S. went to war with the Taliban in 2001 to help Unocal construct an oil pipeline through Afghanistan—a project that was, in fact, shelved in 1998. *Capitalism: A Love Story* suggested that the financial debacle of 2008 was a Wall Street plot to wheedle a huge bail-out from Congress. Such economic reductionism enabled critics on the right and elsewhere to mount attacks that undercut Moore's appeal. Repeated in each film, his verbal stunts, while still amusing, also became predictable. *Fahrenheit 9/11*, which Moore made in order to thwart the re-election of George W. Bush, probably enraged as many voters as it converted.[43]

But Moore could not become the Harriet Beecher Stowe of the postmodern left absent the kind of mass outrage that had inspired the writing of *Uncle Tom's Cabin* and enabled it to change minds. Some on the left criticized Moore for having "little faith in the working people whose misfortunes he shows" in his films. But with organized labor in perhaps terminal decline and no institution stepping into the breach, it would have required a gifted fantasist—or a dogmatic sectarian—to construct a more uplifting portrait of wage-earning Americans. In mass-market films produced at the end of the twentieth century and the beginning of the twenty-first, the only collective resistance to the piggish powers-that-be came from indigenous people fighting foreign imperialists: *Pocahontas*, *Dances with Wolves*, and *Avatar* (whose blue-skinned natives reside in another solar system). Once again, a racial narrative seemed more credible than one based on class resentments.

Thus, although certain individuals proved, in the age of Reagan and after, that radical ideas could still gain a wide hearing, the alarm of such foes as Patrick Buchanan was quite overblown. Millions of Americans were happy to see Michael Moore or George Clooney expose and embarrass thieving, polluting corporate bigwigs. But their joy did not lead many to join a union or an environmental group or to become community organizers. *The Simpsons* was broadcast on Fox, whose news operation was, in all but name, a vehicle of the rightward-leaning Republican Party. The cultural influence of the post-1960s left thus became a background melody to a political narrative written largely by conservatives. It softened the tone and created some striking ironies, but it did not rewrite the script.

## THE USES OF UTOPIA: A CONCLUSION

The American left strode into history in the early nineteenth century with a set of grievances and a dream of absolute social equality. By the end of the twentieth century, the sustained and arduous efforts of radicals, both theists and non-believers, had helped eliminate the most flagrant injustices in the capitalist republic: slavery was abolished, African Americans and women of all races enjoyed full civil and political rights, and the state was able to assure a modicum of security to the poor and disabled and had the power to regulate the worst abuses of large corporations.

The left was certainly more successful when it sought to expand personal liberty than when it struggled to advance the collective might of workers and the poor. Fanny Wright and David Walker would have applauded the freedoms that African Americans and women of all races enjoy. But Thomas Skidmore would likely be as angry as ever; his general division of property never gained many supporters, even among his fellow wage earners. By the late twentieth century, the grand vision of a classless society survived, for the most part, among a dwindling minority that was largely of a secular mind and, ironically, pursued professional careers.

Almost two centuries later, it can be difficult to recall the old passion for beginning the world over again. The Cold War is history, and where Communist parties still rule, most do so as aggressive managers of market economies. The once great social-democratic parties of Europe struggle to keep their welfare states from unraveling. In the United States, progressive young Americans threw themselves heart and soul into campaigning for a charismatic black Democrat. But their enthusiasm slackened after Obama took office and tried to initiate a new era of modest reform, which irate conservatives branded as "socialism."

At a nadir of the historical left, perhaps utopia could use a few words in its defense. A world of freebooting capitalisms has delivered neither material abundance nor social harmony to most of the world's people. Failed states, religious wars, environmental disasters, clashes between immigrants and the native-born are common features of current history, as they were in earlier times. But the perception that there is no alternative to chronic crisis except to somehow muddle through exacerbates the problem. As Max Weber wrote, just after his famous line that politics is the "boring of hard boards": "Certainly all historical experience confirms the truth—that man would not have attained the possible unless time and again he had reached out for the impossible."[44]

Surely this is a time for awakening the better angels of our nature, for rescuing the virtues of the non-Communist radical faith from the junk pile of history. Workers who organize themselves could brake the wild ride of the free marketeers, open-minded secularists and tolerant believers might form a third force to disarm the armies of fundamentalists; pacifists could challenge the myth that perpetual war delivers either national security or global democracy. In the United States no less than in the Islamic world, we need a moral equivalent of the passion that drives vengeful believers.

Communism did teach a brutal, unforgettable lesson about the perils of utopianism as a governing faith. "If we have learned nothing else from the twentieth century," cautioned the historian Tony Judt, "we should at least have grasped that the more perfect the answer, the more terrifying its consequences." A moral capitalism is certainly preferable to an authoritarian socialism that bred some of the most antisocial regimes in history. But when Judt added the caution that "imperfect improvements upon unsatisfactory circumstances are the best that we can hope for, and probably all we should seek," he ignored what, since the abolitionist crusade, has always motivated large numbers of people to join mass movements.[45] Who would throw themselves into a left that renounced any vision of a better world and admitted that it would, at best, be able to make only tiny changes in the human condition?

Since the New Left died, most progressives have engaged in limited, if worthy, campaigns; a few have become expert at crafting legislation to nudge the country closer to a kind of social-democratic order. Some of it has even become law.

But the utopian impulse should not be smothered under a patchwork quilt of policy prescriptions. It has always been a boon to those who pursue more limited gains. Reformers from above always needed the pressure of left-wing movements from below—from the abolitionists, the Socialists, and the Popular Front to the advocates of black and Latino power, radical feminism, and environmental rescue. The challenge of uncompromising dissenters made governing liberals and progressives appear to be problem-solvers and soothers of the body politic. Without powerful left movements, neither Bill Clinton nor Barack Obama could become the transformative figure each aspired to be, and liberalism retained the baleful image it acquired in the 1970s: as an ideology out of touch with the interests and beliefs of ordinary men and women.

Then, suddenly, in the fall of 2011, a wave of innovative "occupations" gave radicals an opportunity to reach millions of Americans whose anger about the economic crisis no leading politician in either party knew how to address. Beginning in a small park in lower Manhattan on September 17, thousands of mostly young occupiers quickly set up tent camps in scores of towns and cities around the nation. Claiming, "We are the 99 percent," they thrust the problems of Wall Street greed and malfeasance and the corruption of the political system by big money onto front pages, home pages, and into the hot center of political debate. Polls showed that a majority of Americans agreed with the grievances of the occupiers, although few yearned to camp out in the middle of a city. "I support what they are doing," said a retired judge from the Boston suburbs. "It affects our democracy. Until we can stop corporations from buying all our congressmen, we will not have a democracy worth having."[46] For the first time since the 1930s, the inequality of wealth had become a passionate cause and an inescapable political issue.

The aim of these protests represented a leap beyond what most left activists had been saying since the 1960s. Gender equality, multiculturalism, opposition to military intervention, and global warming were all worthy causes. But each represented the passions of discrete groups whose opponents on the right were able to belittle them as "special interests." But the Great Recession that began in 2007 injured most Americans and left many open to hearing about egalitarian remedies. The occupiers' creative use of the new social media and their knack for pithy one-liners such as "Dear Banks: I pay my mom's rent; the taxpayers pay yours. How is that fair?" helped turn them in a matter of weeks from a curiosity into a growing national phenomenon.

A fondness for anarchism on the part of a vocal, articulate minority of the occupiers at first helped build their protests but then ensnared them in endless meetings and pointless battles with police. On the one hand, the "horizontal" nature of a movement brought to life and sustained on cyberspace gave the tent camps a necessary taste of utopian élan. They fit snugly inside the romantic vision of a future in which autonomous, self-governing communities would link up with one another, quite voluntarily of course. But bygone anarchists like Emma Goldman were never able to combine their stirring idealism with a politics of the possible—and the new breed may fail at the task as well. Whether the occupiers will be remembered as the beginning of a newer, more inclusive left or a spirited remnant of an older, less attractive one depends on their ability to do so.

In 1954, Lewis Coser and Irving Howe wrote an essay for the new *Dissent* magazine in which they sought to preserve the utopian idea from the deadly embrace of tyrannical rulers and their ideas. "*Socialism is the name of our desire,*" they remarked, a "twist" of a statement Leo Tolstoy had made about his longing for God. They emphasized that socialists would have a future only if they inspired large numbers of working people to take action to liberate themselves. They welcomed the fact that few individuals of any class either live for politics or wish to give up other kinds of allegiances, to an ethnic or racial group, a religion, even to a sports team.

In an era when the fortunes of democratic radicals in the United States were quite low, Coser and Howe acknowledged that "to will the image of socialism is a constant struggle for definition, almost an act of pain." Then they added, "But it is the kind of pain that makes creation possible." Socialism has never been the name most Americans would choose for their dream society; today, many doubt such a society is either feasible or desirable. However, without such an egalitarian ideal, whatever we name it, the real world will be ever harder to change.[47]

# Good Reading

There may be as many published books and articles about the history of the American left as there are contemporary leftists in the United States. But certain studies were indispensable to my understanding of the subject. With gratitude, I list them here.

## GENERAL WORKS

Daniel Bell, *Marxian Socialism in the United States*
Mari Jo Buhle, Paul Buhle, and Dan Georgakas, eds., *Encyclopedia of the American Left*
Paul Buhle, *Marxism in the United States*
John Patrick Diggins, *The Rise and Fall of the American Left*
Geoff Eley, *Forging Democracy: The History of the Left in Europe, 1850–2000*
Richard Flacks, *Making History: The American Left and the American Mind*
Eric Foner, *The Story of American Freedom*
Eric Hobsbawm, *The Age of Empire, 1875–1914* and *The Age of Extremes: A History of the World, 1914–1991*
Irving Howe, *Socialism and America*
Christopher Lasch, *The Agony of the American Left*
Richard Rorty, *Achieving Our Country: Leftist Thought in Twentieth-Century America*
Doug Rossinow, *Visions of Progress: The Left-Liberal Tradition in America*
Christine Stansell, *The Feminist Promise, 1792 to the Present*

## WORKS ON INDIVIDUAL PERIODS AND MOVEMENTS

James Brewer Stewart, *Holy Warriors: The Abolitionists and American Slavery*
John Stauffer, *The Black Hearts of Men: Radical Abolitionists and the Transformation of Race*
Sean Wilentz, *Chants Democratic: New York City and the Rise of the American Working Class*
Eric Foner, *Politics and Ideology in the Age of the Civil War*
Ellen Carol DuBois, *Feminism and Suffrage: The Emergence of an Independent Women's Movement in America, 1848–1869*
Adam Tuchinsky, *Horace Greeley's New-York Tribune: Civil War–Era Socialism and the Crisis of Free Labor*
John L. Thomas, *Alternative America: Henry George, Edward Bellamy, Henry Demarest Lloyd and the Adversary Tradition*
Leon Fink, *Workingmen's Democracy: The Knights of Labor and American Politics*
Charles Postel, *The Populist Vision*
James R. Green, *Grass-Roots Socialism: Radical Movements in the Southwest, 1895–1943*

Christine Stansell, *American Moderns: Bohemian New York and the Creation of a New Century*

Nick Salvatore, *Eugene V. Debs: Citizen and Socialist*

James Weinstein, *The Decline of Socialism in America, 1912–1925*

Mari Jo Buhle, *Women and American Socialism, 1870–1920*

Irving Howe, *The World of Our Fathers*

Tony Michels, *A Fire in Their Hearts: Yiddish Socialists in New York*

Michael Denning, *The Cultural Front: The Laboring of American Culture in the Twentieth Century*

Maurice Isserman, *Which Side Were You On? The American Communist Party During the Second World War*

Mark Naison, *Communists in Harlem During the Depression*

Richard Minnear, *Dr. Seuss Goes to War*

Harvey Klehr, *The Heyday of American Communism: The Depression Decade*

David Guiterrez, *Walls and Mirrors: Mexican Americans, Mexican Immigrants, and the Politics of Ethnicity*

Todd Gitlin, *The Sixties: Years of Hope, Days of Rage*

Van Gosse, *Rethinking the New Left*

Ruth Rosen, *The World Split Open: How the Modern Women's Movement Changed America*

Clayborne Carson, *In Struggle: SNCC and the Black Awakening of the 1960s*

Peniel Joseph, *Waiting 'Til the Midnight Hour: A Narrative History of Black Power in America*

Thomas Jackson, *From Civil Rights to Human Rights: Martin Luther King, Jr., and the Struggle for Economic Justice*

Paul Berman, *A Tale of Two Utopias: The Political Journey of the Generation of 1968*

Lawrence Levine, *The Opening of the American Mind: Canons, Culture, and History*

# Notes

ACKNOWLEDGMENTS

1. Richard Hofstadter, *The Progressive Historians: Turner, Beard, Parrington* (New York, 1968), 120.


INTRODUCTION: WHAT DIFFERENCE DID IT MAKE?

1. Quoted in Michael Egan, *Barry Commoner and the Science of Survival: The Remaking of American Environmentalism* (Cambridge, Mass., 2007), 1.
2. Richard Minnear, *Dr. Seuss Goes to War* (New York, 1999); Philip Nel, *Dr. Seuss: American Icon* (New York, 2004), esp. 39–62. The latter book includes an extensive bibliography of works by and about Seuss/Geisel. Also see Ron Lamothe's revealing film *The Political Dr. Seuss.*
3. E. J. Kahn, "Children's Friend," *The New Yorker*, Dec. 17, 1960.
4. J. F. C. Harrison, *Quest for the New Moral World: Robert Owen and the Owenites in Britain and America* (New York, 1969), 249.
5. George Orwell, "Why I Write," 1947, orwell.ru/library/essays/wiw/English (accessed Oct. 26, 2010).
6. Quoted in Timothy Messer-Kruse, *The Yankee International: Marxism and the American Reform Tradition, 1848–1876* (Chapel Hill, N.C., 1998), 258.
7. Greil Marcus, *Mystery Train: The Image of America in Rock 'n' Roll* (New York, 1975), 22. For a dyspeptic but insightful critique of Americanism from the depression-era left, see Leon Samson, *Toward a United Front: A Philosophy for American Workers* (New York, 1933).
8. "Historical movements," the historian Mari Jo Buhle observes, "are rarely judged solely in the light they cast themselves." Mari Jo Buhle, *Women and American Socialism, 1870–1920* (Urbana, Ill., 1981), 323. Christopher Lasch, *The Agony of the American Left* (New York, 1969), viii–ix.
9. Richard Flacks, *Making History: The American Left and the American Mind* (New York, 1988), 106–7.


CHAPTER ONE: FREEDOM SONGS, 1820S–1840S

1. Henry David Thoreau, *Cape Cod* (1865; West Dennis, Mass., 2002), 103.
2. On Wright see Frances Wright, *Reason, Religion, and Morals* (Amherst, N.Y., 2004), 111; Celia Morris Eckhardt, *Fanny Wright: Rebel in America* (Cambridge,

Mass., 1984); Raymond Lee Muncy, *Sex and Marriage in Utopian Communities: 19th-Century America* (Bloomington, Ind., 1973), 198. On Walker, see *David Walker's Appeal* (New York, 1995), 2; Peter P. Hinks, *To Awaken My Afflicted Brethren: David Walker and the Problem of Antebellum Slave Resistance* (University Park, Pa., 1997). On Skidmore, see Amos Gilbert, *The Life of Thomas Skidmore*, with an introduction by Mark A. Lause (Chicago, 1984). Charles Sellers, *The Market Revolution: Jacksonian America, 1815–1846* (New York, 1991), 287; Sean Wilentz, *Chants Democratic: New York City and the Rise of the American Working Class, 1788–1850* (New York, 1984), 183, 5.

3. Flacks, *Making History*, 113. The quote may be apocryphal, unfortunately.

4. For an extended argument about the primacy of narratives about race over those of class, see my review essay, "The *Other* American Dilemma," *American Prospect* 37 (March–April, 1998), 91–95.

5. Gustave de Beaumont, *Marie or Slavery in the United States*, as quoted by Karl Marx, "On the Jewish Question," 1844, at www.marxists.org.

6. Garrison quoted in Daniel J. McInerney, *The Fortunate Heirs of Freedom: Abolitionist and Republican Thought* (Lincoln, Neb., 1994), 63.

7. On perfectionism, see Sydney Ahlstrom *A Religious History of the American People* (New Haven, 1972), 474–78.

8. The term "feminist" was not coined until the late nineteenth century or widely used until the early twentieth. But the female activists I describe in this chapter, who typically defined their cause as that of "woman's rights," clearly articulated the same types of grievances and remedies as later feminists. Thus, scholars of the movement routinely apply the term to them, despite the anachronism. See, for example, *A History of Women in the West, IV: Emerging Feminism from Revolution to World War*, ed. Genevieve Fraisse and Michelle Perrot (Cambridge, Mass.: 1993).

9. The phrase was reminiscent of Tom Paine's 1792 statement, "My country is the world and my religion is to do good." But as a pious evangelical, Garrison avoided mentioning the connection and claimed that he didn't read Paine until the mid-1840s. See Harvey J. Kaye, *Thomas Paine and the Promise of America* (New York, 2005), 148–50.

10. Quoted in Patrick Allitt, *The Conservatives: Ideas and Personalities Throughout American History* (New Haven, Conn., 2009), 39.

11. See Thomas Wentworth Higginson, "The Eccentricities of Reformers," in his *Reformers* (1899), 329–48; William Leach, *True Love and Perfect Union: The Feminist Reform of Sex and Society* (New York, 1982), 135. Even the few activists who changed ideological sides remained absolutely certain about the virtue of their new position. Orestes Brownson, an eloquent Boston-born intellectual, began his political career in the 1830s as a disciple of Fanny Wright's. At the end of the decade, he was editing a Democratic newspaper in New York City for which he penned a fiery, pro-worker manifesto predicting an international class war. By the early 1840s, Brownson was touting the pro-slavery ideas of John Calhoun, and soon after, he embraced the traditionalist creed of the Roman Catholic Church. At each stage, he thoroughly repudiated his earlier enthusiasms and condemned former comrades who didn't follow his lead. "The Past has always stood in the gate," wrote Brownson in 1840, "and forbid the Future to enter; and it has been only in mortal encounter, that the Future has as yet been able to force its entrance." Brownson, "The Laboring Classes," quoted in *The Transcendentalists*, ed. Perry Miller (Cambridge, Mass., 1950), 445.

12. Weld in 1885, quoted in Merton L. Dillon, "The Abolitionists as a Dissenting Minority," in *Dissent: Explorations in the History of American Radicalism*, ed. Alfred F. Young (De Kalb, Ill., 1968), 95.

13. Quoted in Robert H. Abzug's excellent biography, *Passionate Liberator: Theodore Dwight Weld and the Dilemma of Reform* (New York, 1980), 88.

14. Ibid., 126.

15. For insights about the collective biography of abolitionists, see Donald M. Scott, "Abolition as a Sacred Vocation," in *Antislavery Reconsidered: New Perspectives on the Abolitionists*, ed. Lewis Perry and Michael Fellman (Baton Rouge, La., 1979), 51–74; James Brewer Stewart, *Holy Warriors: The Abolitionists and American Slavery*, rev. ed. (New York, 1997), 40–43; Michael P. Young, *Bearing Witness Against Sin: The Evangelical Birth of the American Social Movement* (Chicago, 2006), passim.

16. Quoted in Carolyn L. Karcher, *The First Woman in the Republic: A Cultural Biography of Lydia Maria Child* (Durham, N.C., 1994), 201.

17. In 1838, James Birney claimed the AAS had at least 112,000 members, but no official statistics were kept. See John Ashworth, *Slavery, Capitalism, and Politics in the Antebellum Republic*, vol. 1 (Cambridge, UK, 1995), 129. Due in part to a lack of good documents, there is no definitive analysis of the social composition of this or any other abolitionist group. But see the pioneering attempt by Edward Magdol, *The Antislavery Rank and File: A Social Profile of the Abolitionists' Constituency* (New York, 1986).

18. *North Star*, Dec. 3, 1847, 2.

19. May quoted in Waldo E. Martin Jr., *The Mind of Frederick Douglass* (Chapel Hill, N.C., 1984), 30.

20. Delany, "Domestic Economy" (1849), in *Martin R. Delany: A Documentary Reader*, ed. Robert S. Levine (Chapel Hill, N.C., 2003), 151.

21. On the emerging racial consciousness of Irish immigrants, see David Roediger, *The Wages of Whiteness: Race and the Making of the American Working Class* (London, 1991), 133–63.

22. See Gilbert Osofsky, "Abolitionists, Irish Immigrants, and the Dilemmas of Romantic Nationalism," *American Historical Review* 80 (October 1975), 889–912; quotes on 898 and 900.

23. Wilentz, *Chants Democratic*, 332.

24. Hughes quoted in Sean Wilentz, *The Rise of American Democracy: Jefferson to Lincoln* (New York, 2005), 680. For an excellent summary of the intra-Christian clash throughout U.S. history, see Mary Jo Bane, "Democracy and Catholic Christianity in America," in Hugh Heclo, *Christianity and American Democracy* (Cambridge, Mass., 2007), 145–66.

25. Max Weber, "Politics as a Vocation" (1919), www.sscnet.ucla.edu/polisci/ethos (accessed Oct. 25, 2010). The historian Aileen Kraditor argued that the Garrisonians were more "practical" than their opponents because they understood that to uncouple abolition from racial equality would ensure the perseverance of a racist order. She added a larger point about the role of radical agitators: "If politics is the art of the possible, agitation is the art of the desirable. The practice of each must be judged by criteria appropriate to its goal . . . To criticize the agitator for not trimming his demands to the immediately realizable—that is, for not acting as a politician—is to miss the point . . . [Unrealistic demands] can be useful to the political bargainer; the more extreme demand of the agitator makes the politician's demand seem acceptable . . . Also, the agitator helps define the value, the principle, for which the politician bargains. The ethical values placed on various possible political courses are put there partly by agitators working on the public opinion that creates political possibilities." Aileen S. Kraditor, *Means and Ends in American Abolitionism: Garrison and His Critics on Strategy and Tactics, 1834–1850* (New York, 1969), 28.

26. Quoted in Michael Bennett, *Democratic Discourses: The Radical Abolition Movement*

*and Antebellum American Literature* (New Brunswick, N.J., 2005), 24. For a wonderful description of these events, see pp. 25–36.

27. Alexis de Tocqueville, *Democracy in America* (New York, 1981 [1855]), 141.

28. Luke 10:1; *The Public Years of Sarah and Angelina Grimké: Selected Writings, 1835–1839*, ed. Larry Ceplair (New York, 1989), 23–24.

29. Quotes from James Brewer Stewart, *Wendell Phillips: Liberty's Hero* (Baton Rouge, La.: 1986), 184; Ottilie Assing, quoted in William S. McFeely, *Frederick Douglass* (New York, 1991), 96.

30. Stewart, *Wendell Phillips*, 185–86; McFeely, *Frederick Douglass*, 178.

31. Stanzas 9 and 10 of "Get Off the Track!" Reprinted in Scott Gac, *Singing for Freedom: The Hutchinson Family Singers and the Nineteenth-Century Culture of Reform* (New Haven, Conn., 2007), 250–51; ibid., 181.

32. Ibid., 269.

33. *North Star*, Oct. 27, 1848, 2.

34. Quoted in Bennett, *Democratic Discourses*, 52. Also see Dickson D. Bruce Jr., "Print Culture and the Antislavery Community: The Poetry of Abolitionism, 1831–1860," in *Prophets of Protest: Reconsidering the History of American Abolitionism*, ed. Timothy Patrick McCarthy and John Stauffer (New York, 2006), 220–34.

35. For critical responses to the novel, see *The Annotated Uncle Tom's Cabin*, ed. with an introduction and notes by Henry Louis Gates Jr. and Hollis Robbins (New York, 2006), ix–xlv; Edmund Wilson, *Patriotic Gore: Studies in the Literature of the American Civil War* (New York, 1962), 3–11; Jane Tompkins, *Sensational Designs: The Cultural Work of American Fiction, 1790–1860* (New York, 1986), 122–46 ("sentimental power" is her term); Joan D. Hedrick, *Harriet Beecher Stowe: A Life* (New York, 1994), passim.

36. Quotes from John Stauffer's fascinating study, *The Black Hearts of Men: Radical Abolitionists and the Transformation of Race* (Cambridge, Mass., 2002), 1, 16.

37. Garrison quoted in Leslie M. Harris, "From Abolitionist Amalgamators to 'Rulers of the Five Points,' " in *Sex, Love, Race: Crossing Boundaries in North American History*, ed. Martha Hodes (New York, 1999), 194; Brown quoted in W. E. B. DuBois, *John Brown* (1909; New York, 1972), 192.

38. Quoted in Lawrence J. Friedman, *Gregarious Saints: Self and Community in American Abolitionism, 1830–1870* (Cambridge, UK, 1982), 169.

39. On debates within the movement during the 1830s, see Katherine Samford Takvorian, "The Sex Factor: Abolitionist Outsiders, Amalgamation, and the Search for Social Equality in America, 1825–1843," undergraduate thesis in history and literature, Harvard College, 2007.

40. Quotes from Nathan Irvin Huggins, *Slave and Citizen: The Life of Frederick Douglass* (Boston, 1980), 158; McFeely, *Frederick Douglass*, 314. Also see Maria Diedrich, *Love Across Color Lines: Ottilie Assing and Frederick Douglass* (New York, 1999).

41. Quoted in McFeely, *Frederick Douglass*, 312.

42. Quoted in Blanche Glassman Hersh, *The Slavery of Sex: Feminist-Abolitionists in America* (Urbana, Ill., 1978), 19.

43. See Carroll Smith-Rosenberg, "Beauty, the Beast, and the Militant Woman: A Case Study in Sex Roles and Social Stress in Jacksonian America," in Carroll Smith-Rosenberg, *Disorderly Conduct: Visions of Gender in Victorian America* (New York, 1986), 109–28, quote on 111–12; Daniel S. Wright, *"The First of Causes to Our Sex": The Female Moral Reform Movement in the Antebellum Northeast, 1834–1848* (New York, 2006). At least in Boston, 70 percent of officials of the Boston Moral Reform Society were anti-slavery activists. Anne M. Boylan, *The Origins of Women's Activism: New York and Boston, 1797–1840* (Chapel Hill, N.C., 2002), 73.

44. Stewart quoted in Jean Fagan Yellin, *Women and Sisters: The Antislavery Feminists in American Culture* (New Haven, Conn., 1989), 47. For an insightful treatment

of the Grimkés' tour, see Kathryn Kish Sklar, *Women's Rights Emerges Within the Antislavery Movement: A Brief History with Documents* (Boston, 2000), 16–39.

45. Quotes from Sklar, *Women's Rights Emerges*, 103, 120, 105, 38.

46. Quotes from *History of Woman Suffrage*, 2nd ed., vol. 1, ed. Elizabeth Cady Stanton, Susan B. Anthony, and Matilda Joslyn Gage (Rochester, N.Y., 1889), 334–37. Also see Ira V. Brown, "Racism and Sexism: The Case of Pennsylvania Hall," *Phylon* 37 (2nd qtr., 1976): 126–36.

47. Bonnie Anderson, *Joyous Greetings: The First International Women's Movement, 1830–1860* (New York, 2000), quote on 8. "From Wollstonecraft to Mill: What British and European Ideas and Social Movements Influenced the Emergence of Feminism in the Atlantic World, 1792–1869?" http://womhist.alexanderstreet .com.awrm/intro.htm; D. C. Bloomer, *Life and Writings of Amelia Bloomer* (Boston, 1895), 65–81.

48. On the local context, see Judith Wellman, *The Road to Seneca Falls: Elizabeth Cady Stanton and the First Woman's Rights Convention* (Urbana, Ill., 2004).

49. Stanton et al., *History*, vol. 1, 73.

50. *Woman's Rights Conventions: Seneca Falls and Rochester, 1848* (1870; New York, 1969), 4–5.

51. Ibid., 72. On this question, see Ellen Carol DuBois, *Feminism and Suffrage* (Ithaca, N.Y., 1978). The sole survivor was Rhoda Palmer, aged 102. Wellman, *Road to Seneca Falls*, 231.

52. Grimké's book was published in 1838. Quoted in Karcher, *First Woman*, 226.

53. Quoted in Stanton et al., *History*, 535–36.

54. Ibid., 536–37.

55. See Carol Kolmerten, *The American Life of Ernestine L. Rose* (Syracuse, N.Y., 1999).

56. Ibid., 153.

57. Hersh, *Slavery of Sex*, 142; Kolmerten, *American Life*, 238–39.

58. Hersh, *Slavery of Sex*, 236.

59. Abzug, *Passionate Liberator*, 193–95; Hersh, *Slavery of Sex*, 90–92. On the general pattern of marriage among radical reformers, see Hersh, 218–51; Anderson, *Joyous Greetings*, 57.

60. Anderson, *Joyous Greetings*, 132.

61. Lillian Faderman, *To Believe in Women: What Lesbians Have Done for America—A History* (Boston, 1999), 20–22; J. Matthew Gallman, *America's Joan of Arc: The Life of Anna Elizabeth Dickinson* (New York, 2006), 110. For an influential argument that even married white middle-class women felt closer to their female friends than to their husbands, see Carroll Smith-Rosenberg, "The Female World of Love and Ritual: Relations Between Women in Nineteenth-Century America," in Smith-Rosenberg, *Disorderly Conduct*, 53–76.

62. Stanton quoted by Theodore Tilton in *Eminent Women of the Age* (Hartford, Conn., 1872), 360.

63. Ralph Waldo Emerson in "The American Scholar." The great essayist was no socialist, but his psychological critique of capitalism was reminiscent of Marx's in the *Economic and Philosophical Manuscripts*, written in the early 1840s.

64. Collins quoted in John L. Thomas, "Antislavery and Utopia," in *The Antislavery Vanguard: New Essays on the Abolitionists*, ed. Martin Duberman (Princeton, N.J., 1965), 257.

65. Stanton quoted in Carl J. Guarneri, *The Utopian Alternative: Fourierism in Nineteenth-Century America* (Ithaca, N.Y., 1991), 396; Douglass quoted in *Socialism in America*, ed. Albert Fried (New York, 1970), 108.

66. Quotes from Adam-Max Tuchinsky, "'The Bourgeoisie Will Fall and Fall Forever': The *New-York Tribune*, the 1848 French Revolution, and American Social-Democratic Discourse," *Journal of American History* 92 (September 2005),

470–97; Adam Tuchinsky, *Horace Greeley's New-York Tribune: Civil War-Era Socialism and the Crisis of Free Labor* (Ithaca, N.Y., 2009), 104.

67. Owen quoted in *Socialism in America: From the Shakers to the Third International, A Documentary History* (Garden City, N.Y., 1970), 108.

68. Engels, "Description of Recently Founded Communist Colonies Still in Existence," published in German in 1845. At www.marxists.org (accessed Oct. 25, 2010).

69. See Mark Lause, *Young America: Land, Labor, and the Republican Community* (Urbana, Ill., 2005).

70. On the young labor movement and the short-lived workingmen's parties that existed in several northern cities besides New York, see Walter Licht, *Industrializing America: The Nineteenth Century* (Baltimore, 1995), 48–63; Wilentz, *Chants Democratic*, passim, quote on 198. Neither the "Workies" nor the trade unions had much support among free blacks in northern cities.

71. Lippard also described the French Revolution as a modern-day Calvary: "it was for this same principle that Jesus toiled—endured—died!" Quotes in *George Lippard: Prophet of Protest: Writings of an American Radical, 1822–1854,* ed. David S. Reynolds (New York, 1986), 27, 128.

72. William H. and Jane H. Pease, *Black Utopia: Negro Communal Experiments in America* (Madison, Wisc., 1963); Gail Bederman, "Revisiting Nashoba: Slavery, Utopia, and Frances Wright in America, 1818–1826," *The Best American History Essays, 2007,* ed. Jacqueline Jones (New York, 2007), 89–109.

73. Guarneri, *Utopian Alternative,* 153–54, 407–408, quote on 13.

74. Quoted in Barbara Taylor, *Eve and the New Jerusalem: Socialism and Feminism in the Nineteenth Century* (New York, 1983), 44.

75. Robert David Thomas, *The Man Who Would Be Perfect: John Humphrey Noyes and the Utopian Impulse* (Philadelphia, 1977), quote on 174. For an overview of the subject, see Raymond Lee Muncy, *Sex and Marriage in Utopian Communities: 19th Century America* (Bloomington, 1973).

76. Muncy, *Sex and Marriage,* 215. Gail Bederman, "A 'Great Red Harlot of Infidelity': How Frances Wright Was Converted to Sexual Radicalism (and What Came Afterward), unpublished paper delivered at the annual convention of the American Historical Association, Jan. 7, 2010.

CHAPTER TWO: THE HALFWAY REVOLUTION, 1840S–1870S

1. Rayner quoted in Eric Foner, *Freedom's Lawmakers: A Directory of Black Officeholders During Reconstruction* (New York, 1993), xxx.

2. Stevens, c. 1865, quoted in Eric Foner, "Thaddeus Stevens, Confiscation, and Reconstruction," in Foner, *Politics and Ideology in the Age of the Civil War* (New York, 1980), 129.

3. Fuller quoted in Adam Tuchinsky, *Horace Greeley's New-York Tribune: Civil War-Era Socialism and the Crisis of Free Labor* (Ithaca, N.Y., 2009), 85. Alexis de Tocqueville, *Recollections: The French Revolution of 1848* (New York, 1987), 98.

4. Douglass in *North Star,* Nov. 10, 1848, 2.

5. David Herreshoff, *American Disciples of Marx: From the Age of Jackson to the Progressive Era* (Detroit, 1967), 59–63.

6. Quotes from Zoe Trodd, "Writ in Blood: John Brown's Charter of Humanity, the Tribunal of History, and the Thick Link of American Political Protest," *Journal for the Study of Radicalism* 1 (2006), 2; Sean Wilentz, "Homegrown Terrorist," *The New Republic,* Oct. 24, 2005.

7. Brown quoted in Trodd, "Writ in Blood," 3. On the Radical Abolitionists, see Stauffer, *Black Hearts of Men,* 8–44.

8. Quotes from Mark A. Lause, *Race and Radicalism in the Union Army* (Urbana, Ill., 2009), 9; DuBois, *John Brown*, 254, 6.

9. Lincoln quoted in James Oakes, *The Radical and the Republican: Frederick Douglass, Abraham Lincoln, and the Triumph of Antislavery Politics* (New York, 2007), 106. For contrasting views on Brown's significance, see David S. Reynolds, *John Brown, Abolitionist: The Man Who Killed Slavery, Sparked the Civil War, and Seeded Civil Rights* (New York, 2005), and Sean Wilentz's lengthy review of it, "Homegrown Terrorist."

10. On the interracial Union force (an exception to the segregated rule), see Lause, *Race and Radicalism*, passim.

11. Stanton et al., *History*, vol. 1, 747.

12. *Life and Times of Frederick Douglass Written by Himself* (1892; New York, 1962), 365–66.

13. Quoted in Chandra Manning, *What This Cruel War Was Over: Soldiers, Slavery, and the Civil War* (New York, 2007), 85.

14. Quote from Leon F. Litwack, *Been in the Storm So Long: The Aftermath of Slavery* (New York, 1979), 102.

15. For the fullest history of these events, see Iver Bernstein, *The New York City Draft Riots: Their Significance for American Society and Politics in the Age of the Civil War* (New York, 1990).

16. David Montgomery, *Beyond Equality: Labor and the Radical Republicans, 1862–1872* (New York, 1967), 127–30; William D'Arcy, *The Fenian Movement in the United States, 1858–86* (Washington, D.C., 1947).

17. Labor activist, "Mr. Beales," quoted in Karl Marx, "A London Workers' Meeting," marxists.org/archive/marx/works/1862/02.htm. Adams quoted in James McPherson, *Battle Cry of Freedom: The Civil War Era* (New York, 1988), 549. For a balanced account of British opinion, see R. J. M. Blackett, *Divided Hearts: Britain and the American Civil War* (Baton Rouge, La., 2001).

18. McKim quoted in James Brewer Stewart, *Holy Warriors: The Abolitionists and American Slavery*, rev. ed. (New York, 1997), 196.

19. Quotes from James Brewer Stewart, *Wendell Phillips: Liberty's Hero* (Baton Rouge, La., 1986), 98; Richard Hofstadter, *The American Political Tradition* (New York, 1948), 159.

20. Timothy Messer-Kruse, *The Yankee International: Marxism and the American Reform Tradition, 1848–1876* (Chapel Hill, N.C., 1998), 43. His "reasonable estimate" of IWA members is on p. 261.

21. Marx quoted in ibid., 172, and Tilton in ibid., 105.

22. Stanton quoted in Ellen Carol DuBois, *Feminism and Suffrage: The Emergence of an Independent Women's Movement in America* (Ithaca, N.Y., 1978), 65.

23. Quoted in DuBois, ibid., 59, 60.

24. In 1869, another suffrage group, the American Woman Suffrage Association, also began its work. Composed mainly of women from New England, AWSA depended on the Republican Party to support its efforts and was never the energetic center of activism and propaganda that its counterpart was. Its leaders were also given to snide, nativist remarks that limited their reach. Lucy Stone, for example, complained that male immigrants "who cannot even speak the mother tongue correctly" were welcome at polling stations that barred her and her respectable, native-born sisters. Quoted in Kolmerten, *American Life*, 94.

25. Stevens in September 1865, quoted in W. E. B. DuBois, *Black Reconstruction* (1935).

26. The best study of these events, and the period as a whole, remains Eric Foner's *Reconstruction: America's Unfinished Revolution* (New York, 1988).

27. Quote (the individual is unnamed) from Steven Hahn, *A Nation Under Our Feet* (Cambridge, Mass., 2003), 215.

28. For details, see Foner, *Freedom's Lawmakers*. Orville Vernon Burton, *The Age of Lincoln* (New York, 2007), 277.

29. See Silvana R. Siddali, *From Property to Person: Slavery and the Confiscation Acts, 1861-1862* (Baton Rouge, La., 2005).

30. Bayley quote from http://www.gwu.edu/~folklife/bighouse/panel9.html (accessed Oct. 25, 2010); unnamed soldier quoted in Manning, *What This Cruel War Was Over*, 218.

31. E. B. Callender, *Thaddeus Stevens: Commoner* (Boston, 1882), 141, 145. The most prominent Republicans to back Stevens's bill were senators Charles Sumner and Benjamin Wade, both former abolitionists.

32. Quoted in Foner, "Thaddeus Stevens, Confiscation, and Reconstruction," in Foner, *Politics and Ideology*, 143.

33. Sumner quoted in ibid., 142.

34. Wade quoted in H. L. Trefousse, *Benjamin Franklin Wade: Radical Republican from Ohio* (New York, 1963), 287.

35. Quoted in Trefousse, *Thaddeus Stevens: Nineteenth-Century Egalitarian* (Chapel Hill, N.C., 1997), xi.

36. Quoted in Hahn, *One Nation Under Our Feet*, 195.

37. Foner, *Freedom's Lawmakers*, xxvii. Also see the perceptive analysis by August Meier, "Afterword: New Perspectives on the Nature of Black Political Leadership During Reconstruction," in *Southern Black Leaders of the Reconstruction Era*, ed. Howard N. Rabinowitz (Urbana, Ill., 1982), 393–406.

38. Details about Bradley are drawn from Foner, *Freedom's Lawmakers*, 23–24; Joseph P. Reidy, "Aaron A. Bradley: Voice of Black Labor in the Georgia Lowcountry," in Rabinowitz, ed., *Southern Black Leaders*, 281–308; Jacqueline Jones, *Saving Savannah: The City and the Civil War* (New York, 2008), passim.

39. Reidy, "Aaron A. Bradley," 291. Jones, *Saving Savannah*, 358.

40. DuBois, *Black Reconstruction*, 67, 16, 670.

41. Eric Foner, "Reconstruction and the Crisis of Free Labor," in Foner, *Politics and Ideology*, 106–107.

42. Douglass quoted in Heather Cox Richardson, *West from Appomattox: The Reconstruction of America after the Civil War* (New Haven, Conn., 2007), 127.

43. David Montgomery, *Beyond Equality* (New York, 1967), 446. For an illuminating exchange on the issue of white workers, slavery, and abolition, see Bruce Laurie, "Workers, Abolitionists, and the Historians" and responses by James L. Huston, Joanne Pope Melish, and Brian Kelly, *Labor* 5 (Winter 2008): 17–82.

44. Phillips quoted in Richard Hofstadter, *The American Political Tradition and the Men Who Made It* (New York, 1948), 161.

CHAPTER THREE: THE SALVATION OF LABOR, 1870S–1890S

1. Quoted in Kathryn Kish Sklar, *Florence Kelley and the Nation's Work: The Rise of Women's Political Culture* (New Haven, Conn., 1995), 132–33.

2. Wilde, "The Soul of Man Under Socialism," originally published in 1891, as quoted in Carl J. Guarneri, "Edward Bellamy's *Looking Backward:* The International Impact of an American Socialist Utopia, 1888–1945," in *Visualizing Utopia*, ed. Mary G. Kemperink and Willemien H. S. Roenhorst (Leuven, Belgium, 2007), 1.

3. Quotes from George's speech on October 5, 1886, in *Henry George's 1886 Campaign*, prepared by Louis F. Post and Fred C. Leubuscher (1887; New York, 1961), 20–29.

4. Henry George, *Progress and Poverty* (1879; New York, 1962), 272, 552.

5. On exiles in New York, see Alessandra Lorini, "Cuba Libre and American Imperial Nationalism: Conflicting Views of Racial Democracy in the Post-Reconstruction

United States," in *Contested Democracy: Freedom, Race, and Power in American History*, ed. Manisha Sinha and Penny Von Eschen (New York, 2007), 191–214.

6. McGlynn quoted in Edward T. O'Donnell, " 'Though Not an Irishman': Henry George and the American Irish," *American Journal of Economics and Sociology* 56 (October 1997): 414. The best study of the Land League is Eric Foner's essay "Class, Ethnicity, and Radicalism in the Gilded Age: The Land League and Irish-America," in Foner, *Politics and Ideology in the Age of the Civil War* (New York, 1980), 150–200.

7. This is just a partial list, of course. For details, see Charles Albro Barker, *Henry George* (New York, 1955), 469–71. McCabe quoted in *Henry George's 1886 Campaign*, 152.

8. Quote in Eric Hobsbawm, *The Age of Empire* (New York, 1987), 112. On the most extensive socialist network in Europe, see Vernon Lidtke, *The Alternative Culture: Socialist Labor in Imperial Germany* (New York, 1985). On the growth of socialist parties themselves, see Geoff Eley, *Forging Democracy: The History of the Left in Europe, 1850–2000* (New York, 2002), 13–118 (and the chart on p. 66).

9. "Accepted by Mr. George," *New York Times*, Oct. 6, 1886.

10. Bellamy quoted in Edward K. Spann, *Brotherly Tomorrows: Movements for a Cooperative Society in America, 1820–1920* (New York, 1989), 200. For the most complete statements of this view, see the once-popular books by Matthew Josephson, *The Robber Barons* (New York, 1934) and *The Politicos* (1938; New York, 2008).

11. The phrase "carboniferous capitalism" was coined by Lewis Mumford in his *Technics and Civilization* (New York, 1934).

12. Lester Frank Ward, *The Psychic Factors of Civilization* (1892), 275. books.google.com (accessed Oct. 25, 2010).

13. Jane Addams, "The Subjective Value of a Social Settlement," delivered in 1892. Accessed at http://pds.lib.harvard.edu/pds/view/3613929?n=4&s=4 (accessed Oct. 25, 2010); Alan Trachtenberg, *The Incorporation of America*, rev. ed. (New York, 2007).

14. For numerical trends in organizational history, see Gerald Gamm and Robert D. Putnam, "The Growth of Voluntary Associations in America, 1840–1940," *Journal of Interdisciplinary History* 29 (Spring 1999): 511–57.

15. On the attitudes of Protestant clergy toward labor in the Gilded Age, see Robin Archer, *Why Is There No Labor Party in the United States?* (Princeton, N.J., 2007), 182–87.

16. Henry George, undated quote, from John L. Thomas, *Alternative America: Henry George, Edward Bellamy, Henry Demarest Lloyd and the Adversary Tradition* (Cambridge, Mass., 1983), 61.

17. George, *Progress and Poverty*, 548.

18. Richard J. Ellis, *To the Flag: The Unlikely History of the Pledge of Allegiance* (Lawrence, Kans., 2005), 1–23.

19. Edward Bellamy, *Looking Backward* (New York, 1960 [1888]), 99.

20. Bellamy, "How I Came to Write *Looking Backward*," *The Nationalist*, May 1889, 4; George, *Progress and Poverty*, 538; George on the Chinese quoted in Simon Schama, *The American Future: A History* (New York, 2009), 276. The "petroleuses" were female supporters of the Paris Commune, who were suspected, on scant evidence, of having burned down large sections of Paris during the final days of the Commune in 1871.

21. Peter D'Autremont Jones, *Henry George and British Socialism* (New York, 1991), 124, 184. Marx added, "The whole thing is simply an attempt, decked out with Socialism, to save capitalist domination and indeed to establish it afresh." Ibid., 123.

22. N. I. Markhov, quoted in Alexander Nikoljukin, "A Little-Known Story: Bellamy

in Russia," in Sylvia Bowman et al., *Edward Bellamy Abroad: An American Prophet's Influence* (New York, 1962), 74; Wallace quoted in Peter Marshall, "A British Sensation," ibid., 112; Bebel quoted in "The German Acceptance and Reaction," ibid., 195. On Canada, see Ian McKay, *Rebels, Reds, and Radicals: Rethinking Canada's Left History* (Toronto, 2005), 148–50.

23. Geoff Eley makes a similar point about the "robust eclecticism" of the European left and provides evidence that "Marx was read mainly by movement intellectuals." Eley, *Forging Democracy*, 43–46. Quote is on p. 43. As pamphlets, both *The Communist Manifesto* and Engels's "Socialism: Utopian and Scientific" did reach many workers, however.

24. Harry Thurston Peck, quoted in Howard H. Quint, *The Forging of American Socialism: Origins of the Modern Movement* (Indianapolis, Ind., 1953), 95. For the list of clubs, see *The Nationalist*, June 1890, 281–82. Almost half the clubs were located in just one state: California.

25. Thomas, *Alternative America*, 356; Postel, *Populist Vision*, 228–32; Daniel Rodgers, *Atlantic Crossings: Social Politics in a Progressive Age* (Cambridge, Mass., 1998), 139–40; Robert D. Johnston, *The Radical Middle Class: Populist Democracy and the Question of Capitalism in Progressive Era Portland, Oregon* (Princeton, N.J.,), 159–76. Guttstadt quoted in Michael Kazin, *Barons of Labor: The San Francisco Building Trades and Union Power in the Progressive Era* (Urbana, Ill., 1987), 159.

26. Postel, *Populist Vision*, 230–31; Clarence Darrow, *The Story of My Life* (1932; New York, 1996), 41–42. Dewey, "An Appreciation of Henry George" (1928), at www.cooperativeindividualism.org/dewey-john_appreciation-of-henry-george .html (accessed Oct. 25, 2010).

27. Bellamy, *Looking Backward*, 91.

28. Willard quoted in Mari Jo Buhle, *Women and American Socialism, 1870–1920* (Urbana, Ill., 1981), 80. On Flynn, see Leslie Fishbein, *Rebels in Bohemia: The Radicals of* The Masses, *1911–1917* (Chapel Hill, N.C., 1982), 9.

29. Herron, *The New Redemption* (1893), quoted in *Socialism in America: A Documentary History*, ed. Albert Fried (Garden City, N.Y., 1970), 368.

30. Bellamy, *Looking Backward*, 26–29.

31. Quoted in Quint, *Forging*, 55. The SLP was originally named the Socialistic Labor Party; it was the successor to the Workingmen's Party of the United States, formed just a year before.

32. Liebknecht quoted in Hartmut Keil, "German Working-Class Radicalism in the United States from the 1870s to World War I," in *"Struggle a Hard Battle": Essays on Working-Class Immigrants*, ed. Dirk Hoerder (De Kalb, Ill., 1986), 88; Engels quoted in Daniel Bell, *Marxian Socialism in the United States* (1952; Ithaca, N.Y., 1998), 36; Sklar, *Florence Kelley and the Nation's Work*, 128–29.

33. Buhle, *Women and American Socialism*, 32.

34. The French writer and activist Pierre Proudhon described himself as an anarchist in 1840. But the first American publication to use the term favorably was *The An-archist*, a short-lived Boston magazine edited by the multilingual revolutionary Dr. Edward Nathan-Ganz, which first appeared in 1881. Paul Avrich, *The Haymarket Tragedy* (Princeton, N.J., 1984), 57.

35. According to a contemporary writer friendly to the cause, the number of anarchists in Chicago was about half the total in the U.S. as a whole. There were about 2,500 in New York City, 700 in Milwaukee, and scattered groups in a few other industrial cities. Tom Goyens, *Beer and Revolution: The German Anarchist Movement in New York City, 1880–1914* (Urbana, Ill., 2007), 147.

36. Quotes from Avrich, *Haymarket*, 65, 12–13; www.lucyparsonsproject.org/about_ lucyparsons.html (accessed Oct. 25, 2010). For the fullest description of the Chicago movement, see James Green, *Death in the Haymarket* (New York, 2006).

37. Parsons quoted in Avrich, *Haymarket*, 115.
38. Ibid., 112–13.
39. George Schilling quoted in Avrich, *Haymarket*, 455.
40. Quotes in ibid., 268.
41. David Montgomery, *The Fall of the House of Labor: The Workplace, the State, and American Labor Activism, 1865–1925* (Cambridge, UK, 1987), quote on 161. The name of the Knights was a deliberate attempt by its founders, a group of skilled garment cutters in Philadelphia in 1869, to keep their membership and purposes hidden from anti-union employers. Under Powderly, the group gradually shed its secrecy and rituals while retaining the name.
42. Pledge quoted in Michael Kazin, *The Populist Persuasion: An American History*, rev. ed. (Ithaca, N.Y., 1998), 81.
43. The editor was from Rhode Island. Quoted in Richard Oestreicher, "Terence Powderly, the Knights of Labor, and Artisanal Republicanism," in *Labor Leaders in America*, ed. Melvyn Dubofsky and Warren Van Tine (Urbana, Ill., 1987), 48.
44. Craig Phelan, *Grand Master Workman: Terence Powderly and the Knights of Labor* (Westport, Conn., 2000), 180. Powderly quoted on 181.
45. For details and analysis, see Leon Fink's splendid study, *Workingmen's Democracy: The Knights of Labor and American Politics* (Urbana, Ill., 1983).
46. Gompers testimony before the U.S. Strike Commission, Aug. 25, 1894, quoted in *The Samuel Gompers Papers*, vol. 3, ed. Stuart B. Kaufman and Peter J. Albert (Urbana, Ill., 1989), 579.
47. Quote from Kaufman, *Samuel Gompers and the Origins of the American Federation of Labor, 1848–1896* (Westport, Conn., 1973), 168; *The Samuel Gompers Papers*, vol. 1, ed. Stuart B. Kaufman (Urbana, Ill., 1986), 21.
48. Gompers quoted in Kazin, *Populist Persuasion*, 55; Gompers to Engels, Jan. 9, 1891, Kaufman and Albert, *Gompers Papers*, vol. 3, 10. Italics added.
49. See the thoughtful biographical introduction by Nick Salvatore to Samuel Gompers, *Seventy Years of Life and Labor*, abridged version (Ithaca, N.Y., 1984), xi–xli. In the summer of 1886, Powderly signed a combative letter from the Knights leadership that included the line, "The General Executive Board has never had the pleasure of meeting with Mr. Gompers when he was sober." Kaufman, *Gompers Papers*, vol. 1, 410.
50. Eley, *Forging Democracy*, 81.
51. Joseph Gerteis, *Class and the Color Line: Interracial Class Coalition in the Knights of Labor and the Populist Movement* (Durham, N.C., 2007), 96–98, quote on 96.
52. Quoted in Steven Hahn, *A Nation Under Our Feet: Black Political Struggles in the Rural South from Slavery to the Great Migration* (Cambridge, Mass., 2003), 420.
53. Ibid., 420–21.
54. Danielewicz quoted in Alexander Saxton, *The Indispensable Enemy: Labor and the Anti-Chinese Movement in California* (Berkeley, 1971), 221; London quoted in Richard O'Connor, *Jack London: A Biography* (Boston: 1964), 220.
55. Kearney quoted in Saxton, *Indispensable Enemy*, 118. On the utility of anti-Asian sentiment for white-led unions from the late nineteenth century until World War I, see Kazin, *Barons of Labor*, 162–71.
56. See Barbara Goldsmith, *Other Powers: The Age of Suffrage, Spiritualism, and the Scandalous Victoria Woodhull* (New York, 1998), and Amanda Frisken, *Victoria Woodhull's Sexual Revolution: Political Theater and the Popular Press in Nineteenth-Century America* (Philadelphia, 2004).
57. Catt at the 1895 NAWSA convention, quoted in *The Concise History of Woman Suffrage*, ed. Mari Jo Buhle and Paul Buhle (Urbana, Ill., 2005), 338.
58. Elizabeth Cady Stanton, *The Woman's Bible* (1895; Boston, 1993), 10, 11.
59. Stanton quoted in Leila R. Brammer, *Excluded from Suffrage History: Matilda Joslyn*

292 · NOTES TO PAGES 100–111

*Gage, Nineteenth-Century American Feminist* (Westport, Conn., 2000), 104. Gage was a close ally of Stanton's on religious matters.

60. For the brief exchange, which probably took place in 1903 in Rochester, see Ray Ginger, *Eugene V. Debs: A Biography* (1949; New York, 1962), 240.

61. This paragraph is adapted from Kazin, *Populist Persuasion*, 83, where sources for the quotes can be found.

62. Episcopal minister Richard Heber Newton, quoted in Suzanne M. Marilley, *Woman Suffrage and the Origins of Liberal Feminism in the United States, 1820–1920* (Cambridge, Mass., 1996), 111.

63. Willard quoted in ibid., 107. On her religious views, see Willard, *Woman in the Pulpit* (Boston, 1888).

64. Willard quoted in Jean H. Baker, *Sisters: The Lives of America's Suffragists* (New York, 2005), 173.

65. Field quoted in Josephson, *The Politicos*, 57.

66. Quoted in Nick Salvatore, *Eugene V. Debs: Citizen and Socialist* (Urbana, Ill., 1982), 153.

67. Rebecca Edwards, "Mary Elizabeth Lease: Advocate for Political Reform," in *John Brown to Bob Dole: Movers and Shakers in Kansas History*, ed. Virgil W. Dean (Lawrence, Kans., 2006), 127–39; Marilley, *Woman Suffrage*, 124–58.

68. On Doyle and black populism generally, see Omar Ali, *In the Lion's Mouth: Black Populism in the New South* (Jackson, Miss., 2010). Donnelly quote on 91.

69. Kelley, quoted in Sklar, *Florence Kelley and the Nation's Work*, 275 (italics added); George quoted in Postel, *Populist Vision*, 231.

70. Quotes from Robert C. McMath Jr., *Populist Vanguard: A History of the Southern Farmers' Alliance* (Chapel Hill, N.C., 1975), 68; Joseph W. Creech Jr., "Righteous Indignation: Religion and Populism in North Carolina, 1886–1906," PhD diss., University of Notre Dame, 2000, 230–31; Postel, *Populist Vision*, 264; *Holy Trinity v. United States* 143 U.S. 457 (1892).

71. Bellamy quoted in Thomas, *Alternative America*, 314.

72. W. B. McCormick to Bryan, quoted in Michael Kazin, *A Godly Hero: The Life of William Jennings Bryan* (New York, 2007), 75.

73. William Jennings Bryan, *The First Battle* (Chicago, 1896), 378.

74. Wilson quoted in Steve Fraser, "The 'Labor Question,'" *The Rise and Fall of the New Deal Order, 1930–1980*, ed. Steve Fraser and Gary Gerstle (Princeton, N.J., 1989), 55. On Wilson, see Martin J. Sklar, *The Corporate Reconstruction of American Capitalism, 1890–1916* (New York, 1988), 401–12. On the continuing influence of populism, see Elizabeth Sanders, *Roots of Reform: Farmers, Workers, and the American State* (Chicago, 1999), and Kazin, *Godly Hero*. The philosopher Richard Rorty carelessly called for doing away with "the leftist-versus-liberal distinction" in U.S. history. But he correctly observed, "The history of leftist politics is a story of how top-down initiatives and bottom-up initiatives have interlocked." Rorty, *Achieving Our Country*, 53.

CHAPTER FOUR: A TALE OF THREE SOCIALISMS, 1890–1920S

1. Garin Burbank, *When Farmers Voted Red: The Gospel of Socialism in the Oklahoma Countryside, 1910–1924* (Westport, Conn., 1976), 19–20.

2. Quoted in Irving Howe, *The World of Our Fathers* (New York, 1976), 315.

3. Lippmann in *A Preface to Politics*, quoted in Leslie Fishbein, *Rebels in Bohemia: The Radicals of The Masses, 1911–1917* (Chapel Hill, 1982), 69.

4. Bryan quote in Kazin, *Godly Hero*, 128; T. Roosevelt quoted in Martin J. Sklar, *The Corporate Reconstruction of American Capitalism, 1890–1916: The Market, the Law, and Politics* (Cambridge, UK, 1988), 359; Wilson quoted in ibid., 407.

5. Irving Howe, *Socialism and America* (New York, 1985), 5. On the electoral fortunes of Socialists in Europe, Australia, and New Zealand, see Seymour Martin Lipset and Gary Marks, *It Didn't Happen Here: Why Socialism Failed in the United States* (New York, 2000), 188. For a list of where SP members won local office in the U.S., see James Weinstein, *The Decline of Socialism in America, 1912–1925* (New York, 1967), 116–18. Socialists also occupied 150 seats in state legislatures at some time between 1910 and 1920. Weinstein, 118.

6. For references to these quotes, see Michael Kazin, "The Agony and Romance of the American Left," *American Historical Review* 100 (December 1995): 1488–1512. The best summary and analysis of the question is Lipset and Marks, *It Didn't Happen Here*. But also see Eric Foner, "Why Is There No Socialism in the United States?," in Foner, *Who Owns History?: Rethinking the Past in a Changing World* (New York, 2002), 110–45.

7. Quoted in Kazin, "Agony and Romance."

8. Quoted in John Patrick Diggins, *The Rise and Fall of the American Left* (New York, 1992), 100.

9. Lippmann, *A Preface to Politics* (New York, 1914), 309.

10. *If You Don't Weaken: The Autobiography of Oscar Ameringer* (1940; Norman Okla., 1983), 228, 227.

11. Ibid., 229.

12. On the SP program, see Burbank, *When Farmers Voted Red*, 9; quote from Ameringer, *If You Don't Weaken*, 233.

13. Quoted in Burbank, *When Farmers Voted Red*, 25.

14. Ameringer, *If You Don't Weaken*, 267.

15. Quote from Burbank, *When Farmers Voted Red*, 30.

16. *Letters of Eugene V. Debs*, vol. 1, ed. J. Robert Considine (Urbana, Ill., 1990), 560. Debs was writing in 1912 to Fred D. Warren, editor of *The Appeal to Reason*.

17. Quoted in Burbank, *When Farmers Voted Red*, 78. In 1915, the U.S. Supreme Court struck down the clause as a blatant violation of the Fourteenth Amendment. On the scant presence of blacks in the Oklahoma SP, see Jimmy Lewis Franklin, *Journey Toward Hope: A History of Blacks in Oklahoma* (Norman, Okla., 1982), 118–19.

18. On the Appeal Army, see James R. Green, *Grass-Roots Socialism: Radical Movements in the Southwest, 1895–1943* (Baton Rouge, La., 1978), 128–35. For examples of ads, see Elliott Shore, *Talkin' Socialism: J. A. Wayland and the Role of the Press in American Radicalism, 1890–1912* (Lawrence, Kans., 1988), 136, and from the monthly *International Socialist Review* in Paul Buhle and Edmund B. Sullivan, *Images of American Radicalism* (Hanover, Mass., 1998), 111.

19. Bohn quoted in Nick Salvatore, *Eugene V. Debs: Citizen and Socialist* (Urbana, Ill, 1982), 239–40. For a list of SP officials elected from 1911 to 1920, see Weinstein, *Decline of Socialism*, 116–18.

20. Quotes from Marvin Wachman, *History of the Social-Democratic Party of Milwaukee, 1897–1910* (Urbana, Ill., 1945), 77–81, 11.

21. Berger quoted in Sally Miller, *Victor Berger and the Promise of Constructive Socialism, 1910–1920* (Westport, Conn., 1973), 72.

22. An anecdote from the 1908 campaign, quoted in Ray Ginger, *Eugene V. Debs: A Biography* (1949; New York, 1962), 294.

23. Quoted in Salvatore, *Eugene V. Debs*, 49.

24. Quoted in ibid., 81.

25. Ibid., 161–62.

26. Debs, "Speech at Indianapolis, 1904," in *Socialism in America: A Documentary History*, ed. Albert Fried (Garden City, N.Y., 1970), 402; Dos Passos, quoted in Daniel Bell, *Marxian Socialism in the United States* (1952; Ithaca, N.Y., 1996), 88.

27. Debs, "Speech at Indianapolis, 1904," 404.

28. Quoted in John P. Enyeart, "Revolution or Evolution: The Socialist Party, Western Workers, and Law in the Progressive Era," *Journal of the Gilded Age and Progressive Era* 2 (October 2003): 392.

29. For the history and lyrics of IWW songs, see *The Big Red Songbook*, ed. Archie Green et al. (Chicago, 2007).

30. For a lively, if inflated, survey of Hill's influence, see Franklin Rosemont, *Joe Hill: The IWW & the Making of a Revolutionary Workingclass Counterculture* (Chicago, 2003).

31. Dreiser quoted in a Flynn obituary, published in *Time*, http://www.time.com/time/magazine/article/0,9171,830712-1,00.html (accessed Oct. 26, 2010).

32. A member of the Philadelphia Women's Committee, quoted in Melvyn Dubofsky, *We Shall Be All: A History of the Industrial Workers of the World* (New York, 1969), 252.

33. Quoted in ibid., 253.

34. See *The Lost World of Italian-American Radicalism*, ed. Philip Cannistraro and Gerald Meyer (Westport, Conn., 2003).

35. In 1913, the Finnish Federation reported 12,651 members in 260 locals; in 1910, there were about 130,000 Finnish immigrants in the country. A. William Hoglund, "Finns," *Harvard Encyclopedia of American Ethnic Groups*, ed. Stephan Thernstrom (Cambridge, Mass., 1980), 367, 365.

36. For examples of this cultural breadth, see *A Living Lens: Photographs of Jewish Life from the Pages of the Forward*, ed. Alana Newhouse (New York, 2007).

37. Undated Cahan quote from Tony Michels, *A Fire in Their Hearts: Yiddish Socialists in New York* (Cambridge, Mass., 2005), 80; Isaiah 16:3, New Revised Standard Version.

38. Quoted in Irving Howe, *World of Our Fathers*, 301.

39. Michels, *Fire in Their Hearts*, 254.

40. Howe, *World of Our Fathers*, 323.

41. Goldman in 1909, quoted in Candace Serena Falk, *Love, Anarchy, and Emma Goldman* (New Brunswick, N.J., 1984), 82.

42. Quoted in ibid., xi.

43. On her lectures, see Christine Stansell, *American Moderns: Bohemian New York and the Creation of a New Century* (New York, 2000), 128–29. On the decline of the anarchists, see Tom Goyens, *Beer and Revolution: The German Anarchist Movement in New York City, 1880–1914* (Urbana, Ill., 2007).

44. Oscar Ameringer, *Life and Deeds of Uncle Sam* (1909; Chicago, 1985), 1.

45. Sanger, "Family Limitation" (1914), quoted in Ellen Chesler, *Woman of Valor: Margaret Sanger and the Birth Control Movement in America* (1992; New York, 2007), 103.

46. *The Selected Papers of Margaret Sanger*, vol. 1, *The Woman Rebel, 1900–1928*, ed. Esther Katz (Urbana, Ill., 2003), 85.

47. Testimony of March 5, 1912, in ibid., 32.

48. Quoted in Chesler, *Woman of Valor*, 114.

49. Eric Hobsbawm, "Revolution and Sex" (1969), in Hobsbawm, *Revolutionaries: Contemporary Essays* (New York, 1973), 216.

50. Engels quoted by Eleanor Marx-Aveling in 1896, http://www.marxists.org/archive/eleanor-marx/1896/11/proletarian-home.htm (accessed Oct. 26, 2010). On the links between "sexual emancipation" and the left in this period, see Mari Jo Buhle, *Women and American Socialism, 1870–1920* (Urbana, Ill., 1981), 246–87.

51. See Sarah Burns, *Inventing the Modern Artist: Art and Culture in Gilded Age America* (New Haven, 1996), 247–73. Max Eastman, *Love and Revolution: My Journey Through an Epoch* (New York, 1964), 4. There were clusters of "bohemians" in other American cities at the same time, but no other combined artistic innovation

with political radicalism to any great degree. For example, see Kevin Starr's survey of the San Francisco milieu that included Frank Norris, George Sterling, and Ambrose Bierce: *Americans and the California Dream, 1850–1915* (New York, 1973), 239–87.

52. Max Eastman, *Enjoyment of Living* (New York, 1948), 445, 449.

53. For fine examples, see Rebecca Zurier, *Art for the Masses: A Radical Magazine and Its Graphics* (New Haven, 1985). Eastman, *Enjoyment of Living*, 416.

54. Hutchins Hapgood, *The Spirit of Labor* (1907; Urbana, Ill., 2004), 392.

55. Stansell, *American Moderns*, 12.

56. Quoted in Alfred Kazin, *On Native Grounds: An Interpretation of Modern Prose Literature* (1942; New York, 1995), 170.

57. *Current Opinion* from 1913, quoted in http://historymatters.gmu.edu/d/5648 (accessed on Dec. 9, 2008).

58. The essay is in the public domain. I am quoting from a copy posted at www .swarthmore.edu/SocSci/rbannis1/AIH19th/Bourne.html (accessed on Dec. 9, 2008).

59. There were a few exceptions among Marxists. Most notably, the Austrian Socialist Party, operating in the multiethnic empire of Austria-Hungary, "advocated the establishment of a democratic federation within which national minorities would be protected and nations would have local autonomy in matters of 'cultural or national significance.'" Sheri Berman, *The Primacy of Politics: Social Democracy and the Making of Europe's Twentieth Century* (New York, 2006), 64.

60. Bourne expressed his praise for Zionism in a lecture given in the same year and published as "The Jew and Trans-National America," in *The Menorah Journal* 2 (December 1916): 277–84. For a sensitive reading of Bourne's transnational essays and their limits, see Jonathan M. Hansen, *The Lost Promise of Patriotism: Debating American Identity, 1890–1920* (Chicago, 2003), 111–15.

61. Ovington quoted in David Levering Lewis, *W. E. B. DuBois: Biography of a Race, 1868–1919* (New York, 1993), 496. On Emilie Hapgood, see Harold Cruse, *The Crisis of the Negro Intellectual* (New York, 1967), 31.

62. On Harrison, see *A Hubert Harrison Reader*, ed. Jeffrey B. Perry (Middletown, Conn., 2001).

63. Berger quoted in Weinstein, *Failure of Socialism*, 66; DuBois quoted in Fishbein, *Rebels in Bohemia*, 164.

64. Stansell, *American Moderns*, 3.

65. Eastman, *Enjoyment of Living*, 463.

66. Burbank, *When Farmers Voted Red*, 36–37.

67. Eastman, *Love and Revolution*, 22.

68. Reprinted in Zurier, *Art for the Masses*, 60.

69. Quotes from Weinstein, *Decline of Socialism*, 126. For a perceptive discussion of the People's Council, see Doug Rossinow, *Visions of Progress: The Left-Liberal Tradition in America* (Philadelphia, 2008), 70–74.

70. Herbert Mahler, quoted in Dubofsky, *We Shall Be All*, 358.

71. In Chicago, the judge who tried most of the IWW cases as well as those of Berger and other SP leaders was Kenesaw Mountain Landis. Landis refused any leniency to defendants he regarded as traitors. John Reed described him as "a wasted man with untidy white hair, an emaciated face in which two burning eyes are set like jewels, parchment skin split by a crack for a mouth; the face of Andrew Jackson three years dead." Quoted in Miller, *Victor Berger*, 208. But Landis's tough behavior made him a favorite of employers all over the nation. In 1920, the owners of major league baseball teams appointed him the first commissioner and gave him near-absolute power to run the affairs of a sport sullied by the Black Sox scandal of the previous year—a scandal largely caused by the refusal of Chicago White Sox owner Charles Comiskey to pay decent wages to his first-place team.

72. Ludwig Frank quoted in Geoff Eley, *Forging Democracy: The History of the Left in Europe, 1850–2000* (New York, 2002), 126. Frank died at the front during the first Geman offensive.

73. Weinstein, *Decline of Socialism*, 153.

74. Quote by J. C. St. Clair Drake in Theodore Kornweibel Jr., *No Crystal Stair: Black Life and the Messenger, 1917–1928* (Westport, Conn., 1975), 19. Randolph and Owen quoted in Jervis Anderson, *A. Philip Randolph: A Biographical Portrait* (Berkeley, Calif., 1986), 94.

75. Green, *Grass-Roots Socialism*, 359, 360; Bissett, *Agrarian Socialism in America: Marx, Jefferson, and Jesus in the Oklahoma Countryside, 1904–1920* (Norman, Okla., 1999), 142–53.

76. The anarchists who wrote the plan while sitting in a Mexican prison imagined a race war in which every Anglo male over the age of sixteen would be killed. But the gunmen who tried to implement it had abandoned that genocidal vision. James A. Sandos, *Rebellion in the Borderlands: Anarchism and the Plan of San Diego, 1904–1923* (Norman, Okla., 1992), 81–85 and passim.

77. Haywood to Sanger, Feb. 1, 1919, *Margaret Sanger Papers*, vol. 1, 246.

78. Berger quoted in Weinstein, *Decline of Socialism*, 180.

79. Eastman quoted in Salvatore, *Debs*, 320; Boudin quoted in David Shannon, *The Socialist Party of America: A History* (Chicago, 1967), 148. The best narrative of these complicated, wrenching events is still Weinstein, *Decline of Socialism*, 177–257.

80. Quoted in Ernest Freeberg, *Democracy's Prisoner: Eugene V. Debs, the Great War, and the Right to Dissent* (Cambridge, Mass., 2008), 177. Debs's total of 919,000 votes was slightly higher than the number he received in 1912. But, due to woman suffrage, it was only about half the percentage of all ballots cast.

81. Baldwin quoted in Rossinow, *Visions of Progress*, 83. For an engaging history of the amnesty campaign, see Freeberg, *Democracy's Prisoner*.

CHAPTER FIVE: THE PARADOX OF
AMERICAN COMMUNISM, 1920S–1950S

1. Quoted in Aileen S. Kraditor, *"Jimmy Higgins": The Mental World of the American Rank-and-File Communist, 1930–1958* (New York, 1988), 81.

2. Quoted in D. D. Guttenplan, *American Radical: The Life and Times of I. F. Stone* (New York, 2009), 165.

3. The analogy between converts to religion and to Communism is not an exact one, of course. In each case, the consequences of such a change of heart and mind were often quite different. But the abundance of memoirs of those who embraced Communism as a burning faith that explained *everything* cannot be dismissed. For example, see such accounts of "the god that failed" as Arthur Koestler's: "to say one had 'seen the light' is a poor description of the intellectual rapture which only the convert knows . . . The new light seems to pour from all directions across the skull." Quoted in Vivian Gornick, *The Romance of American Communism* (New York, 1977), 257. Some African-American ministers did make temporary alliances with the CP in the 1930s and '40s, but they did not join the Party, in contrast to the hundreds of preachers, mostly white, who joined the Socialist Party before World War I.

4. Vito Marcantonio, who served seven terms in Congress during the 1930s and '40s, was a reliable supporter of Communist positions on both domestic and foreign policy. But he ran first as a Republican and later as the nominee of the American Labor Party and always denied he was a CP member. See Gerald Meyer, *Vito Marcantonio: Radical Politician* (Albany, N.Y., 1989).

5. *The Gallup Poll: Public Opinion, 1935–1971*, vol. 1, *1935–1948* (New York, 1972),

277, 285. These polls were taken toward the end of the period of the Hitler-Stalin pact, but the CP's temporary anti-war stand was shared by major figures like John L. Lewis and Charles Lindbergh. On espionage, see Harvey Klehr, John Earl Haynes, and Fridrikh Igorevich Firsov, *The Secret World of American Communism* (New Haven, Conn., 1995); Haynes and Klehr, *In Denial: Historians, Communism and Espionage* (San Francisco, 2003); Haynes, Klehr, and Alexander Vassiliev, *Spies: The Rise and Fall of the KGB in America* (New Haven, Conn., 2009).

6. Daniel Bell, *Marxian Socialism in the United States* (1952; Ithaca, N.Y., 1995), 193.

7. Michael Denning, *The Cultural Front: The Laboring of American Culture in the Twentieth Century* (London, 1996), 230–58. Of the nine books, three were detective novels by Dashiell Hammett, and one book each by John Steinbeck, Betty Smith, Ruth McKenney, Ernest Hemingway, Lillian Smith, and Richard Wright. Only Hammett, McKenney, and Wright were members of the Party. For the list, see Frank Luther Mott, *Golden Multitudes* (New York, 1947), 303–31.

8. Rovere quoted in Guttenplan, *American Radical*, 81–82.

9. On the preponderance of Jewish New Yorkers in the CPUSA, see Nathan Glazer, *The Social Basis of American Communism* (1961; Westport, Conn.: 1974), 130–68, 220–22; Harvey Klehr, *Communist Cadre: The Social Background of the American Communist Party Elite* (Stanford, Calif., 1979), 37–52.

10. Harvey Klehr and John Earl Haynes, *The American Communist Movement: Storming Heaven Itself* (New York, 1992), 50–51.

11. Eric Hobsbawm, *Interesting Times* (New York, 2002), 133–34, 135.

12. Stalin, "A Year of Great Change," 1929, at http://marxists.org/reference/archive/stalin/works/1929/11/03.htm (accessed Oct. 26, 2010).

13. Stalin quoted in Klehr and Haynes, *American Communist Movement*, 49. "Reds Oust 9 More in Lovestone Row," *New York Times*, Aug. 15, 1929, 8. The *Times* did not even mention Cannon's expulsion. American Trotskyists soon fragmented into a number of organizations, the largest of which, the Socialist Workers Party, still exists. During the 1930s, the Lovestoneites gathered in the tiny Communist Party Opposition, later renamed the International Labor League of America, but abandoned that effort in 1941. During the Cold War, Lovestone became an influential architect of anti-Communist unionism and a close ally of AFL-CIO president George Meany.

14. Michael Gold, "Why I Am a Communist," *New Masses*, September 1932, 9.

15. The membership of the CP grew from 7,500 in 1930 to 23,467 in 1934. Irving Howe and Lewis Coser, *The American Communist Party: A Critical History* (New York, 1957), 225. In 1932, besides the 885,000 votes which Thomas received (2.2% of the total), Socialists also found hope in the quarter-million votes (12.6% of the total) which Morris Hillquit won as candidate for mayor of New York City.

16. Stalin quoted in Howe and Coser, *American Communist Party*, 178; ibid., 183. The "first period" of revolutionary hope and fervor began with the Bolshevik triumph in 1917 and ended with an aborted German revolution in 1923; the "second period" of compromise and united fronts with social democrats, left-wing nationalists, and other reform groups—including the AFL in the United States—ended in 1928.

17. Foster's book (which may have been co-written), quoted in Edward P. Johanningsmeier, *Forging American Communism: The Life of William Z. Foster* (Princeton, 1994), 263, 264. Quote from Howe and Coser, *American Communist Party*, 223.

18. Harvard Sitkoff, *A New Deal for Blacks*, 30th anniversary ed. (New York, 2009), 120.

19. Transcript of 1979 interview with Howard Johnson, Oral History of the American Left, Tamiment Institute, New York University, 6; Sol Harper to the Negro Department, Aug. 28, 1933, CPUSA Collection, Reel 247, Library of Congress.

20. Frederick Schuman, quoted in Richard H. Pells, *Radical Visions and American*

*Dreams: Culture and Social Thought in the Depression Years* (New York, 1973), 64. Edmund Wilson, *The American Earthquake: A Documentary of the Jazz Age, the Great Depression, and the New Deal* (Garden City, N.Y., 1964), 428, 521, 12, 464.

21. "Culture and the Crisis" quoted in Michael Denning, *The Cultural Front: The Laboring of American Culture in the Twentieth Century* (London, 1996), 98.

22. *The Maltese Falcon*, quoted in Joan Mellen, *Hellman and Hammett: The Legendary Passion of Lillian Hellman and Dashiell Hammett* (New York, 1996), 105.

23. James T. Farrell, *Studs Lonigan* (1935; Urbana, Ill., 1993), 840–44.

24. Ashley Pettis, "Marching with a Song," *New Masses*, May 1, 1934. On the song's reception, see Howard Pollack, *Aaron Copland: The Life and Work of an Uncommon Man* (Urbana, Ill., 2000), 275. I am grateful to the composer Susan Blaustein for helping me to describe Copland's music.

25. Quoted in Harvey Klehr, *The Heyday of American Communism: The Depression Decade* (New York, 1984), 178.

26. Louis Goldblatt, *Working Class Leader in the ILWU, 1935–1977*, 2 vols., ed. Estolv Ethan Ward (Berkeley, Calif., 1980), 425.

27. Irving Howe, "The Brilliant Masquerade: A Note on 'Browderism,'" in Irving Howe, *Socialism and America* (New York, 1985), 87–104, quote on 91.

28. Quoted in Howe and Coser, *American Communist Party*, 338.

29. For good summaries of CP gains during the late 1930s from opposing ideological positions, see Mark Naison, "Remaking America: Communists and Liberals in the Popular Front," in *New Studies in the Politics of U.S. Communism*, ed. Michael E. Brown et al. (New York, 1993), 45–73; Harvey Klehr, *Heyday of American Communism*, 186–385. There are no reliable statistics about the precise number of members in the CP during these years, in part because an unknown number kept their membership secret. For estimates, see Glazer, *Social Basis*, 92–93; Klehr, *Heyday*, 365–68; Klehr and Haynes, *American Communist Movement*, 85–86.

30. "Answers on the Air: An Interview with Earl Browder," *New Masses*, Oct. 20, 1936, 6.

31. The figure of 40 percent comes from Klehr and Haynes, *American Communist Movement*, 83. Robert Zieger, in his authoritative study of the CIO, quotes a reporter who estimated that "the [pro-CP] left" controlled about one-third of the delegates to the union federation's 1946 convention—just before the Cold War eroded the party's support. Robert H. Zieger, *The CIO, 1935–1955* (Chapel Hill, N.C., 1997), 254.

32. Some of this paragraph is adapted from Michael Kazin, *The Populist Persuasion: An American History*, rev. ed. (Ithaca, N.Y., 1998).

33. At one point, Franklin and Eleanor Roosevelt mocked petitions demanding Browder's release. Eleanor marked one, "For your amusement," and her husband responded, "I think I will send Browder as ambassador to Berlin. The place is vacant!" James G. Ryan, *Earl Browder: The Failure of American Communism*, 2nd ed. (Tuscaloosa, Ala., 2006), 204–205.

34. *New Masses*, July 1, 1941, 2, 8.

35. Browder quoted in Maurice Isserman, *Which Side Were You On? The American Communist Party During the Second World War* (Middletown, Conn., 1982), 156.

36. On the CPA and its critics within Communist ranks, see Isserman, *Which Side*, 187–213.

37. Al Richmond, *A Long View from the Left: Memoirs of an American Revolutionary* (New York, 1972), 248.

38. On the meaning and power of these documents, see Harold Meyerson and Ernie Harburg, *Who Put the Rainbow in The Wizard of Oz: Yip Harburg, Lyricist* (Ann Arbor, Mich., 1993), 45–52; Linda Gordon, "Dorothea Lange: The Photographer as Agricultural Sociologist," *Journal of American History* 93 (December 2006), www

.historycooperative.org/journals/jah/93.3/gordon.html (accessed Oct. 26, 2010). Lawrence W. Levine, "The Historian and the Icon: Photography and the History of the American People in the 1930s and 1940s," *Documenting America, 1935–1943*, ed. Carl Fleischhauer and Beverly W. Brannan (Berkeley, Calif., 1988), 15–42.

39. Gordon, "Dorothea Lange"; Samuel Sillen, "Censoring 'The Grapes of Wrath,' " *New Masses*, Sept. 12, 1939, 23–24.

40. Alfred Kazin, *On Native Grounds: An Interpretation of Modern American Prose Literature* (1942; New York, 1995) , 364.

41. Seeger, quoted in Robbie Lieberman, *"My Song Is My Weapon": People's Songs, American Communism, and the Politics of Culture, 1930–1950* (Urbana, Ill., 1989), 34, 37.

42. Quoted in Jabari Asim, "Josh White, Caught in the Middle," *Washington Post*, Jan. 2, 2001, C2.

43. Ibid.; Denning, *Cultural Front*, 351.

44. Elijah Wald, "Josh White and the Protest Blues," *Living Blues*, posted at http://www.elijahwald.com/joshprotest.html (accessed Oct. 26, 2010). David W. Stowe, "The Politics of Café Society," *Journal of American History* 84 (March 1998): 1384–1406.

45. Quoted in Lieberman, *"My Song Is My Weapon,"* 39.

46. Quoted in Ed Cray, *Ramblin' Man: The Life and Times of Woody Guthrie* (New York, 2004), 151.

47. Steinbeck, *Grapes of Wrath*, quoted in Jay Parini, *John Steinbeck* (New York, 1999), 222.

48. Lyrics at www.woodyguthrie.org/Lyrics/Jesus_Christ.htm; Klein, *Woody Guthrie*, 128. In contrast, William Gropper, a regular cartoonist for the *New Masses* during the late 1930s and early 40s, had the wit of a sledgehammer. In 1941, for example, he drew FDR consulting *Mein Kampf* as he directs U.S. troops, outfitted as stormtroopers, to bust up strikes at defense plants. *New Masses*, June 24, 1941, 15. Two days before the date on the cover, the real armies of Nazi Germany had invaded the USSR.

49. Quoted in Klein, *Woody Guthrie*, 172.

50. Ibid., 143–44.

51. Quoted in Lieberman, *"My Song Is My Weapon,"* 39.

52. David Thomson, *The New Biographical Dictionary of Film* (New York, 2004), 462–63 (in the entry on Pauline Kael).

53. For opposing views, see Paul Buhle and Dave Wagner, *Radical Hollywood: The Untold Story Behind America's Favorite Movies* (New York, 2002), especially v–xviii, and Larry Ceplair and Steven Englund, *The Inquisition in Hollywood: Politics in the Film Community, 1930–1960* (Berkeley, Calif., 1983), especially 49–50.

54. The estimate of three hundred Communists is that of Ceplair and Englund, *Inquisition in Hollywood*, 65–66. They do not cite the sources they used to come up with that number.

55. On Reagan's politics at the time, see Steven J. Ross, *Hollywood Left and Right: How Movie Stars Shaped American Politics* (New York, 2011).

56. *Mission to Moscow*, a clumsy production, was directed by Michael Curtiz, the same man responsible for the masterful *Casablanca*.

57. Quotes from Joseph McBride, *Frank Capra: The Catastrophe of Success* (New York, 1992), 420, 421. Harry Cohn, head of Columbia Pictures, turned Kennedy down, in part because the film was doing well at the box office.

58. Quotes from a 1969 interview which appears in Bertrand Tavernier, *Amis Américains: Entretiens avec les grand Auteurs d'Hollywood* (Arles, France, 1993), 469–70. The translations are my own.

59. Peter Novick, *That Noble Dream: The "Objectivity Question" and the American His-*

*torical Profession* (Cambridge, UK, 1988), 172–74, 239–47; Arthur S. Link, "The American Historical Association, 1884–1984: Retrospect and Prospect," *American Historical Review* 90 (February 1985): 4–5. Unlike their elders, graduate students in history were often willing to do political work while pursuing an engaged style of scholarship. In the early 1930s, the Arkansas-born C. Vann Woodward visited the Soviet Union and then assisted a Communist organizer during a nationwide textile strike. He would go on to write such books as *The Strange Career of Jim Crow* and *Origins of the New South* that demolished conservative notions about his region's past. See Glenda Gilmore, *Defying Dixie: The Radical Roots of Civil Rights, 1919–1950* (New York, 2008), 133.

60. Leo Huberman, *We, the People*, rev. ed. (New York, 1947), 160; Andrew Hemingway, *Artists on the Left: American Artists and the Communist Movement, 1926–1956* (New Haven, Conn., 2002), 201–204.

61. Matthew Josephson, *The Politicos, 1865–1896* (New York, 1938), 182, 183. A few sentences from this portrait are borrowed from my introduction to a new edition of this work published by Commons in 2007. Josephson was no relation to the owner of Café Society.

62. Matthew Josephson, *The Robber Barons* (1934; San Diego, 1962), 275, 38, 441.

63. Quoted in David Shi, *Matthew Josephson: Bourgeois Bohemian* (New Haven, Conn., 1981), 165.

64. Ibid., 12; Matthew Josephson, *Life Among the Surrealists: A Memoir* (New York, 1962), 31.

65. Shi, *Matthew Josephson*, 283.

66. War and Navy Departments, *Instructions for American Servicemen in France During World War II* (1944; Chicago, 2008), 38–39.

67. Quoted in Sitkoff, *A New Deal for Blacks*, 118; the sociologists were Horace Cayton and St. Clair Drake, quoted in Eric Arnesen, "No 'Graver Danger': Black Anticommunism, the Communist Party, and the Race Question," *Labor: Studies in Working-Class History of the Americas* 3 (Winter 2006): 32. According to Nathan Glazer, whose work is still the best statistical study of the subject, "The party steadily recruited about twice as many Negro members as the rolls showed at any time." Seldom did black membership top 10 percent of the total. Glazer, *Social Basis*, 175. The CP, it seems, did not report separate totals of Latino or Asian-American members. In fact, neither category was widely employed anywhere until the 1960s.

The Los Angeles CP did report that it recruited over 200 "Spanish and Mexican workers" in 1936 and 1937. Douglas Monroy, "*Anarquismo y Comunismo*: Mexican Radicalism and the Communist Party in Los Angeles During the 1930s," *Labor History* 24 (Winter 1983): 53. According to one longtime Communist from California, there were no more than forty Japanese Americans in the Party in the late 1920s and even fewer Chinese Americans. The opposition of the former to the emperor system in Japan made it difficult for them to work with other Japanese organizations during the Popular Front. Karl Yoneda, transcript of interview with Oral History of the American Left, conducted Nov. 7, 1983. Tamiment Library, NYU.

68. Quoted in Arnesen, "No 'Graver Danger,' " 15. On the Party's racial policies during wartime, see Maurice Isserman, *Which Side Were You On?: The American Communist Party During the Second World War* (Middletown, Conn., 1982). Yoneda is quoted on 144–45.

69. Some New Deal liberals, particularly in northern cities, also promoted the idea of ethnic diversity as well as civil rights—but skirted the social roots of inequality. See Diana Selig, *Americans All: The Cultural Gifts Movement* (Cambridge, Mass., 2008).

70. For the history and legacy of the PLM in the U.S., see Monroy, "*Anarquismo y Comunismo*," 34–59.

71. Quotes from David Guiterrez, *Walls and Mirrors: Mexican Americans, Mexican Immigrants, and the Politics of Ethnicity* (Berkeley, Calif., 1995), 113, 109.

72. Quotes from a reprint of the article in *Herencia: The Anthology of Hispanic Literature of the United States*, ed. Nicolas Kanellos (New York, 2001), 156–63.

73. See Zaragosa Vargas, *Labor Rights Are Civil Rights: Mexican American Workers in Twentieth-Century America* (Princeton, N.J., 2005), 140.

74. Ibid., 133.

75. Howard Johnson, a black leader of the Young Communist League, quoted in Naison, *Communists in Harlem*, 193.

76. Transcript of oral interview with Queen Mother Moore by Ruth Prego, Dec. 23, 1981, 12–13, 9. Oral History of the American Left, Tamiment Institute.

77. This was the Party's view during the revolutionary "third period," as well, despite occasional trials of members for "white chauvinism." For example, see the illustrations by William Siegel in 1930 which depict white workers viewing black people as fellow proletarians while a bourgeois couple sees them only as licentious entertainers, gamblers, and overemotional evangelists. *New Masses*, May 1930, 7.

78. James Dugan, "G'wan with the Wind," *New Masses*, Jan. 2, 1940, 28.

79. Quotes from Irwin Silber, *Press Box Red: The Story of Lester Rodney, the Communist Who Helped Break the Color Line in American Sports* (Philadelphia, 2003), 3, 5.

80. Rodney in *Daily Worker*, Aug. 13, 1936, quoted in Silber, ibid., 53.

81. Gold, Oct. 26, 1945, quoted in Silver, ibid., 91. For a masterful study of the larger subject, see Jules Tygiel, *Baseball's Great Experiment: Jackie Robinson and His Legacy* (New York, 1983).

82. Richard Wright, *Black Boy (American Hunger)*, in Richard Wright, *Later Works* (New York, 1991), 351–52.

83. Quoted in Hazel Rowley, *Richard Wright: The Life and Times* (New York, 2001), 200.

84. Quotes from ibid., 117; Richard Wright, *12 Million Black Voices* (1941), excerpted in *The American Writer and the Great Depression*, ed. Harvey Swados (Indianapolis, Ind., 1966), 370.

85. Junius Scales, a white Communist from North Carolina, quoted in Martin Bauml Duberman, *Paul Robeson: A Biography* (New York, 1989), 258.

86. Quoted in ibid., 273. Harold Cruse, an ex-Communist, later pointed out that Robeson was an "interpretive" artist rather than a "creative" one like Wright and so found it easier to adhere to "the canons of Communist aesthetics." Harold Cruse, *The Crisis of the Negro Intellectual: A Historical Analysis of the Failure of Black Leadership* (1967; New York, 1984), 289.

87. Quoted in ibid., 342.

88. Ibid., 358. In 1951, Robeson offered to join the CP, whose top officials were about to go to prison for violating the Smith Act, which proscribed advocating the violent overthrow of the federal government. But those leaders rejected him, thinking membership would ensure his political irrelevance. Ibid., 420. The Civil Rights Congress helped defend black men and women accused of violent crimes and may have had as many as ten thousand members at its height in the late 1940s.

89. Isserman, *Which Side*, 216–21; Ryan, *Earl Browder*, 262.

90. Statement by John Howard Lawson to the House Committee on Un-American Activities, *Hearings Regarding the Communist Infiltration of the Motion Picture Industry*, 80th Congress, 1st Session, October 1947 (Washington, D.C., 1947), accessed in http://historymatters.gmu.edu/d/6441 (accessed October 8, 2010).

91. Cooper quoted in *Life*, Nov. 3, 1947, 40. The researcher in Harlem was John Graves, cited in Glazer, *Social Basis*, 237. One reason for the CP's popularity in Harlem is that the CP and its fronts continued to be a force in the black freedom

movement there. For details, see Martha Biondi, *To Stand and Fight: The Struggle for Civil Rights in Postwar New York City* (Cambridge, Mass., 2003).

92. On these subjects, see Julia L. Mickenberg, *Learning from the Left: Children's Literature, the Cold War, and Radical Politics in the United States* (New York, 2006); Dr. Seuss, *Yertle the Turtle and Other Stories* (New York, 1958); Arthur Miller, *Timebends: A Life* (New York, 1987), 265–67; Tony Kushner, "Kushner on Miller," *The Nation*, May 26, 2005, at http://www.thenation.com/doc/20050614/kushner; Judith Smith, *Visions of Belonging: Family Stories, Popular Culture, and Postwar Democracy, 1940–1960* (New York, 2004).

93. Quoted in Guttenplan, *American Radical: The Life and Times of I. F. Stone*, 333.

94. Quoted in Kate Weigand, *Red Feminism: American Communism and the Making of Women's Liberation* (Baltimore, 2001), 1.

95. See Daniel Horowitz, "Rethinking Betty Friedan and *The Feminine Mystique*: Labor Union Radicalism and Feminism in Cold War America," *American Quarterly* 48 (1996): 1–42. In her autobiography, Friedan admits that after graduating from college, she routinely attended "Communist Front meetings and rallies" and "thought of myself as a revolutionary." She also asked to join the Party, but it is unclear if the offer was accepted. Betty Friedan, *Life So Far: A Memoir* (New York, 2000), 57–58.

96. For a good sample of the Hooverite view, see Haynes and Klehr, *In Denial*, and Klehr and Haynes, *American Communist Movement*. For the rosier interpretation, see most of the essays in *New Studies*, ed. Brown et al., and the summary by Paul Buhle and Dan Georgakas in *Encyclopedia of the American Left*, 2nd ed., 146–56.

97. Quoted in Julian Barnes, "Such, Such Was Eric Blair," *New York Review of Books*, March 12, 2009, 19.

98. Naison, *Communists in Harlem*, xx.


CHAPTER SIX: NOT WITH MY LIFE, YOU DON'T, 1950S–1980S

1. Quoted in James Miller, *"Democracy Is in the Streets": From Port Huron to the Siege of Chicago* (New York, 1987), 374.

2. Quoted in Eric Hobsbawm, *The Age of Extremes: A History of the World, 1914–1991* (New York, 1994), 333.

3. Available at donnadarko.wordpress.com/2008/02/05 (accessed June 24, 2009).

4. Richard Rorty, *Achieving Our Country: Leftist Thought in Twentieth-Century America* (Cambridge, Mass., 1998), 70.

5. See the application form at www.slp.org (accessed June 29, 2009).

6. King quoted in Thomas F. Jackson, *From Civil Rights to Human Rights: Martin Luther King, Jr., and the Struggle for Economic Justice* (Philadelphia, 2007), 69, 72.

7. C. Wright Mills, *The Power Elite* (New York, 1956); lecture given at the London School of Economics, 1959, published in *The Politics of Truth: Selected Writings of C. Wright Mills*, ed. John H. Summers (New York, 2008), 199.

8. Ginsberg, "Howl" in *Howl and Other Poems* (San Francisco, 1956), 9. Emma Goldman had inveighed against "the merciless Moloch of capitalism" in a famous 1911 essay, "The Traffic in Women." But Ginsberg's Moloch was driven more by the need to repress free souls than by profit.

9. Van Gosse, *The Movements of the New Left, 1950–1975: A Brief History with Documents* (Boston, 2005).

10. http://www.bartleby.com/73/1828.html. Jerry Rubin later turned the jibe into a warning.

11. By 1980, more than 12 percent of the population was attending college, compared to only 2.5 percent in 1950. Doug Rossinow, *The Politics of Authenticity: Liberalism, Christianity, and the New Left in America* (New York, 1998), 255.

12. For a survey of poll results on these matters, see Louis Harris, *Inside America* (New

York, 1987). A few sentences in this paragraph are borrowed from "The Failure and Success of the New Radicalism," an article I co-wrote with Maurice Isserman that was published in *The Rise and Fall of the New Deal Order, 1930–1980* (Princeton, N.J., 1989), 212–42. They are used with Isserman's permission.

13. Clancy Sigal, *Going Away: A Report, a Memoir* (1961; New York, 1984), 141, 512. Sigal had once been close friends with C. Wright Mills, although the two had fallen out by 1961. See John H. Summers, "The Epigone's Embrace, Part 2: C. Wright Mills and the New Left," *Left History* 13 (Fall/Winter 2008): 110.

14. The historian John Patrick Diggins summed up the view nicely: "The historical context of the Old Left was the abundance of poverty; that of the New Left, the poverty of abundance." Diggins, *The Rise and Fall of the American Left* (New York, 1992), 232. Such reformist intellectuals as Arthur Schlesinger Jr. and John Kenneth Galbraith had earlier made a similar critique of "quantitative liberalism," but the solutions they offered, such as better television programming and curbing urban sprawl, were not likely to inspire a mass movement.

15. Ellen Willis, "The Family: Love It or Leave It," in Willis, *Beginning to See the Light: Sex, Hope, and Rock-and-Roll* (Hanover, N.H., 1992), 164; Marshall Berman, *The Politics of Authenticity: Radical Individualism and the Emergence of Modern Society* (New York, 1970), 324.

16. In his *Politics of Authenticity*, p. x, Marshall Berman writes, "The New Left's complaint against democratic capitalism was not that it was too individualistic, but rather that it wasn't individualistic enough."

17. Michael Harrington, "Harlem Today," *Dissent*, July 1961, 371.

18. Bayard Rustin, "From Protest to Politics: The Future of the Civil Rights Movement," in *The Radical Papers*, ed. Irving Howe (Garden City, N.Y., 1966), 355. The article was originally published in the February 1965 issue of *Commentary*.

19. Rustin, "From Protest to Politics," 358, 354. On the budget and its failure, see John D'Emilio, *Lost Prophet: The Life and Times of Bayard Rustin* (New York, 2003), 430–39.

20. King quoted in Thomas F. Jackson's essential text, *From Civil Rights to Human Rights*, 42.

21. King quoted in Nancy MacLean, *Freedom Is Not Enough: The Opening of the American Workplace* (Cambridge, Mass., 2006), 105.

22. Jackson, *From Civil Rights to Human Rights*, 363–64.

23. Lorraine Hansberry, address to Roosevelt University (her alma mater), in *Women and the Civil Rights Movement, 1954–1965*, ed. David W. Houck and David E. Dixon (Jackson, Miss., 2009), 94–95; James Baldwin, *The Fire Next Time* (New York, 1963), 7; John Edgar Wideman, introduction to Stokely Carmichael with Ekwueme Michael Thelwell, *Ready for Revolution: The Life and Struggles of Stokely Carmichael (Kwame Ture)* (New York, 2003), 6.

24. Quoted in Clayborne Carson, *In Struggle: SNCC and the Black Awakening of the 1960s* (Cambridge, Mass., 1981), 17.

25. http://www.marxists.org/history/usa/workers/black-panthers/1966/10/15.htm (accessed Oct. 26, 2010). For a sympathetic history of the phenomenon, see Peniel E. Joseph, *Waiting 'til the Midnight Hour: A Narrative History of Black Power in America* (New York, 2006).

26. I saw the Stalin poster on a visit to the Black Panther Party office during the summer of 1969. For a critical perspective on the party's history, see Hugh Pearson, *The Shadow of the Panther: Huey Newton and the Price of Black Power in America* (Reading, Mass., 1994). For friendly ones, see Kathleen Cleaver and George Katsiaficas, eds., *Liberation, Imagination, and the Black Panther Party: A New Look at the Panthers and Their Legacy* (New York, 2001). A more balanced view is Curtis J. Austin's *Up Against the Wall: Violence in the Making and Unmaking of the Black Panther*

*Party* (Fayetteville, Ark., 2006). For media coverage of the group, see Jane Rhodes, *Framing the Black Panthers: The Spectacular Rise of a Black Power Icon* (New York, 2007). On Newton's admiration of the Dylan song, which he saw as a comment on American racism, see Bobby Seale, *Seize the Time*, at http://lemming.mahost.org/library/seize/index.htm (accessed Oct. 25, 2010).

27. Newton speech at Boston College, November 18, 1970. Printed in *To Die for the People: The Writings of Huey P. Newton* (New York, 1972), 22. The editor of this collection was Toni Morrison.

28. Genet quoted in Thomas Sugrue, *Sweet Land of Liberty: The Forgotten Struggle for Civil Rights in the North* (New York, 2008), 344. For the influence of the BPP on Chicano and Japanese-American radicals, see Laura Pulido, *Black, Brown, Yellow and Left: Radical Activism in Los Angeles* (Berkeley, Calif., 2006), and Jeffrey O. G. Ogbar, "Rainbow Radicalism: The Rise of Radical Ethnic Nationalism," in *The Black Power Movement: Rethinking the Civil Rights–Black Power Era*, ed. Peniel E. Joseph (New York, 2006), 193–228. Among young whites, the allure of the Panthers stretched beyond the ranks of New Left stalwarts. A poster of the handsome Huey Newton, pike in one hand and rifle in the other, sitting in a wicker chair and half glaring, half grinning at the camera, was hung on the walls of innumerable apartments and dormitory rooms. One day in 1969, I gave a long ride to a young, white working-class hitchhiker from the Central Valley of California whose repeated response to my criticisms of the Panthers was "Well, you know, they *are* the vanguard."

29. For details on these groups, see Michael L. Clemons and Charles E. Jones, "Global Solidarity: The Black Panther Party in the International Arena," in Cleaver and Katsiaficas, eds., *Liberation, Imagination, and the Black Panther Party*, 20–39. In West Germany, the example of the Panthers also inspired some radicals "to pick up the gun" to attack the "fascist" business and political establishments in that nation. The notorious terrorist group, the Red Army Faction, emerged from this milieu. See Martin Klimke, *The Other Alliance: Student Protest in West Germany and the United States in the Global Sixties* (Princeton, N.J., 2010), 108–42.

30. Unnamed informant, quoted in Pulido, *Black, Brown, Yellow, and Left*, 102.

31. Carmichael, *Ready for Revolution*, 93. According to one historian, Carmichael was also friendly with a number of Jews on the socialist left and the first demonstration he attended was one in support of Israel. Cheryl Lynn Greenberg, *Troubling the Waters: Black-Jewish Relations in the American Century* (Princeton, N.J., 2006), 219.

32. Quoted in Carmichael, *Ready for Revolution*, 263.

33. Peniel E. Joseph, "Black Power's Powerful Legacy," *Chronicle of Higher Education*, July 21, 2006, B7; Carmichael, *Ready for Revolution*, 601.

34. Clayborne Carson, "Black Power After Ten Years," *The Nation*, Aug. 14, 1976, reprinted in *A History of Our Time: Readings on Postwar America*, 2nd ed., ed. William H. Chafe and Harvard Sitkoff (New York, 1987), 199.

35. On the cultural legacy of the BPP, see Rhodes, *Framing the Black Panthers*, 307–36.

36. For Toni Morrison's 1993 lecture, see http://nobelprize.org/nobel_prizes/literature/laureates/1993/morrison-lecture.html (accessed Oct. 26, 2010). For an insightful critique of identity politics from the left, see Todd Gitlin, *The Twilight of Common Dreams: Why America Is Wracked by Culture Wars* (New York, 1995).

37. Quotes from Miller, *"Democracy Is in the Streets,"* 329; Carson, *In Struggle*, 176.

38. Carl Oglesby, "Democracy Is Nothing If Not Dangerous," SDS Papers, Microfilm Edition, reel 38, no. 265.

39. Isserman and Kazin, *America Divided: The Civil War of the 1960s*, 3rd ed. (New York, 2008), 191.

40. Flacks quoted in Jonah Goldberg, *Liberal Fascism: The Secret History of the American*

*Left* (New York, 2008), 185. Kenneth Keniston, *Young Radicals: Notes on Committed Youth* (New York, 1968), 113.

41. Ginsberg, "America," writing.upenn.edu/affiliates/88/america.html (accessed Oct. 26, 2010).

42. Hayden quoted in Isserman and Kazin, *America Divided*, 191; Berman, *Tale of Two Utopias*, 81. On the paucity of left-wing parents among black and Latin radicals, see Pulido, *Black, Brown, Yellow and Left*, 63. On the radical love affair with the Vietnamese, see Todd Gitlin, *The Sixties: Years of Hope, Days of Rage*, rev. ed. (New York, 1993), 261–82.

43. Glenn W. Jones, "Gentle Thursday: An SDS Circus in Austin, Texas, 1966–1969," in *Sights on the Sixties*, ed. Barbara L. Tischler (New Brunswick, N.J., 1992), 75–85. Gitlin, *The Sixties*, 344.

44. Interagency Security Memo, quoted in Dick Cluster, "The Anti-War Movement: It Did Make a Difference," in *They Should Have Served That Cup of Coffee*, ed. Dick Cluster (Boston, 1979), 134; Nitze quoted in Tom Wells, *The War Within: America's Battle Over Vietnam* (Berkeley, 1994), 247.

45. For good analytical surveys, see Jeremi Suri, "The Rise and Fall of an International Counterculture, 1960–1975," *American Historical Review* 114 (February 2009): 45–68; Geoff Eley, *Forging Democracy: The History of the Left in Europe, 1850–2000* (New York, 2002), 341–65.

46. A new People's Party did run Dr. Benjamin Spock in the 1972 election, but the sixty-nine-year-old "baby doctor" was an undistinguished speaker, and most left activists could find no reason to work or vote for him after George McGovern became the Democratic nominee. That year, Spock won about 79,000 votes, less than the total gained by the Trotskyist Socialist Workers Party, which ran candidates whose names were familiar only to party members.

47. http://www.4president.org/speeches/mcgovern1972acceptance.htm (accessed Oct. 26, 2010).

48. For a full, albeit too sympathetic, narrative, see Max Elbaum, *Revolution in the Air: Sixties Radicals Turn to Lenin, Mao and Che* (London, 2002).

49. Quoted in Summers, *The Politics of Truth*, 9.

50. The target for the abortive bombing was a dance at Fort Dix in New Jersey. This was the first and, to my knowledge, the last time the group planned an action whose purpose was to kill rather than to destroy property.

51. Among the many excellent works on the history of recent feminism, two stand out: Ruth Rosen, *The World Split Open: How the Modern Women's Movement Changed America* (New York, 2000), and Christine Stansell, *The Feminist Promise: From 1792 to the Present* (New York, 2010). On labor feminism, also see Dorothy Sue Cobble, *The Other Women's Movement: Workplace Justice and Social Rights in Modern America* (Princeton, N.J., 2004).

52. On WITCH, see Rosen, *World Split Open*, 204–205; Anne Koedt, "The Myth of the Vaginal Orgasm," *Radical Feminism: A Documentary Reader*, ed. Barbara A. Crow (New York, 2000), 377.

53. Robin Morgan, *Saturday's Child: A Memoir* (New York, 2001), 30.

54. In 1973, while en route to a speaking engagement, Morgan wrote to the four-year-old boy, "I am so glad you are interested in these stories . . . because that means to me that you are already fighting hard to grow up and not be like the bad men who are mean to women." Robin Morgan, *Going Too Far: The Personal Chronicle of a Feminist* (New York, 1977), 56.

55. "Goodbye to All That," originally published in the women's issue of *Rat*, reprinted in Morgan, *Going Too Far*, 122–30.

56. The girl's poem: "A hen / is useful to men. / She lays eggs / between her legs." *Sis-*

*terhood Is Powerful: An Anthology of Writings from the Women's Liberation Movement*, ed. Robin Morgan (New York, 1970), 567.

57. Stansell, *The Feminist Promise*, 272.

58. For details, see ibid., 273–352; "How to Start Your Own Consciousness-Raising Group," Chicago Women's Liberation Union (1971), at www.cwluherstory.com/CWLUArchive/crcwlu.html (accessed Oct. 26, 2010).

59. Quoted in Rosen, *World Split Open*, 83.

60. Quoted in Berman, *Tale of Two Utopias*, 148.

61. Quote from the inside cover of *The Ladder*, published by Daughters of Bilitis until 1970. Ironically, the driving force of the Mattachine Society was an ex-Communist named Harry Hay, an actor from Los Angeles. Hay successfully urged the Party to expel him in 1950, fearing he would be a "security risk."

62. Berman, *Tale of Two Utopias*, 165.

63. Rachel Carson, *Silent Spring* (1962; Boston, 1987), 297. On the history of environmentalism in the U.S., see Robert Gottlieb, *Forcing the Spring: The Transformation of the American Environmental Movement* (Washington, D.C., 2003).

64. The paper was *The Willamette Bridge*.

65. Wiley quoted in Edward P. Morgan, *The 60s Experience: Hard Lessons About Modern America* (Philadelphia, 1991), 241; slogan quoted in Michael Egan, *Barry Commoner and the Science of Survival: The Remaking of American Environmentalism* (Cambridge, Mass., 2007), 146.

66. Nixon quoted in Isserman and Kazin, *America Divided*, 288. On Earth Day, see Adam Rome, " 'Give Earth a Chance': The Environmental Movement and the Sixties," *Journal of American History* 90 (September 2003), 525–54. Egan, *Barry Commoner*, 109–11.

67. Egan, *Barry Commoner*, 112; Dr. Seuss, *The Lorax* (New York, 1971).

68. Quote from Commoner, *Closing Circle*, in Egan, *Barry Commoner*, frontispiece; "Paul Revere of Ecology," *Time*, Feb. 2, 1970.

69. Egan, *Barry Commoner*, 19; on the AASW, see Peter Kuznick, *Beyond the Laboratory: Scientists as Political Activists in 1930s America* (Chicago, 1987), 227–52.

70. On radical pacifists, see Isserman, *If I Had a Hammer*, 127–69. "Fighting to Save the Earth from Man," *Time*, Feb. 2, 1970.

71. Commoner, *The Closing Circle* (New York, 1971), 9–10, 282.

72. Gottlieb, *Forcing the Spring*, 113; Barry Commoner, *The Poverty of Power* (New York, 1976); Egan, *Barry Commoner*, 163–64.

73. Egan, *Barry Commoner*, 168; Philip Shabecoff, "Commoner Says Victory Is Not Object of His Drive," *New York Times*, Oct. 30, 1980, B19.

74. In Berkeley, Commoner received 6.3 percent of the vote, Reagan 14.4 percent. Thanks to Leshaun Yopack of the Alameda Registrar of Voters office for sending me these totals. The party persevered through one more presidential contest. In 1984, it nominated Sonia Johnson, an ex-Mormon feminist, for the White House. But she fared even worse than Commoner, winning just over 72,000 votes.

75. In the West German case, the main New Left organization, whose initials were also SDS, had begun as the youth group of the SPD. So radicals there returned to their original political home, albeit with different aims in mind. On the impact of the New Left on the politics of post-1960s Europe, see Geoff Eley, *Forging Democracy*, 366–83, 457–69; Gerd-Rainier Horn, *The Spirit of '68: Rebellion in Western Europe and North America, 1956–1976* (Oxford, UK, 2007), passim.

76. Daniel Yankelovich, *The New Morality: A Profile of American Youth in the 70s* (New York, 1974), 10–11. At the time, no right-wing conspiracy theorist seems to have noticed that the senior vice president of Yankelovich's firm was Ruth Clark, a former Communist and the wife of Joseph Clark, onetime Moscow correspondent for the *Daily Worker*. In addition, the Clarks' daughter Judy was then a member of

the Weather Underground, although her parents had become simply good liberals who shunned her politics.

77. For contrasting explanations of the power of feminism after the 1960s, see Jeremy Rabkin, "Feminism: Where the Spirit of the Sixties Lives On," 46–81, and Martha Nussbaum, "Women in the Sixties," 82–101, in *Reassessing the Sixties: Debating the Political and Cultural Legacy*, ed. Stephen Macedo (New York, 1997).

78. Sara Evans, "Sons, Daughters, and Patriarchy: Gender and the 1968 Generation," *American Historical Review* 114 (April 2009); Eley, *Forging Democracy*, 475–76.

79. Berman, *Tale of Two Utopias*, 60.

80. Marshall Berman, "Modernism in the Streets," *Dissent*, Fall 2008.

81. Unnamed informant, quoted in Richard Sennett and Jonathan Cobb's insightful study, *The Hidden Injuries of Class* (New York, 1972), 205.

82. Quoted in Miller, *"Democracy Is in the Streets,"* 332.

## CHAPTER SEVEN: REBELS WITHOUT A MOVEMENT, 1980S–2010

1. Randy Newman, "The World Isn't Fair," from the 1999 CD, *Bad Love*.

2. Buchanan, quoted in David Frum, *Dead Right* (New York, 1994), 30.

3. For example, the *Washington Post* reported, "Seeger made sure to include stanzas of the song not often sung at events of this official magnitude, including protest sentiments and references to Depression-era poverty." Richard Leiby and DeNeen L. Brown, "The Stars Align, with Egos in Check; Celebrity-Studded Concert Offers Heady Mix of History & Hollywood," Jan. 19, 2009, C1.

4. Richard Rorty, *Achieving Our Country: Leftist Thought in Twentieth-Century America* (Cambridge, Mass., 1998), 80–81.

5. Quote from Nader's 2000 Green Party acceptance speech, http://www.ratical.org/co-globalize/RalphNader/062500.html (accessed Oct. 26, 2010).

6. In early 2010, for example, the *New York Times*, in reporting on Osama bin Laden's praise of Chomsky for comparing " 'the U.S. policies to those of the Mafia,' " identified Chomsky as "the American linguist and liberal political activist." Jack Healy, "Bin Laden Adds Climate Change to List of Grievances Against U.S.," *New York Times*, Jan. 30, 2010, A6.

7. Quote from Obama's speech on the night of the New Hampshire primary, at http://www.nytimes.com/2008/01/08/us/politics/08text-obama.html (accessed Oct. 26, 2010); Bob Dylan, "Love Minus Zero/No Limit."

8. King quoted in David L. Hostetter, *Movement Matters: American Antiapartheid Activism and the Rise of Multicultural Politics* (New York, 2006), 31.

9. "Sun City" by Steven Van Zandt, quoted in ibid., 95.

10. Robinson quoted in *The Progressive*, October 2005, at http://www.progressive.org/mag_intv1005 (accessed Oct. 26, 2010).

11. Quotes from Christian Smith's excellent study, *Resisting Reagan: The U.S. Central America Peace Movement* (Chicago, 1996), 368, 367.

12. For details by one of the breed, see Steve Early, *Embedded with Organized Labor: Journalistic Reflections on the Class War at Home* (New York, 2009). Also see Nelson Lichtenstein, "Why American Unions Need Intellectuals," *Dissent*, Spring 2010, 69–73.

13. Early, *Embedded with Organized Labor*, 9. On these strategies, see Rick Fantasia and Kim Voss, *Hard Work: Remaking the American Labor Movement* (Berkeley, Calif., 2004), 120–59.

14. Betty Friedan, "History's Geiger Counter," *Audacious Democracy: Labor, Intellectuals, and the Social Reconstruction of America*, ed. Steven Fraser and Joshua B. Freeman (New York, 1997), 22.

15. Molly McGrath, quoted in Liza Featherstone, *Students Against Sweatshops* (Lon-

don, 2002), viii; Naomi Klein, *No Logo: Taking Aim at the Brand Bullies* (New York, 1999), 445.

16. Klein, *No Logo*, xxi. For a lively, if somewhat simplistic, critique of Klein, see Joseph Heath and Andrew Potter, *Nation of Rebels: Why Counterculture Became Consumer Culture* (New York, 2004), 205–208; 328–31.

17. See my overly optimistic op-ed, "Saying No to W.T.O," *New York Times*, Dec. 5, 1999, 17.

18. One sign of its decline was the lack of an audience for the 2007 movie *Battle in Seattle*, which starred Academy Award–winning actress Charlize Theron as well as the popular actors Woody Harrelson and Ray Liotta. Although the film received generally positive reviews, it earned less than $900,000 in box-office receipts, two-thirds of which came from its overseas release. http://www.boxofficemojo.com/movies/?id=battleinseattle.htm.

19. Quoted in William Finnegan, "After Seattle: Anarchists Get Organized," *The New Yorker*, April 17, 2000, 44.

20. Nicholas D. Kristof and Sheryl W. Dunn, *China Wakes: The Struggle for the Soul of a Rising Power* (New York, 1994); Featherstone, *Students Against Sweatshops*, 34; Michael Hardt and Antonio Negri, *Empire* (Cambridge, Mass., 2000), 400. Italics in original. That Negri, an Italian political scientist, was serving a long prison sentence for his involvement in the violent Red Brigades during the 1970s and '80s added a frisson of revolution to what is otherwise a work suffused with such puzzling assertions as "History has a logic only when subjectivity rules it, only when (as Nietzsche says) the emergence of subjectivity reconfigures efficient causes and final causes in the development of history. The power of the proletariat consists precisely in this" (235).

21. Jennifer Egan, in Finnegan, "After Seattle," 48.

22. On Chomsky's anarchism, see his *For Reasons of State* (New York, 1973), 370–86 and passim. The title comes from an essay by Bakunin, iii.

23. Noam Chomsky, *Chronicles of Dissent: Interviews with David Barsamian* (Monroe, Maine, 1992), xiii. Chomsky, interview by Eric French, posted in January 2010, at http://www.zmag.org/znet/viewArticle/23595 (accessed June 10, 2010).

24. http://news.bbc.co.uk/2/hi/5379650.stm (accessed Oct. 26, 2010).

25. Quote from Chomsky, *Chronicles of Dissent*, 142; Michael Kazin and Joseph A. McCartin, "Introduction," *Americanism: New Perspectives on the History of an Ideal*, ed. Michael Kazin and Joseph A. McCartin (Chapel Hill, N.C., 2006), 6.

26. In 1955, Richard Hofstadter commented, with a certain condescension, about Populists who became prosperous farmers, "The dialectic of history is full of odd and cunningly contrived ironies, and among these are rebellions waged only that the rebels might in the end be converted into their opposites." *The Age of Reform* (New York, 1955), 130.

27. From 1990 to 2010, the fourteen presidents of the Organization of American Historians who have come from the left included Mary Frances Berry, Lawrence Levine, Eric Foner, Gary Nash, Linda Kerber, William Chafe, David Montgomery, Darlene Clark Hine, Ira Berlin, Jacquelyn Dowd Hall, James O. Horton, Vicki Ruiz, Nell Irvin Painter, and Elaine Tyler May. The American Studies Association president quoted was Janice Radway, "What's in a Name? Presidential Address to the ASA, 20 November, 1998," *American Quarterly* 51 (1999): 22, 16–17.

28. Roger Kimball, *Tenured Radicals*, 3rd ed. (New York, 2008), xiv–xv; Arthur Schlesinger Jr., *The Disuniting of America: Reflections on a Multicultural Society* (New York, 1992), 133; David Horowitz, *The Professors: The 101 Most Dangerous Academics in America* (New York, 2006).

29. Quoted in Lawrence Levine, *The Opening of the American Mind: Canons, Culture, and History* (Boston, 1996), 168.

30. In the spring of 2010, pollsters found that Americans under forty-five were markedly more friendly to immigrants and opposed to laws restricting their rights and opportunities than were older citizens. Damien Cave, "A Generation Gap over Immigration," *New York Times*, May 17, 2010 (accessed May 19, 2010).

31. Roy Rosenzweig, "Afterthoughts," in Roy Rosenzweig and David Thelen, *The Presence of the Past: Popular Uses of History in American Life* (New York, 1998), 187.

32. Howard Zinn, *A People's History of the United States, 1492–Present* (New York, 2003), 631

33. Ibid., 632.

34. Chomsky quoted in http://www.boston.com/ae/celebrity/articles/2010/01/28/peoples_history_author_howard_zinn_dies_at_87/ (accessed June 10, 2010).

35. Quotes from Zinn, *People's History*, 59, 237, 573.

36. These comments on Zinn's work are adapted from my article, "Howard Zinn's History Lessons," *Dissent*, Spring 2004, 81–85.

37. Norman Mailer, *The Armies of the Night* (New York: 1968), 61.

38. Several Hollywood studio films made after 1980 also unambiguously presented the left's view of the Red Scare after World War II: *The Front, Goodnight and Good Luck*, and *The Majestic*.

39. Roberta Smith, "As Seen on Television: Sealed with a Simpson," *New York Times*, July 7, 2009, C7. For a sharp analysis of the show's themes, see Nicholas Guehlstorf, Lars Hallstrom, and Jonathan Morris, "The ABCs of *The Simpsons* and Politics: Apathy of Citizens, Basic Government Leaders, and Collective Interests," in *Laughing Matters: Humor and American Politics in the Media Age*, ed. Jody C. Baumgartner and Jonathan S. Morris (New York, 2008), 211–28.

40. http://en.wikipedia.org/wiki/Matt_Groening (accessed June 10, 2010); Carin Chocano, "Matt Groening" http://salon.com/people/bc/2001/01/03/groening/html (accessed Jan. 30, 2001); Paul Andrews, quoted in John Ortved, *The Simpsons: An Uncensored, Unauthorized History* (New York, 2009), 16. For delicious examples, see Matt Groening, *The Huge Book of Hell* (New York, 1997).

41. See the critical biography by Jesse Larner, *Forgive Us Our Spins: Michael Moore and the Future of the Left* (Hoboken, N.J., 2006). In his paper, *The Flint Voice*, Moore did publish a regular column by Ben Hamper, a "rivethead" for General Motors. But both in the paper and in his subsequent films, Moore was always the main character.

42. David Thomson, *The New Biographical Dictionary of Film* (New York, 2004), 627.

43. See the discussion in Robert Brent Toplin, *Michael Moore's Fahrenheit 9/11: How One Film Divided a Nation* (Lawrence, Kans., 2006), 120–36.

44. Weber, "Politics as a Vocation," en.wikipedia.org/wiki/politics_as_a_vocation (accessed Oct. 26, 2010).

45. Tony Judt, "What Is Living and What Is Dead in Social Democracy?," *New York Review of Books*, Dec. 17, 2009, 96.

45. Margaret Zaleski, quoted in Jose Martinez, "Protest Finding Backers in Burbs," *Boston Globe*, October 27, 2011, 8. For documents from and analysis of the movement, see *Occupy! Scenes from Occupied America*, eds. Astra Taylor, Keith Gessen, et al. (London, 2011) and Todd Gitlin, *Occupy Nation: The Roots, the Spirit, and the Promise of Occupy Wall Street* (New York, 2012).

46. Margaret Zaleski, quoted in Jose Martinez, "Protest Finding Backers in Burbs," *Boston Globe*, October 27, 2011, 8. For documents from and analysis of the movement, see *Occupy! Scenes from Occupied America*, eds. Astra Taylor, Keith Gessen, et al. (London, 2011) and Todd Gitlin, *Occupy Nation: The Roots, the Spirit, and the Promise of Occupy Wall Street* (New York, 2012).

47. Lewis Coser and Irving Howe, "Images of Socialism," in *Legacy of Dissent: Forty Years of Writing from* Dissent *Magazine*, ed. Nicolaus Mills (New York, 1994), 30, 47.

# Index